Catchpole and the 'F' words

(F1, F2, F3, F3000, FFord, etc.)

By Barry Foley

Foreword by Ken Tyrrell

To the real Catchpole — always the fastest. Much love. Jim x 1994 - 2015 So far!

tfm Publishing Limited

Publisher

By tfm Publishing

The exclamation mark
on the side of
Catchpole's helmet is a
registered trademark.

tfm Publishing Limited
Brimstree View
Kemberton
Nr. Shifnal
Shropshire
TF11 9LL

Tel: 01952 586408
Fax: 01952 587654
E-mail: nikki@tfmpublishing.co.uk
Web site: www.tfmpublishing.co.uk

Design and layout: Nikki Bramhill

First Edition   December 2000
ISBN 1 903378 04 4
Copyright © 2000 Barry Foley

Printed by Ebenezer Baylis & Son Ltd.
The Trinity Press
London Road
Worcester
WR5 2JH

Tel: 01905 357979
Fax: 01905 354919

Acknowledgements

This book is dedicated to my wife Liz, son and daughter Justin and Amanda, my friend 'Harty' and Karen and Nikki and Paul, all of whom made this book possible. To Ken and John, Martin and Kathy, Richard and Jill, Barbara and Alan, Phil and Jane and the many wonderful people who have been so supportive, who I am honoured to call friends including all the members of the Clubmans Register.

Barry Foley

And finally ....

I'd like to thank my Mum and Dad, my wife, her husband, the sponsors and I wanna say a special thanks to the team, they did a great job all day. I tell you the car was just sensational, we coulda won easy, the car handled just fantastic - it could dodge and miss all the other cars coming straight at us. OK, maybe I shoulda been going anti-clockwise, but if they hadn't black flagged us, we'd a been right there.

By Barry Foley

iii

Introduction

By Simon Taylor

Barry Foley's wonderful strip cartoons, chronicling the life of British grass roots motor sport, were an indelible feature of Autosport every week through the two decades of the 1970s and 1980s. Their gentle humour was always right on target because Barry was a club racer himself; he knew what it was like to stand in the rain at Rufforth, or hit the bank backwards at Lydden Hill, or tow a car all the way to Llandow after an all-nighter, only to find you'd left the diff behind.

Catchpole was born in 1970, when Barry and I were both racing in the clubmen's formula in a team sponsored by St Bruno pipe tobacco - which was highly appropriate, because Barry only ever took his smelly old pipe out of his mouth in order to don his crash helmet. He was a successful commercial artist, while I was then Autosport's editor, and I wanted a cartoon strip in my magazine to reflect the motley characters that we met around the paddocks every weekend. One night over dinner with Barry and his wife, Liz, they showed me a cartoon he'd done. It depicted a monk in a silent order falling over, and breaking his vow of silence as a result. Somehow, as we got into the second bottle, that monk began to metamorphose into a racing driver and his friends.

The only problem was that we couldn't think of a name for our hero. Then, for some reason, into my mind came the name of the very respectable bank manager who'd lived next door to us when I was a kid: Mr Catchpole. Eureka!

Within weeks of the first cartoon, starring our new friend Catchpole and his scruffy and monosyllabic mechanic Demon Tweak, Barry had conjured up a whole supporting cast. All the real people we knew in club racing gave Barry unlimited material on which to base his characters - and in many cases the fiction was so close to the fact that they were not difficult to recognise. But if people did see themselves in his cartoons, they were never offended, because the portrayals were always affectionate. There was even a brief appearance by a motor-racing editor called Simon Hooter, who had to sleep in his new full-face helmet because he couldn't get it off over his sizeable nose. I felt highly flattered, and the original of that cartoon hangs in my loo to this day. The wonderfully curvaceous Booby Galore was inspired by at least two prototypes, and as for Mad Dog Malone, he knows who he is.....

Soon Catchpole became part of the motor-racing establishment, enjoyed by people in the sport at every level, from Formula 1 downwards. Catchpole, as the central character, the narrator if you like, was in many ways Barry himself, and it wasn't long before he too wore a big exclamation mark on both sides of his crash helmet. He would deliver his cartoon each Monday, just as the magazine was starting to go to press, and often it reflected the adventures he'd had over that weekend's racing.

There was never a formal agreement between us, and in the freewheeling 1970s we never even got round to discussing matters like copyright. I'm pretty sure Barry, as Catchpole's only begetter, has the copyright anyway, but in any case we at Autosport are only too happy to grant Barry the right to give all those wonderful characters an airing again between the covers of this book, and remember again the relaxed, unprofessional and fun way club racing used to be.

Simon Taylor
Autosport

The Cartoonist

By Barry Foley

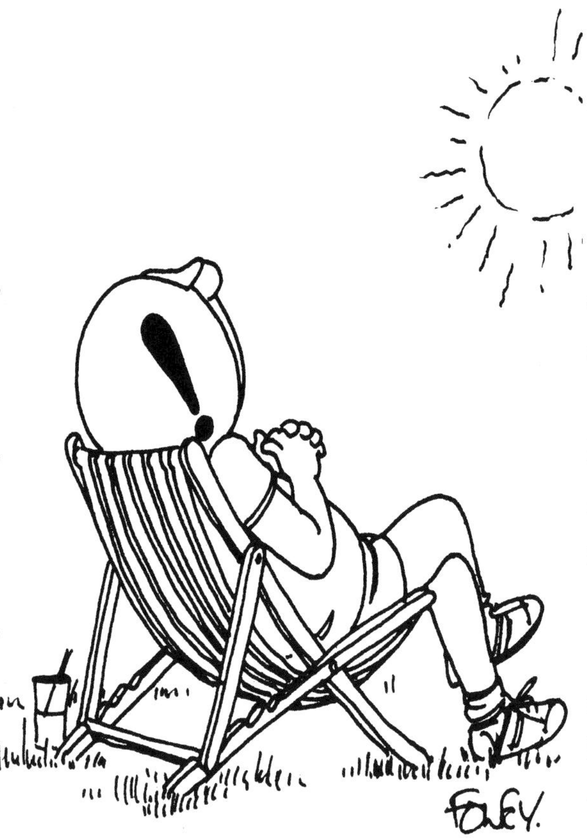
FOLEY.

Catchpole appeared in Autosport for twenty four years. Autosport would go to print on Tuesday morning and because motor sport usually happens on Sunday it was difficult to do anything topical, even a cartoon, before Monday. That meant every Monday morning I had to think up a new cartoon, draw it, have it finished by late evening. Then I would drive it to the printers, often arriving between 2am and 3am in the morning.

Up until the early nineties and the advent of new computer technology, Autosport was pasted together by hand and put to bed at the printers. You can imagine there were all sorts of things that could go wrong and often did, not least the odd error initiated by my dyslexia. Usually the error was spotted by my wife or a sub editor, but at 3am in the morning even sub editors' eagle eyes get a bit blood shot. I would like to thank all those great editors and sub editors that have put up with my last minute deliveries and spelling mistakes!

I remember several funny stories, one in particular. When Mark Thatcher took up motor racing he was of course prime material for the cartoonist. I was introduced to him at Brands Hatch and he asked if he could buy the original of a Catchpole that had featured him. We agreed a price and he suggested I ring him on one of three phone numbers he gave me, and because his mother had recently become Prime Minister he asked me to be discreet.

A couple of weeks later when the cartoon came back I called him at one of the numbers. A young female announced 'Number Ten, can I help you?' 'Oh' I said, 'I need to speak to Mark Thatcher.' 'Just a minute, I think he's in with his mum. I'll put you through.' Suddenly this rather familiar voice said, 'Yes?' 'Is Mark there by any chance?' I asked. 'Who is that?' 'Er, this is Barry Foley,' I replied. 'Oh, I see,' and I heard her shout across the room: 'Mark, that cartoonist is on the phone for you!'

A year or two later Mark was on the Paris Dakar or some rally when he went missing in the desert. The news broke on a Saturday night so, of course, I just had to do a Catchpole on it. By the Tuesday it emerged that aircraft and helicopters were scouring the desert and that he had been missing for well over a week - it was looking pretty serious - so serious that the Prime Minister herself was flying out to supervise the search.

A very agitated publisher in the shape of Simon Taylor rang me on Tuesday morning saying: 'Oh God, we are in deep, deep poo. We'll have to send her a telegram saying how sorry we are, how we didn't mean it, what a grand chap he'd been and how we'll all miss him.' On the Thursday or Friday they found him alive and well and a couple of days later we had a response back from Mrs Thatcher saying all was well and that she rather enjoyed the cartoon.

Well I just hope you all enjoy this book as much as I did putting it together.

Barry Foley

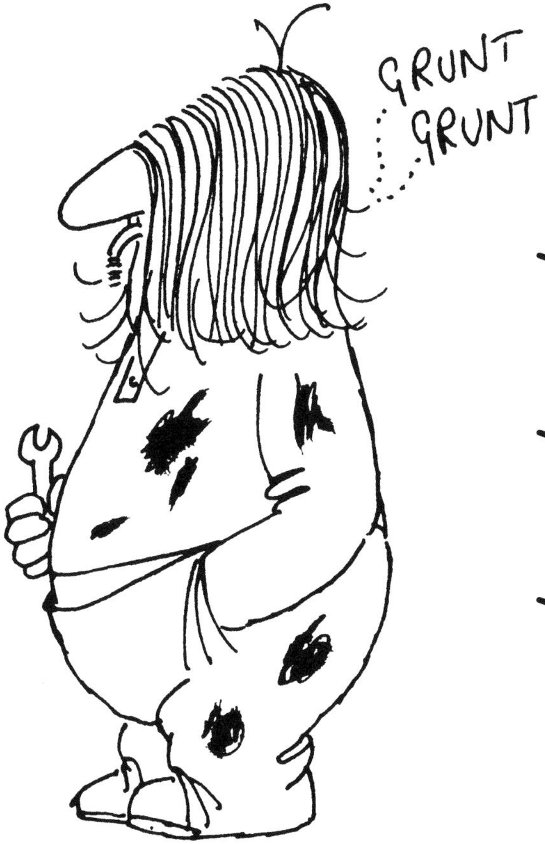
GRUNT
GRUNT

The Characters

By Simon Taylor

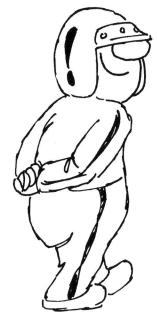

Catchpole

The archetypal club racing driver: endlessly patient and good humoured in the face of all the disappointments that a shoestring season can throw at him. Usually to be seen passing comment on scrutineers, the weather, rules and regulations, marshals and other drivers, always with the same wry, lop-sided smile.

Demon Tweak

Catchpole's monosyllabic and utterly scruffy mechanic, who has only been known ever to utter one syllable ("Grunt"). Has a permanent fag-end in his mouth, oil-smeared overalls that are as dirty at the start of the season as at the end, and a Dougal-dog haircut which renders forward vision marginal at best. Makes a bee-line for the beer tent as soon as Catchpole's car has retired, so has a gut which requires him to hold up his trousers by keeping his hands permanently in his pockets. Has never been seen actually working on a car.

Mad Dog Malone

Driver of ape-like aspect with insufficient brain to feel fear. Drools at the mouth at the prospect of being in the middle of a grid of single-seaters and being able to take at least half of them off at the first corner. On the very rare occasions that he keeps the car on the road, usually wins the race because everyone else is terrified to get near him - or he's already pushed them off.

The Characters

By Simon Taylor

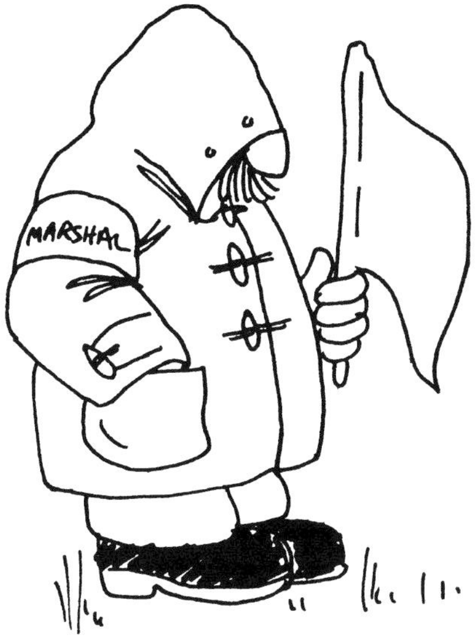
MARSHAL

Mat Dillon

Trusty British flag marshal, dressed permanently in welly boots and all-encompassing duffel coat against the persistent club racing weather, even on the rare occasions when the sun comes out. Off-season, actually hibernates in same duffel and wellies. Hood prevents him from being able to see any track action, so his flag signals are erratic: has been known to give the leader the blue flag because of the proximity of a car that's just been lapped. Every June makes the trip to Le Mans to cheer on the Brits, still in duffel and wellies, in which he gets rather hot and smelly by the end of the race.

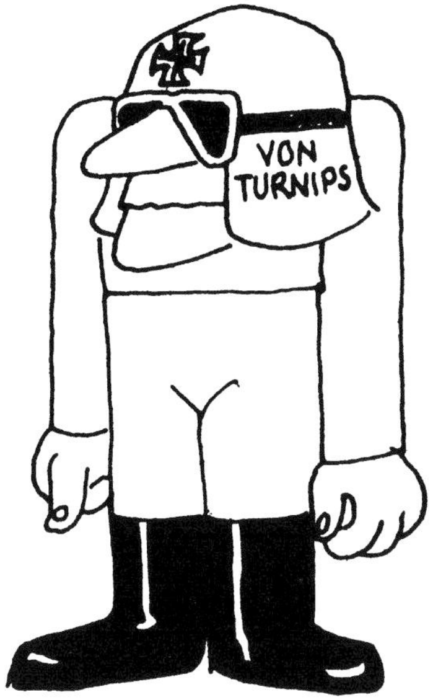
VON TURNIPS

Von Turnips

German traditionalist who should have been born in another era so that he could have been Lautenschlager's team-mate, and gone into battle with the Luftwaffe. Having been denied that, races his car to glory as though it is a Me109, or perhaps a Junkers J88. Wears jackboots over his Nomex bottoms and an unusual crash-helmet with echoes of Kaiser Bill. Has no sense of humour and speaks in strident Germanic tones.

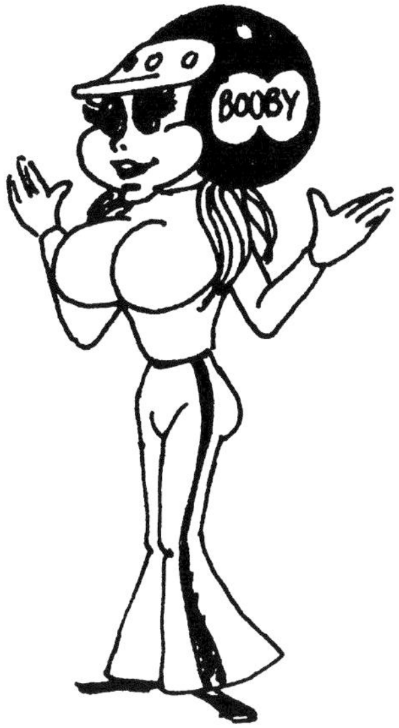
BOOBY

Booby Galore

Extremely curvaceous lady in tight-fitting Nomex overalls who turns every male head in the paddock, but is also a very talented operator in a variety of cockpits. No-one has ever been sure whether she has enormous blue eyes, or wears mascara on top of her goggles. Occasionally asks apparently naïve questions, but actually knows exactly which side her back axle is buttered.

The Characters

By Simon Taylor

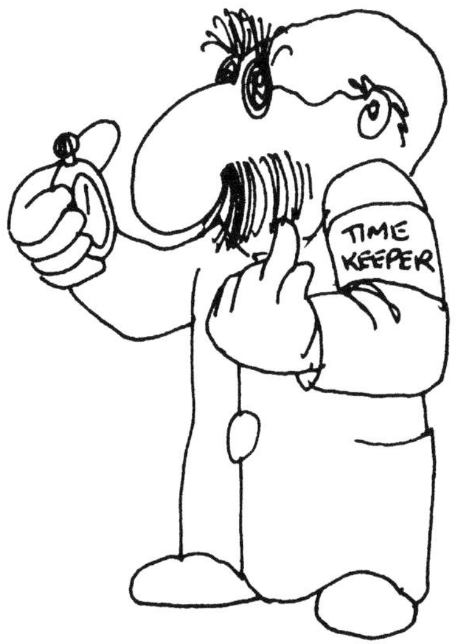
TIME KEEPER

Gerald, the timekeeper

A frustrated and befuddled perfectionist. If only he could have six weeks to produce this morning's practice times he could get them all absolutely right, to six places of decimals. As it is, these impatient racing drivers seem to want to see a starting grid today. Bald apart from three hirsute sources (moustache, neck and eyebrows), peers myopically at an armful of turnip stopwatches through spectacles like the bottom of bottles. Feels permanently harassed and under-appreciated.

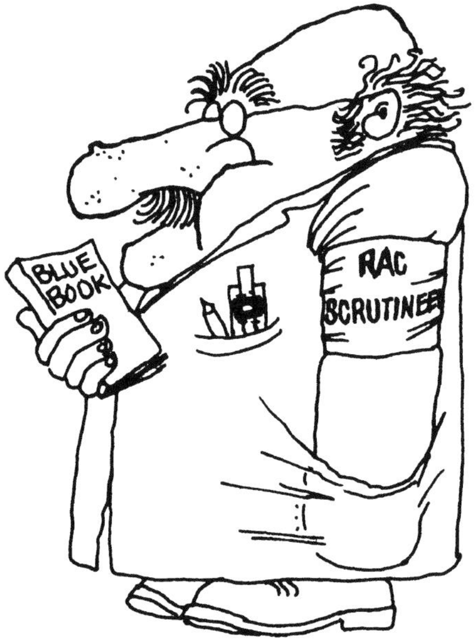
BLUE BOOK
RAC SCRUTINEER

Fred, the scrutineer

In fifty years in the scrutineering bay, has seen every bodge and heard every excuse. Without pity, and impervious to pleading, bribery, lying, imprecations, and threats of suicide or murder. Regards passing any car at its first attempt as a failure in his duty. Ultimate ambition: to scrutineer Michael Schumacher's Formula 1 Ferrari, and fail it for an inadequate throttle return spring. Father and grandfather were both scrutineers before him. Rumoured to be married to a scrutineer and to be bringing up a brood of little scrutineers of the future.

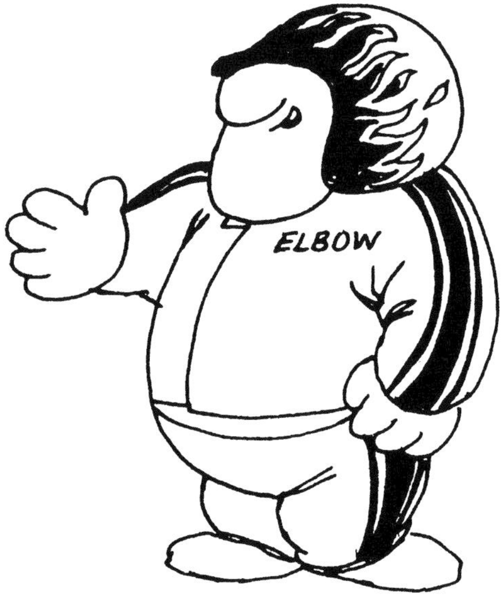
ELBOW

Elbow

Heavyweight touring car driver who claims to have started 700 races in the last seven seasons, and won 800 of them. Car usually rides lower on the right than on the left. Known as Elbow because of his skill both in elbowing rivals off the track, and in bending his elbow in the beer tent afterwards. Heart of gold, especially if it's your round.

The Characters

By Simon Taylor

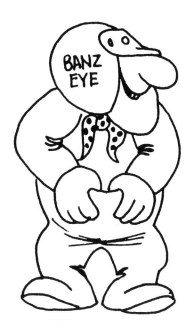

Banz Eye

Australian touring car driver who believes all Poms are poofs and the pedal in the middle between the throttle and the clutch is for sissies. As a result, can be relied upon to lead into the first corner and have the biggest accident as quickly as possible. The scourge of all commentators, because he is liable to express himself in native Australian during a live interview.

Jet Trotter

A smoothy with button-down shirt, smart suit, horn-rimmed glasses and brief case who doesn't quite understand motor-racing but will fasten on any driver who has a little bit of success and offer to manage him and find him sponsorship. Has never been known actually to find any sponsorship, has never even been known to buy a round. Do not trust this man with your credit cards.

Scoop

Keen, anxious hot-shot journalist from Autosport. Always chasing an elusive story, and usually swallowing hook, line and sinker every red herring he's fed around the paddock. Regards food and drink as free substances provided by PR men. Often believes he has personally spotted the next Ayrton Senna, who then proves to be five seconds off the pace.

Contents

Catchpole
and the 'F' words

Contents

MAD DOG

Catchpole and the 'F' words

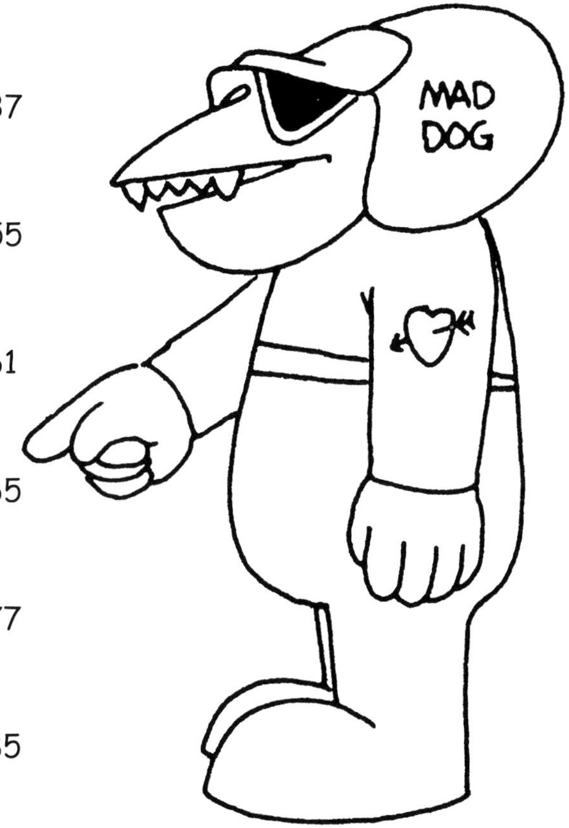

Foreword

By Ken Tyrrell

HOLD IT, HOLD IT JACKIE....
EUROVISION TV
elf
FIRST NATIONAL CITY
TRAVELLERS CHECKS
...THEY ARE STILL ARGUING ABOUT WHICH SPONSOR GETS HIS NAME ON THE CENTRE OF THE STEERING WHEEL.
EUROVISION TV
elf
FIRST NATIONAL CITY
TRAVELLERS CHECKS

It has been my great pleasure to count Barry Foley as a friend for more years than either of us care to remember. Throughout more than three decades, I have never failed to be impressed by Barry's ability to make people laugh and the Catchpole cartoons were an embodiment of his unique, albeit sometimes twisted, sense of humour.

Invariably, the first task on a Thursday morning was to open up Autosport and see what element of the sport Barry had turned his spotlight on that week. Even the people at the very top of our sport were not safe from his parodies.

Of course, from time to time I, along with my racing team, was the butt of Barry's humour. How he could make humour out of something as serious as Formula 1 racing is a mystery, but he always seemed to manage.

What I am certain of, is that if Barry found Formula 1 so amusing, his own efforts to be a team manager, racing driver, engineer and gopher all in one during his own racing career, must have kept him in stitches.

Few people know that Barry designed the colour schemes and graphics of many Formula 1 cars, the wonderful black and gold John Player Special Lotus cars and several Tyrrells, including the First National City six-wheeler. He was also responsible for the promotion of John Player Team Lotus from its launch for some five years.

As time has perhaps mellowed my outlook, I have just about forgiven Barry for most of his jokes at my expense and I am delighted to be associated with this anthology of Catchpoles. I hope everyone will enjoy reading these motorsport vignettes now as much as we all did at the time.

Ken Tyrrell
November 2000

The Early Days

Chapter One

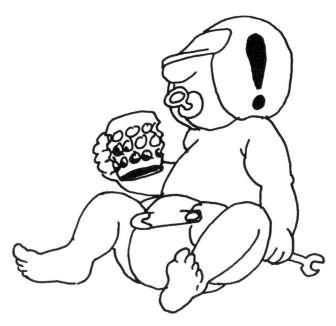

This was the dawn of time, a time of innocence before data logging and cheating were invented. John Webb was the most powerful man in motor racing and Dennis Jenkinson was more famous than Bernie Ecclescake. Earlier Catchpoles were simpler and more naive both in style and drawing - the humour more odd-ball and basic. This was an era when club racing was only a 2.5 secs a lap step from F1.

HALLO, WHO'S THIS IN A NEW BELL STAR?
ANYONE IN?
SPEAK, SPEAK
IT'S ALRIGHT, HE'S A FRIEND

IT'S STARTED RAINING, DAMN AND BLAST IT.....
DEMON TWEAK
.... BETTER PUT ON THE WET BOOTS BEFORE THE RACE
DEMON TWEAK
DEMON TWEAK

12th November 1970

SHAKE SHAKE
SNIFF SNIFF
HEY, TWEAK...
TWEAK, 'YOU BEEN AT MY BEER AGAIN ?

26th November 1970

Chapter One

HERE COMES DEAR OLD VON TURNIPS. I'LL SEE IF I CAN PSYCHE HIM ABOUT HIS OLD NAIL
CATCH-POLE
HEY, TURNIPS, WHEN DID YOU LAST WIN A RACE?
VON TURNIPS
1942
CATCH-POLE

3rd December 1970

GRUNT
SHUFFLE SHUFFLE
GRUNT GRUNT
CATCH-POLE
GRUNT
CATCH-POLE
GRUNT
CATCH-POLE
SHUFFLE SHUFFLE
BLOODY CHATTERBOX
CATCH-POLE

10th December 1970

TWEAK! FOR ME? HOW NICE OF YOU
GRUNT
OH GOODY, GOODY, JUST WHAT I'VE ALWAYS WANTED....
ASSORTED SPLIT-PINS
GRUNT

24th December 1970

TWEAK, I WAS WONDERING IF YOU COULD GIVE VON TURNIPS A HAND, HE'S GOT A BIT OF A MECHANICAL PROBLEM WITH HIS CAR.......
CATCH-POLE
EMON TWEAK
VON TURNIPS
....THE MAGAZINE HAS JAMMED ON HIS MACHINE GUN.
CATCH-POLE
DEMON TWEAK
VON TURNIPS
FARTZ SPECIAL

7th January 1971

Chapter One

The Early Days

LOOK - THAT'S SIMON HOOTER THE FAMOUS EDITOR AND F.1. TESTER.....
GRUNT
.....THEY DO SAY HE HAS TO SLEEP IN HIS BELLSTAR....
...HE CAN'T GET IT OFF OVER HIS NOSE!
GRUNT

21st January 1971

PETROL AND OIL CHECKED? TELL-TALE RESET? .....
GRUNT GRUNT
TYRE PRESSURES? GEAR RATIOS? PLUGS CHANGED? .....
GRUNT GRUNT
... GOOD - THAT'S THE TRANSPORTER DONE, NOW LET'S DO THE RACING CAR.

4th March 1971

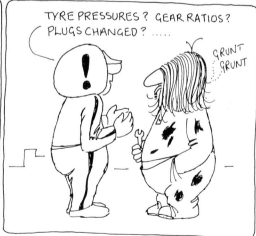

THESE NEW NOMEX OF MINE ARE DAMN UNCOMFORTABLE.....
TUG TUG
I COMPLAINED ABOUT THE FIT WHEN I BOUGHT THEM....
I TOLD LESTON THAT THEY WERE MUCH TOO TIGHT AROUND THE CRUTCH.... AND ALL HE DID, WAS TO MUMBLE SOME NONSENSE......
ABOUT THEM REDUCING THE UNSPRUNG WEIGHT

15th April 1971

COME ON TWEAK, TIDY YOURSELF UP. WE'RE GOING INTO THE CLUBHOUSE FOR A DRINK.
GRUNT
BRUSH
PAT PAT
BRUSH BRUSH
GRUNT
COMB COMB
TUG TUG
BRUSH BRUSH
PAT
SHUFFLE
GRUNT GRUNT
AMAZING! AMAZING! I WOULDN'T HAVE RECOGNIZED YOU

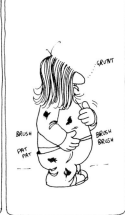

10th June 1971

Chapter One

....ALSO THERE'S TOO MUCH INITIAL UNDERSTEER. PERSONALLY, I WOULD INCREASE THE FRONT ROLL BAR STIFFNESS, GO UP TWO CLICKS ON THE REAR SHOCKERS AND...
INCREASE THE ANGLE OF INCIDENCE OF THE FRONT FLIPPERS BY ONE AND THREE QUARTER DEGREES.
GRUNT
BUT IM SURE YOU'VE GOT A MORE SUBTLE SOLUTION
BRILLIANT, TWEAK, BRILLIANT
GRUNT GRUNT
BIFF

29th July 1971

...IT'S NO GOOD TWEAK, I JUST DONOT LIKE THIS TRACK, THE SURFACE IS LIKE CORRUGATED IRON...
...IT'S FULL OF WHACKING GREAT POT HOLES, AND RIGHT IN THE MIDDLE OF ONE BEND THERE'S THIS....
...UGLY LOOKING HILL
TAP TAP
WATCH IT

12th August 1971

.... I DON'T KNOW, TWEAK. IT'S DIFFICULT TO TELL THESE DAYS, BUT OFFHAND I WOULD SAY.....
12
.... ITS EITHER A NEXT YEARS FORMULA ONE G.P. CAR, OR A LAST YEARS CLUBMANS FORMULA CAR.
GRUNT GRUNT
12

9th September 1971

...AUTUMN, FALLING LEAVES, THE SEASON'S DRAWING TO A CLOSE...
... IT'S SAD TWEAK, REAL SAD, LAST FEW RACES. GATHER UP THE TOOLS, PUT THE CAR AWAY FOR THE WINTER....
... AND THEN IT'S RAIN, SNOW, WIND, FOG, POWER CUTS, BURST PIPES AND ONE LONG CONTINUOUS ROUND....
... OF BIRDS, BOOZE, AND PARTIES.
GRUNT GRUNT

4th November 1971

Chapter One

THIS SHOULD BE A GIGGLE, TWEAK IS WEARING AN **EVENING DRESS**, WOULD YOU BELIEVE? HE'S JUST OFF TO HIS ANNUAL MECHANICS DINNER.
HEY! TWEAK, FOR GOODNESS SAKE DON'T PUT YOUR SPANNER DOWN ON THE DINNER TABLE.
GRUNT
SOMEBODY MIGHT PINCH IT.
GRUNT
GRUNT

17th February 1972

DO YOU KNOW, IN ALL THE YEARS I'VE KNOWN YOU...
GRUNT
.... I'VE NEVER ONCE SEEN YOUR FACE, TWEAK...
......
GRUNT
I SEE HULME WON AT MOSPORT.

15th June 1972

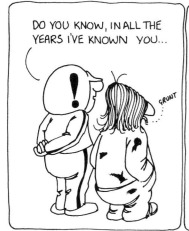

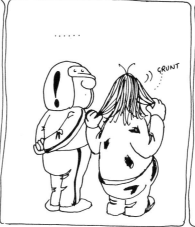

THERE GOES SAM TOW RAG THE FASTEST BREAKDOWN MAN IN THE GAME....
TOW RAG
PART OF KNOCK FOR KNOCK INC
THE MAD FOOL TOWED ME IN THE OTHER DAY AND WE...
...LAPPED THREE SECONDS FASTER THAN MY PREVIOUS BEST.

9th November 1972

THE NEW RAC 'BLUE BOOK' IS OUT I SEE...
....APPARENTLY IT'S CALLED...
..THE 'BLUE BOOK' BECAUSE...
...IT'S FULL OF DIRTY WORDS AND DISGUSTING SUGGESTIONS.

4th January 1973

Chapter One

The Early Days

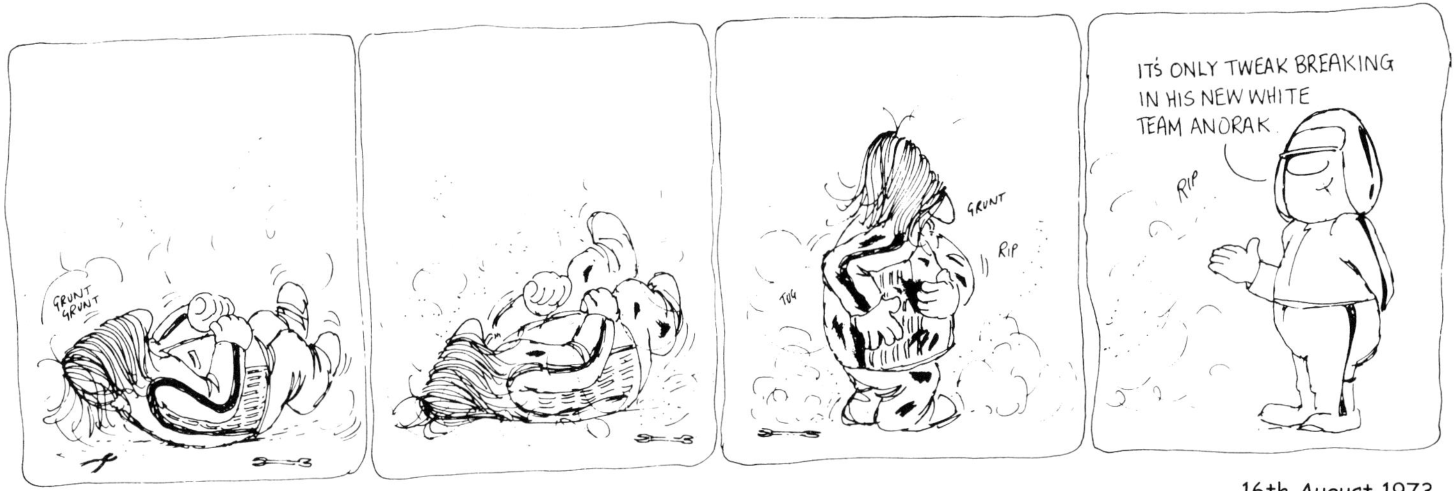

GRUNT GRUNT
TUG
GRUNT
RIP
IT'S ONLY TWEAK BREAKING IN HIS NEW WHITE TEAM ANORAK
RIP

16th August 1973

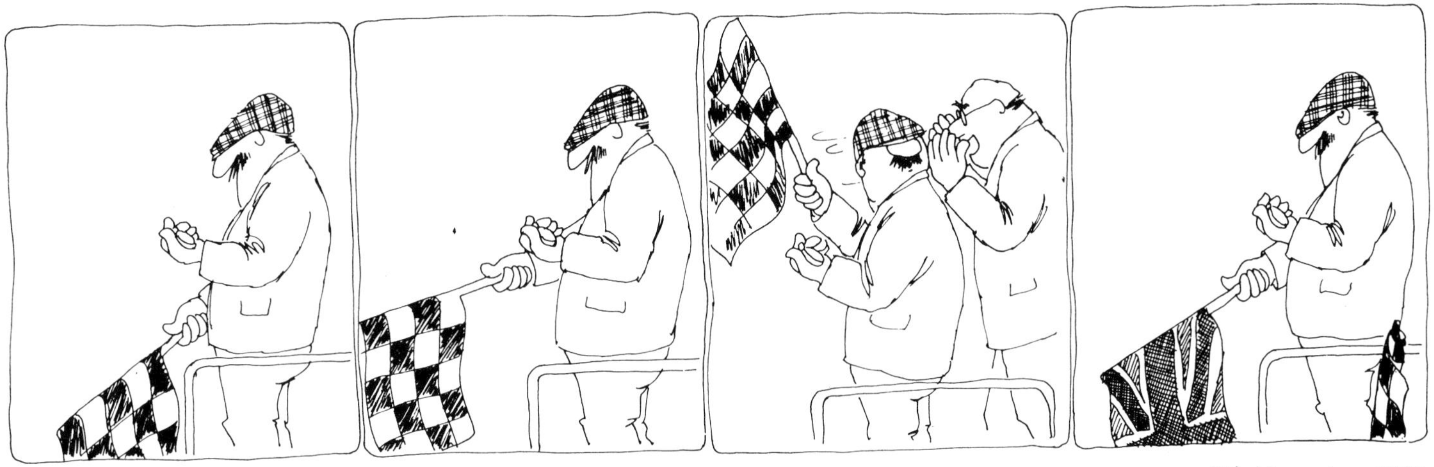

8th November 1973

I KNOW VE ARE IN ZE COMMON MARKET UNT ALL ZAT, BUT....
...VOT IS A GOOD RUSSIAN-JEWISH BEAR LIKE ME VID DE ALL AMERICAN...
...BELL STAR HELMIT ON GOT TO DO VID DE BRITISH RACING TEAM?

6th June 1974

'SUPPOSE IT'S ABOUT TIME I TRIED OUT A FULL FACE HELMET....
...NO, NO, IT'S NO GOOD...
TUG TUG
...FAR TOO SMALL!

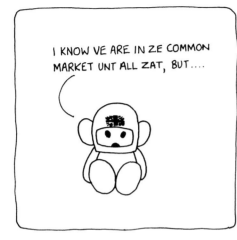

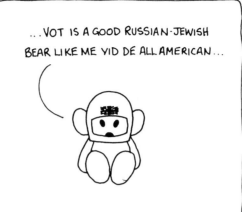

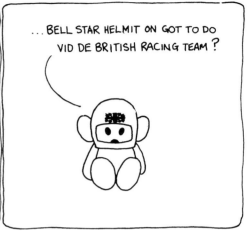

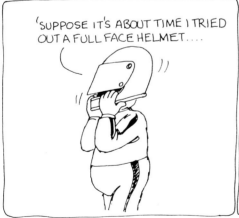

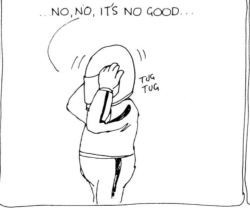

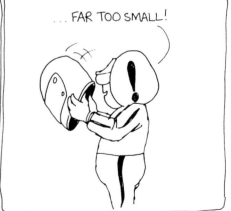

24th October 1974

Chapter One

The Early Days

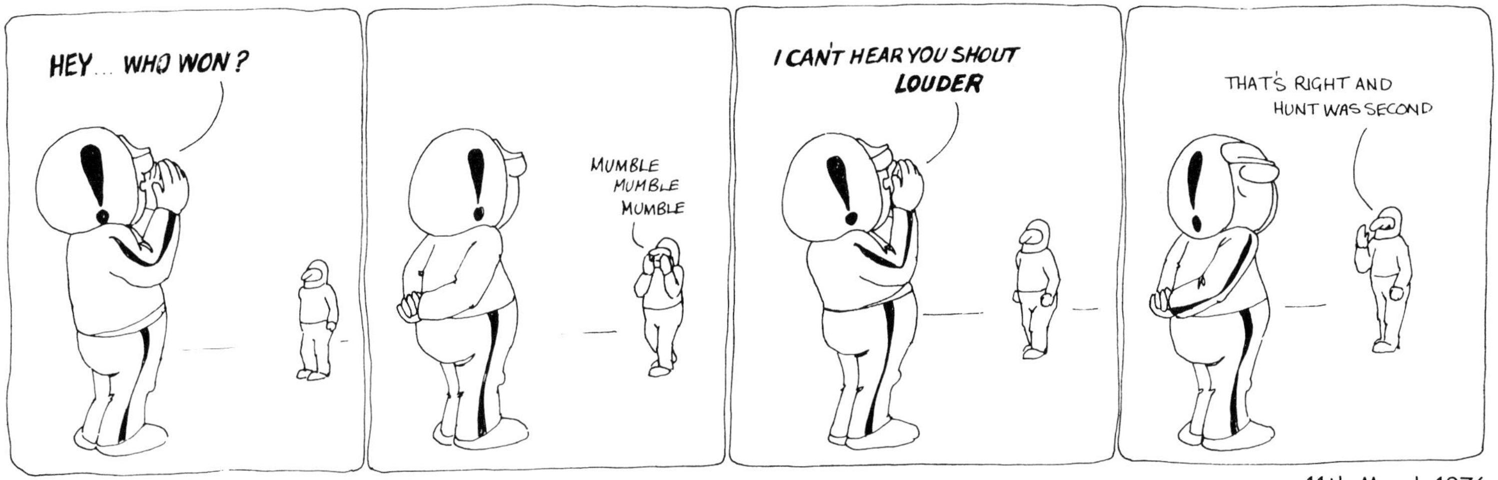

HEY... WHO WON?
MUMBLE
MUMBLE
MUMBLE
I CAN'T HEAR YOU SHOUT
LOUDER
THAT'S RIGHT AND
HUNT WAS SECOND

11th March 1976

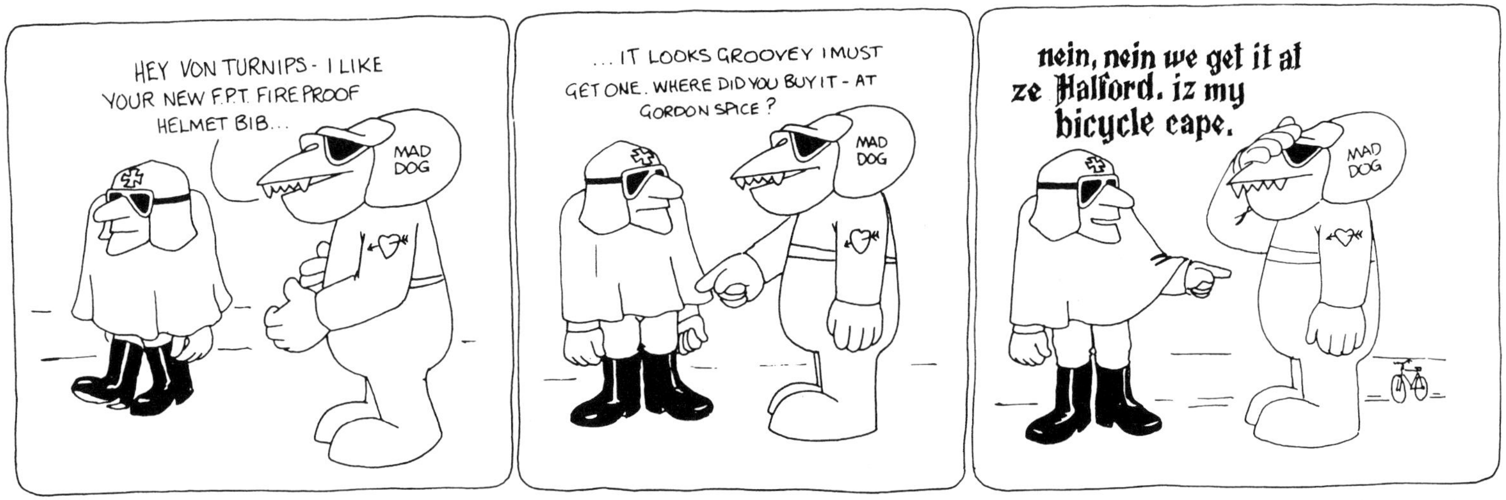

HEY VON TURNIPS - I LIKE YOUR NEW F.P.T. FIRE PROOF HELMET BIB...
MAD DOG
... IT LOOKS GROOVEY I MUST GET ONE. WHERE DID YOU BUY IT - AT GORDON SPICE?
MAD DOG
nein, nein we get it at ze Halford. iz my bicycle cape.
MAD DOG

27th January 1977

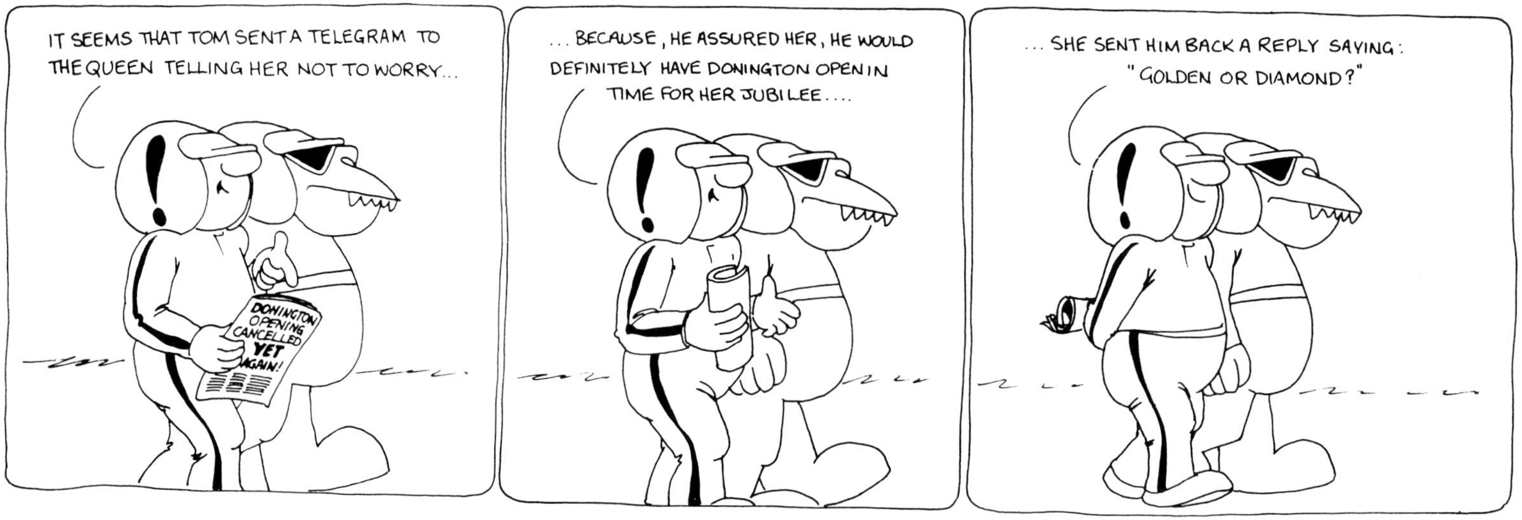
IT SEEMS THAT TOM SENT A TELEGRAM TO THE QUEEN TELLING HER NOT TO WORRY...
DONINGTON OPENING CANCELLED YET AGAIN!
... BECAUSE, HE ASSURED HER, HE WOULD DEFINITELY HAVE DONINGTON OPEN IN TIME FOR HER JUBILEE....
... SHE SENT HIM BACK A REPLY SAYING: "GOLDEN OR DIAMOND?"

17th February 1977

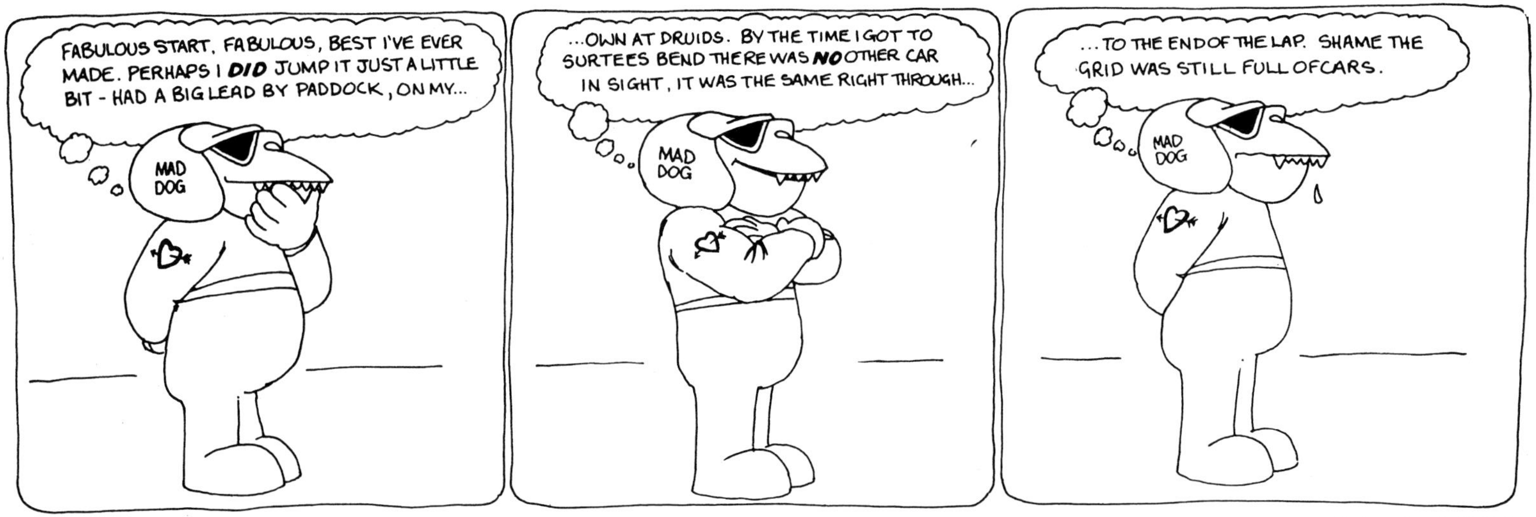
FABULOUS START, FABULOUS, BEST I'VE EVER MADE. PERHAPS I DID JUMP IT JUST A LITTLE BIT - HAD A BIG LEAD BY PADDOCK, ON MY...
MAD DOG
...OWN AT DRUIDS. BY THE TIME I GOT TO SURTEES BEND THERE WAS NO OTHER CAR IN SIGHT, IT WAS THE SAME RIGHT THROUGH...
MAD DOG
...TO THE END OF THE LAP. SHAME THE GRID WAS STILL FULL OF CARS.
MAD DOG

28th April 1977

Rally Stuff

Chapter Two

I've never really been deeply into rallying even though I drove in a few including a works drive for Vauxhall in the Avon Tour of Britain. It was a wonderful event that was half rally, half race and raged throughout the 1970s pitching drivers such as Gerry Marshall and James Hunt against Roger Clark and Jimmy McRae. However rallying has always been a great source of humour and Catchpole and I have always enjoyed having a little jab at all the yumping, crashing and sideways bit. Stages were about too much power and too little grip. Now, of course, they're too quick for tarmac or the forest.

CHEAT!

LET'S TRY TO LOOK AT IT FROM THE POSITIVE SIDE....
... MOST PEOPLE DON'T GET THE CHANCE TO SEE AN UNSPOILT MOUNTAIN SIDE AT CLOSE QUARTERS LIKE THIS, AND....
...IF WE WEREN'T HERE WE'D ONLY BE AT HOME MOWING THE LAWN.

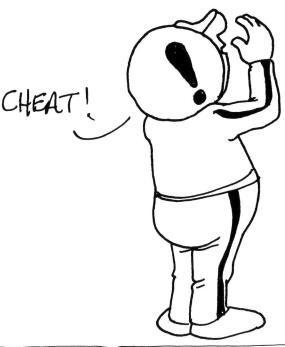

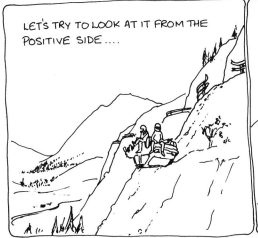

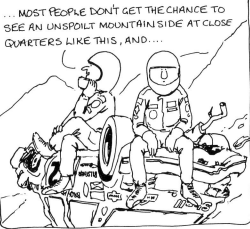

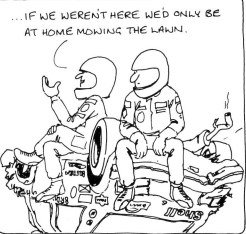

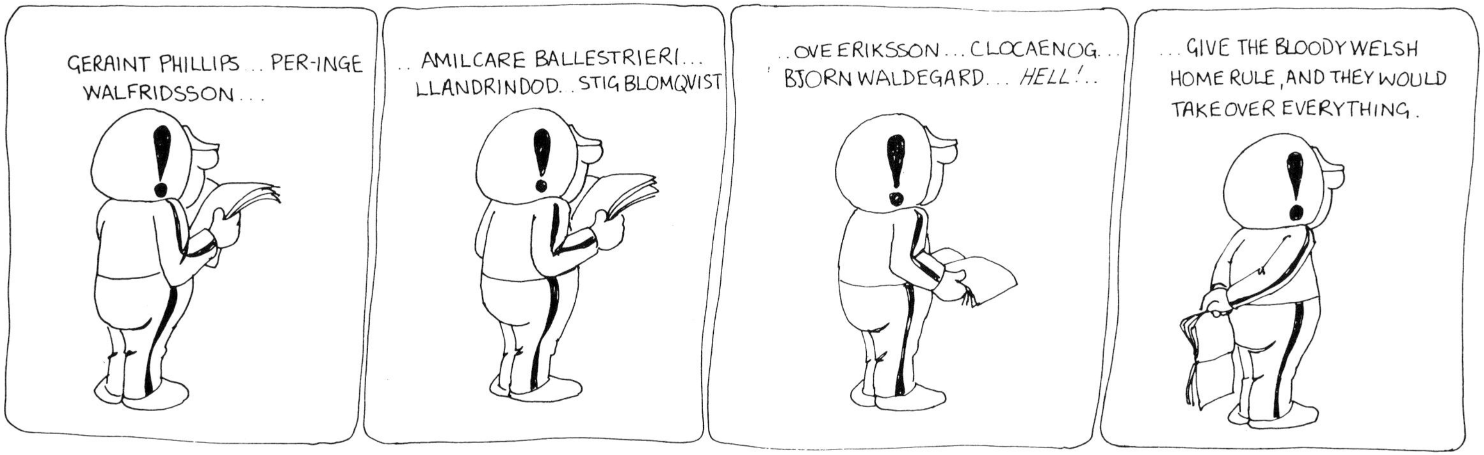
GERAINT PHILLIPS ... PER-INGE WALFRIDSSON ...
.. AMILCARE BALLESTRIERI ... LLANDRINDOD .. STIG BLOMQVIST
.. OVE ERIKSSON ... CLOCAENOG ... BJORN WALDEGARD ... HELL! ..
... GIVE THE BLOODY WELSH HOME RULE, AND THEY WOULD TAKE OVER EVERYTHING.

22nd November 1973

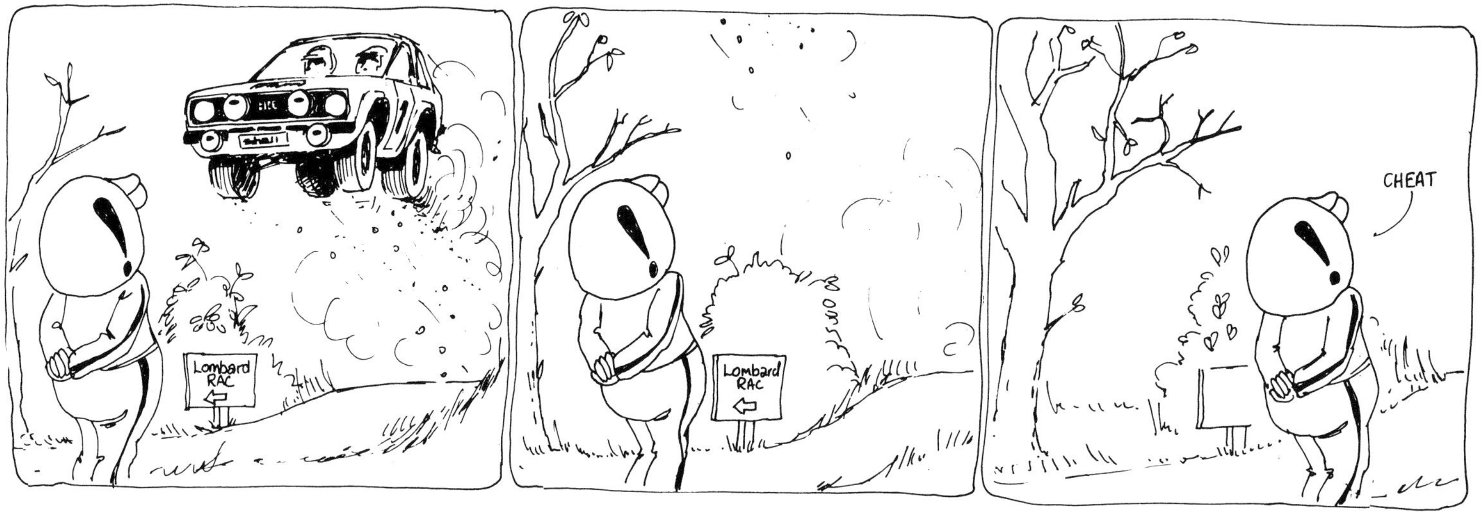
Lombard RAC
Lombard RAC
CHEAT

27th November 1975

Chapter Two

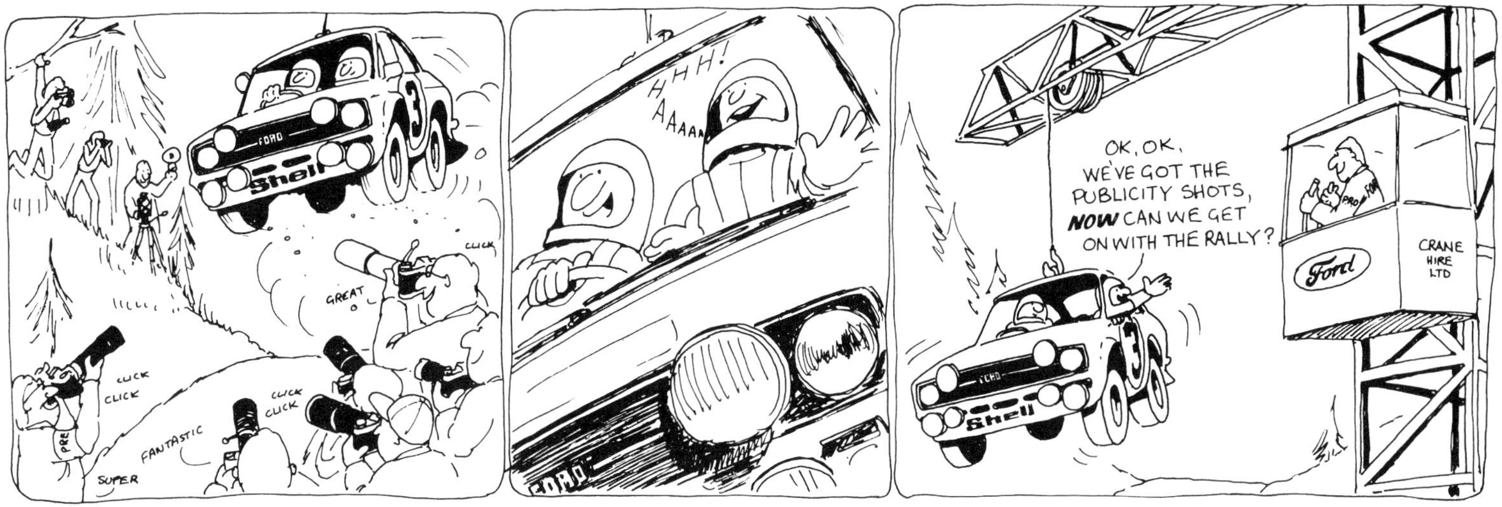

CLICK
GREAT
CLICK
CLICK
CLICK
CLICK
FANTASTIC
SUPER
AAAAHHH!
OK, OK,
WE'VE GOT THE
PUBLICITY SHOTS,
NOW CAN WE GET
ON WITH THE RALLY?
CRANE
HIRE
LTD

23rd September 1976

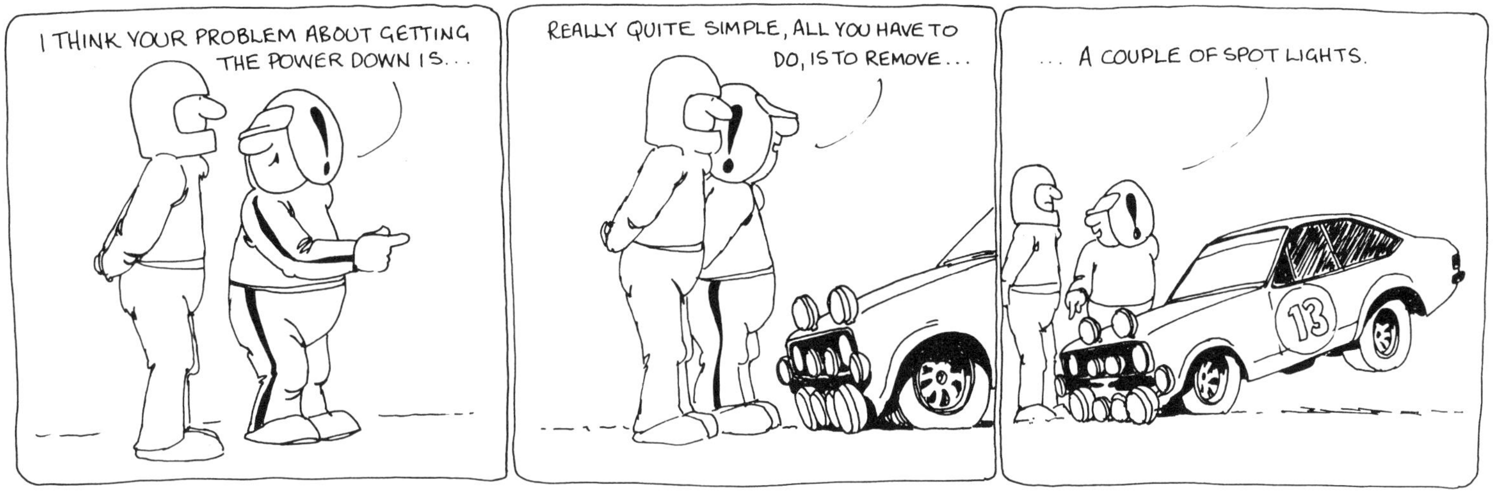

I THINK YOUR PROBLEM ABOUT GETTING THE POWER DOWN IS...
REALLY QUITE SIMPLE, ALL YOU HAVE TO DO, IS TO REMOVE...
... A COUPLE OF SPOT LIGHTS.

21st October 1976

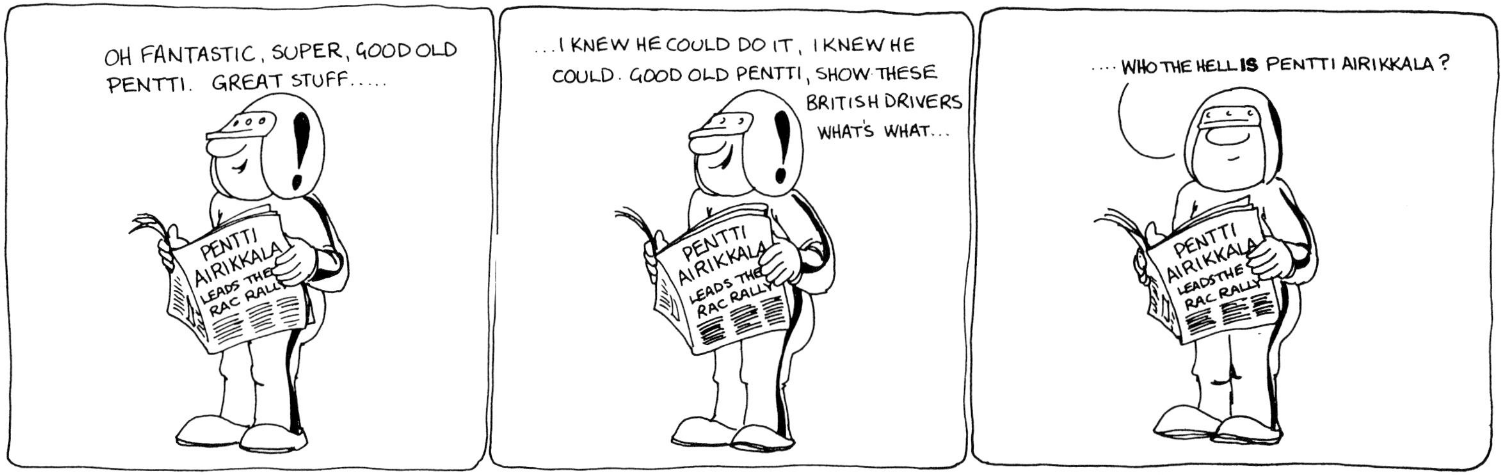
OH FANTASTIC, SUPER, GOOD OLD PENTTI. GREAT STUFF.....
PENTTI AIRIKKALA LEADS THE RAC RALLY
...I KNEW HE COULD DO IT, I KNEW HE COULD. GOOD OLD PENTTI, SHOW THESE BRITISH DRIVERS WHAT'S WHAT...
PENTTI AIRIKKALA LEADS THE RAC RALLY
....WHO THE HELL IS PENTTI AIRIKKALA?
PENTTI AIRIKKALA LEADS THE RAC RALLY

2nd December 1976

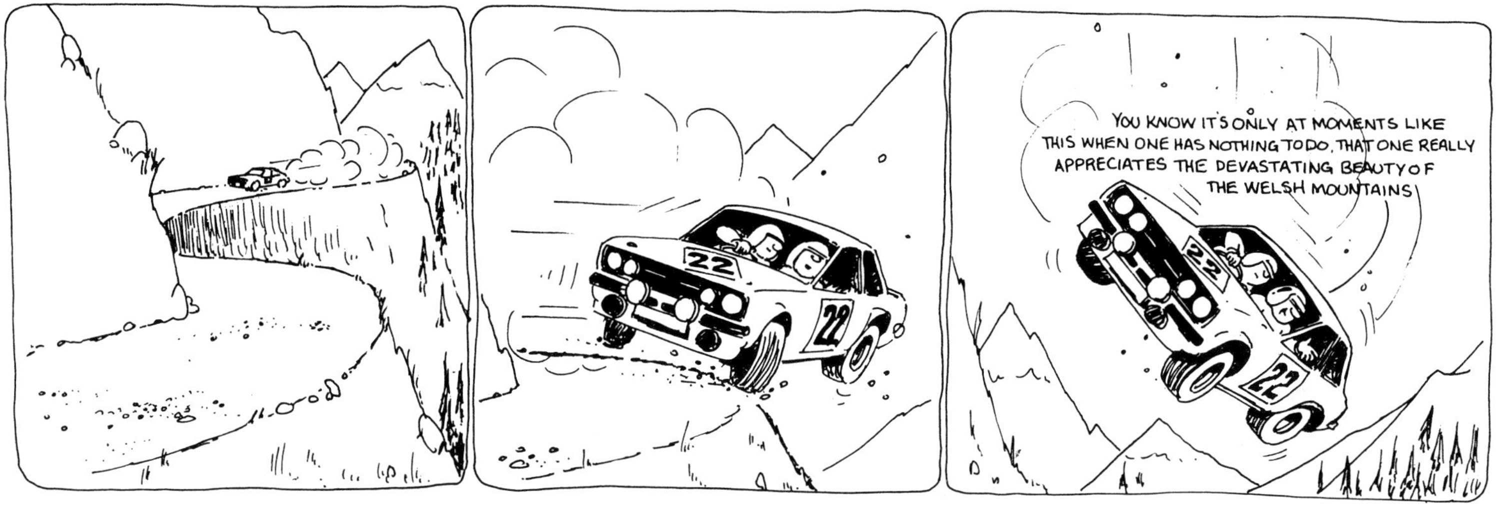
22
22
YOU KNOW IT'S ONLY AT MOMENTS LIKE THIS WHEN ONE HAS NOTHING TO DO, THAT ONE REALLY APPRECIATES THE DEVASTATING BEAUTY OF THE WELSH MOUNTAINS
22
22

16th December 1976

Chapter Two

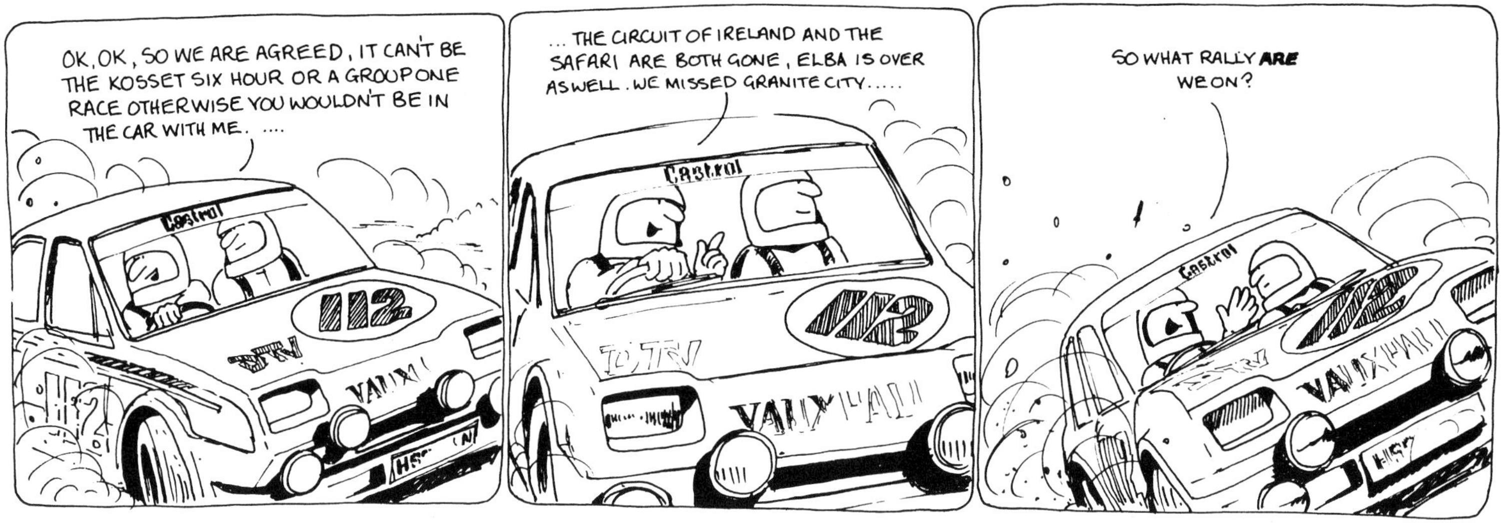
OK, OK, SO WE ARE AGREED, IT CAN'T BE THE KOSSET SIX HOUR OR A GROUP ONE RACE OTHERWISE YOU WOULDN'T BE IN THE CAR WITH ME. ....
Castrol
... THE CIRCUIT OF IRELAND AND THE SAFARI ARE BOTH GONE, ELBA IS OVER AS WELL. WE MISSED GRANITE CITY.....
Castrol
SO WHAT RALLY **ARE** WE ON?
Castrol

5th May 1977

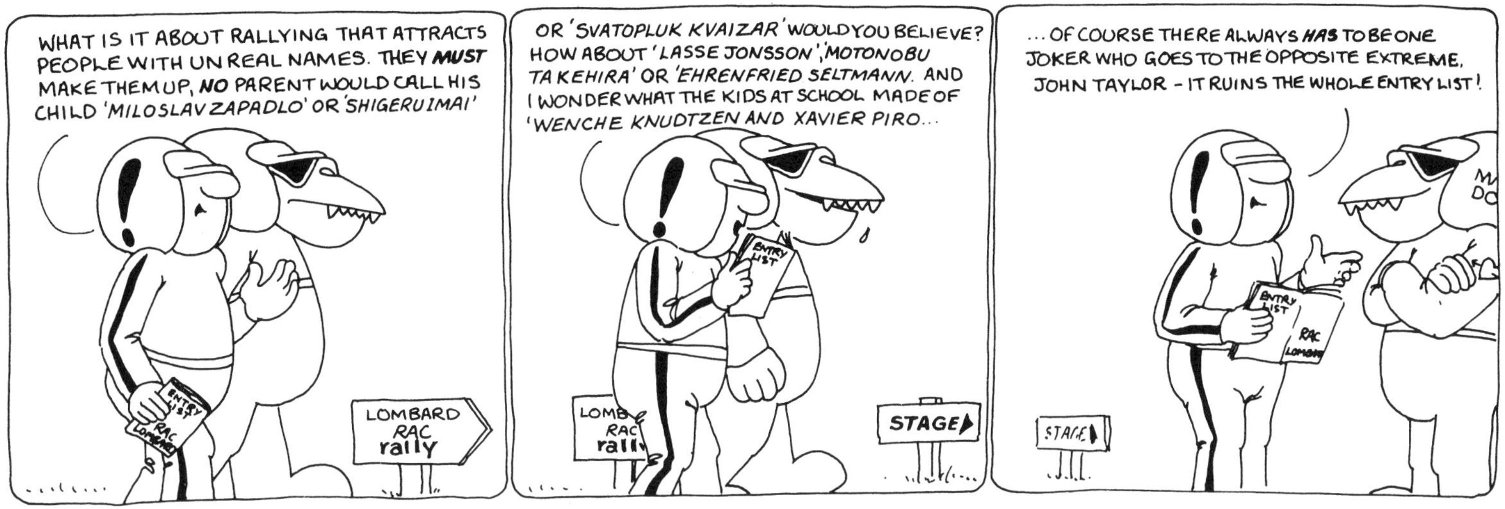
WHAT IS IT ABOUT RALLYING THAT ATTRACTS PEOPLE WITH UNREAL NAMES. THEY ***MUST*** MAKE THEM UP, **NO** PARENT WOULD CALL HIS CHILD '*MILOSLAV ZAPADLO*' OR '*SHIGERU IMAI*'
ENTRY LIST RAC
LOMBARD RAC rally
OR '*SVATOPLUK KVAIZAR*' WOULD YOU BELIEVE? HOW ABOUT '*LASSE JONSSON*', '*MOTONOBU TAKEHIRA*' OR '*EHRENFRIED SELTMANN*'. AND I WONDER WHAT THE KIDS AT SCHOOL MADE OF '*WENCHE KNUDTZEN AND XAVIER PIRO*...
ENTRY LIST
STAGE
... OF COURSE THERE ALWAYS ***HAS*** TO BE ONE JOKER WHO GOES TO THE OPPOSITE EXTREME. JOHN TAYLOR - IT RUINS THE WHOLE ENTRY LIST!
ENTRY LIST RAC
STAGE

7th December 1978

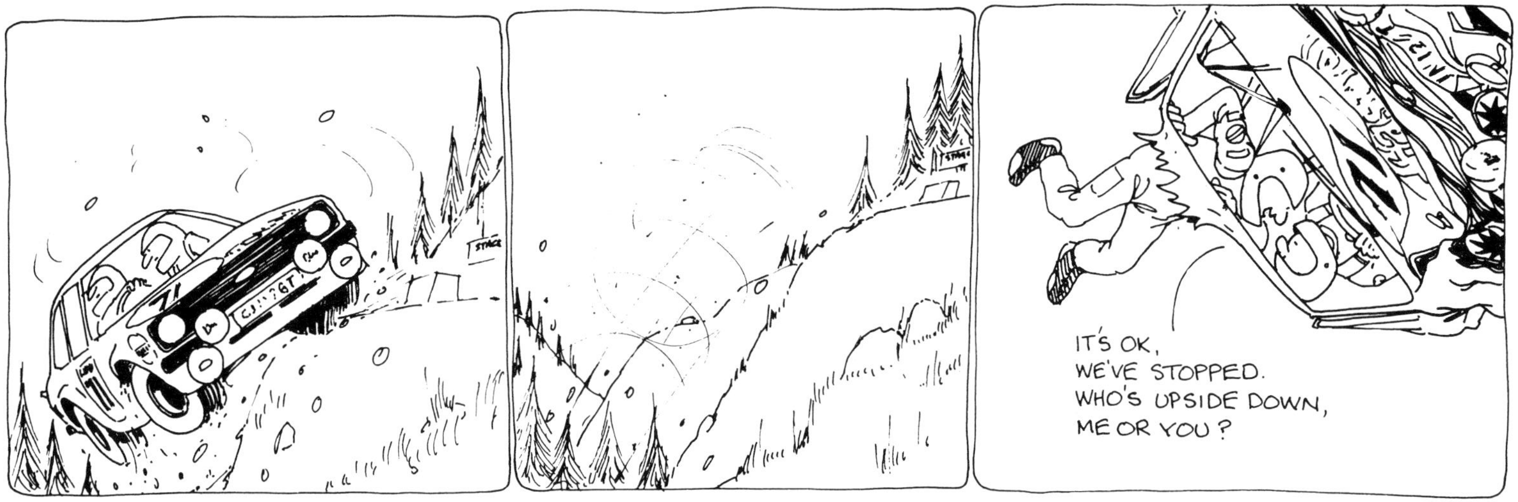
IT'S OK,
WE'VE STOPPED.
WHO'S UPSIDE DOWN,
ME OR YOU?

24th January 1980

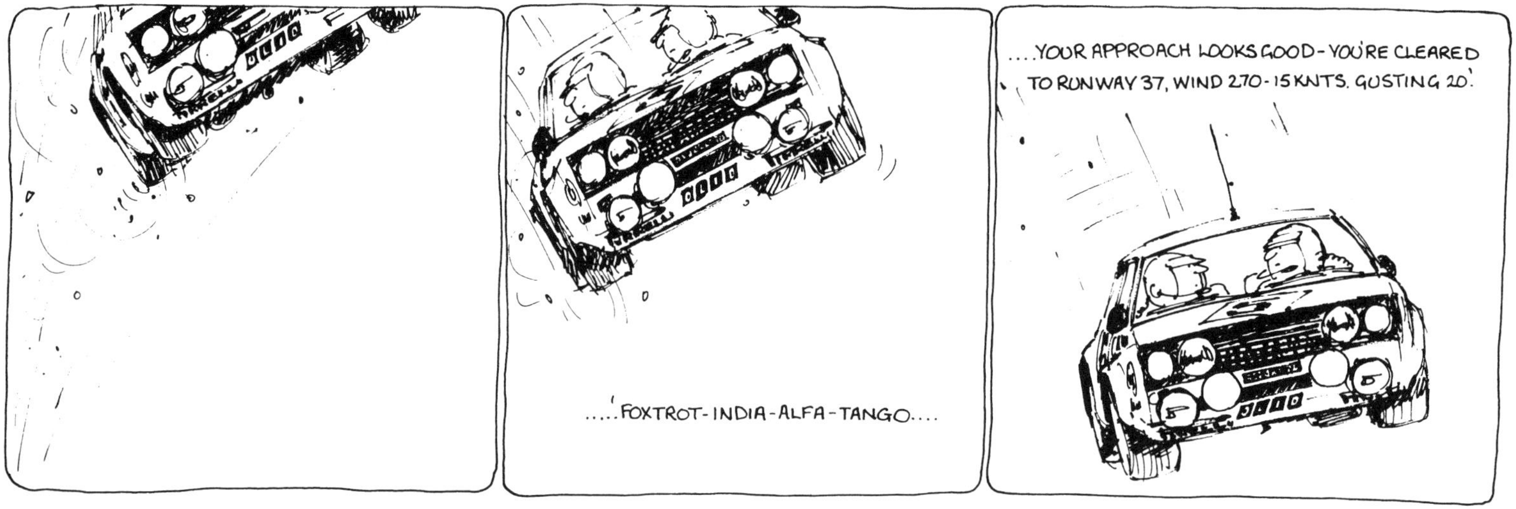
.....FOXTROT-INDIA-ALFA-TANGO....
....YOUR APPROACH LOOKS GOOD - YOU'RE CLEARED TO RUNWAY 37, WIND 270-15 KNTS. GUSTING 20.

22nd January 1981

Chapter Two

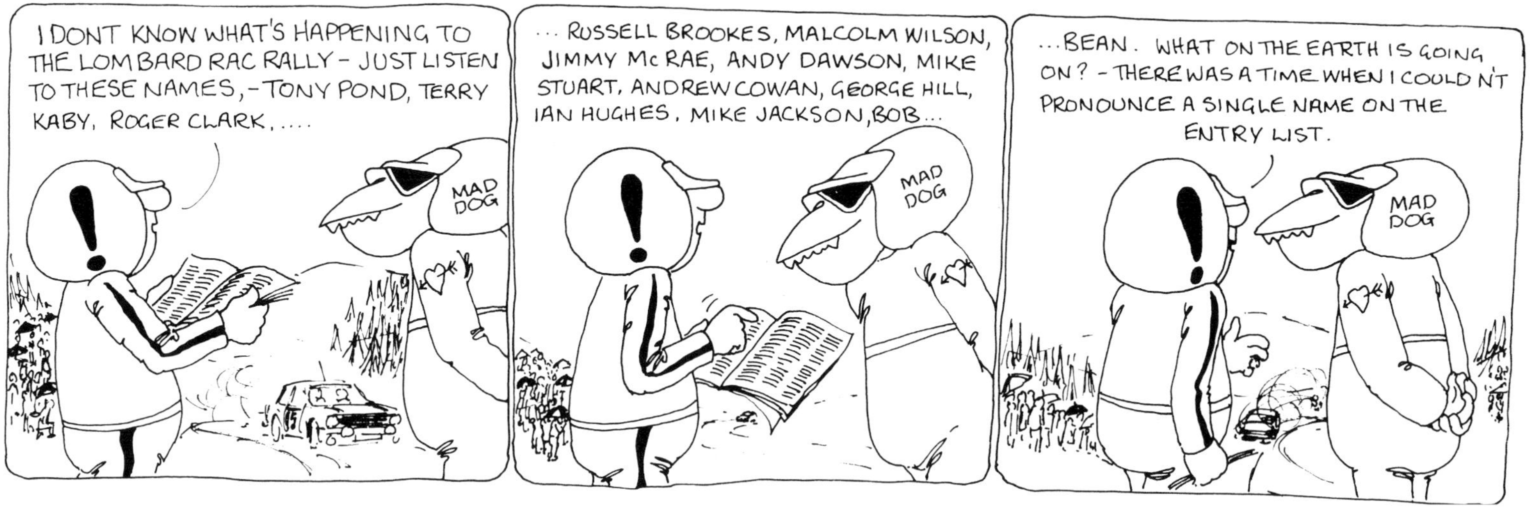
I DONT KNOW WHAT'S HAPPENING TO THE LOMBARD RAC RALLY - JUST LISTEN TO THESE NAMES, - TONY POND, TERRY KABY, ROGER CLARK, ...
MAD DOG
... RUSSELL BROOKES, MALCOLM WILSON, JIMMY McRAE, ANDY DAWSON, MIKE STUART, ANDREW COWAN, GEORGE HILL, IAN HUGHES, MIKE JACKSON, BOB...
MAD DOG
...BEAN. WHAT ON THE EARTH IS GOING ON? - THERE WAS A TIME WHEN I COULDN'T PRONOUNCE A SINGLE NAME ON THE ENTRY LIST.
MAD DOG

26th November 1981

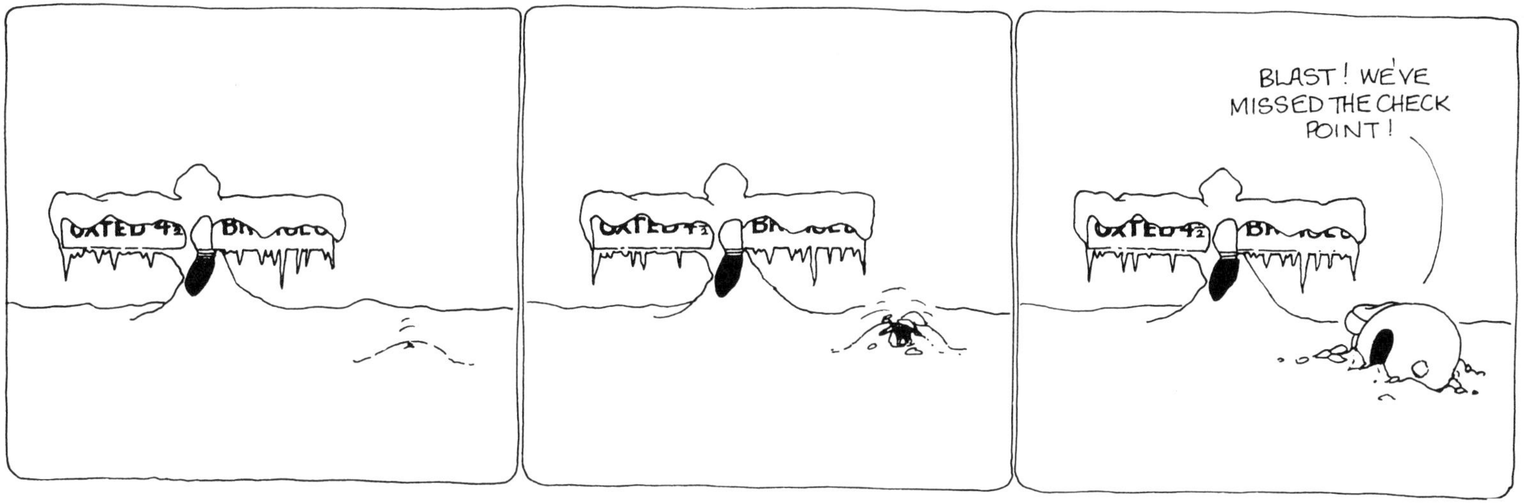
BLAST! WE'VE MISSED THE CHECK POINT!

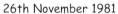

17th December 1981

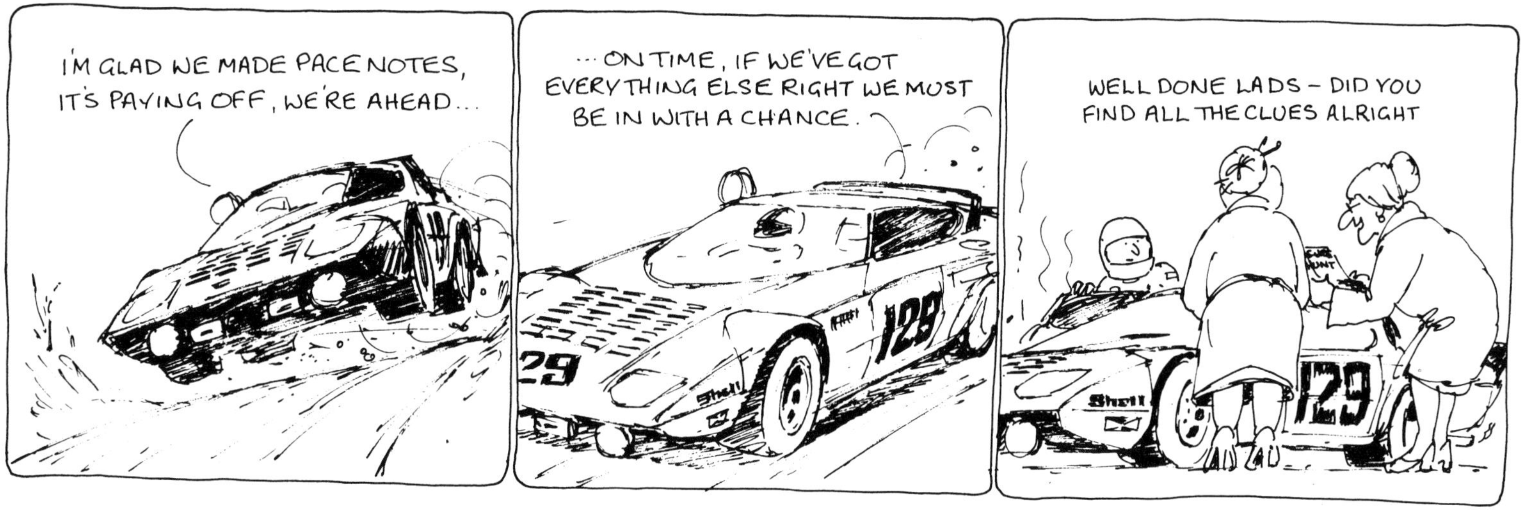
I'M GLAD WE MADE PACE NOTES, IT'S PAYING OFF, WE'RE AHEAD...
... ON TIME, IF WE'VE GOT EVERYTHING ELSE RIGHT WE MUST BE IN WITH A CHANCE.
WELL DONE LADS - DID YOU FIND ALL THE CLUES ALRIGHT

7th January 1982

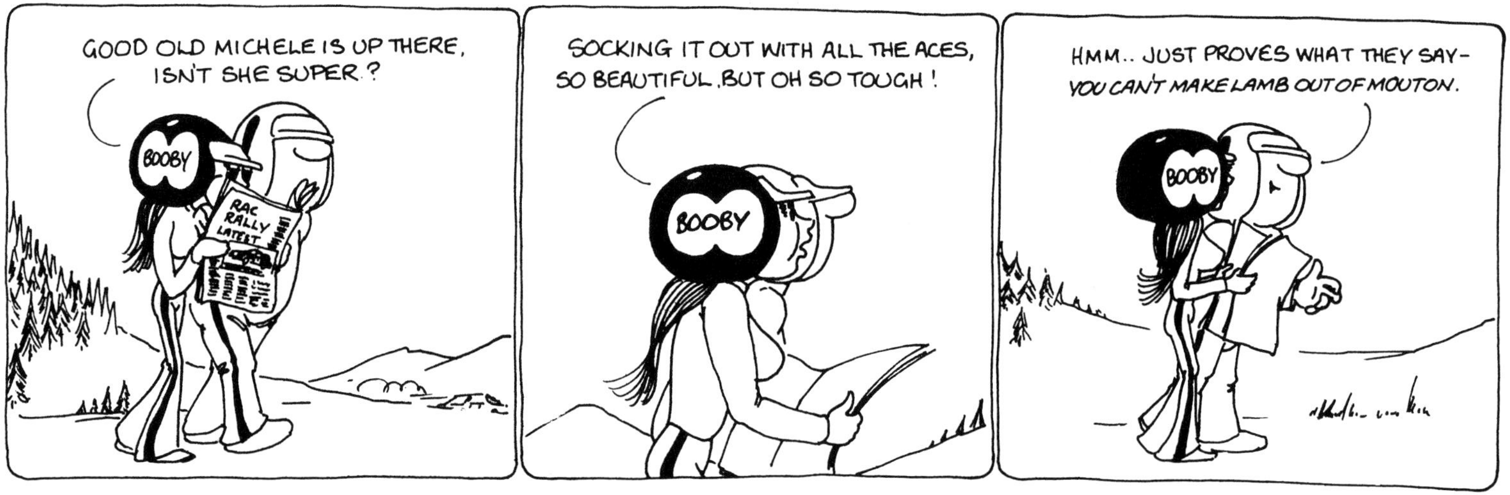
GOOD OLD MICHELE IS UP THERE, ISN'T SHE SUPER?
BOOBY
RAC RALLY LATEST
SOCKING IT OUT WITH ALL THE ACES, SO BEAUTIFUL, BUT OH SO TOUGH!
BOOBY
HMM.. JUST PROVES WHAT THEY SAY - YOU CAN'T MAKE LAMB OUT OF MOUTON.
BOOBY

25th November 1982

Chapter Two

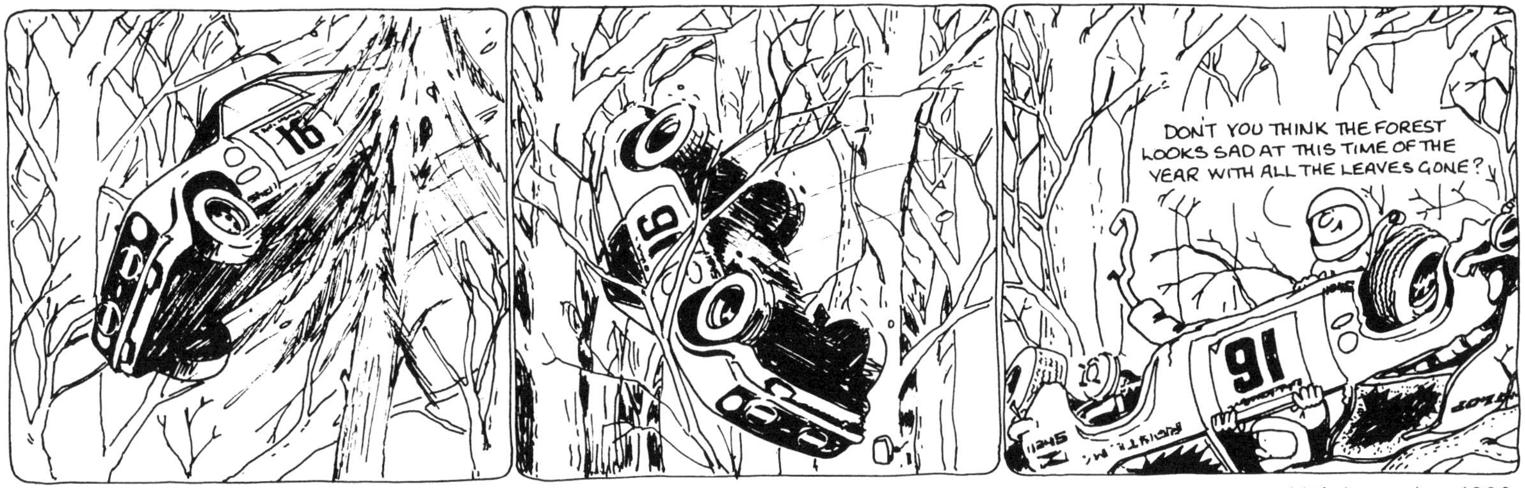
DON'T YOU THINK THE FOREST LOOKS SAD AT THIS TIME OF THE YEAR WITH ALL THE LEAVES GONE?

16th December 1982

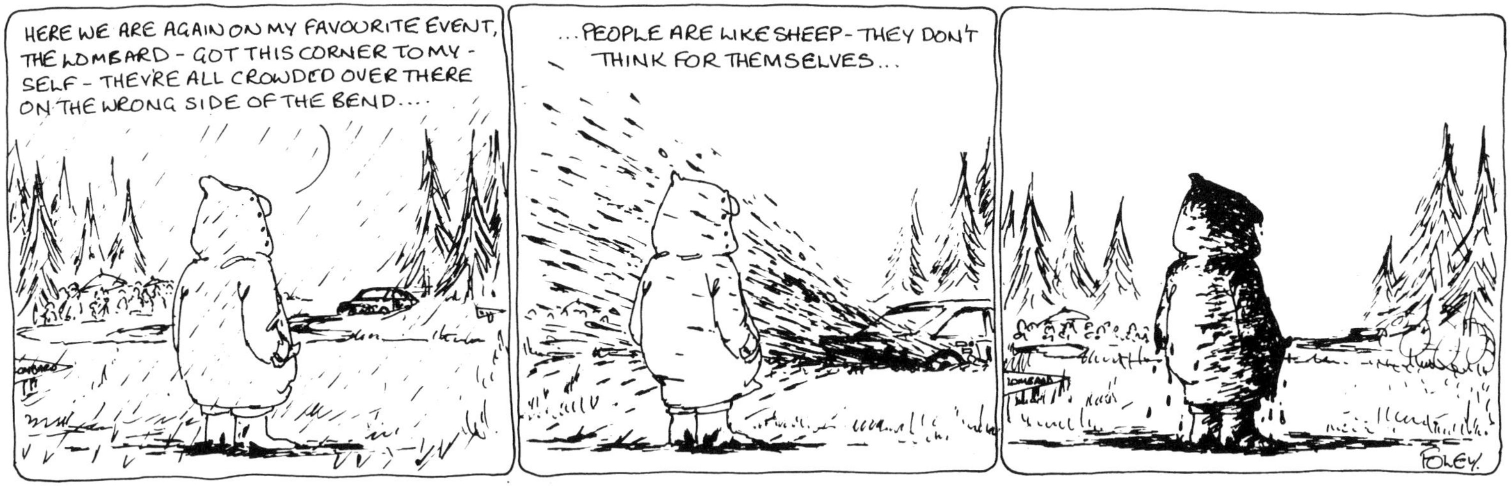
HERE WE ARE AGAIN ON MY FAVOURITE EVENT, THE LOMBARD - GOT THIS CORNER TO MY-SELF - THEY'RE ALL CROWDED OVER THERE ON THE WRONG SIDE OF THE BEND....
...PEOPLE ARE LIKE SHEEP - THEY DON'T THINK FOR THEMSELVES...
FOLEY.

29th November 1984

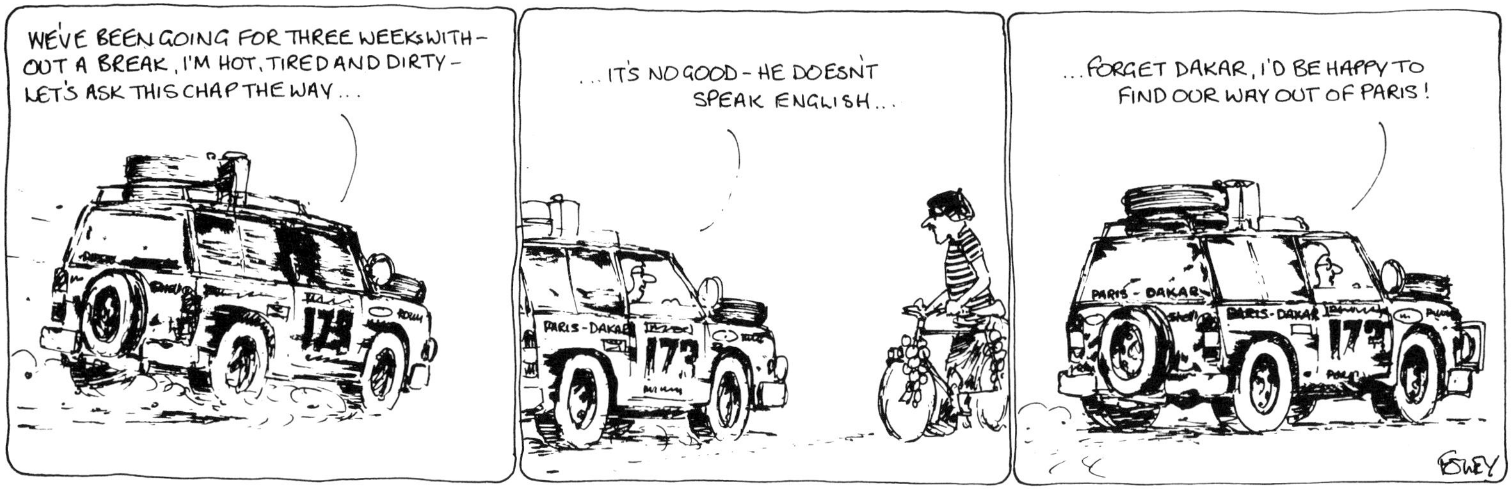
WE'VE BEEN GOING FOR THREE WEEKS WITH-OUT A BREAK, I'M HOT, TIRED AND DIRTY - LET'S ASK THIS CHAP THE WAY...
...IT'S NO GOOD - HE DOESN'T SPEAK ENGLISH...
...FORGET DAKAR, I'D BE HAPPY TO FIND OUR WAY OUT OF PARIS!
FOLEY

7th February 1985

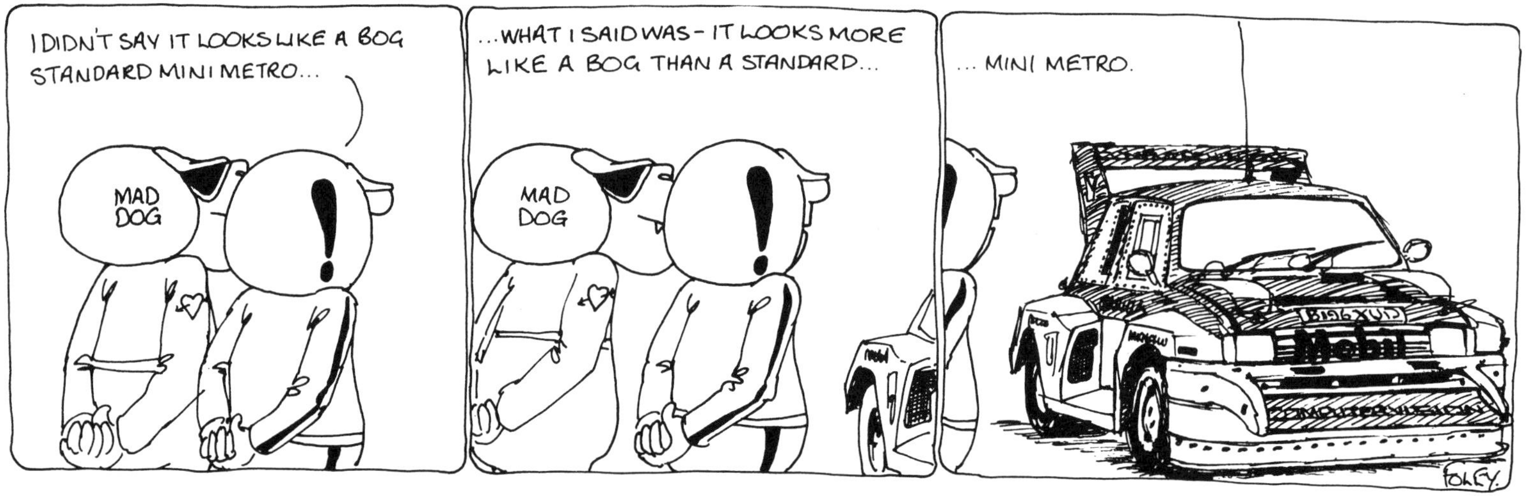
I DIDN'T SAY IT LOOKS LIKE A BOG STANDARD MINI METRO...
MAD DOG
...WHAT I SAID WAS - IT LOOKS MORE LIKE A BOG THAN A STANDARD...
MAD DOG
...MINI METRO.
FOLEY

5th December 1985

Chapter Two

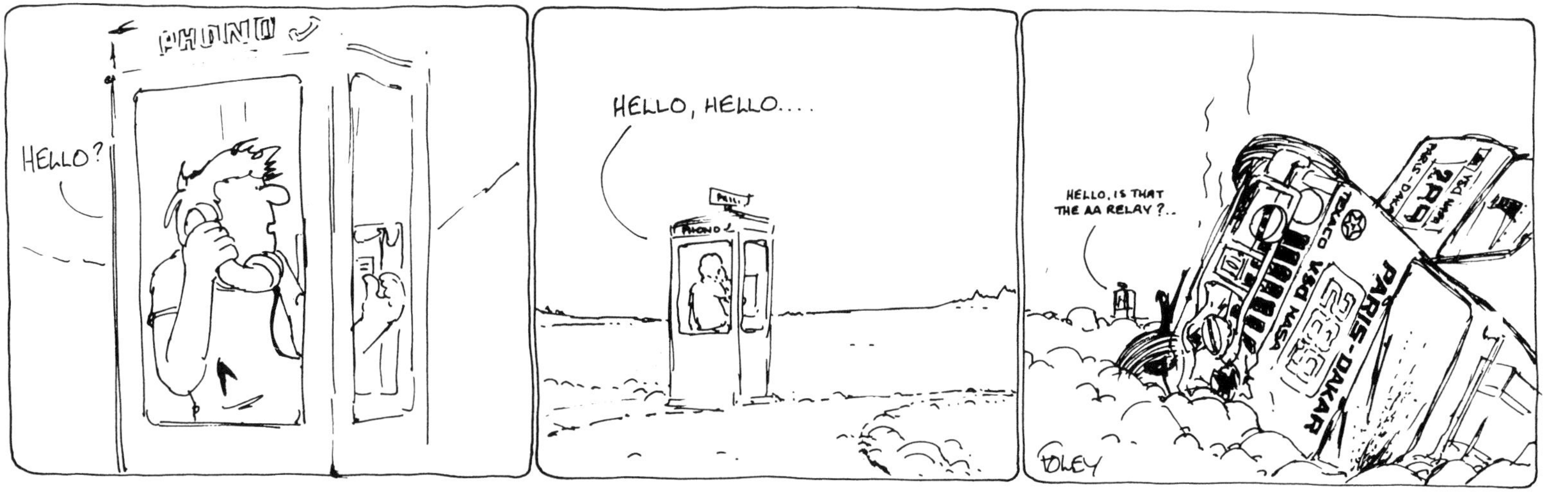
PHONO
HELLO?
HELLO, HELLO....
HELLO, IS THAT THE AA RELAY?..
TEXACO
VSD NASA
PARIS-DAKAR
FOLEY

23rd January 1986

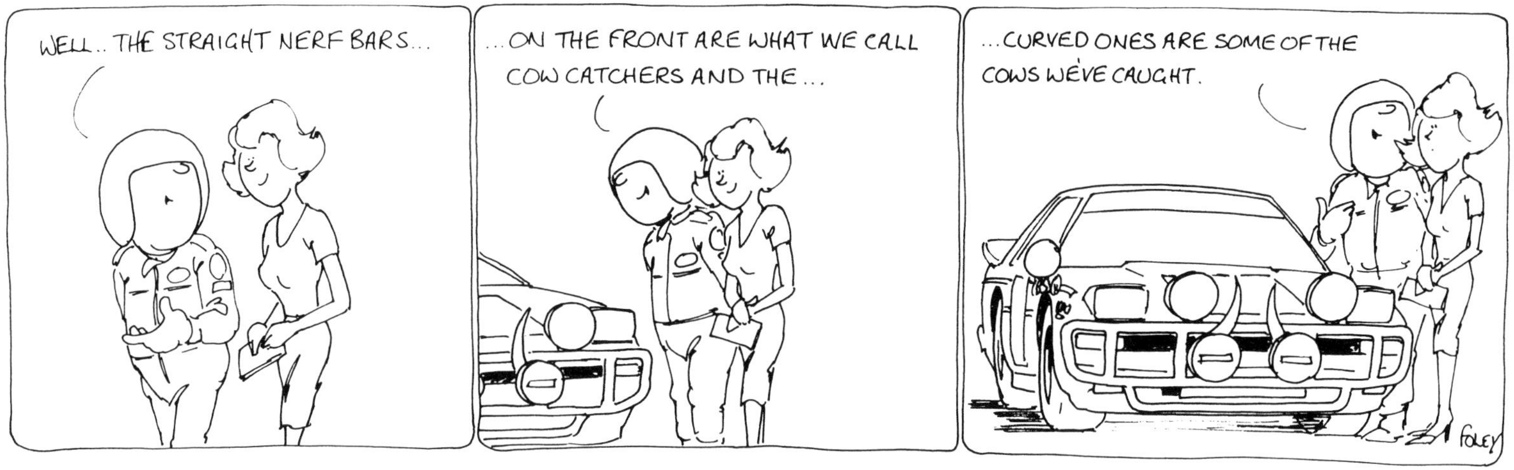
WELL.. THE STRAIGHT NERF BARS...
...ON THE FRONT ARE WHAT WE CALL COW CATCHERS AND THE...
...CURVED ONES ARE SOME OF THE COWS WE'VE CAUGHT.
FOLEY

30th April 1987

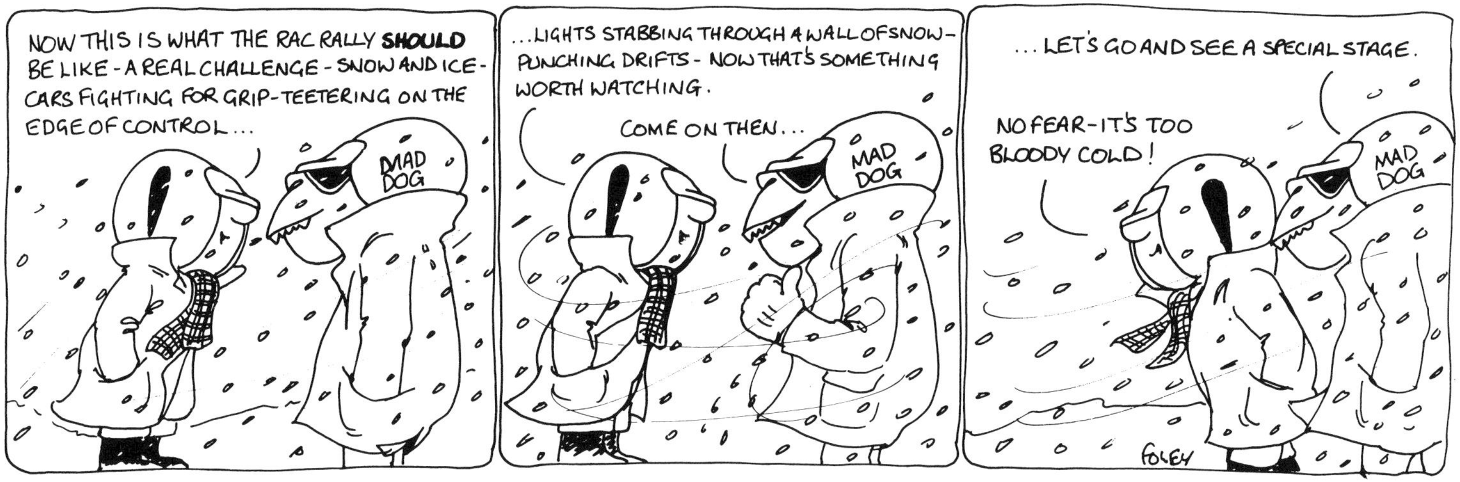
NOW THIS IS WHAT THE RAC RALLY **SHOULD** BE LIKE - A REAL CHALLENGE - SNOW AND ICE - CARS FIGHTING FOR GRIP - TEETERING ON THE EDGE OF CONTROL...
MAD DOG
...LIGHTS STABBING THROUGH A WALL OF SNOW - PUNCHING DRIFTS - NOW THAT'S SOMETHING WORTH WATCHING.
COME ON THEN...
MAD DOG
...LET'S GO AND SEE A SPECIAL STAGE.
NO FEAR - IT'S TOO BLOODY COLD!
MAD DOG
FOLEY

24th November 1988

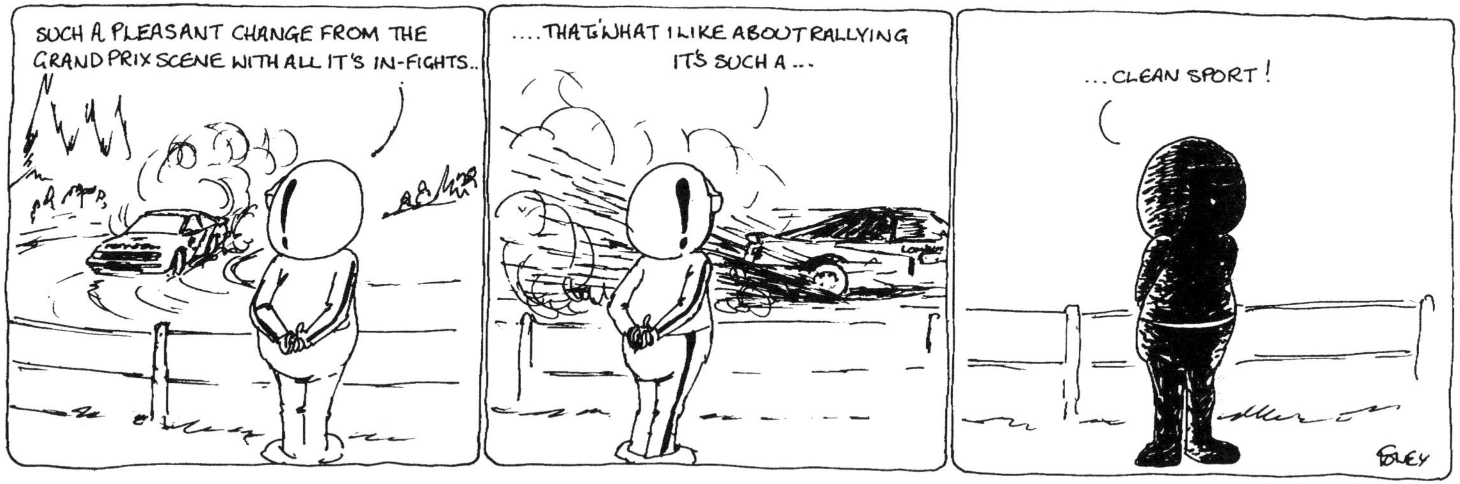
SUCH A PLEASANT CHANGE FROM THE GRAND PRIX SCENE WITH ALL IT'S IN-FIGHTS..
....THAT'S WHAT I LIKE ABOUT RALLYING IT'S SUCH A ...
...CLEAN SPORT!
FOLEY

23rd November 1989

Marshals

Chapter Three

Every one knows marshals are the salt of the earth - that's why they leave so many empty crisp packets about. Dillon is the archetypal marshal, he has difficulty understanding why they call him an anorak when he always wears a duffel coat. Dillon loves racing. Each spring he awakens to go flag marshalling. He spends every weekend at the track unless he's on a fire fighting course or his annual pilgrimage to Le Mans.
As autumn arrives and the weather cools his blood slows, until by the last race of the winter series he goes into full hibernation.

I LIKE THE RED ONES BEST
FLAG MARSHAL

MARSHAL
MARSHAL
MARSHAL
I SAW THAT, NO. 31 PASSING UNDER THE YELLOW FLAG
MARSHAL

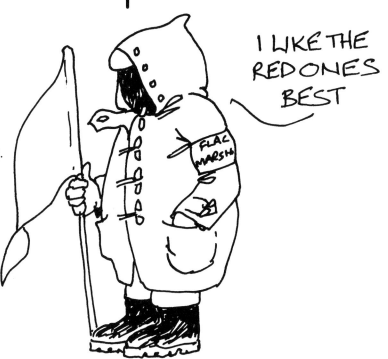

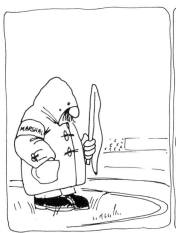

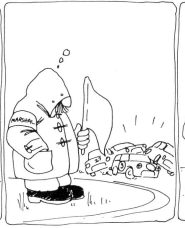

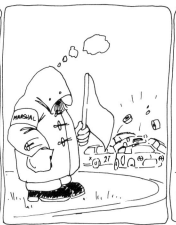

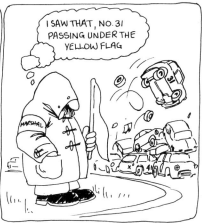

Marshals

TO BE A FLAG MARSHAL YOU'VE GOT 'AVE SPECIAL QUALIFICATIONS, YOU'VE GOT TO 'AVE YER WITS ABOUT YER...
MARSHAL
....YER REFLEXES 'AVE GOT TO BE HONED TO A FINE EDGE. YOU'VE GOT TO BE READY WITH YER FLAG POISED, WAITING...
MARSHAL
..AND THEN WHEN IT 'APPENS YOU'VE GOT TO SIZE THE SITUATION UP COOL AND CALM AND THEN...
MARSHAL
...RUN LIKE HELL
19
19

30th December 1971

HEY, DILLON, WAKE UP! THE RACING SEASON IS OVER. YOU CAN GO HOME NOW....
MARSHAL
FIRE
....DILLON, **DILLON!** WAKE UP DILLON, IT'S ALL OVER
PROD PROD
MARSHAL
FIRE
IT'S NO GOOD, HE'S GONE INTO HIBERNATION
ZZZZ...
MARSHAL
FIRE

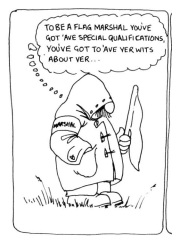

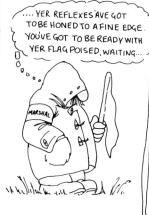

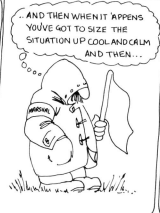

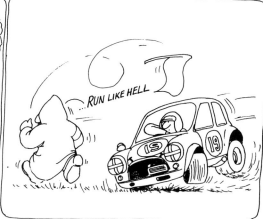

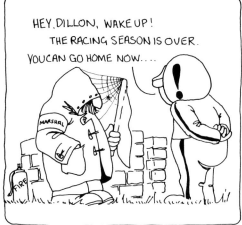

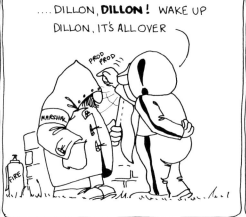

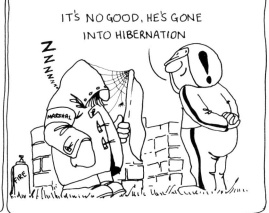

3rd February 1972

Chapter Three

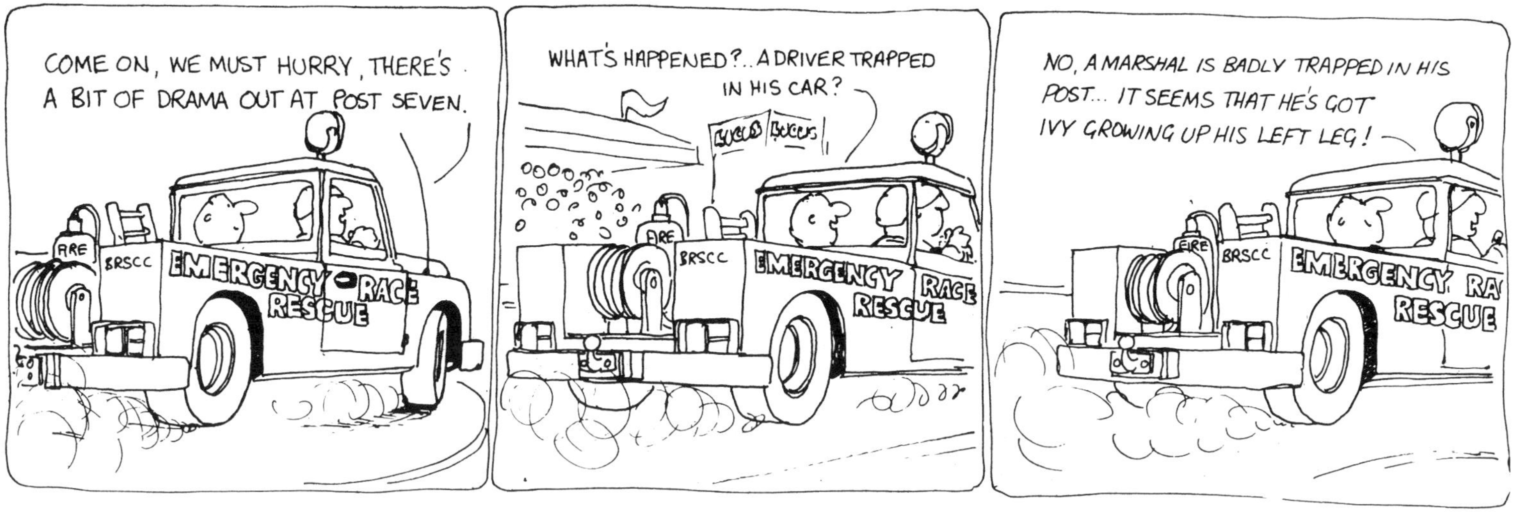
COME ON, WE MUST HURRY, THERE'S A BIT OF DRAMA OUT AT POST SEVEN.
FIRE
BRSCC
EMERGENCY RACE RESCUE
WHAT'S HAPPENED?.. A DRIVER TRAPPED IN HIS CAR?
NO, A MARSHAL IS BADLY TRAPPED IN HIS POST... IT SEEMS THAT HE'S GOT IVY GROWING UP HIS LEFT LEG!

28th August 1975

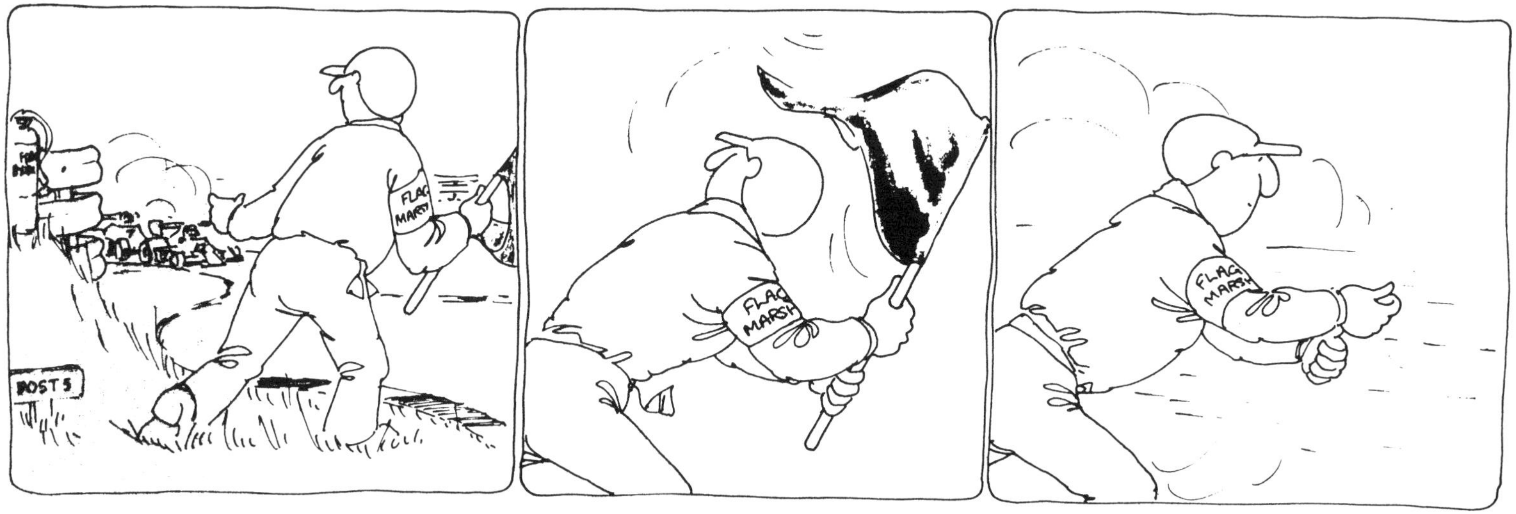
POST 5

10th April 1980

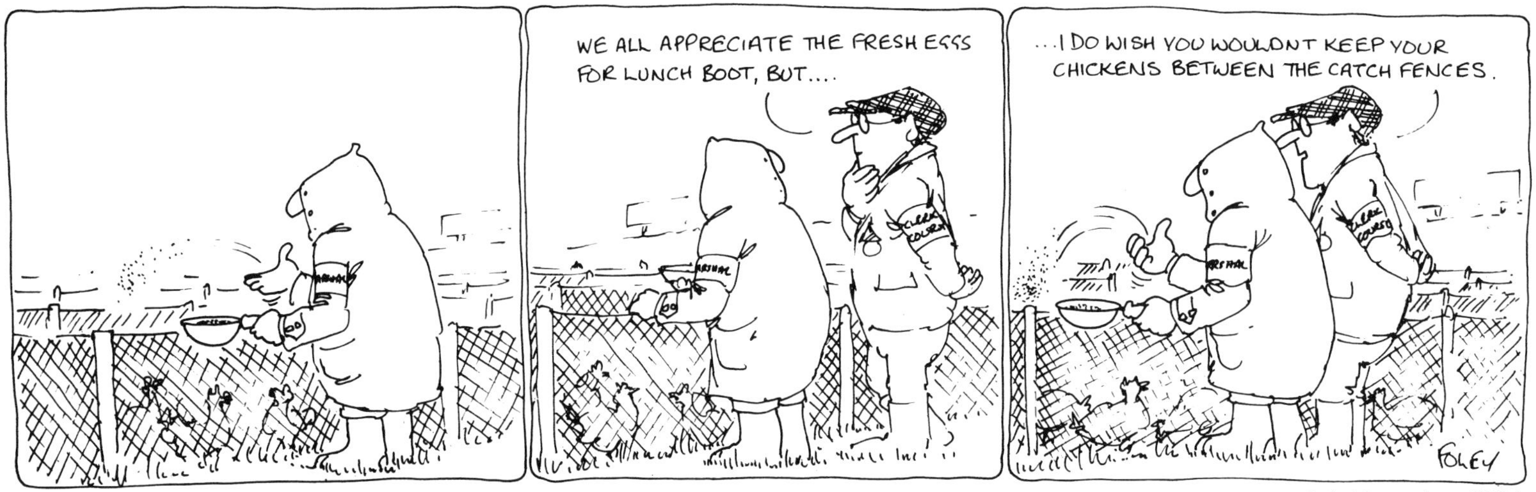
WE ALL APPRECIATE THE FRESH EGGS FOR LUNCH BOOT, BUT....
...I DO WISH YOU WOULDNT KEEP YOUR CHICKENS BETWEEN THE CATCH FENCES.
FOLEY

8th November 1984

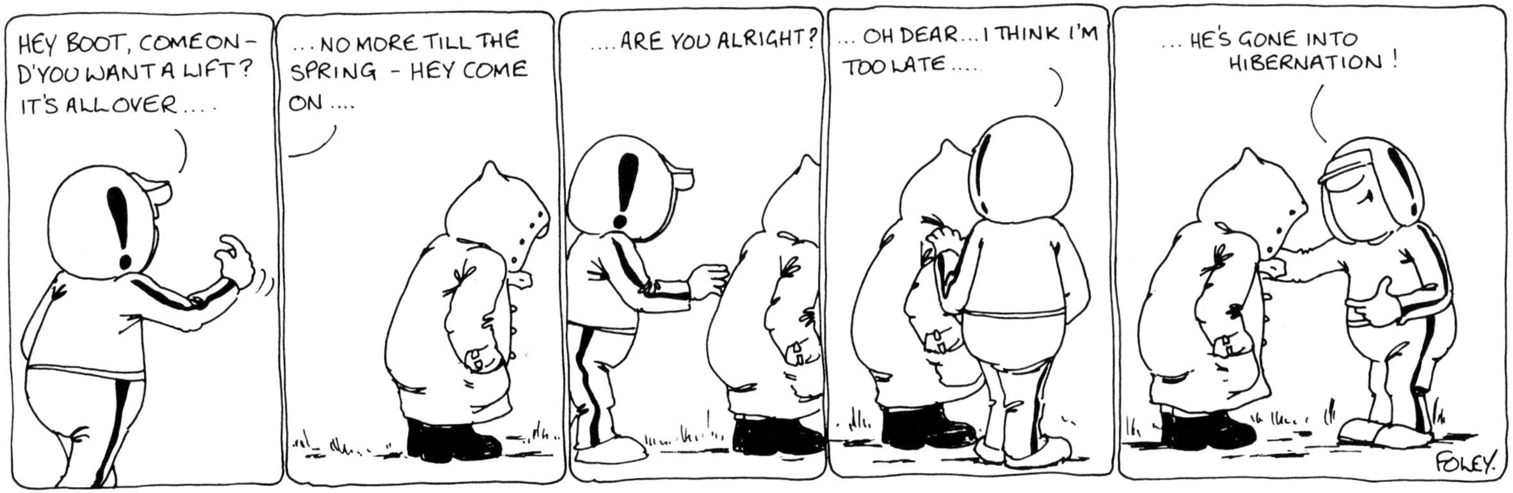
HEY BOOT, COMEON - D'YOU WANT A LIFT? IT'S ALLOVER....
...NO MORE TILL THE SPRING - HEY COME ON ....
....ARE YOU ALRIGHT?
... OH DEAR... I THINK I'M TOO LATE.....
... HE'S GONE INTO HIBERNATION!
FOLEY.

10th January 1985

Chapter Three

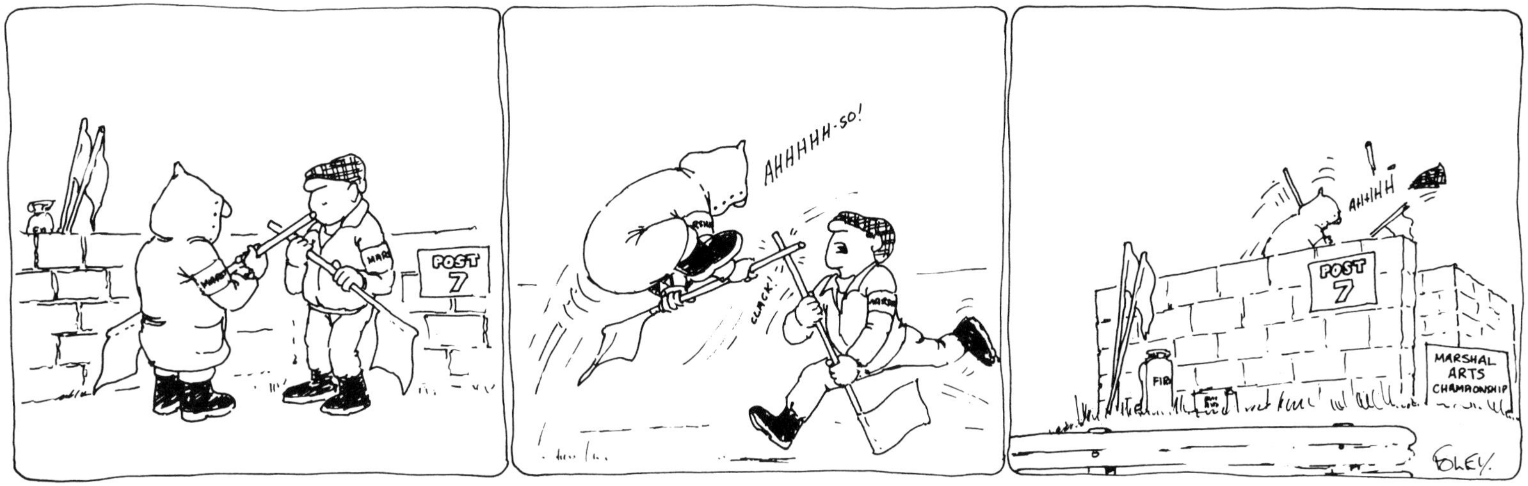

POST 7
AHHHHH-SO!
CLACK!
AHHHH
POST 7
MARSHAL ARTS CHAMPIONSHIP
FOLEY

31st January 1985

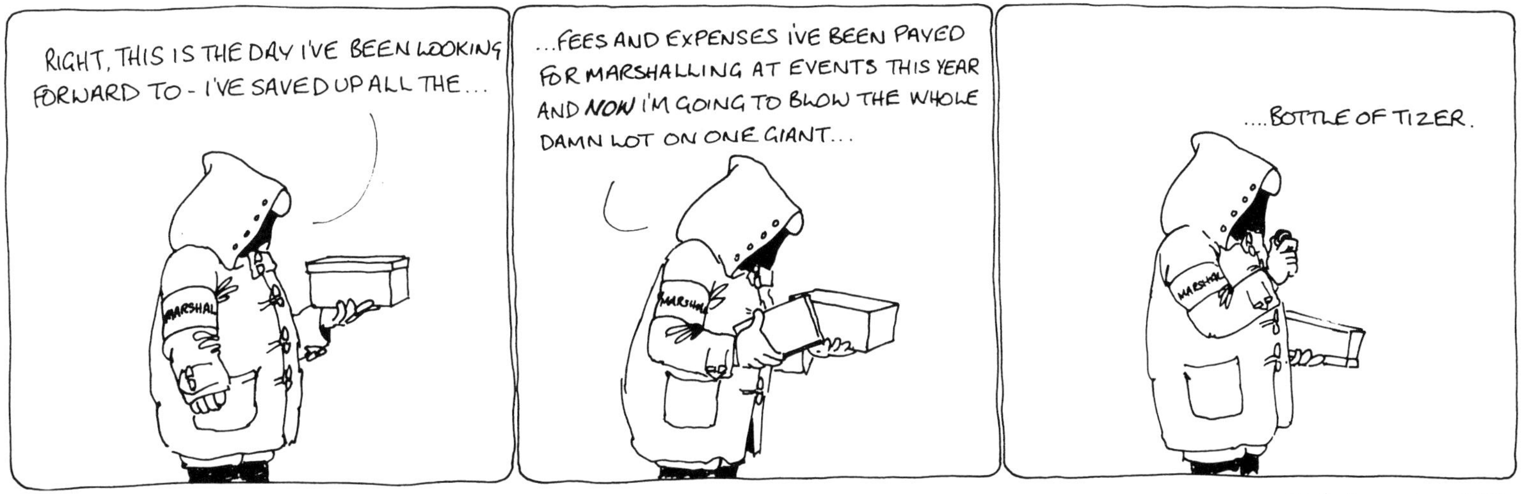

RIGHT, THIS IS THE DAY I'VE BEEN LOOKING FORWARD TO - I'VE SAVED UP ALL THE...
MARSHAL
...FEES AND EXPENSES I'VE BEEN PAYED FOR MARSHALLING AT EVENTS THIS YEAR AND NOW I'M GOING TO BLOW THE WHOLE DAMN LOT ON ONE GIANT...
MARSHAL
....BOTTLE OF TIZER.
MARSHAL

12th December 1985

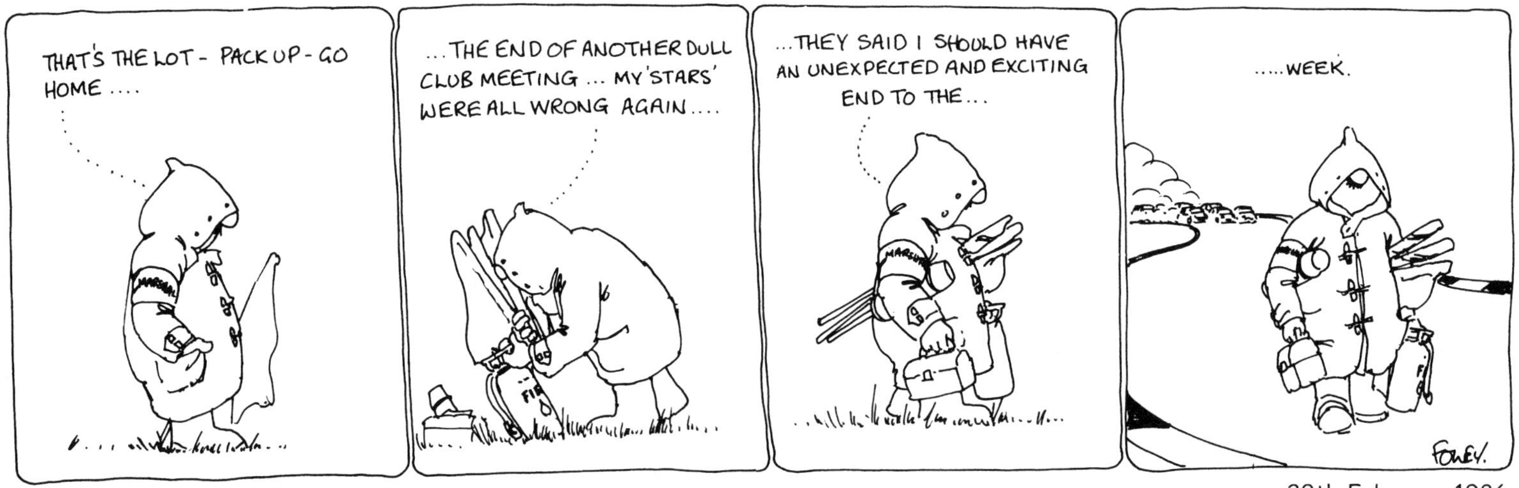
THAT'S THE LOT - PACK UP - GO HOME ....
... THE END OF ANOTHER DULL CLUB MEETING ... MY 'STARS' WERE ALL WRONG AGAIN ....
... THEY SAID I SHOULD HAVE AN UNEXPECTED AND EXCITING END TO THE ...
..... WEEK.
FOLEY.

20th February 1986

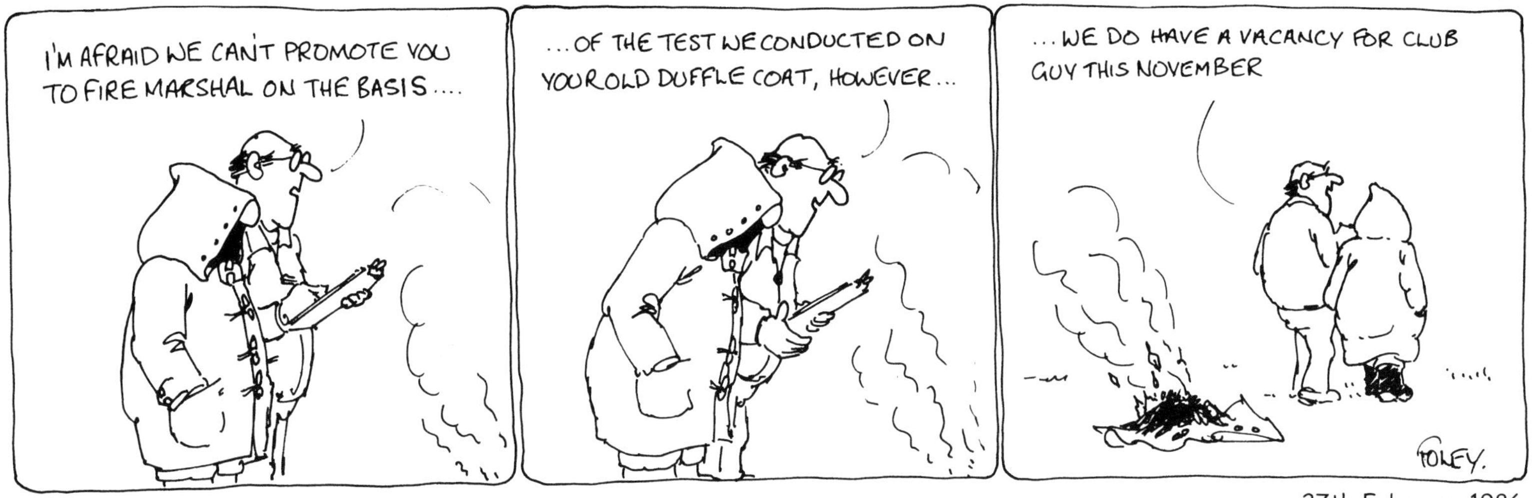
I'M AFRAID WE CAN'T PROMOTE YOU TO FIRE MARSHAL ON THE BASIS ....
... OF THE TEST WE CONDUCTED ON YOUR OLD DUFFLE COAT, HOWEVER ...
... WE DO HAVE A VACANCY FOR CLUB GUY THIS NOVEMBER
FOLEY.

27th February 1986

Chapter Three

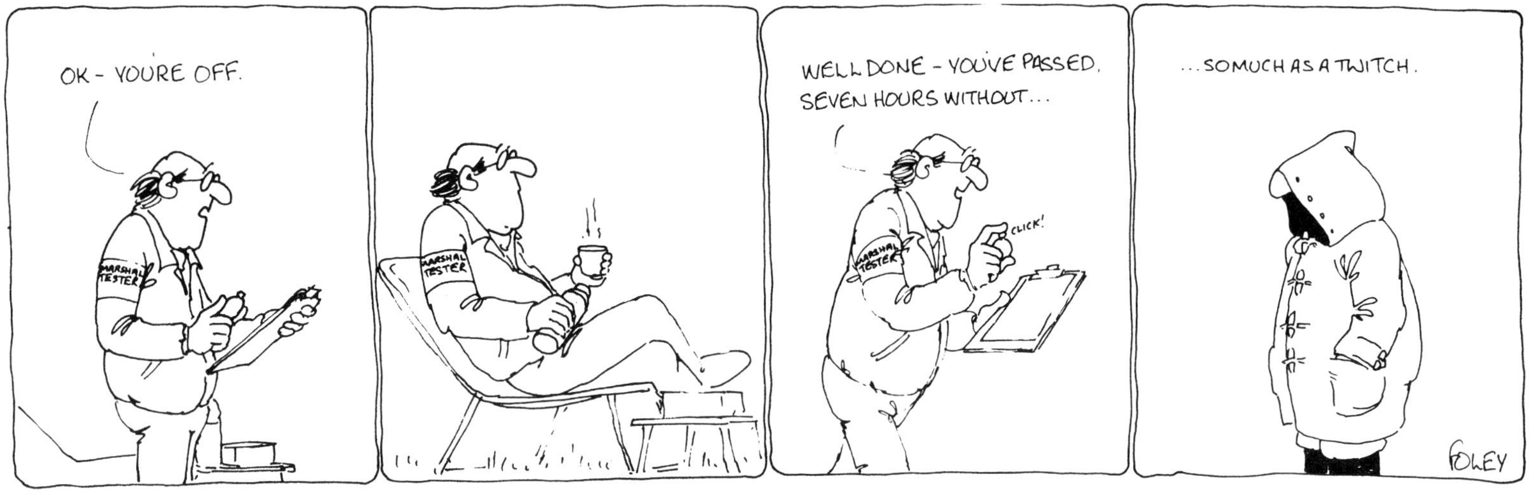
OK - YOU'RE OFF.
MARSHAL TESTER
WELL DONE - YOU'VE PASSED. SEVEN HOURS WITHOUT...
CLICK!
...SO MUCH AS A TWITCH.
FOLEY

15th May 1986

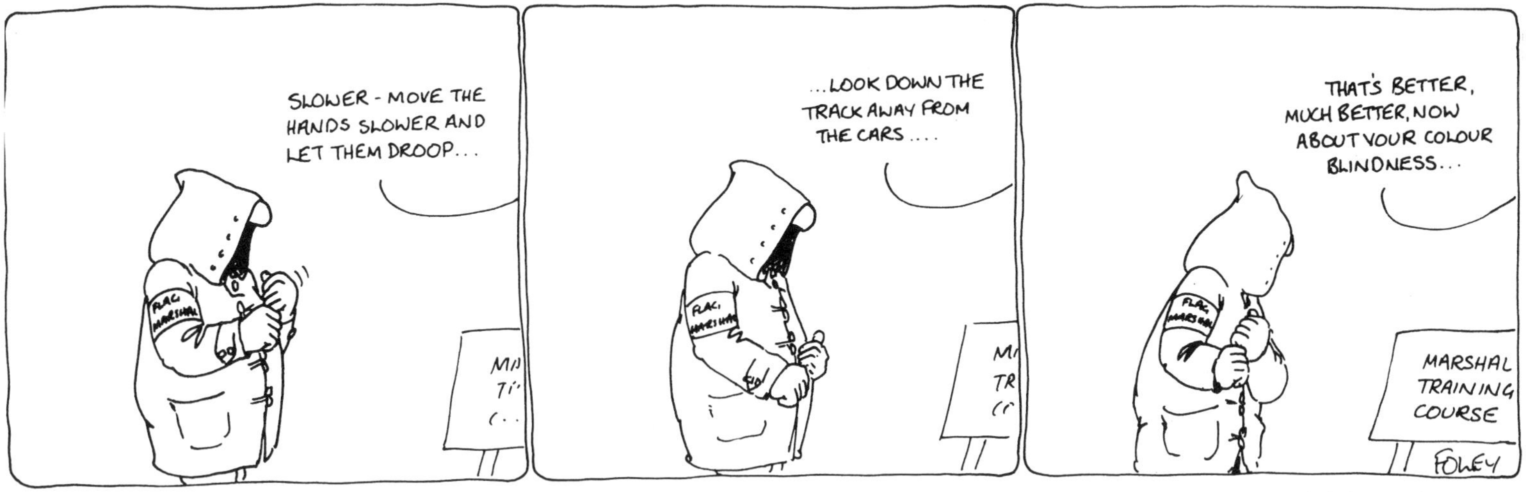
SLOWER - MOVE THE HANDS SLOWER AND LET THEM DROOP...
FLAG MARSHAL
...LOOK DOWN THE TRACK AWAY FROM THE CARS....
THAT'S BETTER, MUCH BETTER, NOW ABOUT YOUR COLOUR BLINDNESS...
MARSHAL TRAINING COURSE
FOLEY

6th November 1986

Marshals

I LIKE THE NEW COAT...
....I BET THAT KEEPS YOU WARM.
'SHOULD DO - I'M TESTING IT FOR A...
...F1 TEAM - IT'S AN ELECTRIC TYRE BLANKET.
FOLEY

6th August 1987

THAT GP WAS A BIT LIKE F3000.
IN WHAT WAY?
WELL, FOR A START IT WAS ACTUALLY EXCITING AND...
....IT HAD **TWO** RESTARTS.
FOLEY

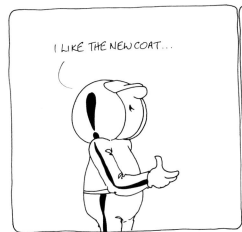

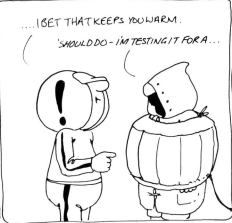

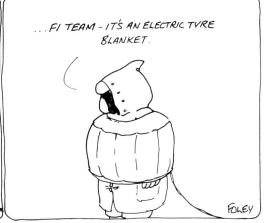

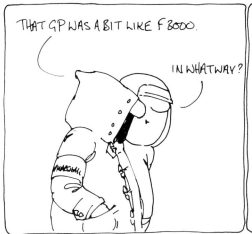

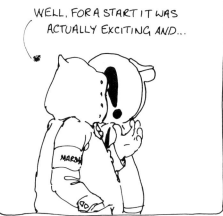

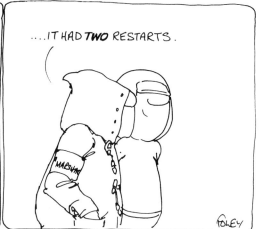

29th September 1988

Politics

This is, of course, the really exciting bit of motor racing. Politics probably use up more headline space in the motoring press than the World Championship. This is because a good political row will run and run, whereas a race is over in a couple of hours. It is debatable now whether there are more dirty tricks in driving or politics.

The reason for this popularity is due to the almost inexhaustible ability of the movers and shakers of motor racing to do something really idiotic with amazing regularity. Mind you the drivers are striking back - the driving is now almost as dirty as the politics.

Chapter Four

I DO LOVE TO GET MY CLAWS INTO A WELL ROTTED BODY

RAC MSA

NOTICE

DUE TO THE OVERWHELMING LIKELIHOOD OF THIS STRIP CARTOON BEING RUDE ABOUT THE F.I. DRIVERS BAN, PRESIDENT J.M. BALESTRE HAS DECIDED TO SUSPEND CATCHPOLE THIS WEEK. BY ORDER OF F.I.S.A.

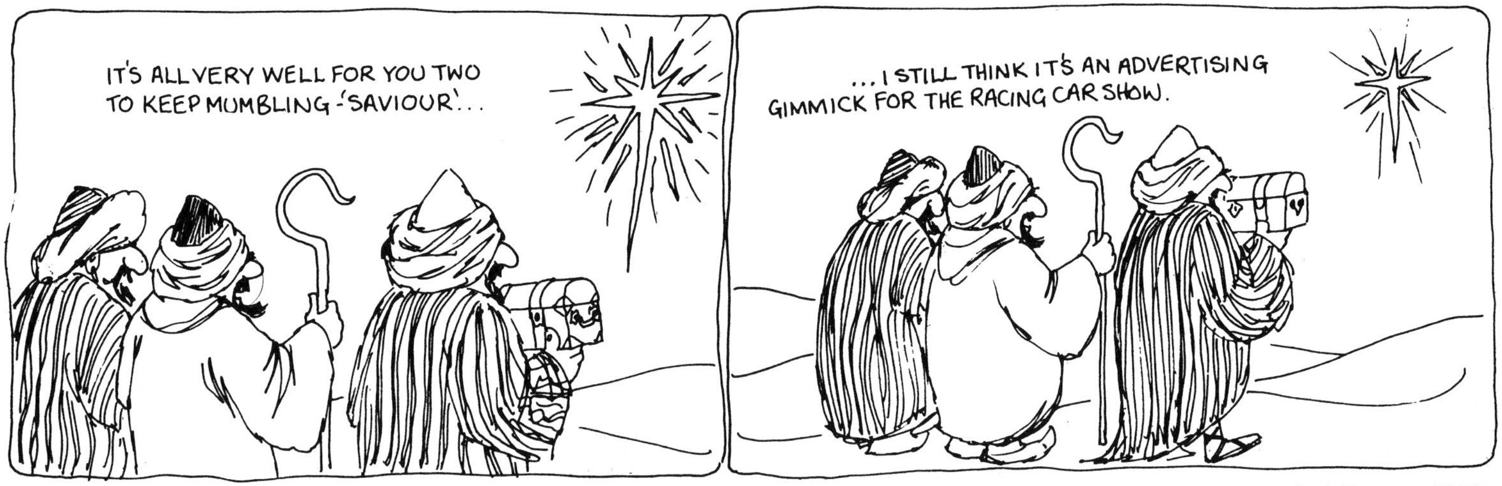
IT'S ALL VERY WELL FOR YOU TWO TO KEEP MUMBLING -'SAVIOUR'...
...I STILL THINK IT'S AN ADVERTISING GIMMICK FOR THE RACING CAR SHOW.

2nd January 1975

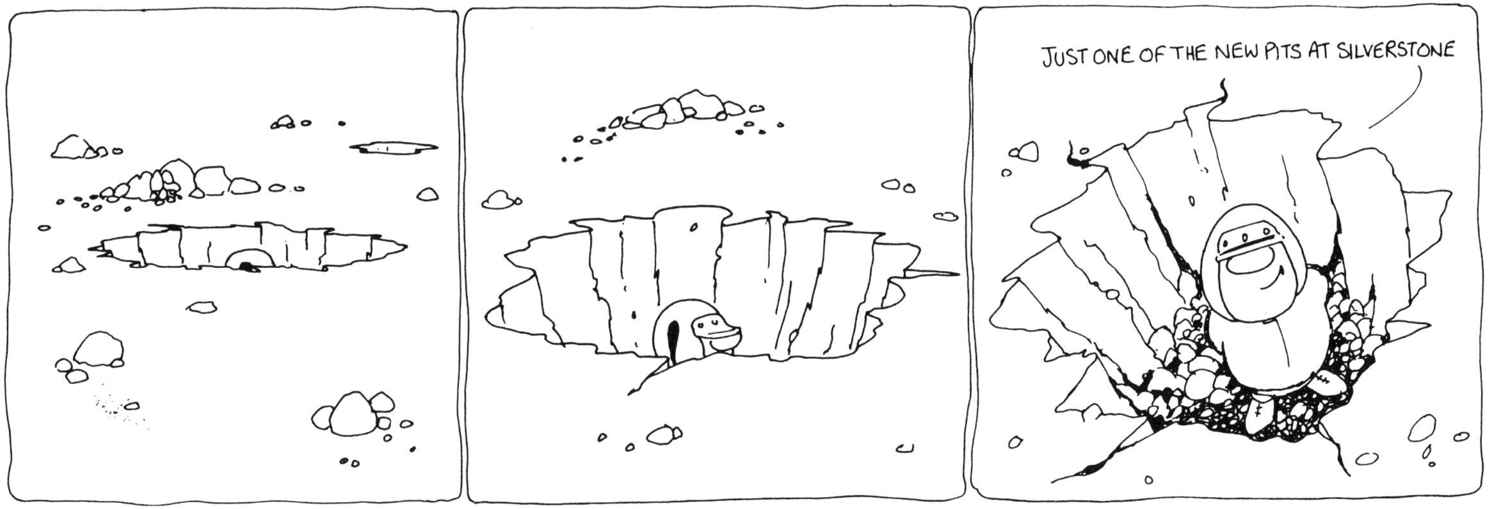
JUST ONE OF THE NEW PITS AT SILVERSTONE

23rd January 1975

Chapter Four

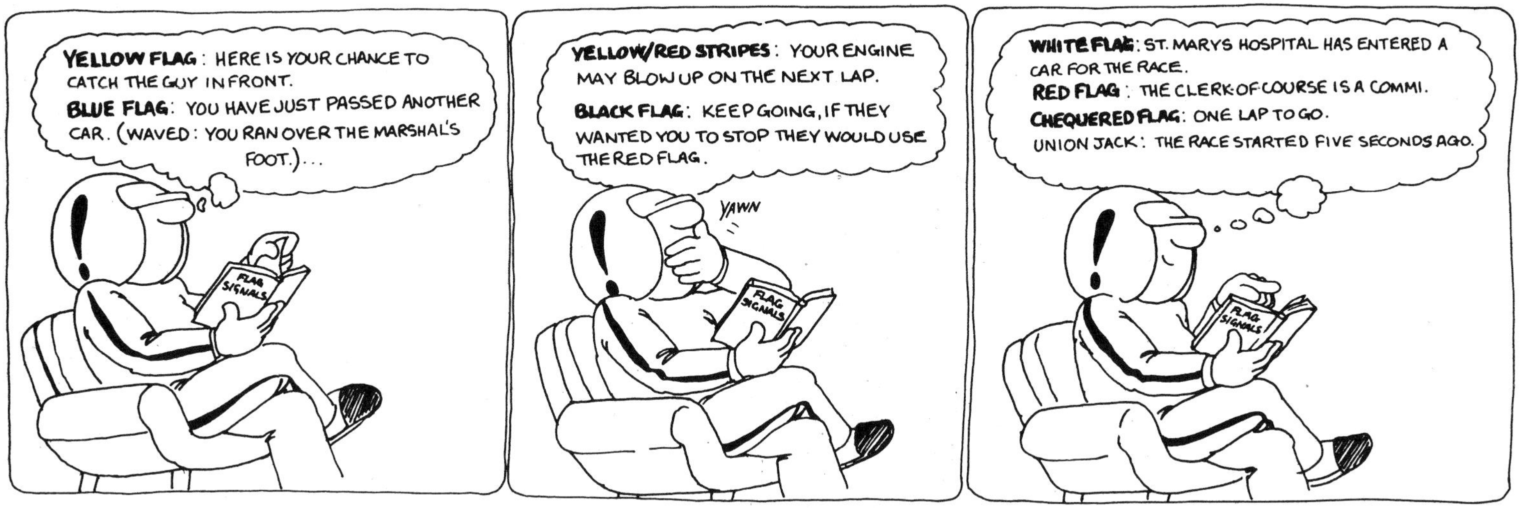
YELLOW FLAG: HERE IS YOUR CHANCE TO CATCH THE GUY IN FRONT.
BLUE FLAG: YOU HAVE JUST PASSED ANOTHER CAR. (WAVED: YOU RAN OVER THE MARSHAL'S FOOT.)...
FLAG SIGNALS
YELLOW/RED STRIPES: YOUR ENGINE MAY BLOW UP ON THE NEXT LAP.
BLACK FLAG: KEEP GOING, IF THEY WANTED YOU TO STOP THEY WOULD USE THE RED FLAG.
YAWN
FLAG SIGNALS
WHITE FLAG: ST. MARYS HOSPITAL HAS ENTERED A CAR FOR THE RACE.
RED FLAG: THE CLERK OF COURSE IS A COMMI.
CHEQUERED FLAG: ONE LAP TO GO.
UNION JACK: THE RACE STARTED FIVE SECONDS AGO.
FLAG SIGNALS

3rd February 1977

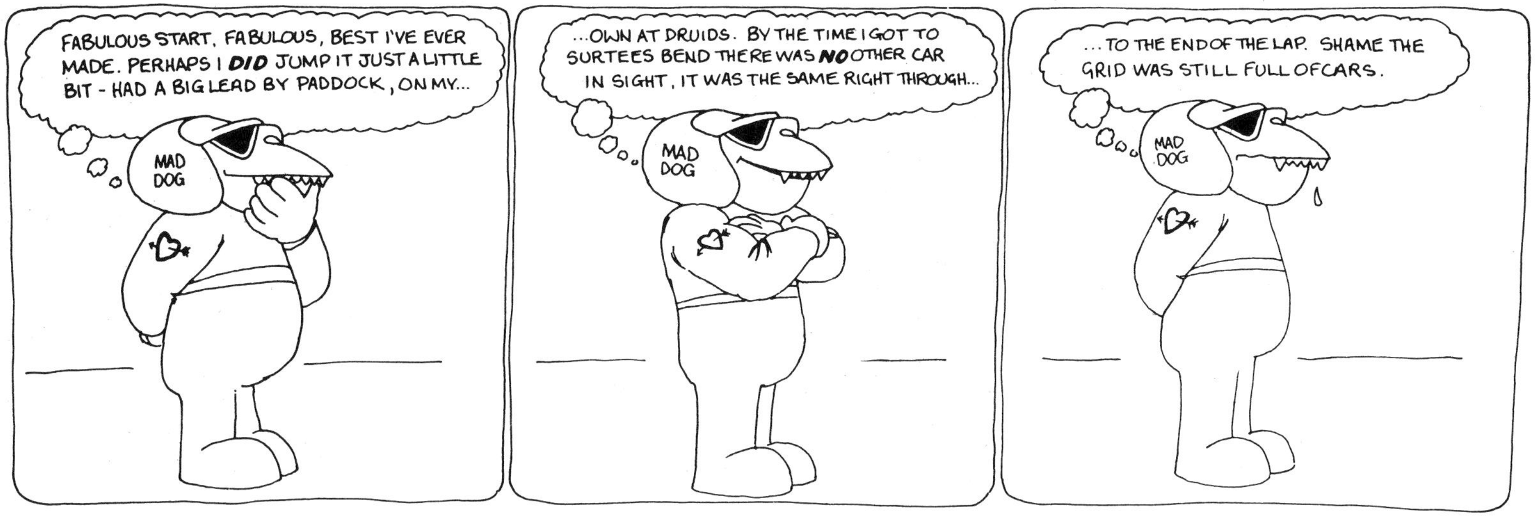
FABULOUS START, FABULOUS, BEST I'VE EVER MADE. PERHAPS I DID JUMP IT JUST A LITTLE BIT - HAD A BIG LEAD BY PADDOCK, ON MY...
MAD DOG
...OWN AT DRUIDS. BY THE TIME I GOT TO SURTEES BEND THERE WAS NO OTHER CAR IN SIGHT, IT WAS THE SAME RIGHT THROUGH...
MAD DOG
...TO THE END OF THE LAP. SHAME THE GRID WAS STILL FULL OF CARS.
MAD DOG

28th April 1977

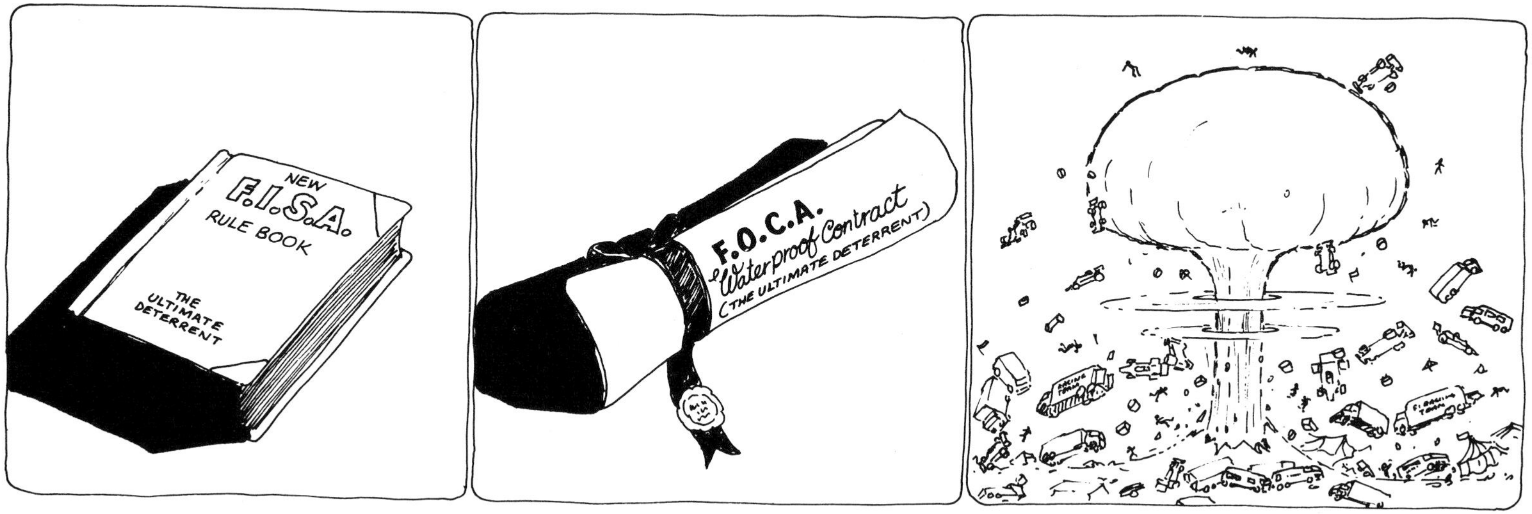
NEW
F.I.S.A.
RULE BOOK
THE ULTIMATE DETERRENT
F.O.C.A.
Waterproof Contract
(THE ULTIMATE DETERRENT)

6th November 1980

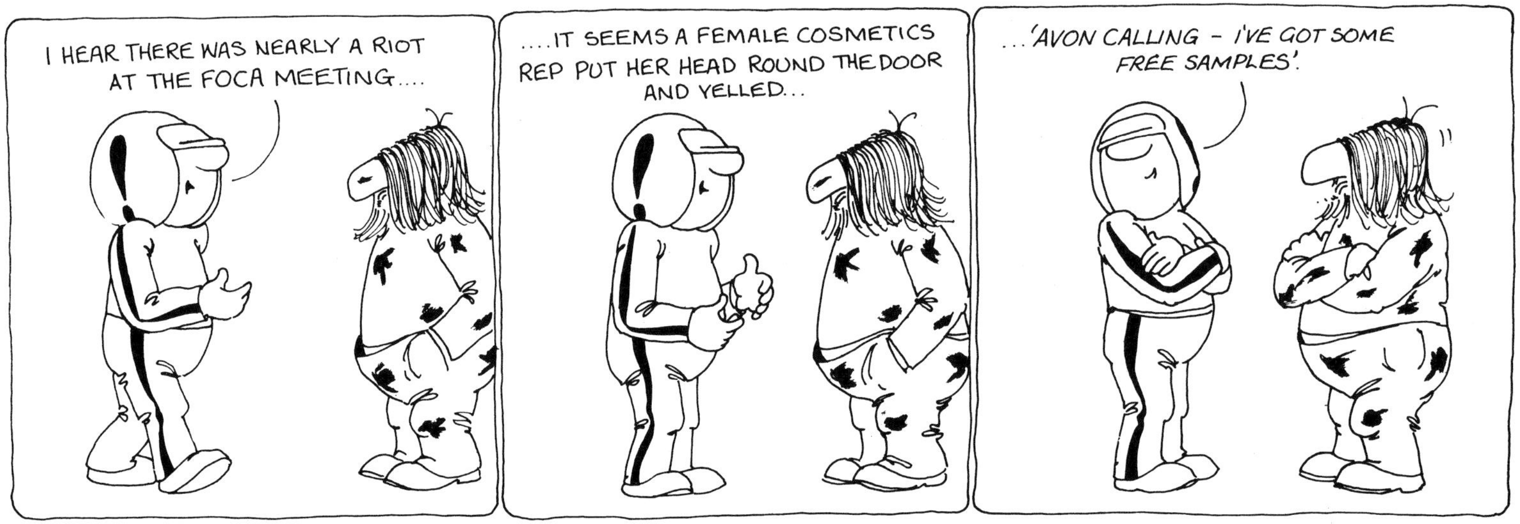
I HEAR THERE WAS NEARLY A RIOT AT THE FOCA MEETING....
....IT SEEMS A FEMALE COSMETICS REP PUT HER HEAD ROUND THE DOOR AND YELLED...
...'AVON CALLING - I'VE GOT SOME FREE SAMPLES'.

5th February 1981

Chapter Four

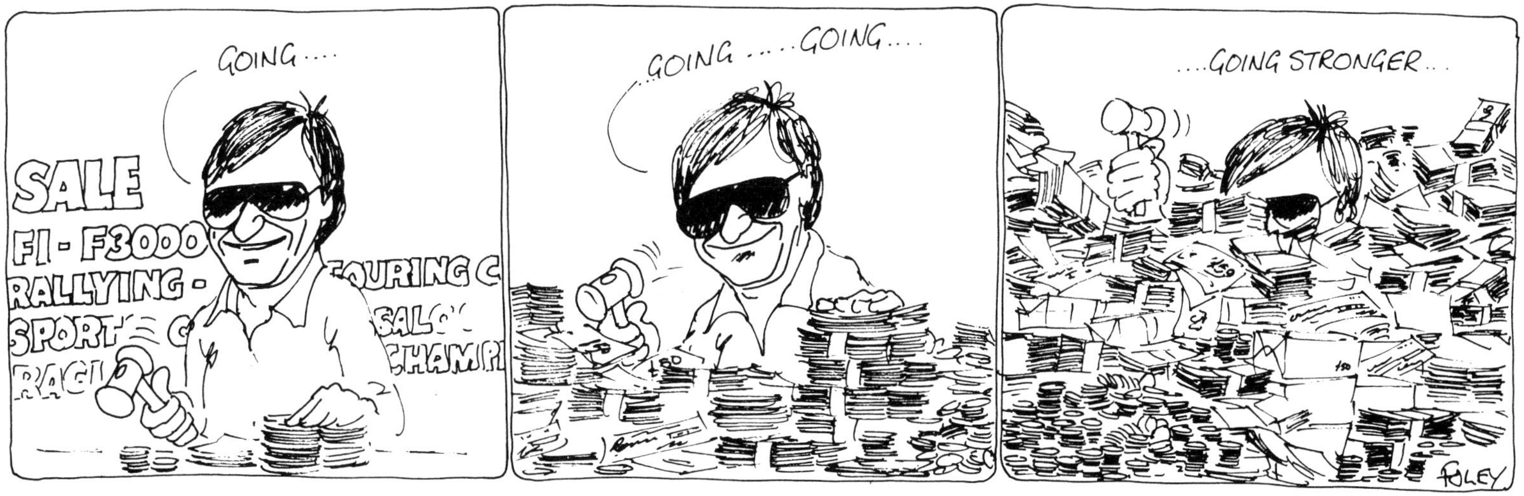
GOING....
SALE
F1 - F3000
RALLYING -
GOING .....GOING....
....GOING STRONGER...
FOLEY

12th March 1987

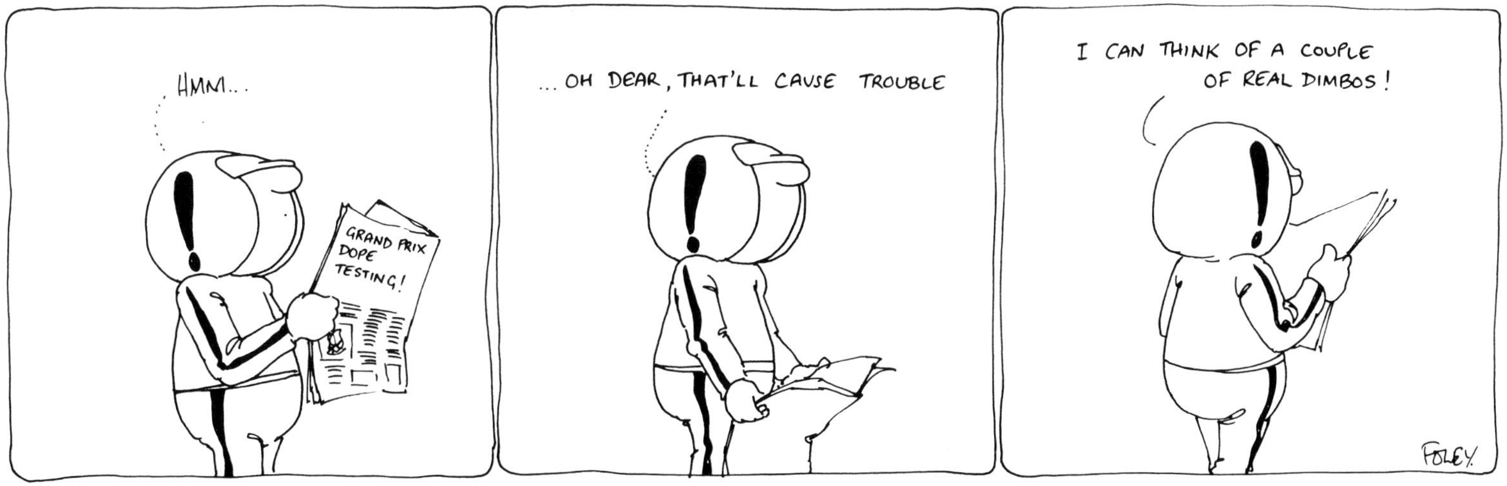
HMM...
GRAND PRIX DOPE TESTING!
...OH DEAR, THAT'LL CAUSE TROUBLE
I CAN THINK OF A COUPLE OF REAL DIMBOS!
FOLEY

17th September 1987

WHAT HAPPENED AT THE APPEAL - DID THEY ACCEPT HIS STORY OF THE BLACK FLAG? - DID THEY BELIEVE?
OH YES, THEY BELIEVED - EVERYONE OF THEM. SOME OF THEM BELIEVED HE WAS TELLING THE TRUTH....
...SOME BELIEVED HE WAS LYING, AND ALL OF THEM BELIEVED THEY'D PUT THE DECISION OFF.
FOLEY

12th October 1989

I HEAR THE NEW SPECIAL COMMISSION ON SAFETY HAS COME UP WITH A DECISION ALREADY
FISA
THAT'S RIGHT - WELL, A RECOMMENDATION REALLY - AN INITIAL SAFETY MEASURE, SHALL WE SAY, WE WON'T BE MAKING A PRESS STATEMENT....
...CONFIDENTIALLY, WE ARE VERY WORRIED ABOUT THE POOR STATE OF THE STAIR CARPET LEADING TO COMMITTEE ROOM 3.
FOLEY

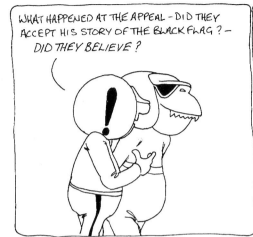

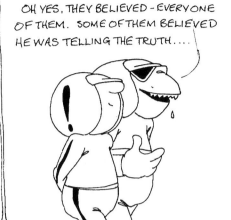

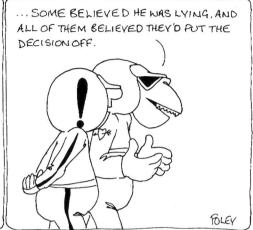

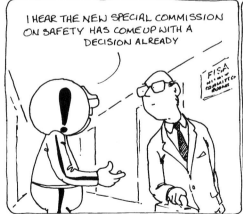

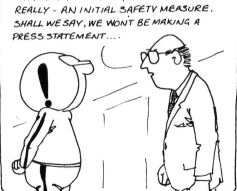

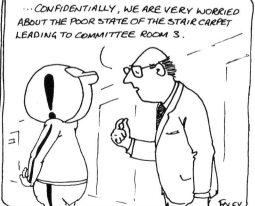

13th December 1990

Chapter Five

The Politically Correct

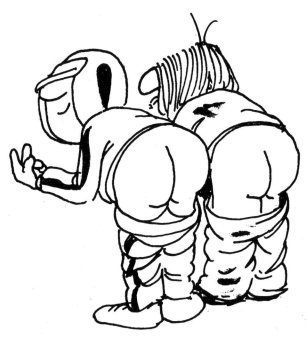

It's surprising to think the term 'politically correct' didn't exist in the era when Booby Galore was born. I remember when even 'sexist' was a fresh, albeit somewhat uncomfortable thought and the smell of smouldering bras was still quite faint. In those halcyon days pictures of pleasantly nubile naked young things adorned every office wall and locker room. Of course we were under the misguided impression that women enjoyed the visual triggers of sex as much as men. Booby was the visual representation of the spinal shiver caused by the presence of a busty young woman in the drivers' changing room.

HALLO, WHAT'S THE RUSH?
SQEEZE UP
ROOM FOR ONE MORE?
DON'T PUSH
MOVE ALONG
GRUNT
DRIVERS CHANGING ROOM
SLAM!
DRIVERS CHANGING ROOM
THE THINGS THAT I MISS!

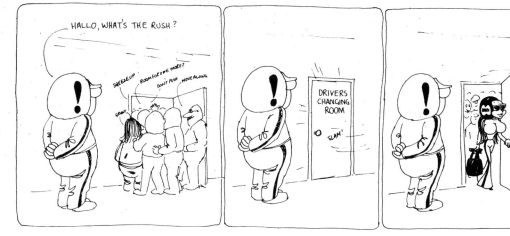

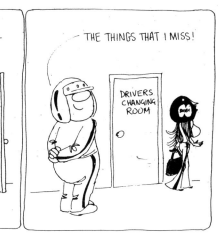

WHEEEE.... THATS ENOUGH TO TURN YOU TO DRINK
...GRUNT ...GRUNT
TWICH TWICH
TWO PINTS OF BITTER PLEASE
CATCH-POLE
DEMON TWEAK

17th December 1970

OH LORD – HERE COMES 'SPIDER' THE TRACKOWNER. THE ARROGANT SLOB. I'LL PRETEND I HAVEN'T SEEN HIM.....
I'LL SHUN HIM. IF HE SAYS A WORD I SHALL JUST TURN MY BACK...
A VERY GOOD MORNING TO YOU, MR. SPIDER, SIR
SOMETIMES I HATE MYSELF

31st December 1970

Chapter Five

GRUNT
GRUNT
HEEL, BOY, HEEL
GRUNT
SCREECH!
TWEAK, DON'T THROW YOURSELF AWAY ON THE FIRST GIRL THAT COMES ALONG.

28th January 1971

HEY, MAD DOG. TELL ME, WHY DO YOU WEAR A HEART ON YOUR ARM?
MAD DOG MALONE
MAD DOG MALONE
MAD DOG MALONE
HE SAID "IT'S PERSONAL"
MAD DOG MALONE

11th February 1971

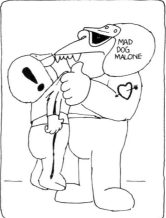

LET'S NIP DOWN TO THE SCRUTING BAY, THERE'S A NEW SCRUTE ON TODAY....
GRUNT
DEMON TWEAK
....HIS NAME IS DAPHNE, I THINK HE FANCIES YOU TWEAK...
DEMON TWEAK
BLOW HIM A KISS AND HE MAY PASS OUR CAR
CHEEKY
GRUNT
DEMON TWEAK

25th February 1971

HALLO THERE, DUCKY
DEMON TWEAK
SCRUTE
GRUNT! GRUNT!
SCRUTE
DEMON TWEAK
OH! BUTCH VERY BUTCH
SCRUTE
DEMON TWEAK

18th March 1971

Chapter Five

LOOK TWEAK, HERE COMES BOOBY GALORE....
GRUNT GRUNT
BOOBY
DEMON TWEAK
....SHE'S A GREAT LITTLE DICER...
'LO CATCHPOLE
BOOBY
DEMON TWEAK
....KEEPS FINISHING TWO ABREAST.
BOOBY
DEMON TWEAK

3rd June 1971

CATCHPOLE, DO YOU THINK I COULD ASK MR TWEAK TO COME AND LOOK AT MY THROTTLE CABLE....
BOOBY
DEMON TWEAK
...I THINK MY NIPPLES ARE COMPLETELY WORN OUT.
GRUNT
BOOBY
DEMON TWEAK
I NEVER SAID A WORD.
BOOBY
DEMON TWEAK

26th August 1971

...ANYWAY, WHEN I CAME IN AFTER THE RACE THE SILLY OLD FORMULA FORD SCRUTES PULLED ME INTO THE....
BOOBY
17
....SCRUTINEERING BAY. THEY SAID THAT I'D HAVE TO BE STRIPPED DOWN AND EXAMINED TO SEE IF I WAS OVERSIZED.
BOOBY
17
THEY MUST BE BLIND!
BOOBY
17

27th January 1972

DID YOU WIN YOUR RACE BOOBY?
BOOBY
YES I DID, BY MILES.
BOOBY
WAY OUT IN FRONT, I SUPPOSE.
BOOBY

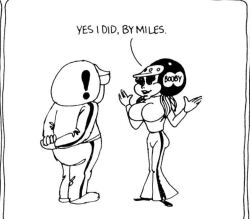

20th April 1972

Chapter Five

The Politically Correct

WHAT'S UP BOOB?
HMMMM...
I DON'T KNOW WHETHER TO FEEL HONOURED....
...OR INSULTED, I HAVE JUST BEEN GIVEN....
....THE MAN OF THE MEETING AWARD.

18th May 1972

LOOK, BANZ EYE - YOU COME FROM 'DOWNUNDER', CAN YOU SETTLE AN ARGUMENT FOR ME?
SURE THING, WHAT'S THE QUESTION?
WHAT'S THE DIFFERENCE BETWEEN AN AUSSIE AND A KIWI?
ABOUT THREE SECONDS A LAP

6th July 1972

The Politically Correct

I ENJOY RACING AGAINST YOU BOOBY, BUT YOU HAVE AN UNFAIR ADVANTAGE
BOOBY
MAD DOG
HOW ?
BOOBY
MAD DOG
I NEVER HIT A WOMAN
BOOBY
MAD DOG

12th October 1972

GRUNT
SNAP!
SNIFF
SNIFF
BONJOUR MATELOT !

9th August 1973

Chapter Five

The Politically Correct

I'VE GOT £25 IN PRIZE MONEY. I CAN'T DECIDE WHAT TO SPEND IT ON... I COULD SPEND IT ON THE RACING CAR.. OR I COULD...
...BLOW THE LOT ON BOOZE.. OR I COULD BUY THE WIFE A NICE PRESENT. I'LL TOSS A COIN TO....
DECIDE. HEADS I SPEND IT ON THE CAR. TAILS I SPEND IT ON BOOZE...
...AND IF IT STANDS ON EDGE I'LL BUY THE WIFE A PRESENT.

17th January 1974

...THE TOP END IS ALL FLOPPY...
ENGINE TEST SHOP
BOOBY
...AND THE BOTTOM IS SO TIGHT THAT SHE MAY...
ENGINE TEST SHOP
BOOBY
...NEED A REGRIND...
ENGINE TEST SHOP
BOOBY
...LET'S GET HER UP ON THE BENCH FOR A QUICK TEST.
ENGINE TEST SHOP

28th February 1974

HOW ABOUT THIS LELLA LOMBARDI ?
MAD DOG
MAD DOG
MAD DOG
WHY NOT - I'LL TRY ANYTHING ONCE.
MAD DOG

8th August 1974

BLUETITS BOOBY ?
BOOBY
NO....
BOOBY
...BUT IT IS COLD.
BOOBY

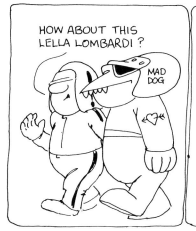

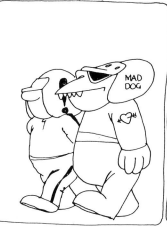

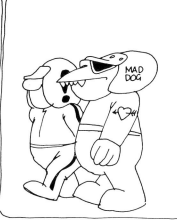

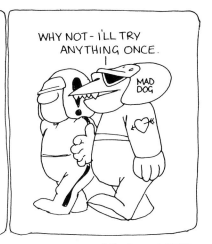

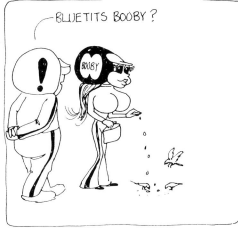

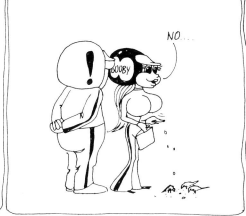

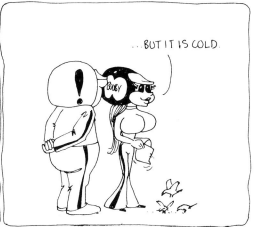

14th November 1974

Chapter Five

The Politically Correct

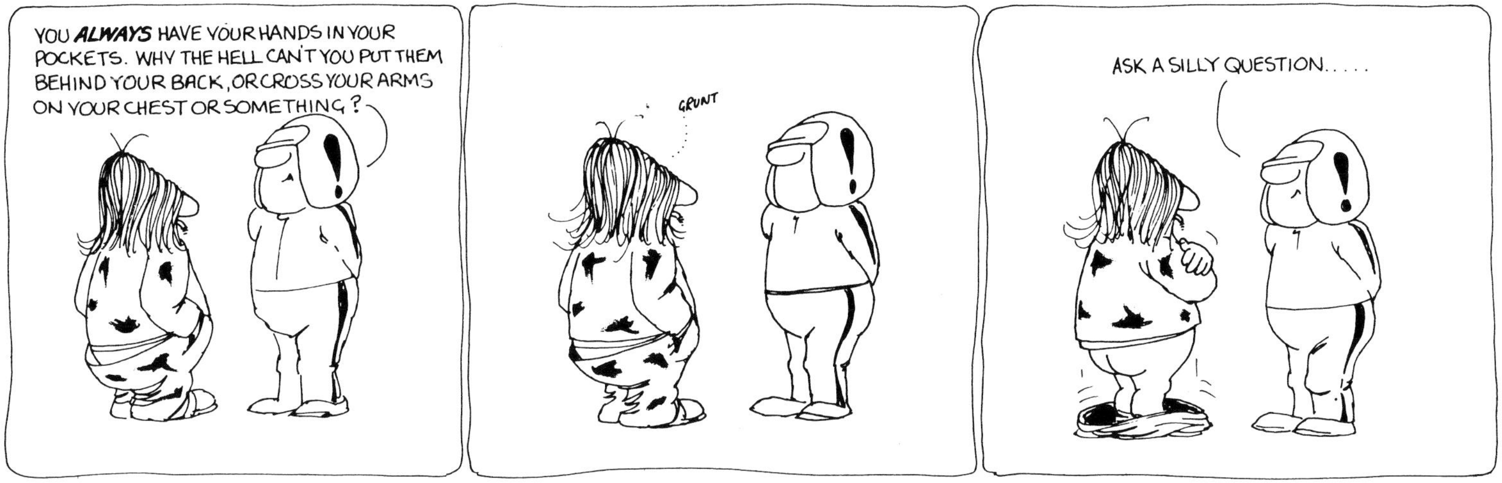

YOU ALWAYS HAVE YOUR HANDS IN YOUR POCKETS. WHY THE HELL CAN'T YOU PUT THEM BEHIND YOUR BACK, OR CROSS YOUR ARMS ON YOUR CHEST OR SOMETHING?
GRUNT
ASK A SILLY QUESTION.....

28th November 1974

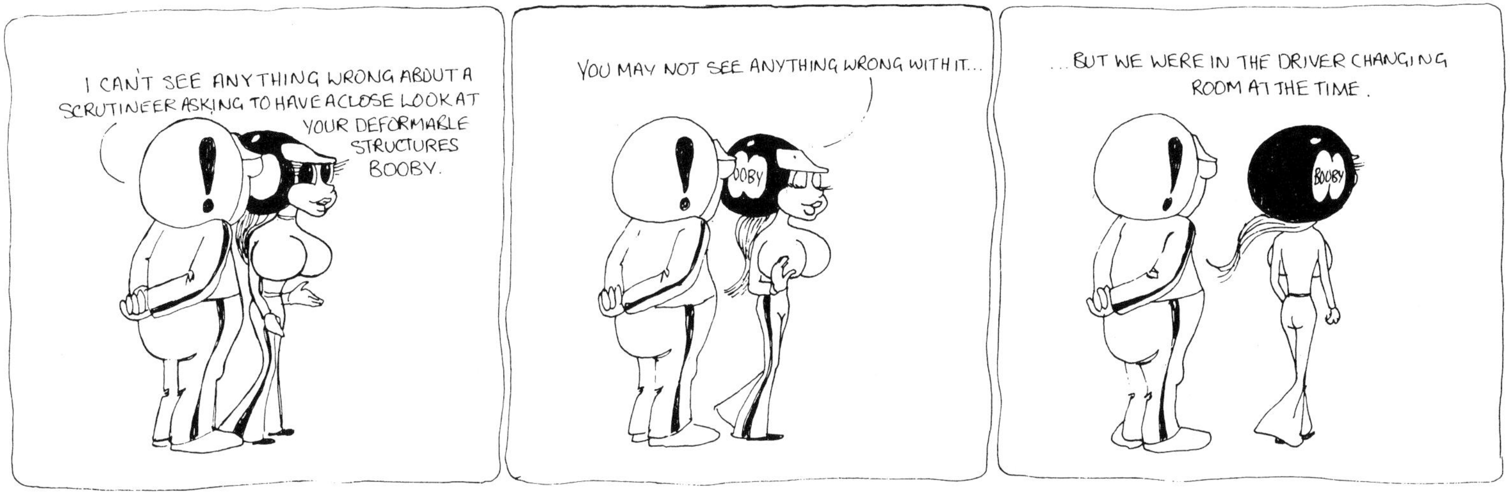

I CAN'T SEE ANYTHING WRONG ABOUT A SCRUTINEER ASKING TO HAVE A CLOSE LOOK AT YOUR DEFORMABLE STRUCTURES BOOBY.
YOU MAY NOT SEE ANYTHING WRONG WITH IT...
OOBY
...BUT WE WERE IN THE DRIVER CHANGING ROOM AT THE TIME.
BOOBY

16th October 1975

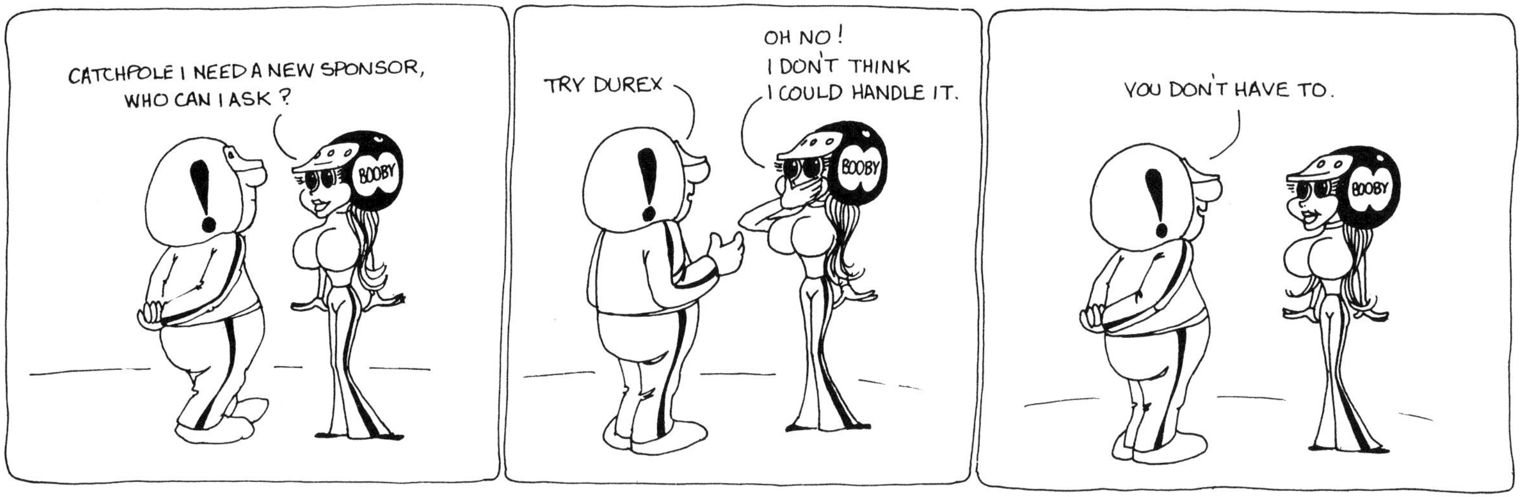
CATCHPOLE I NEED A NEW SPONSOR, WHO CAN I ASK ?
TRY DUREX
OH NO ! I DON'T THINK I COULD HANDLE IT.
BOOBY
YOU DON'T HAVE TO.

1st April 1976

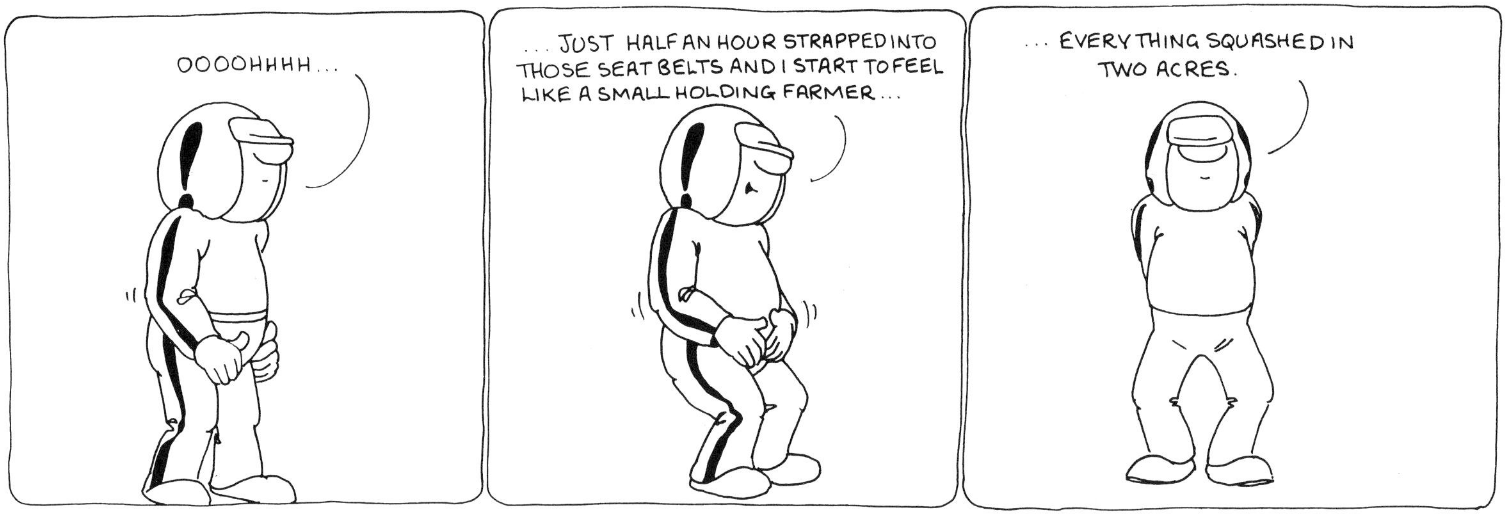
OOOOHHHH ...
... JUST HALF AN HOUR STRAPPED INTO THOSE SEAT BELTS AND I START TO FEEL LIKE A SMALL HOLDING FARMER ...
... EVERY THING SQUASHED IN TWO ACRES.

14th September 1978

Sports Cars

Chapter Six

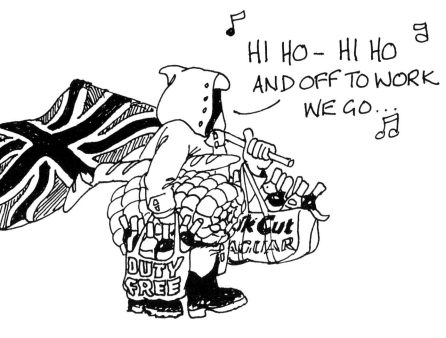

HI HO- HI HO
AND OFF TO WORK
WE GO...
DUTY FREE

If some malevolent force were to drop an atom bomb on the North of France the Friday before Le Mans then it is my belief that around 75% of all the historic and thoroughbred sports cars in the world would be vaporised.
I only went to Le Mans for the first time recently and the amazing thing is that it was every bit as good and enjoyable as I had been told. I love the way this French institution has been totally high-jacked by the British, how a hundred and fifty thousand Brits pile into old MGs, Triumphs, Bentleys, Astons, Jags, TVRs, Lotus, ACs, Austin Healeys, Caterhams, Westfields, etc. etc. and roar down through France at Le Mans speeds. Our man Dillon is there every year, come success or failure.

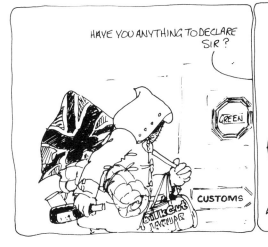

HAVE YOU ANYTHING TO DECLARE SIR?
GREEN
CUSTOMS
YER – I'M TIRED, WET, DIRTY, MY EARS ARE RINGING, I'VE A STINKING HEAD ACHE, I HAVEN'T SLEPT FOR 46 HOURS, I'VE DRUNK SEVEN CANS OF LAGER AND FOUR BOTTLES OF PLONK, EATEN TWELVE CREPES....
...AND SIX WAFFLES, MY MOUTH FEELS LIKE REGAZZONI'S ARM PIT, JAGUAR DIDN'T FINISH IN THE FIRST THREE BUT DEREK BELL WON AND I DON'T KNOW WHETHER TO LAUGH OR CRY SEE YOU NEXT YEAR!
FOLEY

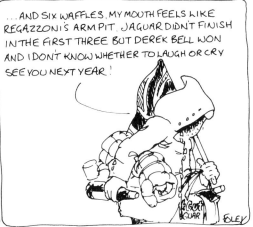

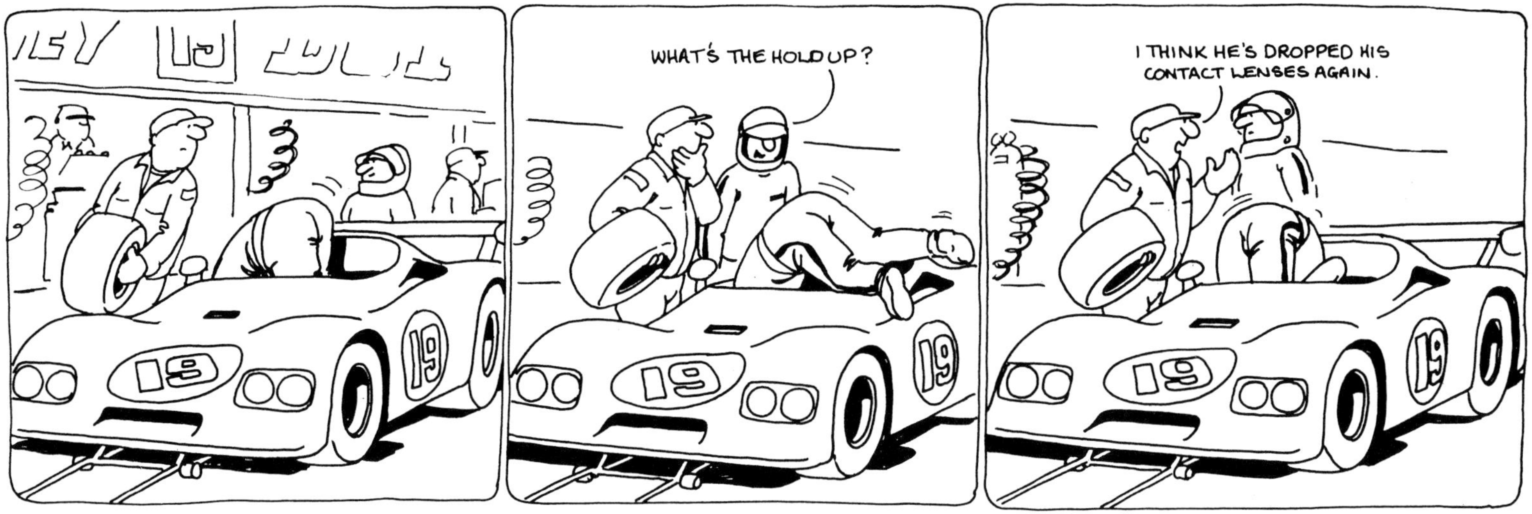
WHAT'S THE HOLD UP?
I THINK HE'S DROPPED HIS CONTACT LENSES AGAIN.

4th May 1978

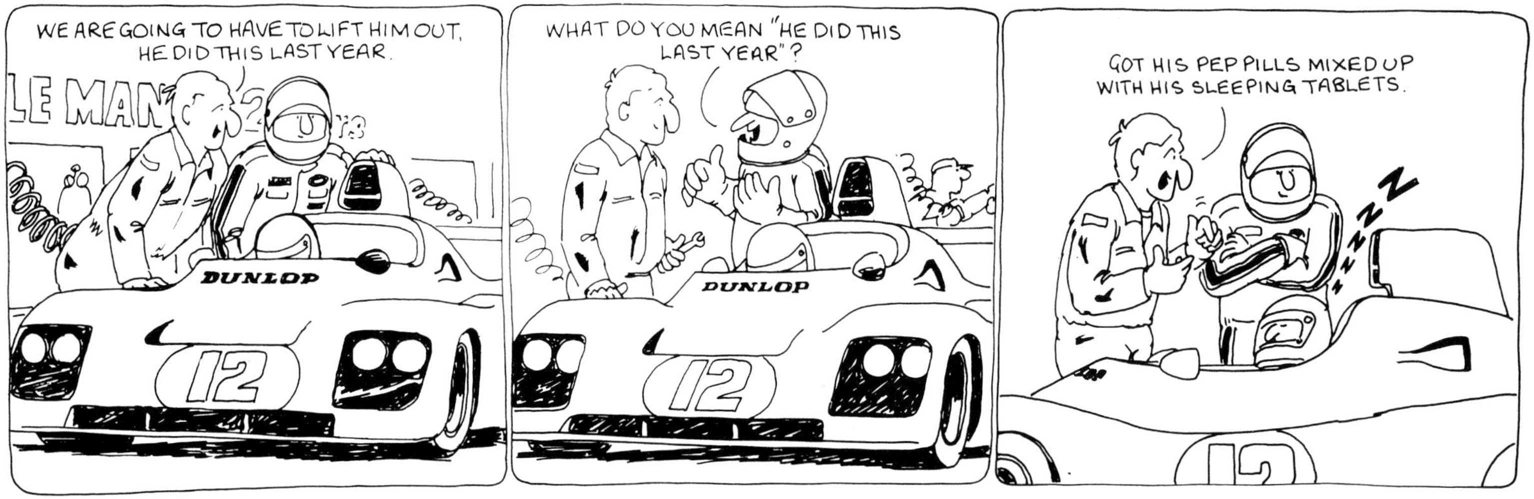
WE ARE GOING TO HAVE TO LIFT HIM OUT, HE DID THIS LAST YEAR.
DUNLOP
WHAT DO YOU MEAN "HE DID THIS LAST YEAR"?
DUNLOP
GOT HIS PEP PILLS MIXED UP WITH HIS SLEEPING TABLETS.

15th June 1978

Chapter Six

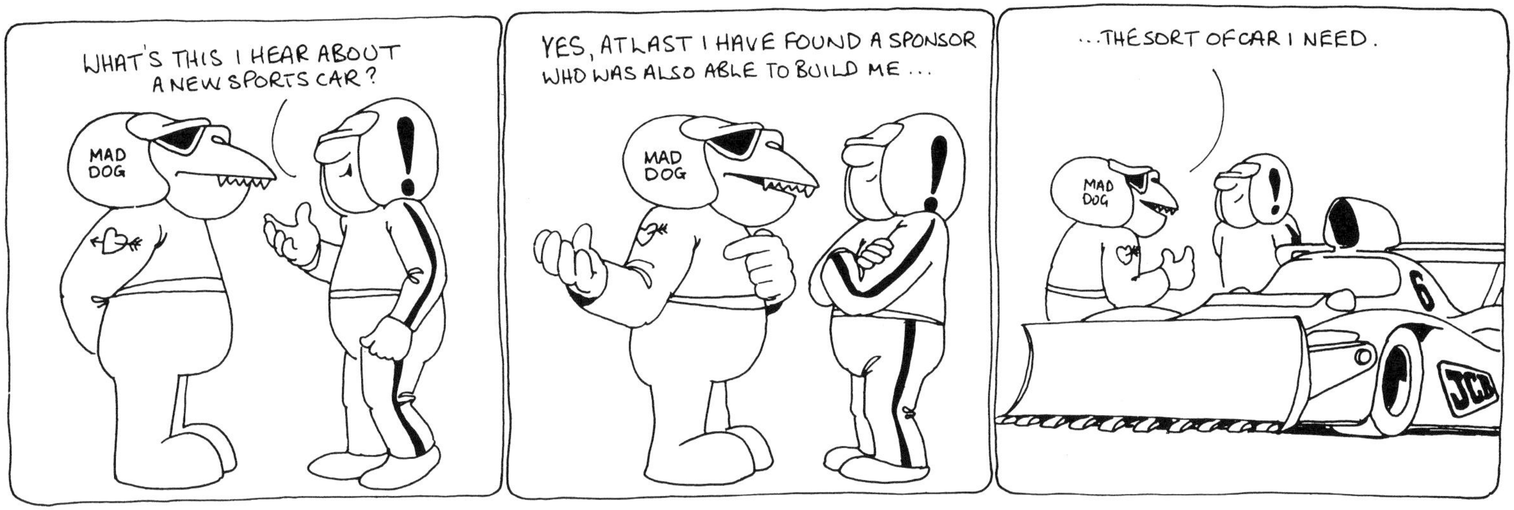

WHAT'S THIS I HEAR ABOUT A NEW SPORTS CAR?
MAD DOG
YES, AT LAST I HAVE FOUND A SPONSOR WHO WAS ALSO ABLE TO BUILD ME ...
MAD DOG
...THE SORT OF CAR I NEED.
MAD DOG
6
JCB

21st September 1978

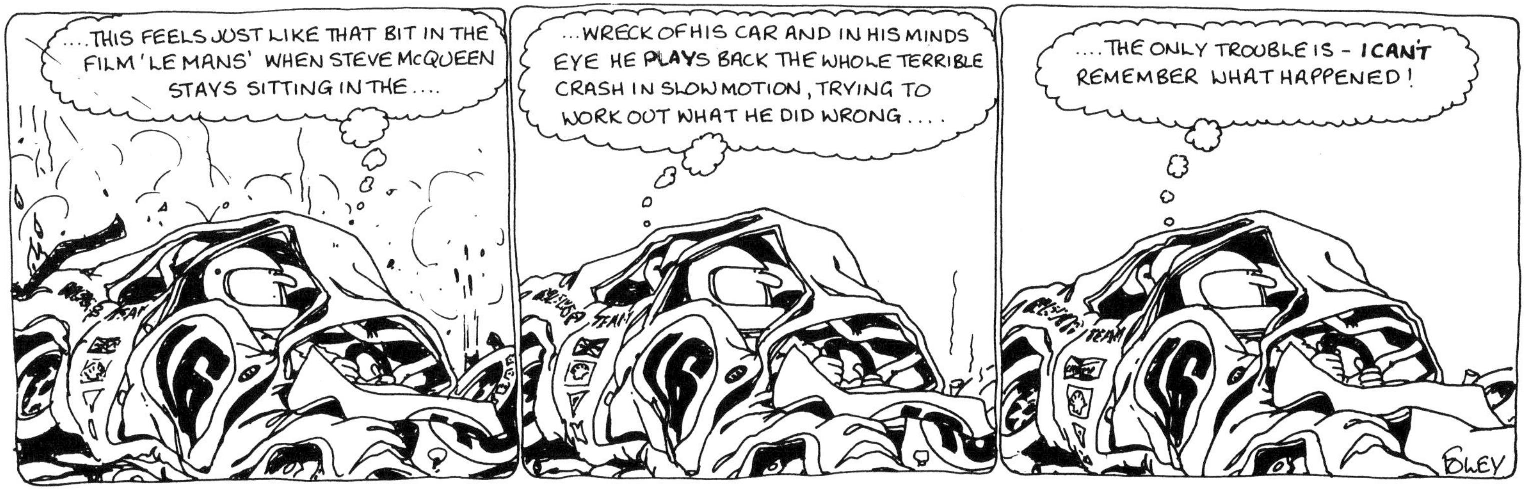

....THIS FEELS JUST LIKE THAT BIT IN THE FILM 'LE MANS' WHEN STEVE McQUEEN STAYS SITTING IN THE....
...WRECK OF HIS CAR AND IN HIS MINDS EYE HE PLAYS BACK THE WHOLE TERRIBLE CRASH IN SLOW MOTION, TRYING TO WORK OUT WHAT HE DID WRONG....
....THE ONLY TROUBLE IS - I CAN'T REMEMBER WHAT HAPPENED!
FOLEY

8th March 1984

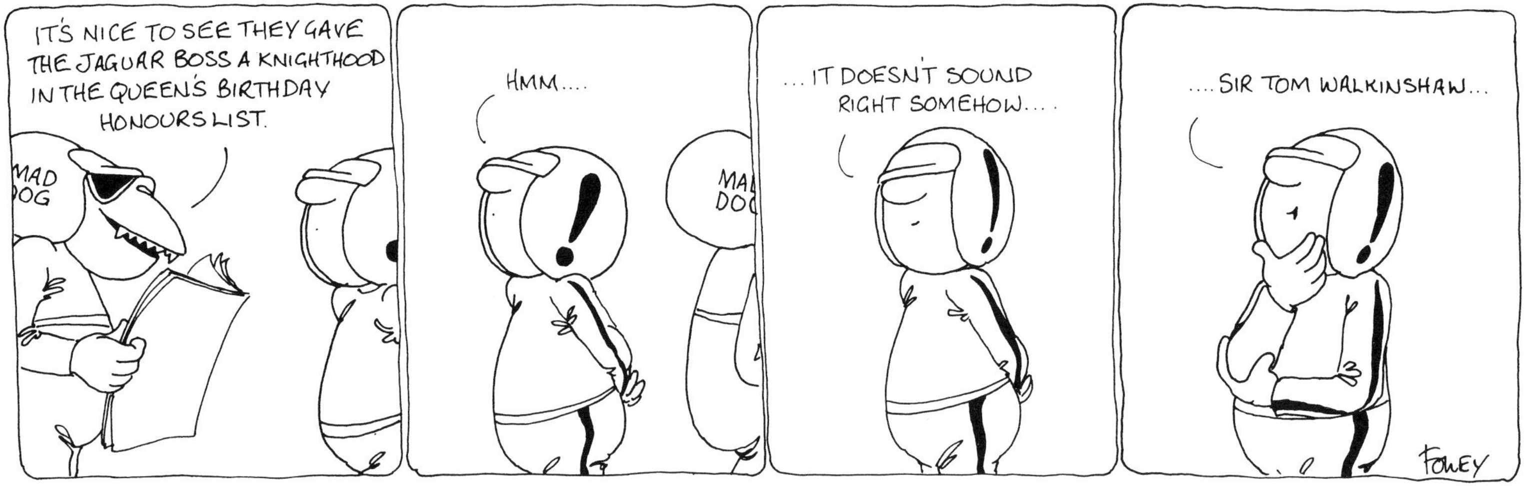
IT'S NICE TO SEE THEY GAVE THE JAGUAR BOSS A KNIGHTHOOD IN THE QUEEN'S BIRTHDAY HONOURS LIST.
MAD DOG
HMM....
...IT DOESN'T SOUND RIGHT SOMEHOW....
....SIR TOM WALKINSHAW...
FOLEY

3rd July 1986

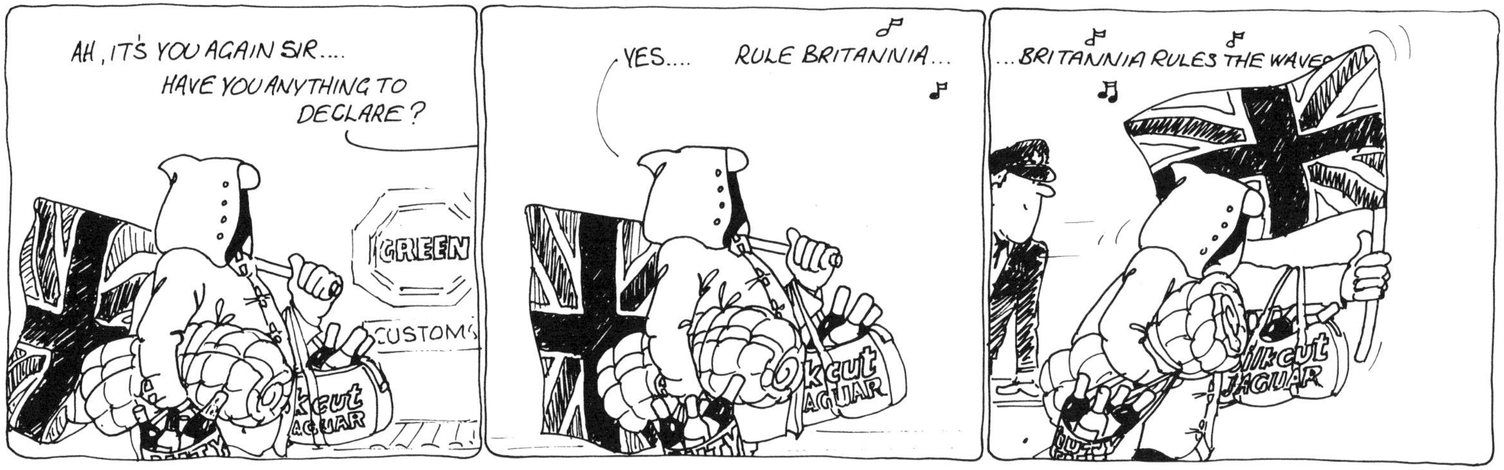
AH, IT'S YOU AGAIN SIR....
HAVE YOU ANYTHING TO DECLARE?
GREEN
CUSTOMS
JAGUAR
YES....
RULE BRITANNIA...
...BRITANNIA RULES THE WAVE

16th June 1988

OH THAT'S NICE.....

....IN HONOUR OF HIS LEMANS WIN,
THEY'VE MADE JAN LAMMERS...

....BRITISH.

FOLEY

30th June 1988

I'VE JUST HAD A SNEAK PREVIEW
OF FISA'S SPORTS-PROTOTYPE
CALENDAR AND REGS.

MAD
DOG

YOU'RE KIDDING - AT LONG LAST -
CAN I SEE THEM?

MAD
DOG

IF YOU CROSS MY PALM
WITH SILVER

MAD
DOG

FOLEY

8th December 1988

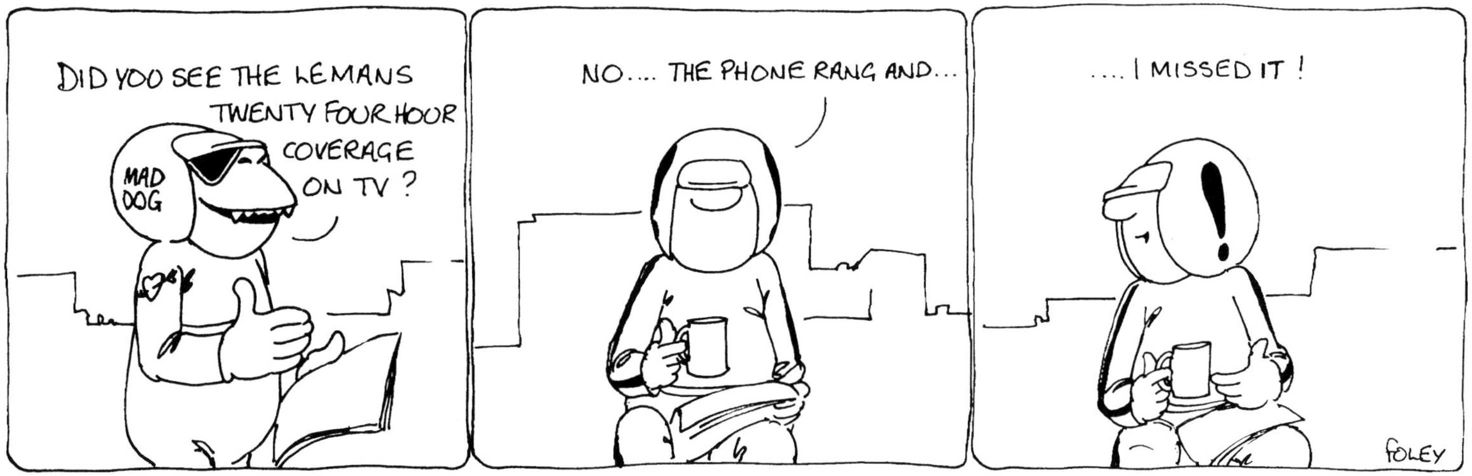
DID YOU SEE THE LEMANS TWENTY FOUR HOUR COVERAGE ON TV ?
MAD DOG
NO.... THE PHONE RANG AND...
....I MISSED IT !
!
FOLEY

15th June 1989

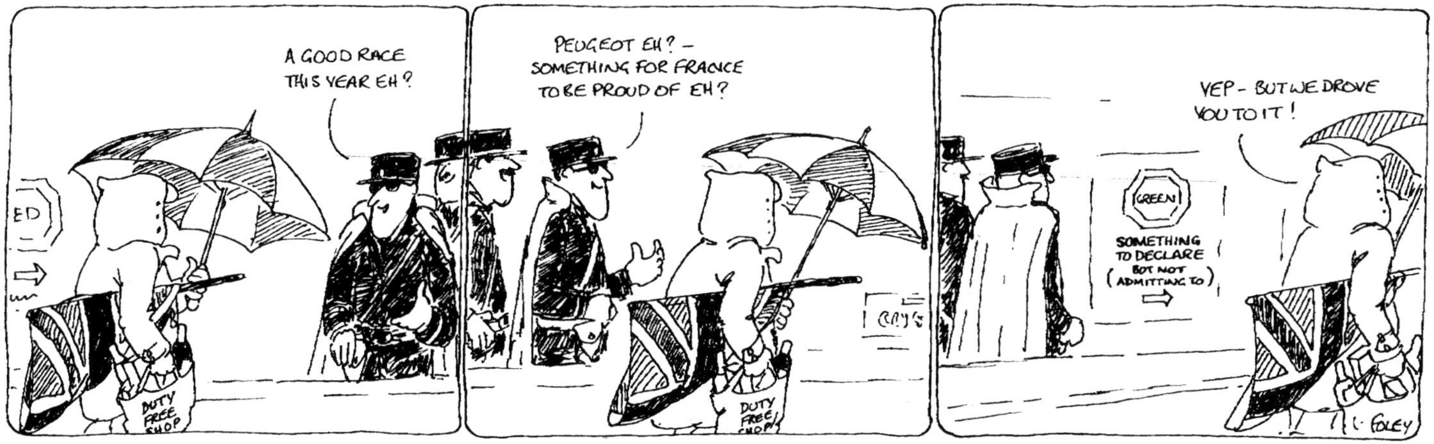
A GOOD RACE THIS YEAR EH?
PEUGEOT EH? - SOMETHING FOR FRANCE TO BE PROUD OF EH?
YEP - BUT WE DROVE YOU TO IT!
DUTY FREE SHOP
GREEN
SOMETHING TO DECLARE
(ADMITTING TO)
FOLEY

25th June 1992

Chapter Seven

Blenkinsop

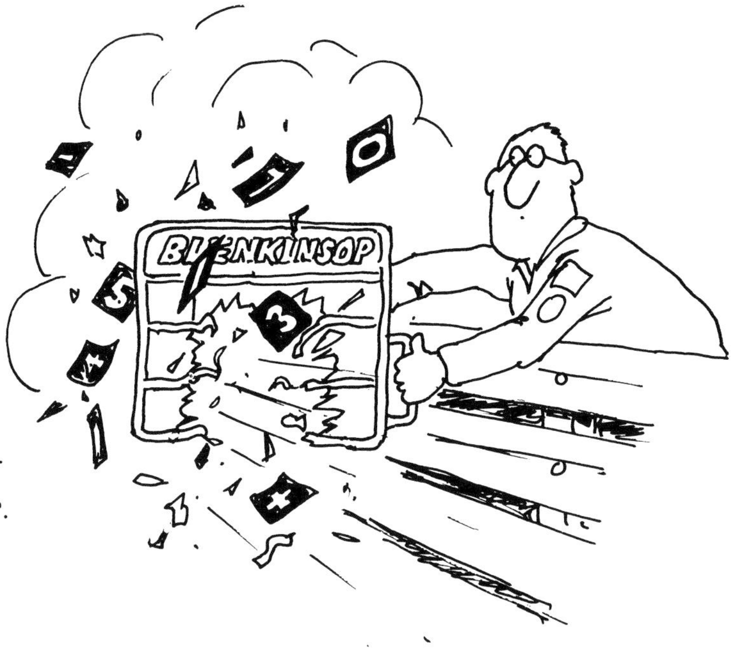
BLENKINSOP

Blenkinsop is one of my favourites. He is the typical characterless, dim, gormless, spotty, highly talented young driver who seeps through to motor racing from karting with sickening regularity. Usually he is someone's son, amazingly the fathers often openly admitting it without the slightest shame.
When I started racing there was a real Blenkinsop in the preparation garage I shared with a bunch of Clubmans racers which included Max Mosley (our glorious leader). He was held in such high esteem that everyone would join in singing the tune of 'Balls to Mr. Blenkinsop, Blenkinsop, Blenkinsop....' The Blenkinsops of this world are a joy to behold and an enduring pain in the arse.

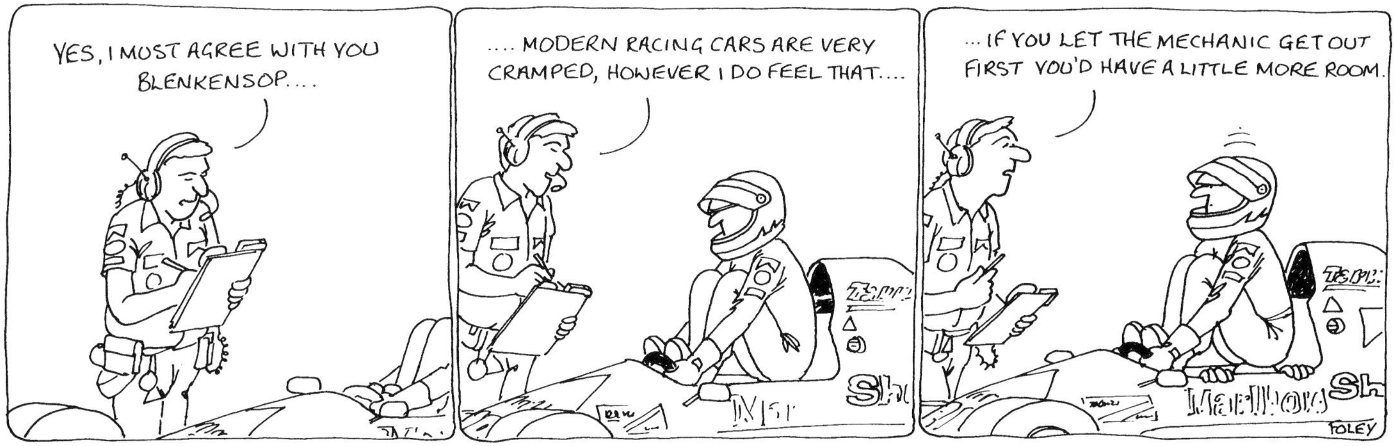
YES, I MUST AGREE WITH YOU BLENKENSOP....
.... MODERN RACING CARS ARE VERY CRAMPED, HOWEVER I DO FEEL THAT....
...IF YOU LET THE MECHANIC GET OUT FIRST YOU'D HAVE A LITTLE MORE ROOM.
FOLEY

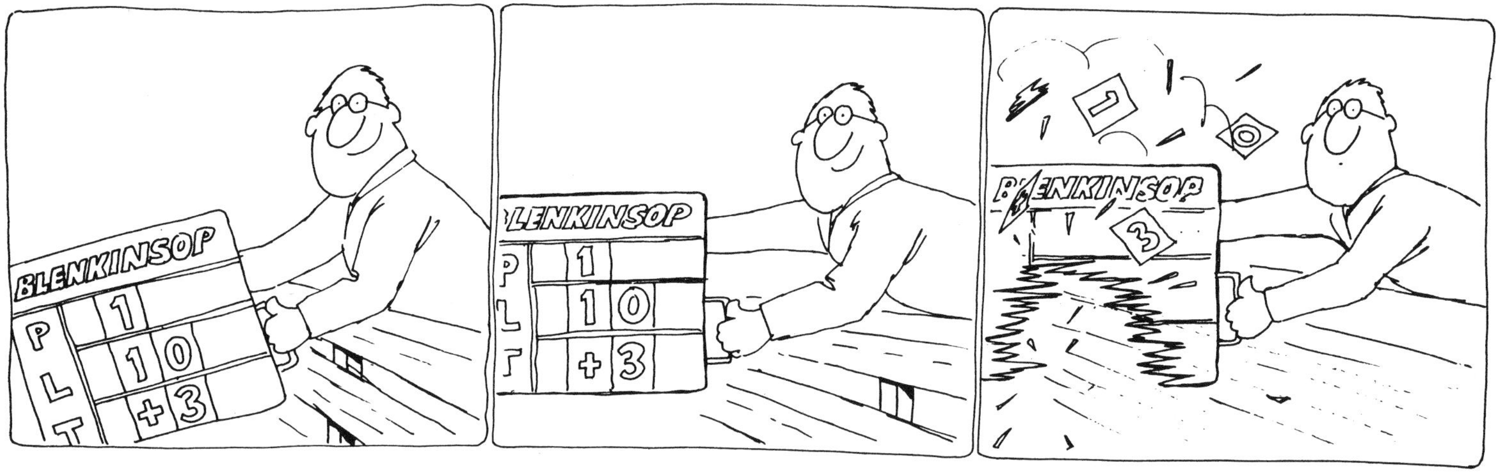
BLENKINSOP
P 1
L 10
T +3

3rd October 1974

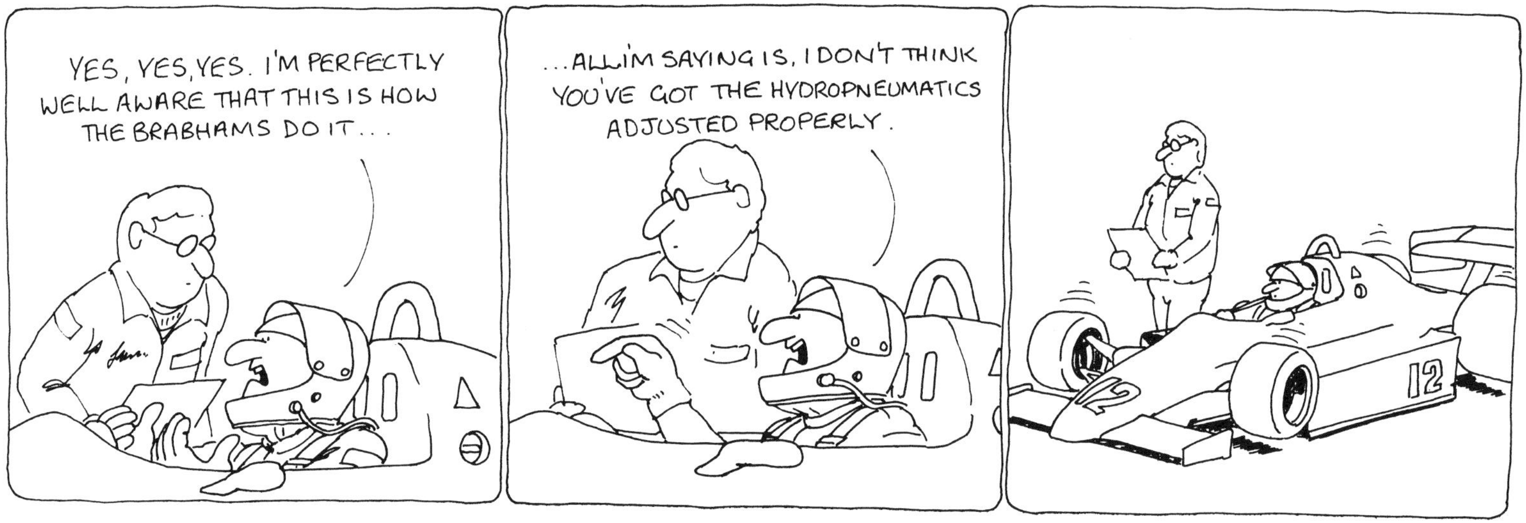
YES, YES, YES. I'M PERFECTLY WELL AWARE THAT THIS IS HOW THE BRABHAMS DO IT...
...ALL I'M SAYING IS, I DON'T THINK YOU'VE GOT THE HYDROPNEUMATICS ADJUSTED PROPERLY.
12

7th May 1981

Chapter Seven

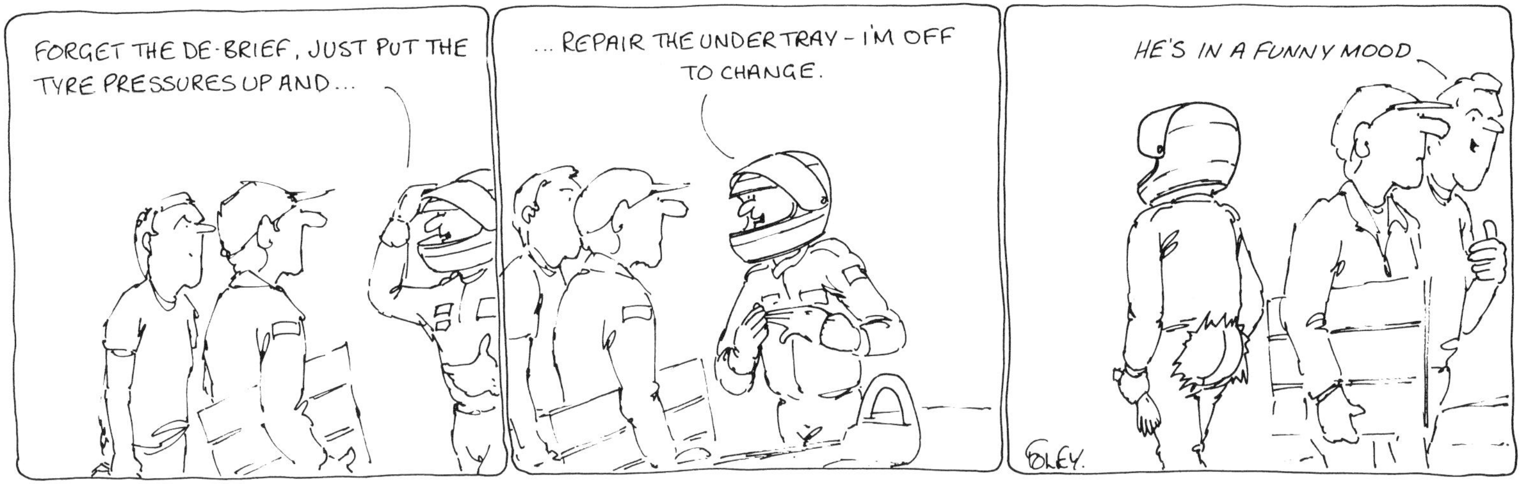
FORGET THE DE-BRIEF, JUST PUT THE TYRE PRESSURES UP AND...
... REPAIR THE UNDERTRAY - I'M OFF TO CHANGE.
HE'S IN A FUNNY MOOD
FOLEY.

8th August 1985

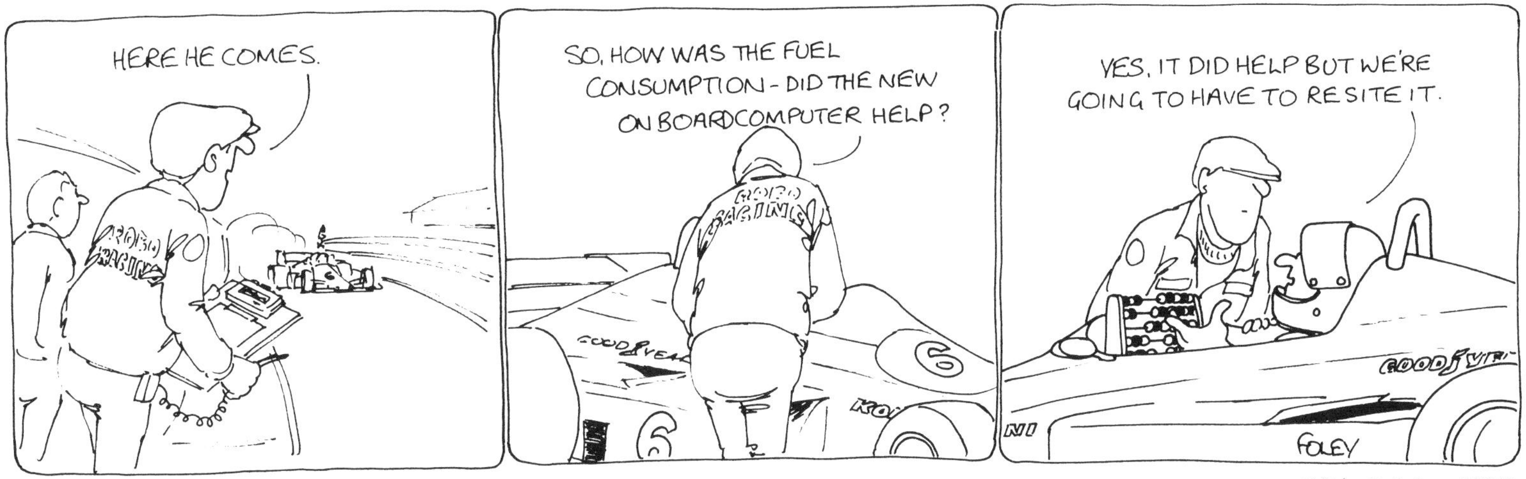
HERE HE COMES.
SO, HOW WAS THE FUEL CONSUMPTION - DID THE NEW ON BOARD COMPUTER HELP?
YES, IT DID HELP BUT WE'RE GOING TO HAVE TO RESITE IT.
FOLEY

24th October 1985

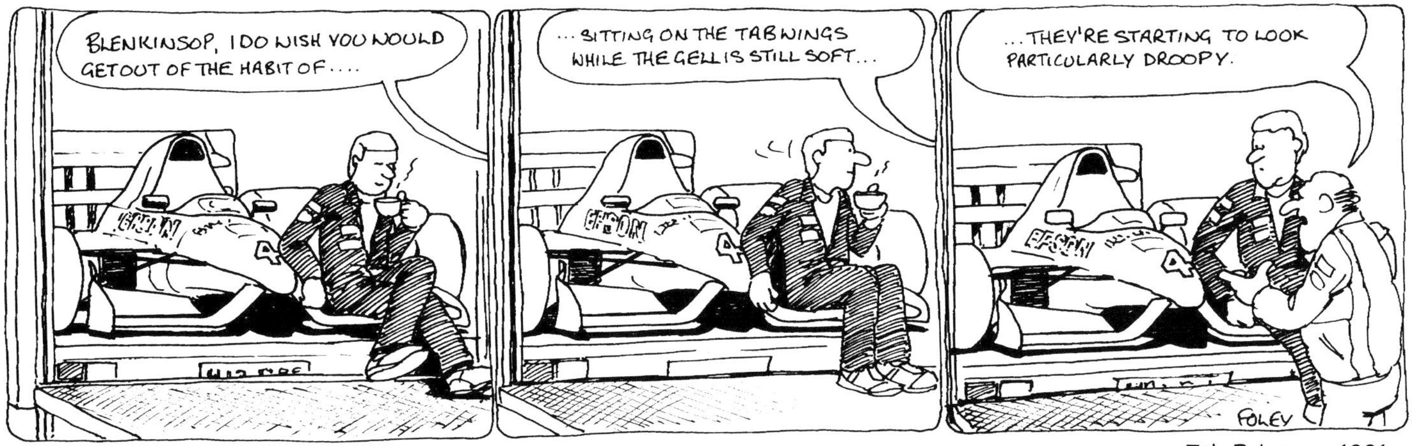
BLENKINSOP, I DO WISH YOU WOULD GET OUT OF THE HABIT OF....
...SITTING ON THE TAB WINGS WHILE THE GELL IS STILL SOFT...
...THEY'RE STARTING TO LOOK PARTICULARLY DROOPY.
FOLEY

7th February 1991

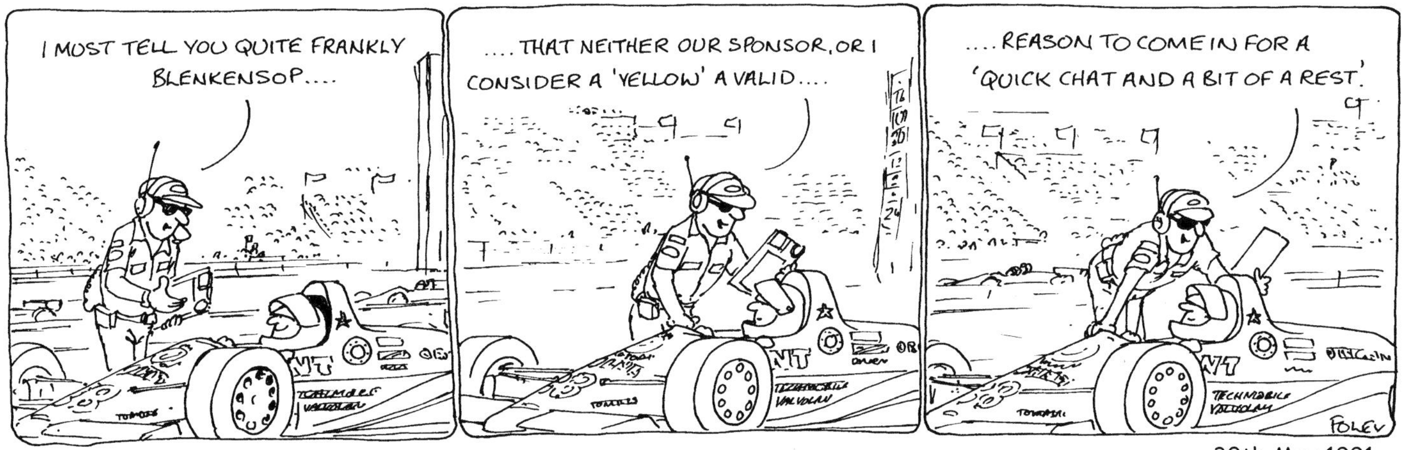
I MOST TELL YOU QUITE FRANKLY BLENKENSOP....
....THAT NEITHER OUR SPONSOR, OR I CONSIDER A 'YELLOW' A VALID....
....REASON TO COME IN FOR A 'QUICK CHAT AND A BIT OF A REST'.
FOLEY

30th May 1991

Chapter Seven

WELL, YOUR TIMES ARE ENCOURAGING BLENKENSOP - JUST ONE THING...
...I KNOW YOU'RE FRESH OUT OF KARTING, BUT WHEN YOU SPIN THE CAR AND STALL THE...
...ENGINE - DON'T TRY TO PICK UP THE BACK END AND TRY TO BUMP START IT, THERE'S A GOOD CHAP.
FOLEY

25th July 1991

FOLEY

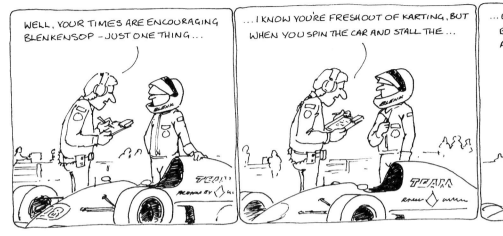

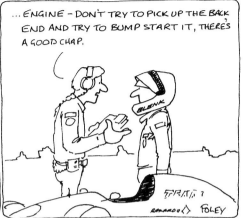

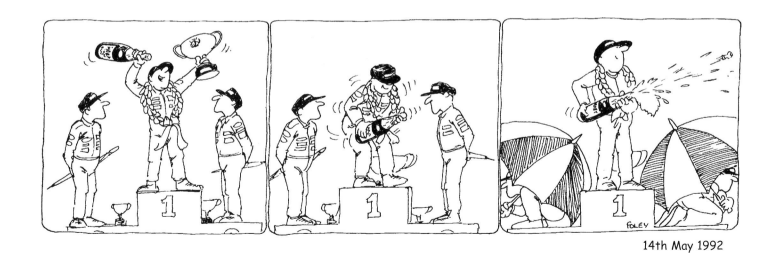

14th May 1992

Blenkinsop

That's Life

Chapter Eight

A man walking along the viewing bank at a track hits his head on a sign that is too low. The sign has words 'MOTOR RACING IS DANGEROUS' on it. The big Italian mechanic who is holding the electric starting handle so tight that the racing car spins round. Or the old time Le Mans driver who runs across the track to get to his sports car - when the dust clears and all the cars have gone our driver is left standing in the middle of the track unable to find his car. These were classic cartoons drawn by the late great Russell Brockbank, past master of this sort of humour, that's life humour. I only wish I could approach Brockbank's wit or purity of line. I hope these Catchpoles make you smile.

OOPS

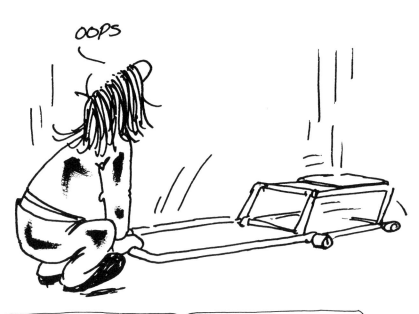

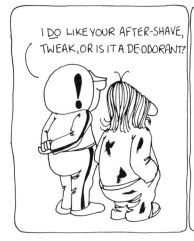

I DO LIKE YOUR AFTER-SHAVE, TWEAK, OR IS IT A DE-ODORANT?
...IT'S A FAMILIAR AND EVOCATIVE SCENT, BUT I CAN'T PUT A NAME TO IT. BUT I WOULD GUESS...
...IT WAS AN INGENIOUS FRAGRANCE COMPOUNDED FROM AN EXOTIC BLEND OF....
...PETROL, SUMPOIL, GUNK AND CELLULOSE THINNERS WITH JUST A SOUPÇON OF SWARFEGA.
GRUNT

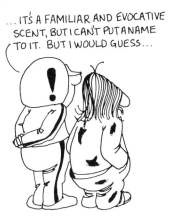

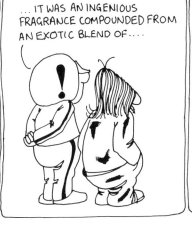

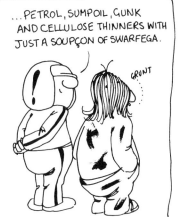

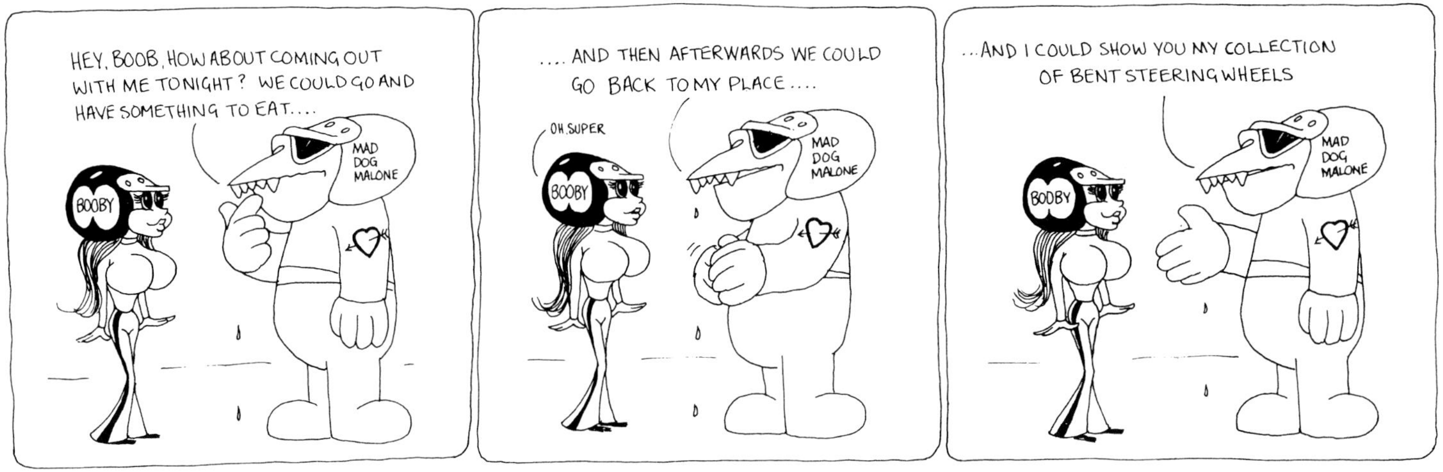
HEY, BOOB, HOW ABOUT COMING OUT WITH ME TONIGHT? WE COULD GO AND HAVE SOMETHING TO EAT....
MAD DOG MALONE
BOOBY
.... AND THEN AFTERWARDS WE COULD GO BACK TO MY PLACE....
OH.SUPER
MAD DOG MALONE
BOOBY
...AND I COULD SHOW YOU MY COLLECTION OF BENT STEERING WHEELS
MAD DOG MALONE
BOOBY

19th August 1971

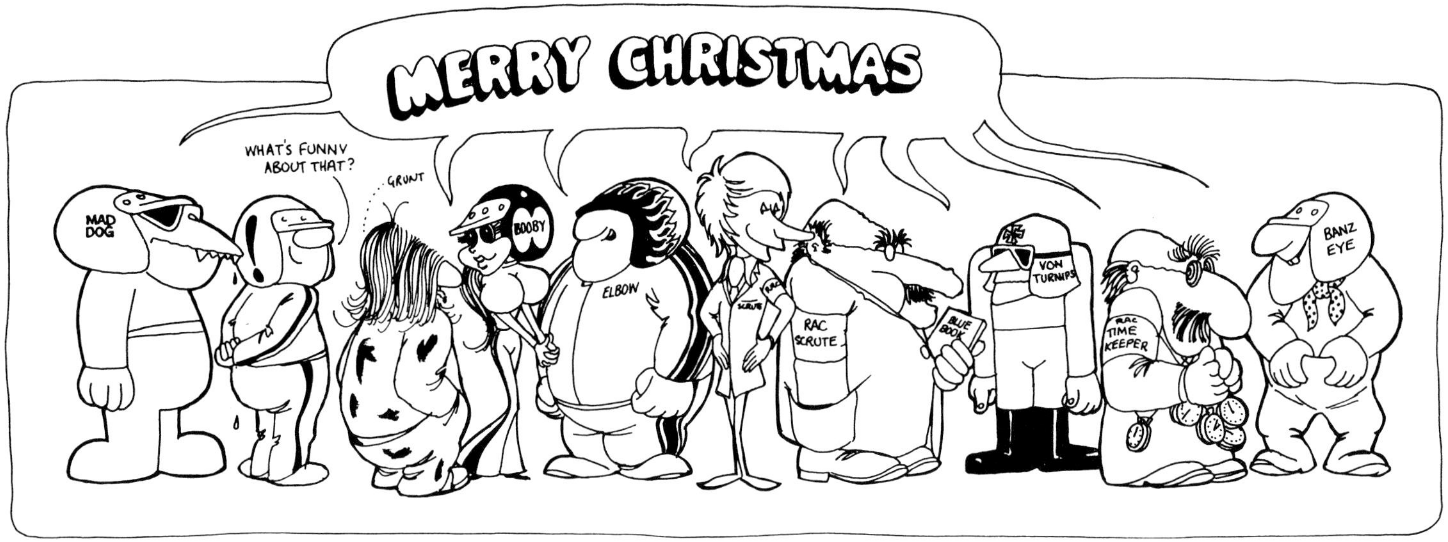
MERRY CHRISTMAS
WHAT'S FUNNY ABOUT THAT?
GRUNT
MAD DOG
BOOBY
ELBOW
SCRUTE
RAC SCRUTE
BLUE BOOK
VON TURNIPS
RAC TIME KEEPER
BANZ EYE

23rd December 1971

Chapter Eight

BULL BULL
RUB RUB
POLISH
SHINE SHINE
POLISH
WHAT TIME IS THE SPONSOR COMING ?
GRUNT
GLINT GLINT
DURA GRIT
POLISH

12th April 1973

PULL OFF MY PANTS..
... LEGS WIDE APART ..
GRUNT
... TUG HARD, HARDER ....
THUMP BUMP
YOU SHOULD TRY CHANGING INTO ONE PIECE OVER-ALLS IN A TENT.

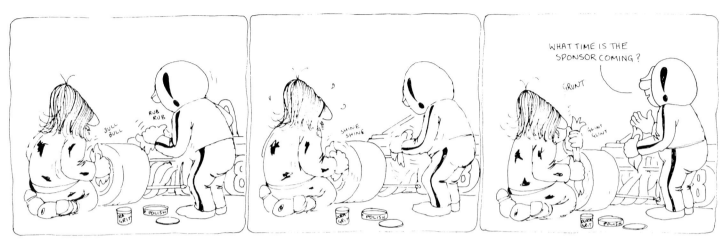

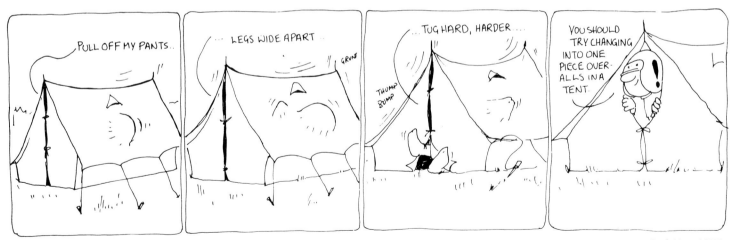

3rd May 1973

TOP UP PETROL, LOOK AT OIL...
...CHECKING TYRE PRESSURES, BOLT CHECKS, TESTING...
...SPRINGS, ADJUSTING THE CORNER WEIGHTS....
BLEEDING BRAKES.
QUITE AGREE
CHECK LIST

25th April 1974

SPLASH
SQUELCH SQUELCH
GRUNT GRUNT
SQUELCH
WHAT A BLOODY FUSS OVER A LITTLE DROP OF RAIN.
SQUELCH SLURP

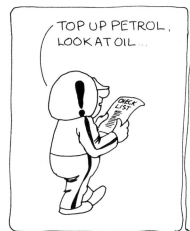

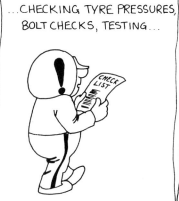

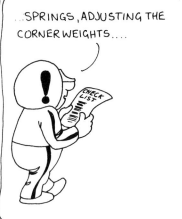

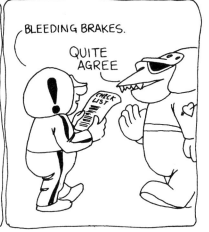

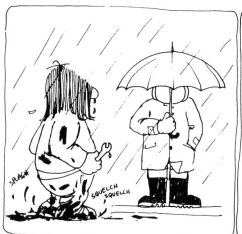

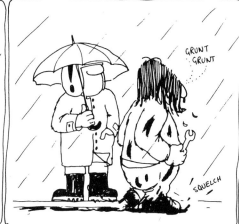

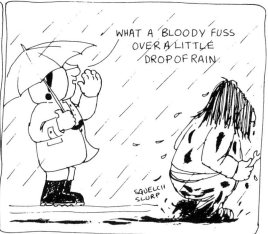

26th September 1974

Chapter Eight

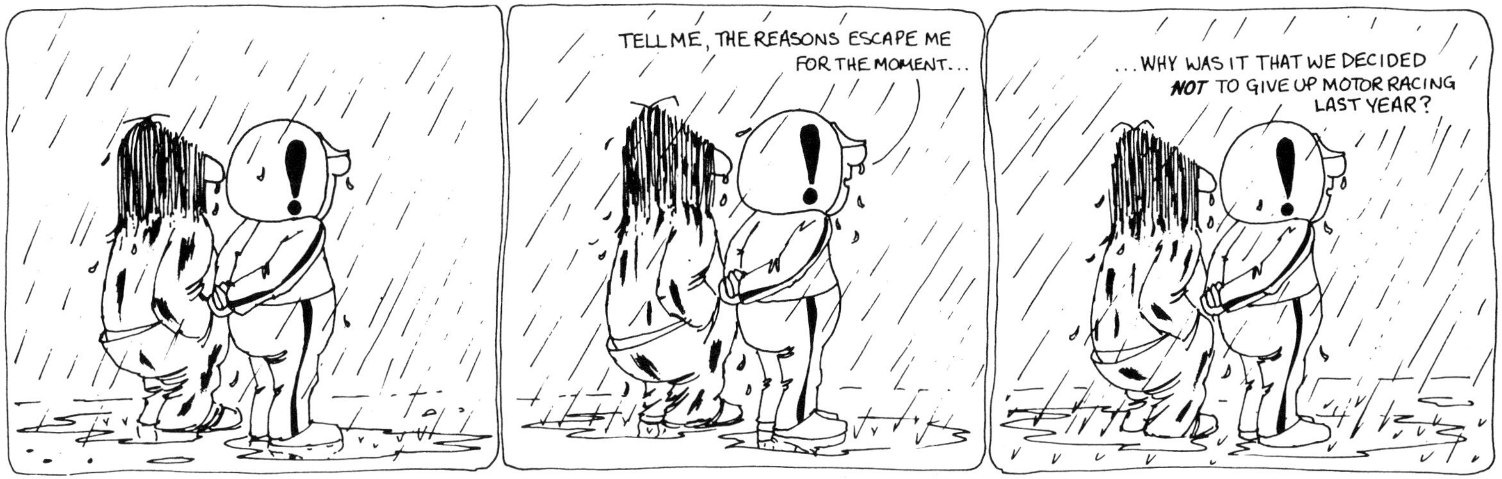
TELL ME, THE REASONS ESCAPE ME FOR THE MOMENT...
...WHY WAS IT THAT WE DECIDED NOT TO GIVE UP MOTOR RACING LAST YEAR?

6th March 1975

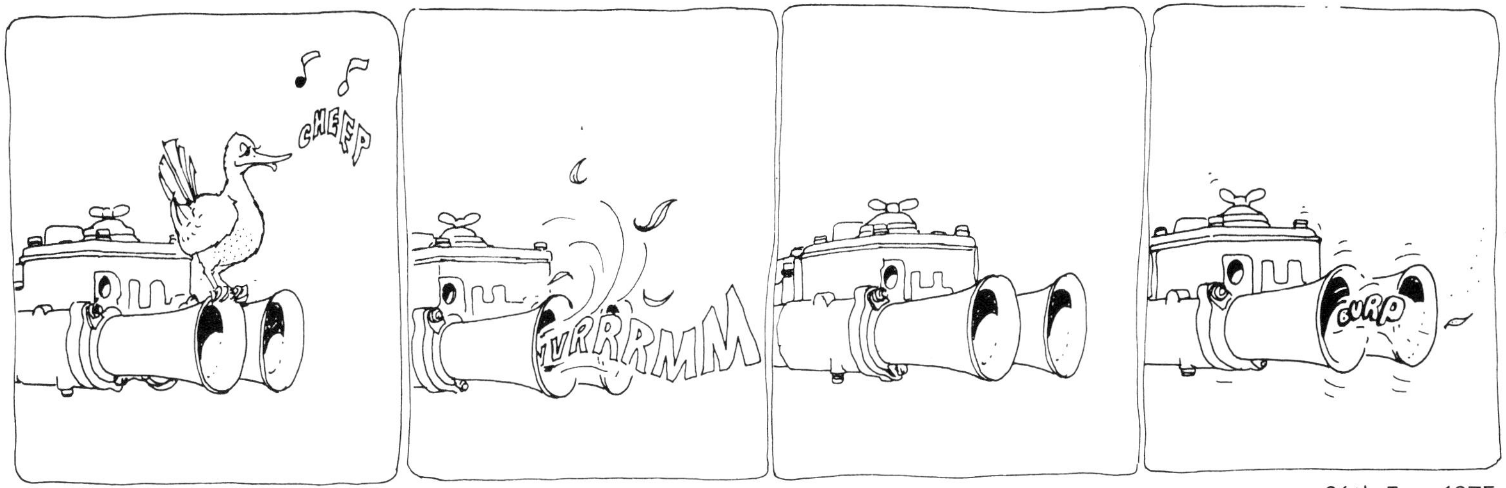
CHEEP
VRRRRMM
BURP

26th June 1975

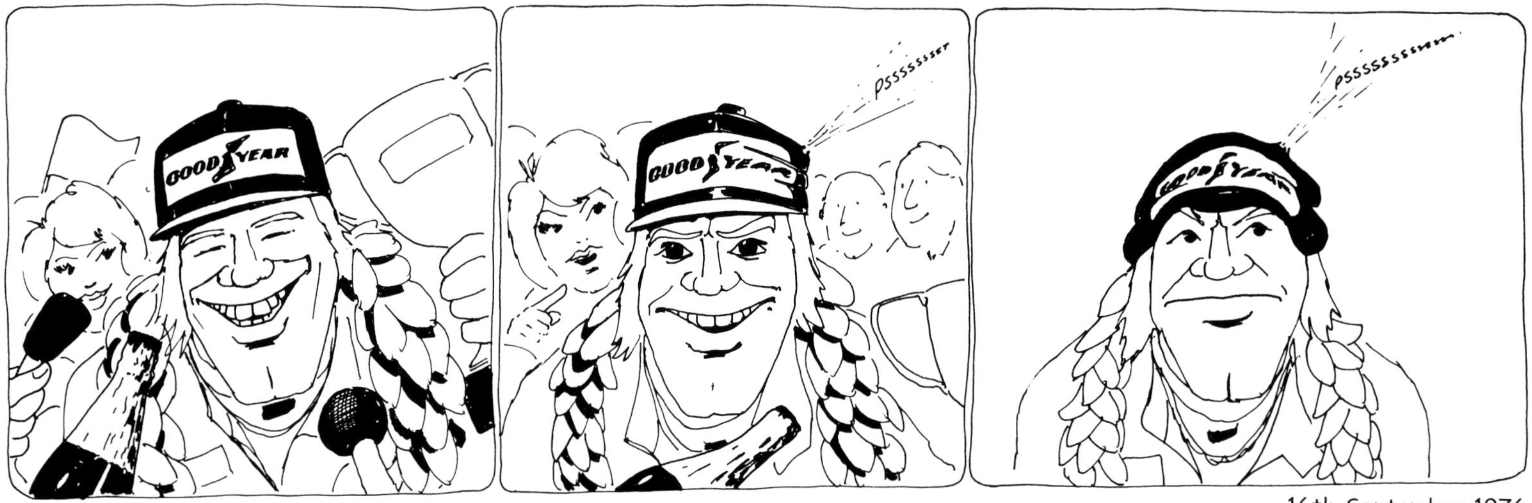
GOOD YEAR
GOOD YEAR
PSSSSSSSST
PSSSSSSSSSHHH
GOOD YEAR

16th September 1976

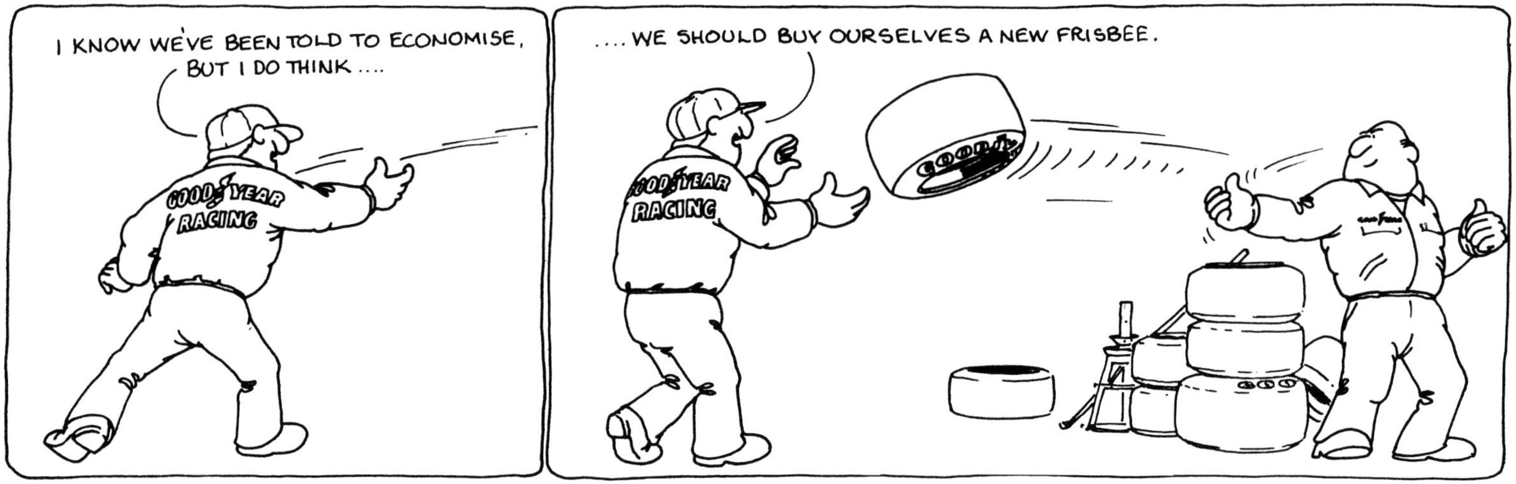
I KNOW WE'VE BEEN TOLD TO ECONOMISE, BUT I DO THINK ....
GOOD YEAR RACING
.... WE SHOULD BUY OURSELVES A NEW FRISBEE.
GOOD YEAR RACING

1st February 1979

Chapter Eight

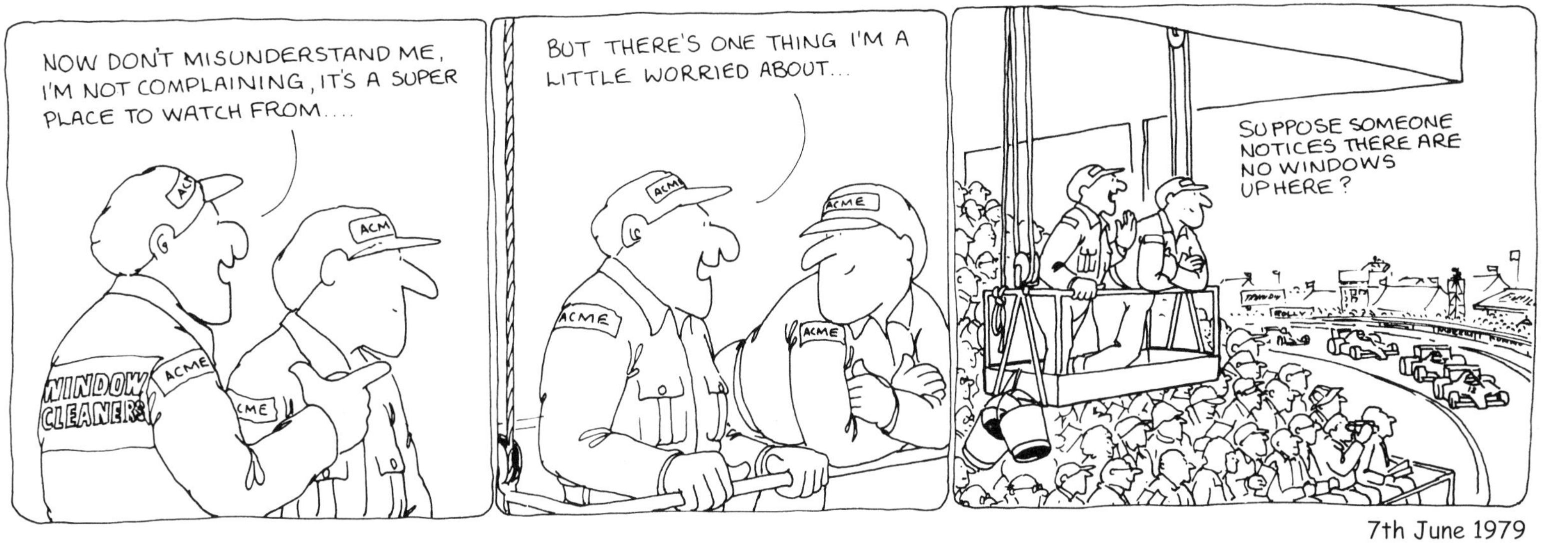
NOW DON'T MISUNDERSTAND ME, I'M NOT COMPLAINING, IT'S A SUPER PLACE TO WATCH FROM....
WINDOW CLEANERS
ACME
BUT THERE'S ONE THING I'M A LITTLE WORRIED ABOUT...
SUPPOSE SOMEONE NOTICES THERE ARE NO WINDOWS UP HERE?

7th June 1979

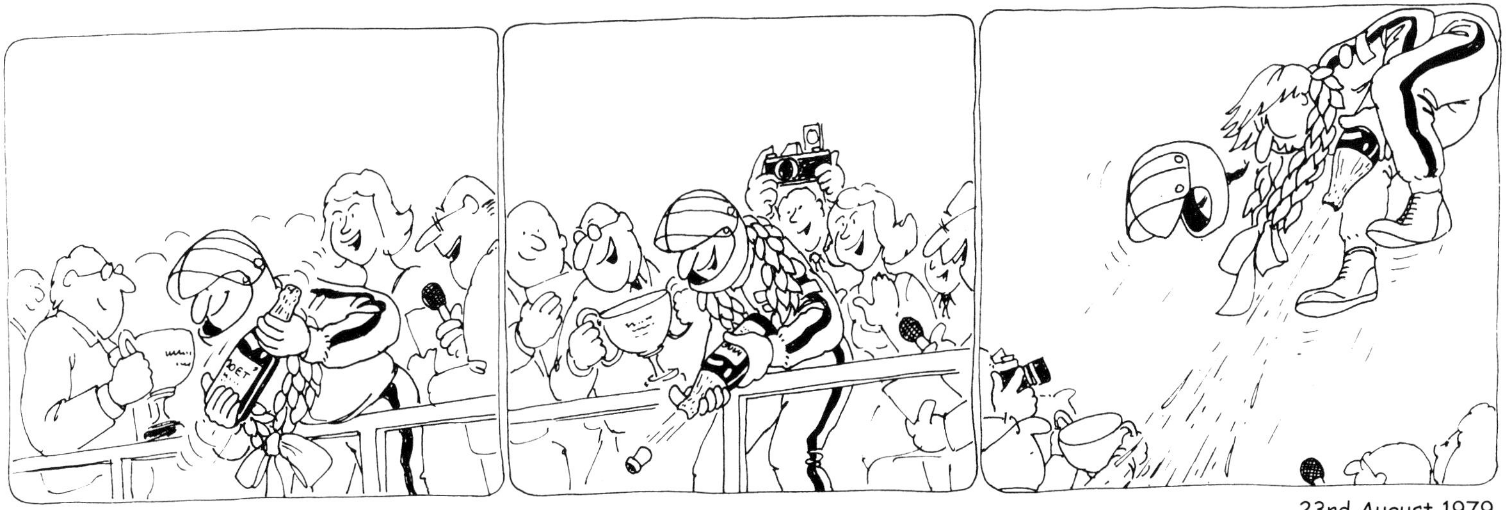

23rd August 1979

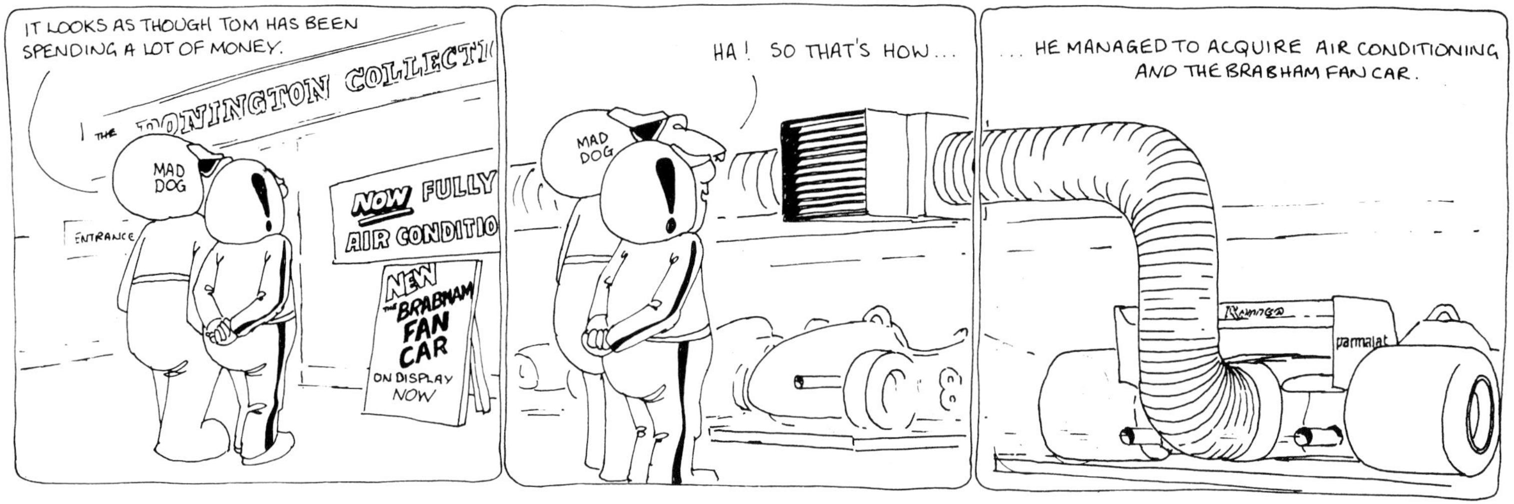
IT LOOKS AS THOUGH TOM HAS BEEN SPENDING A LOT OF MONEY.
MAD DOG
ENTRANCE
NOW FULLY AIR CONDITIO
NEW THE BRABHAM FAN CAR ON DISPLAY NOW
HA! SO THAT'S HOW...
MAD DOG
... HE MANAGED TO ACQUIRE AIR CONDITIONING AND THE BRABHAM FAN CAR.
parmalat

29th November 1979

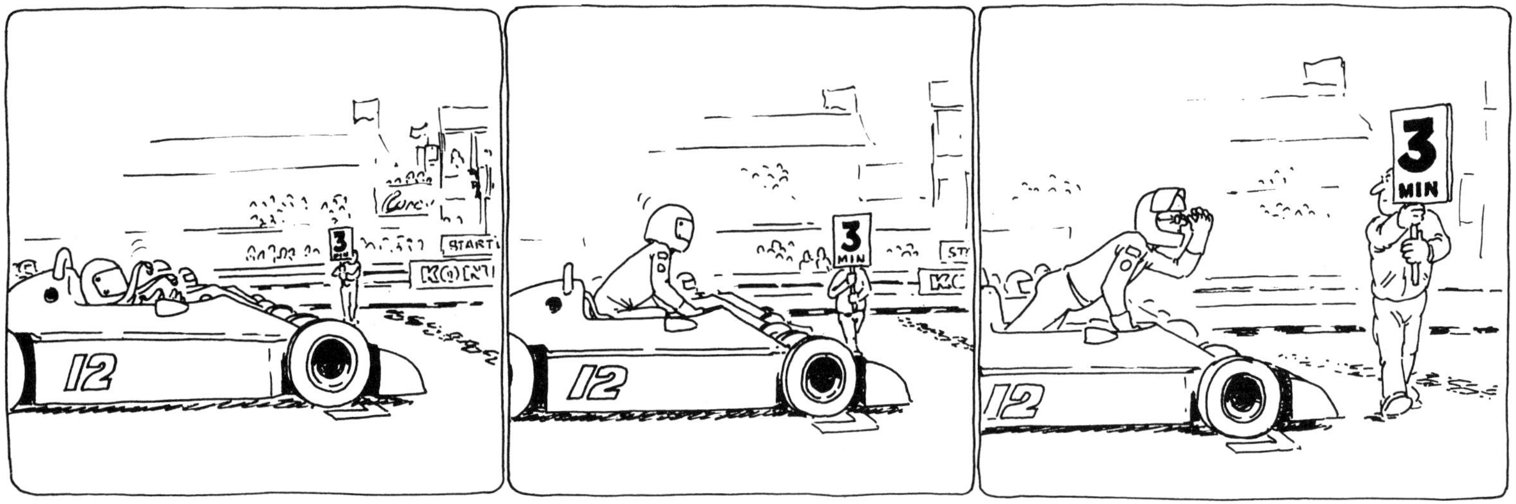
3 MIN
12
START
3 MIN
12
3 MIN
12

16th October 1980

Chapter Eight

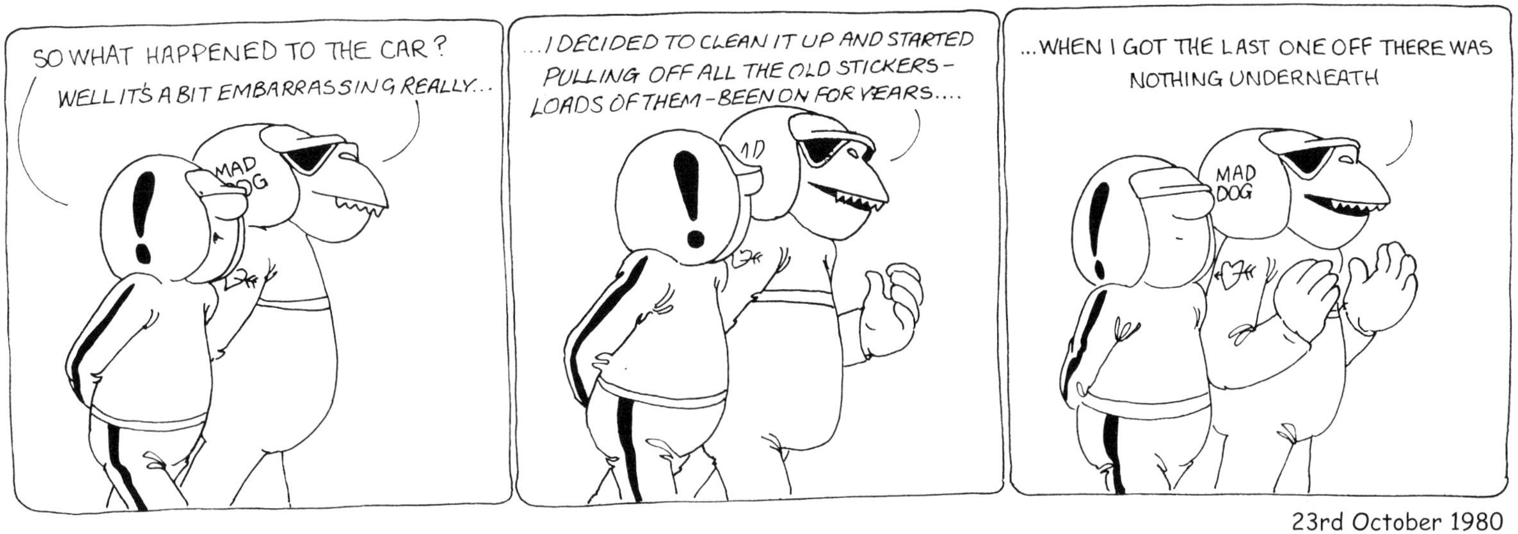
SO WHAT HAPPENED TO THE CAR?
WELL IT'S A BIT EMBARRASSING REALLY...
MAD DOG
...I DECIDED TO CLEAN IT UP AND STARTED PULLING OFF ALL THE OLD STICKERS - LOADS OF THEM - BEEN ON FOR YEARS....
...WHEN I GOT THE LAST ONE OFF THERE WAS NOTHING UNDERNEATH
MAD DOG

23rd October 1980

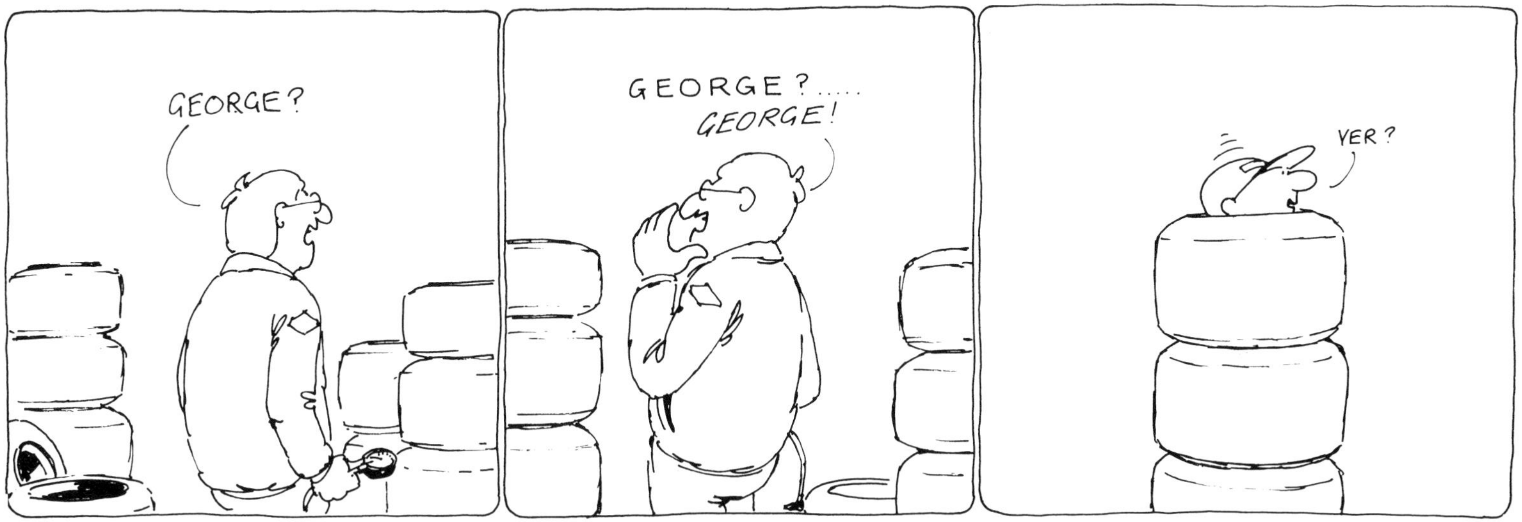
GEORGE?
GEORGE?.....
GEORGE!
YER?

4th June 1981

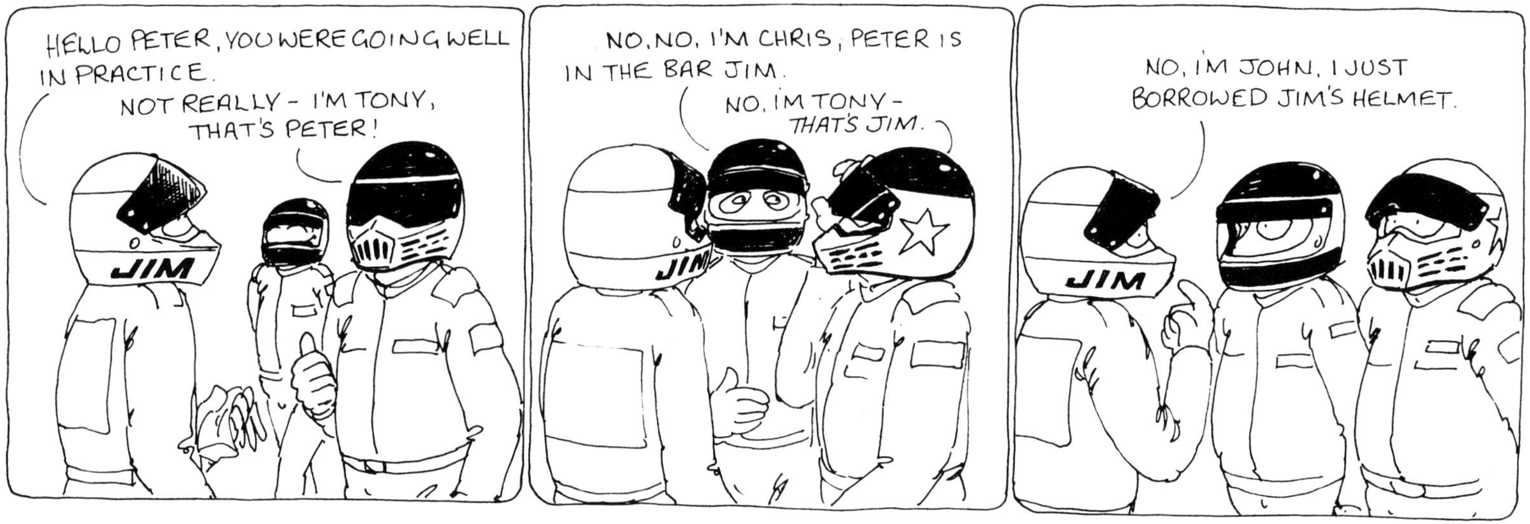
HELLO PETER, YOU WERE GOING WELL IN PRACTICE.
NOT REALLY - I'M TONY, THAT'S PETER!
JIM
NO, NO, I'M CHRIS, PETER IS IN THE BAR JIM.
NO, I'M TONY - THAT'S JIM.
JIM
NO, I'M JOHN, I JUST BORROWED JIM'S HELMET.
JIM

11th June 1981

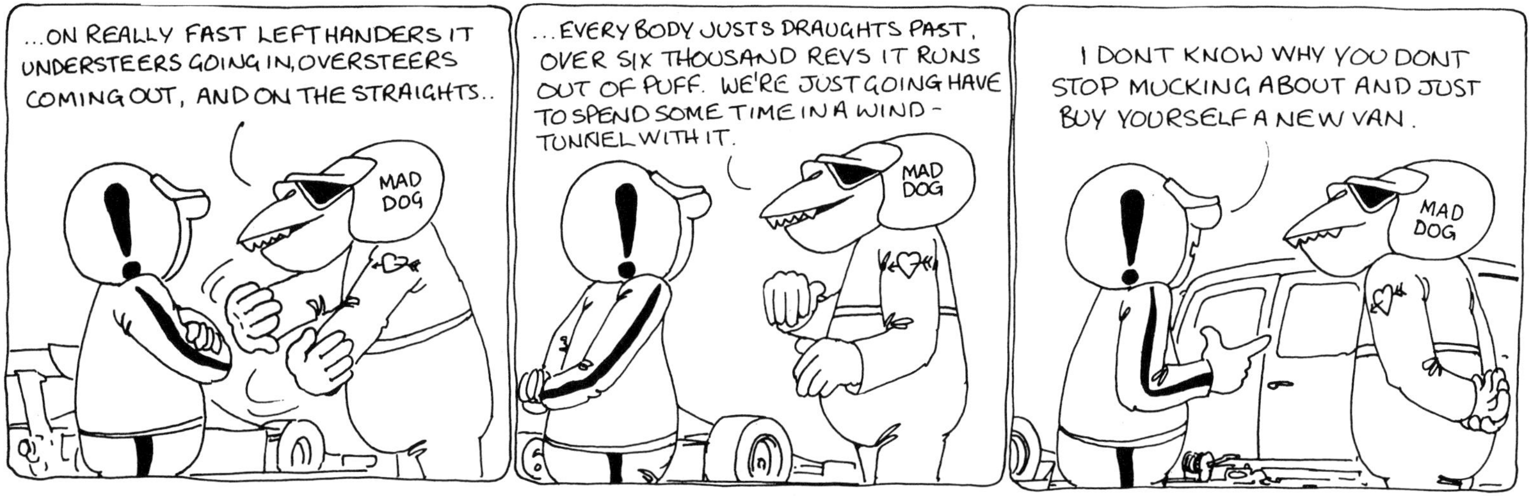
...ON REALLY FAST LEFTHANDERS IT UNDERSTEERS GOING IN, OVERSTEERS COMING OUT, AND ON THE STRAIGHTS..
MAD DOG
...EVERY BODY JUSTS DRAUGHTS PAST, OVER SIX THOUSAND REVS IT RUNS OUT OF PUFF. WE'RE JUST GOING HAVE TO SPEND SOME TIME IN A WIND-TUNNEL WITH IT.
MAD DOG
I DONT KNOW WHY YOU DONT STOP MUCKING ABOUT AND JUST BUY YOURSELF A NEW VAN.
MAD DOG

20th August 1981

Chapter Eight

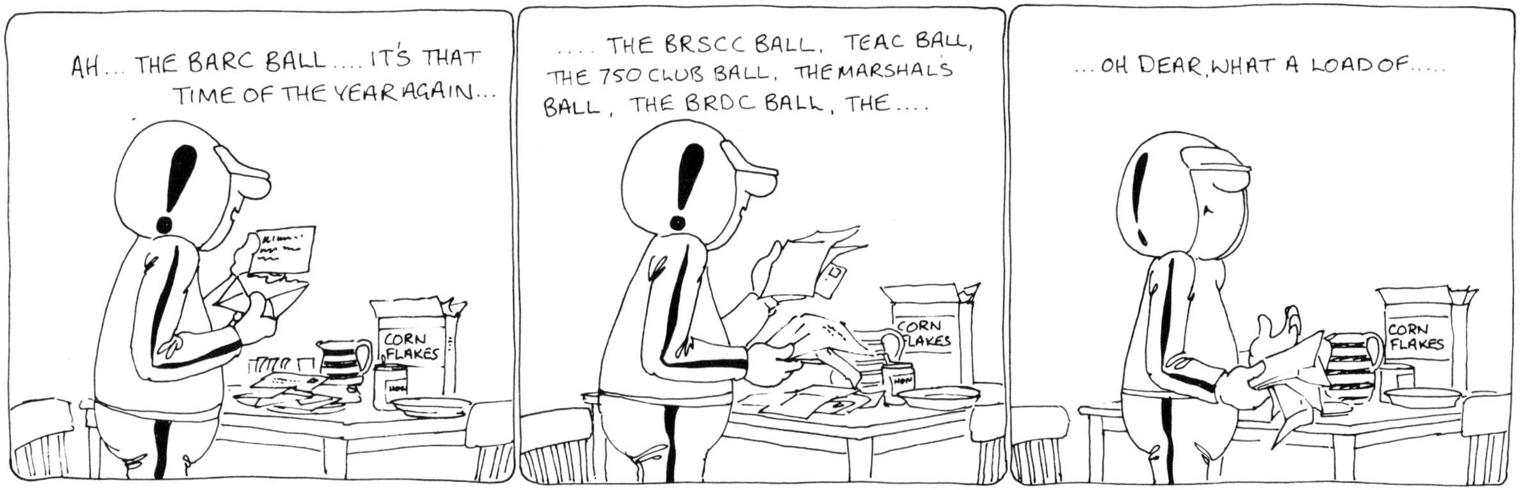
AH... THE BARC BALL.... IT'S THAT TIME OF THE YEAR AGAIN...
CORN FLAKES
.... THE BRSCC BALL, TEAC BALL, THE 750 CLUB BALL, THE MARSHAL'S BALL, THE BRDC BALL, THE....
...OH DEAR, WHAT A LOAD OF.....

5th November 1981

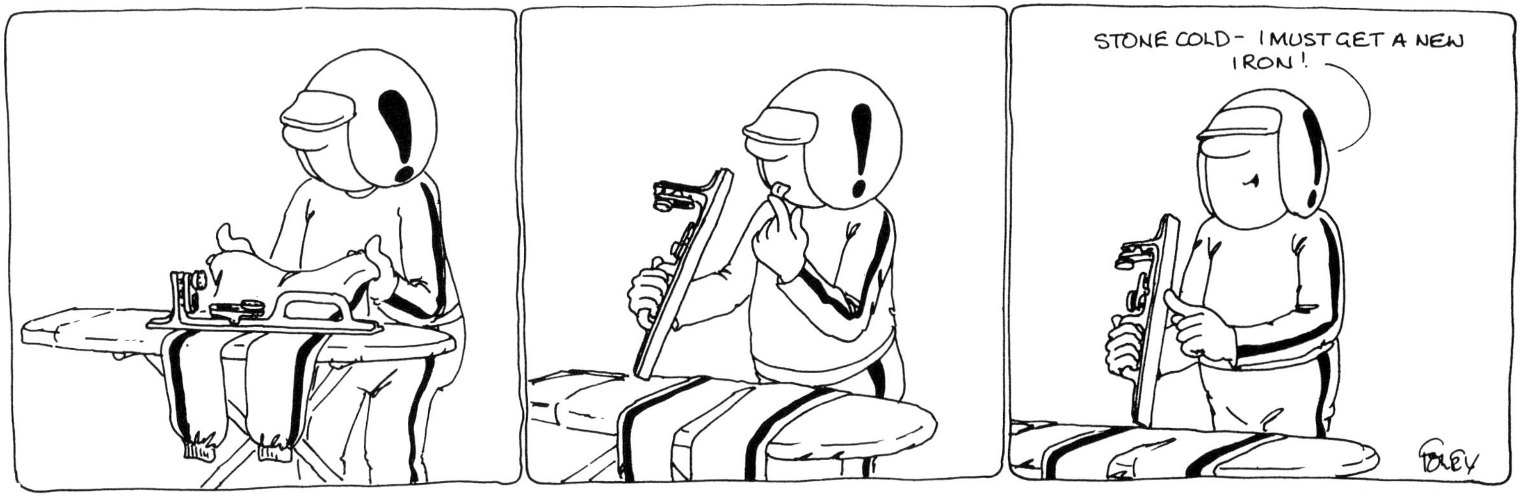
STONE COLD - I MUST GET A NEW IRON!
FOLEY

15th March 1984

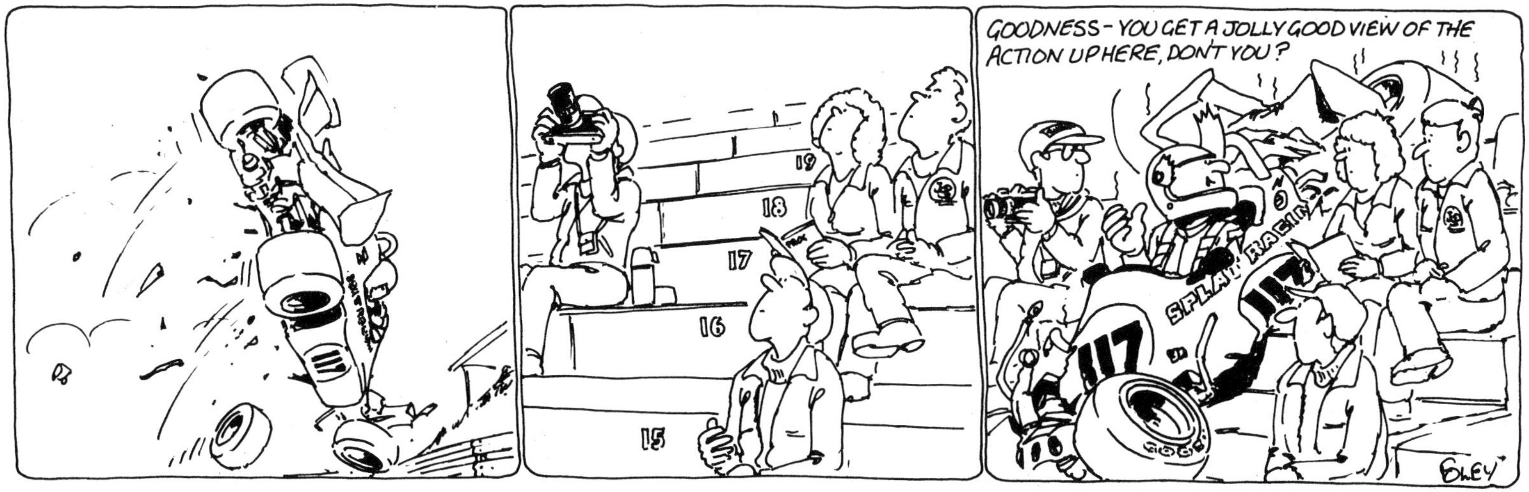
GOODNESS - YOU GET A JOLLY GOOD VIEW OF THE ACTION UP HERE, DON'T YOU?
FOLEY

14th June 1984

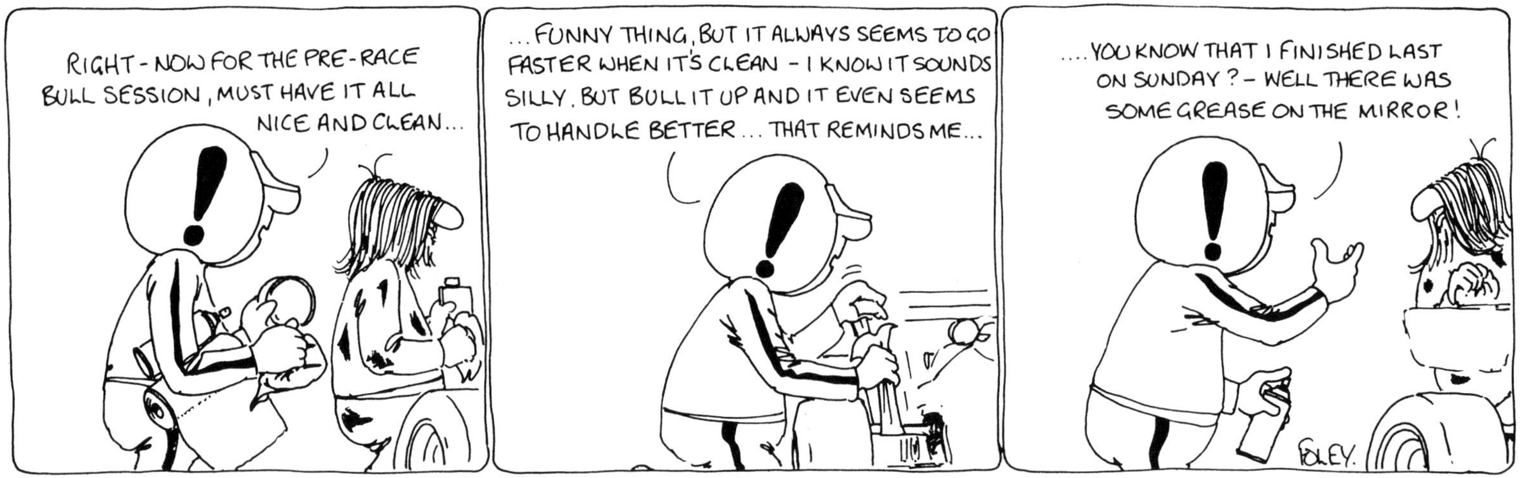
RIGHT - NOW FOR THE PRE-RACE BULL SESSION, MUST HAVE IT ALL NICE AND CLEAN...
...FUNNY THING, BUT IT ALWAYS SEEMS TO GO FASTER WHEN IT'S CLEAN - I KNOW IT SOUNDS SILLY, BUT BULL IT UP AND IT EVEN SEEMS TO HANDLE BETTER... THAT REMINDS ME...
....YOU KNOW THAT I FINISHED LAST ON SUNDAY? - WELL THERE WAS SOME GREASE ON THE MIRROR!
FOLEY

6th September 1984

Chapter Eight

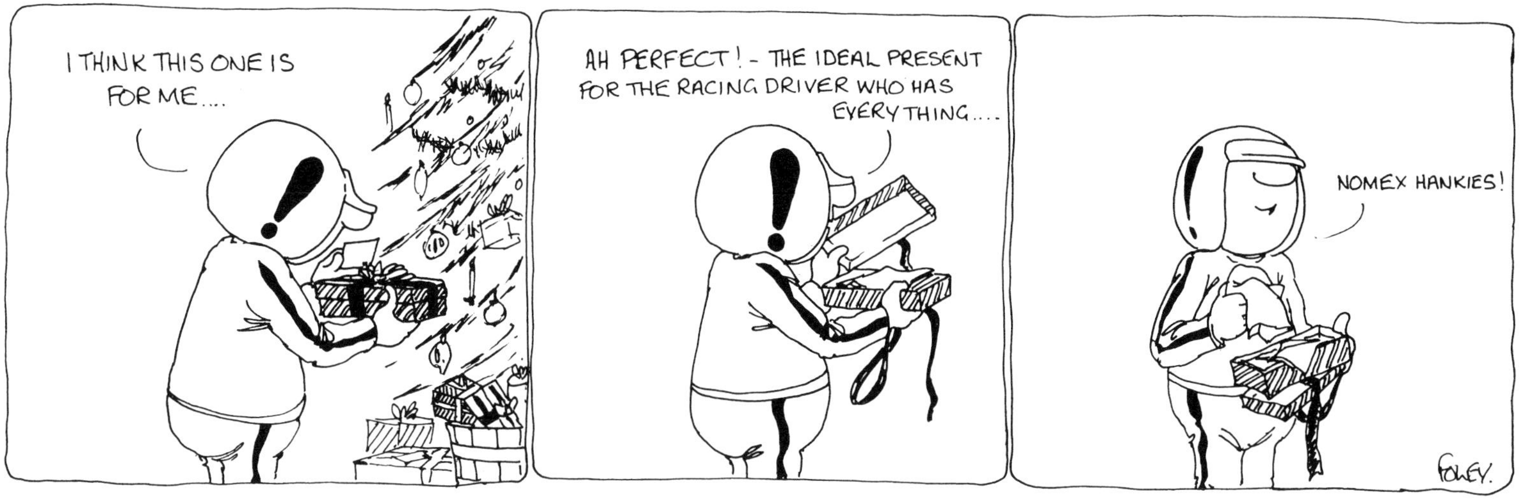
I THINK THIS ONE IS FOR ME....
AH PERFECT! - THE IDEAL PRESENT FOR THE RACING DRIVER WHO HAS EVERYTHING....
NOMEX HANKIES!
FOLEY.

20th December 1984

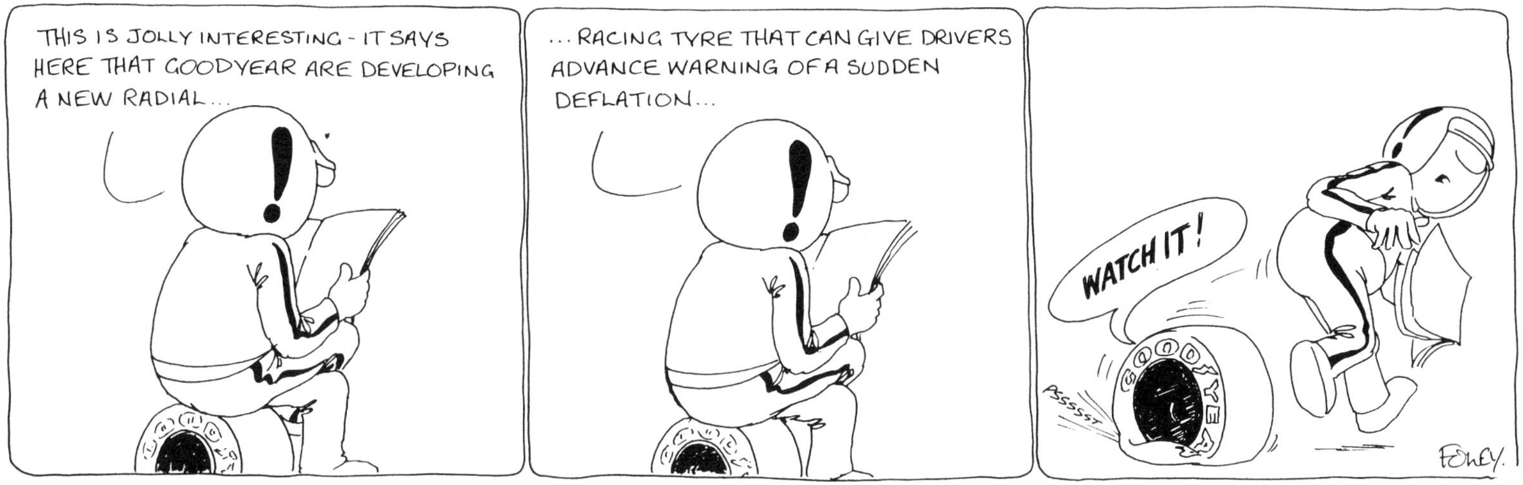
THIS IS JOLLY INTERESTING - IT SAYS HERE THAT GOODYEAR ARE DEVELOPING A NEW RADIAL...
...RACING TYRE THAT CAN GIVE DRIVERS ADVANCE WARNING OF A SUDDEN DEFLATION...
WATCH IT!
PSSSSST
FOLEY.

3rd October 1985

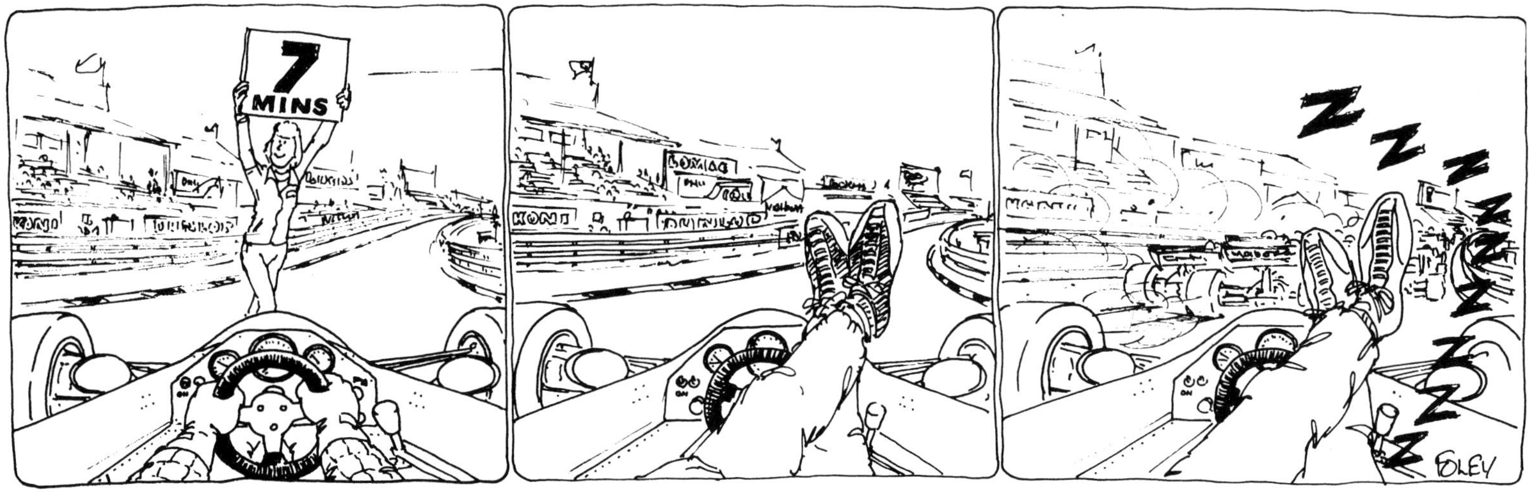
7
MINS
FOLEY

6th March 1986

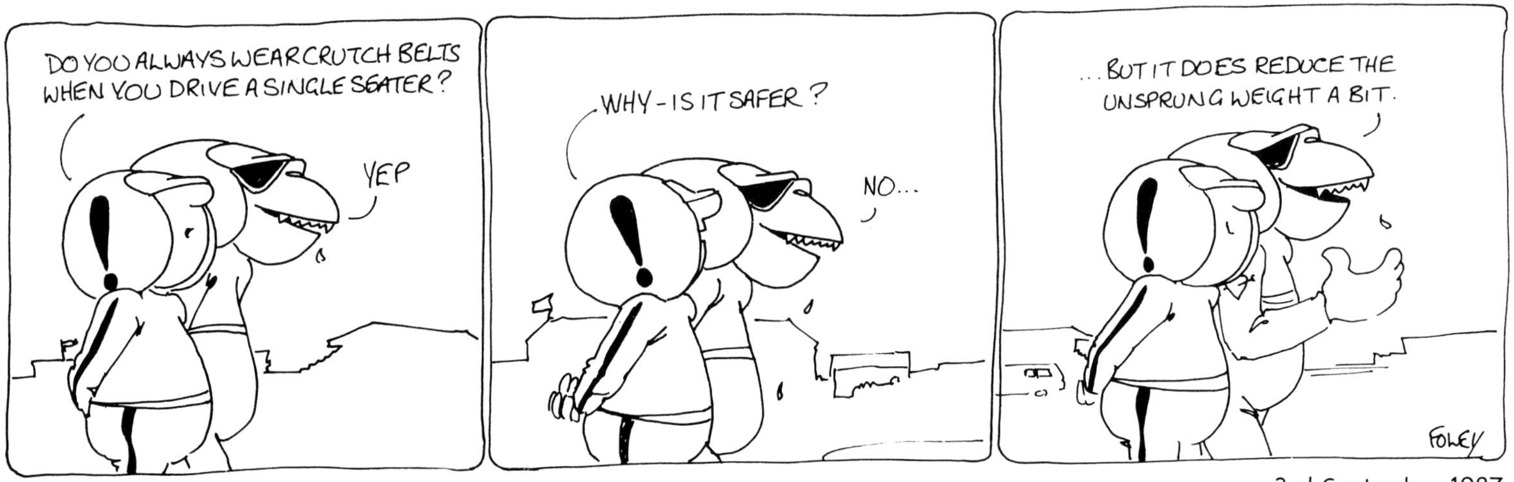
DO YOU ALWAYS WEAR CRUTCH BELTS WHEN YOU DRIVE A SINGLE SEATER?
YEP
WHY - IS IT SAFER?
NO...
...BUT IT DOES REDUCE THE UNSPRUNG WEIGHT A BIT.
FOLEY

3rd September 1987

Chapter Eight

END OF SEASON AGAIN - NO MORE ACTION - OH DEAR WHAT ON EARTH ARE WE GOING TO DO RIGHT THROUGH TO MARCH?....
...IT'S DECEMBER - ALMOST CHRISTMAS, THEN NEW YEAR - COUPLE OF WEEKS OFF - BIT OF A HOLIDAY, THEN...
...DOWN TO THE GARAGE - STRIP THE CAR DOWN, TAKE THE ENGINE OUT - THAT TAKES US TO THE END OF JAN...
...MAKE A FEW MODS - GET THE ENGINE REBUILD DONE - SAY THREE WEEKS - THEN REBUILD THE CAR, PUT THE ENGINE IN - SEND IT OFF FOR..
...A RESPRAY - OVERHAUL THE TRAILER - MY GOD WE'RE NOT GOING TO MAKE IT!
FOLEY

10th December 1987

HOW DID YOU DO WITH THE AUTOSPORT QUIZ?
QUITE WELL REALLY - I FOUND THE PAGE FIRST GO - THEN PUT DOWN ...
...A.J. FOYT AGAINST EVERY QUESTION - I MUST GET AT LEAST ONE RIGHT!
FOLEY

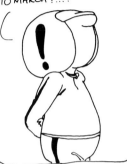

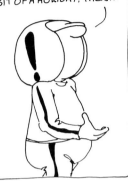

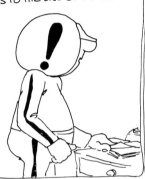

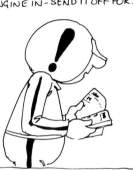

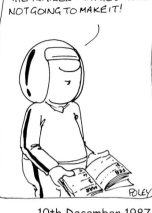

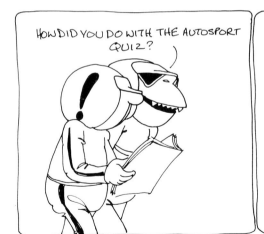

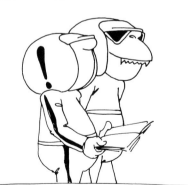

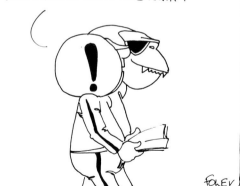

5th January 1989

OH NO - NOT ANOTHER ONE - WOULD YOU BELIEVE McLAREN ARE NOW GOING TO...
...PRODUCE A ROAD CAR - THEY'RE ALL AT IT - FIRST IT WAS MARCH, NOW IT'S McLAREN...
...YOU MARK MY WORDS IT'LL BE LOTUS NEXT.
FOLEY

23rd March 1989

BOOOF
GITANES
3
HARBOUR
FINISH LINE
MONACO POWER BOAT GRAND PRIX
FOLEY

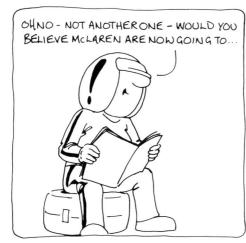

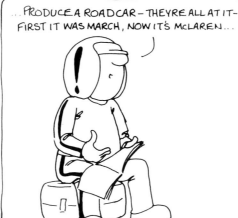

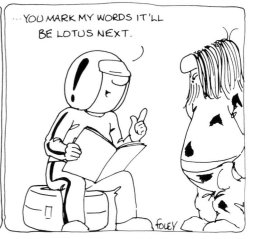

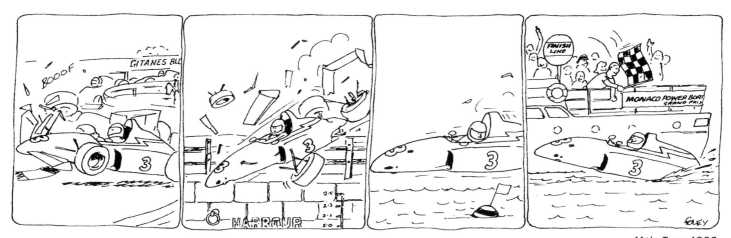

11th June 1992

The Officials

Chapter Nine

The people who organise the sport, the scrutineers, official timers, clerks of the course, doctors and observers. These are people who are essential to the sport, efficient, experienced, skilled, highly motivated, unpaid, selfless, caring people who are far too vulnerable and defenceless to be used as the butt of cartoonists' jokes. The following are some of the cartoons I did before I knew that.

OH DEAR OH DEAR
I THINK I'M LATE AGAIN
TIME KEEPER
FOLEY

HI FRED – HOW'S SCRUTING GOING TODAY?
BLUE BOOK
RAC SCRUTINEER
SPLENDID, SPLENDID JUST PERFECT.....
BLUE BOOK
I'VE TURNED DOWN SEVENTEEN CARS ALREADY

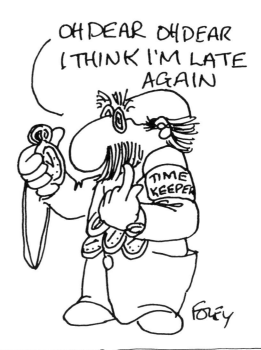

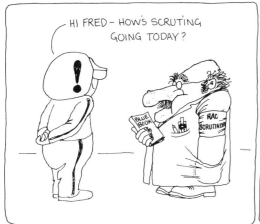

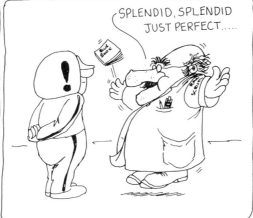

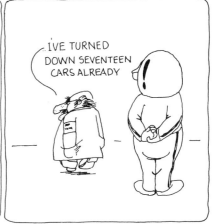

....AND REMEMBER, WHEN YOU TURN A CAR DOWN FOR SCRUT'ING, MAKE SURE YOU FAIL IT FOR A GOOD REASON....
RAC CHIEF SCRUTE
BLUE BOOK
RAC SCRUTE
....IT'S NO GOOD FAILING A CAR FOR SOMETHING SILLY, LIKE LOOSE WHEEL NUTS. BECAUSE....
...THE BLIGHTERS WILL ONLY DO THEM UP, AND BRING THE CAR BACK AGAIN!

20th May 1971

OH DEAR OH DEAR
TIME KEEPER
WHAT'S WRONG GERALD?
WHAT'S THE TIME?
OH DEAR, OH DEAR I THINK I'M LATE AGAIN.

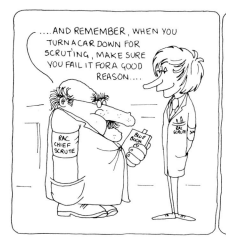

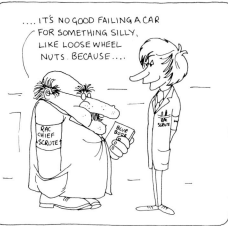

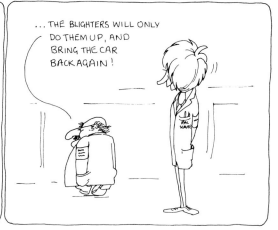

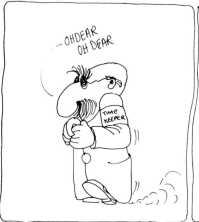

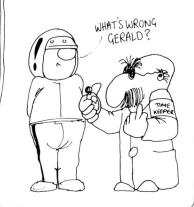

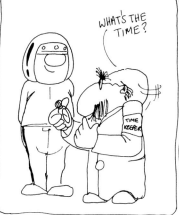

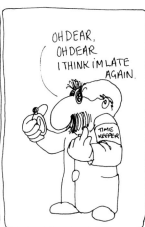

24th June 1971

Chapter Nine

The Officials

'ALT!..... WHER'S YER PASS
OOMPH
SLAP
SECURI HATCH
BUT... BUT...
COME ON SHOW ME YER TRACK PASS
PROD
I HAVEN'T GOT MY PASS WITH ME, BUT I DON'T REALLY NEED ONE. I'M A DRIVER.
YOU'RE THE 'HUNDRED AND FIFTY THIRD JOKER TO SPIN ME THAT YARN THISMORNING – COMEON... OUT!

15th July 1971

....IT'S NOT MY FAULT
TIME KEEPER
....I DON'T SEE HOW THEY CAN BLAME ME...
....SEVEN SPECTACULAR NEW LAP RECORDS..
....SOMEONE SHOULD HAVE TOLD ME THEY WERE USING THE SHORT CLUB CIRCUIT

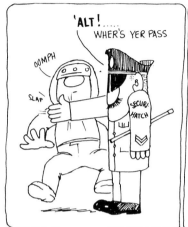

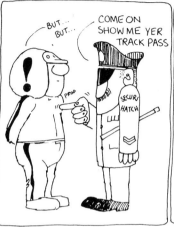

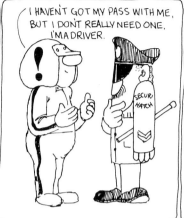

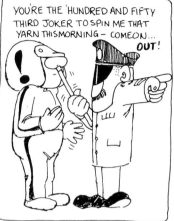

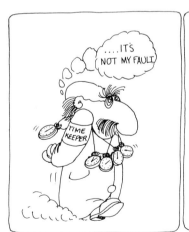

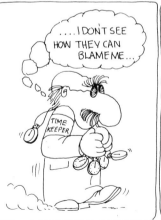

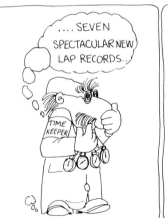

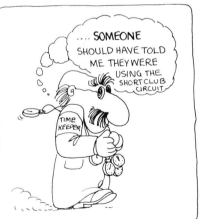

22nd July 1971

RAC TIME KEEPER
RAC TIME KEEPER
RAC TIME KEEPER
I WONDER WHEN THE CLOCKS GO BACK?
RAC TIME KEEPER

20th January 1972

HOLD IT, HOLD IT. YOU'LL HAVE TO DO SOMETHING ABOUT YOUR NUMBERS. I CAN'T...
TIME KEEPER
...SEE THEM AT ALL. YOU'LL HAVE TO STICK THEM IN A MORE OBVIOUS PLACE!
TIME KEEPER
TIME KEEPER

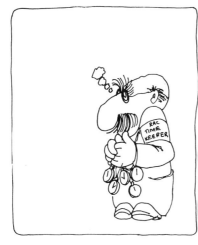

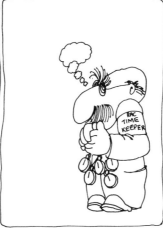

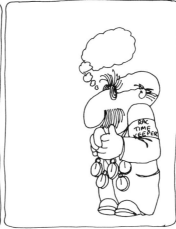

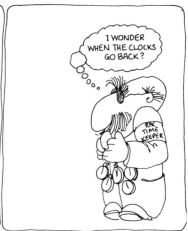

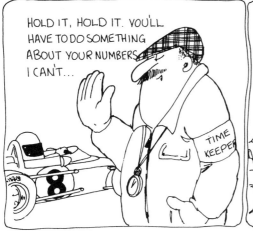

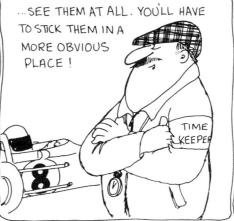

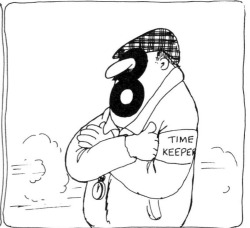

27th January 1972

Chapter Nine

NOW, REPEAT AFTER ME, I SWEAR BY THE ALMIGHTY RAC TO HOLD THE HOLY BLUE BOOK SACRED AT ALL TIMES, EVEN TO THE POINT...
RAC CHIEF SCRUTE
BLUE BOOK
... OF CRASS STUPIDITY. I PROMISE NEVER TO LET FAIR MINDEDNESS, LOGIC, OR PLAIN TRUTH SWAY MY JUDGMENT...
RAC CHIEF SCRUTE
... I WILL DO ALL IN MY POWER TO MINIMIZE THE POSSIBILITY OF A CAR BEING PASSED BEFORE PRACTICE STARTS. I SWEAR TO....
RAC CHIEF SCRUTE

4th May 1972

YOUR TROUBLE, CATCHPOLE, IS YOU'RE ALWAYS CRITICIZING, CARP, CARP, CARP...
...THAT'S ALL YOU EVER DO. YOU NEVER STOP FINDING FAULT, NEGATIVE THAT'S WHAT YOU ARE...
... JUST ONE NEGATIVE CRITICISM AFTER ANOTHER. WHY DON'T YOU SAY SOMETHING POSITIVE FOR A CHANGE?
PROD
DROP DEAD

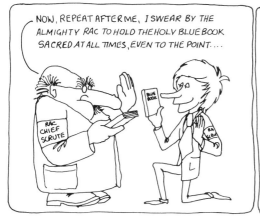

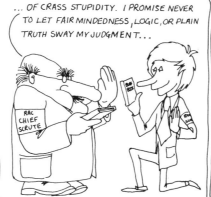

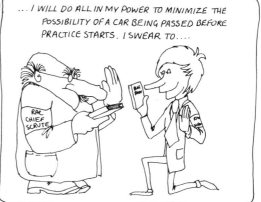

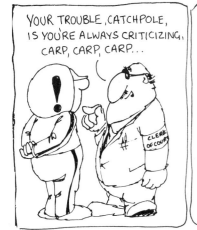

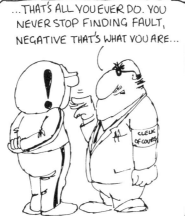

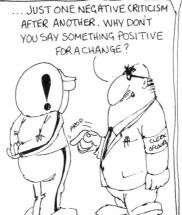

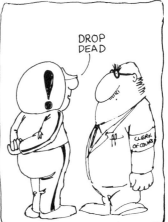

3rd August 1972

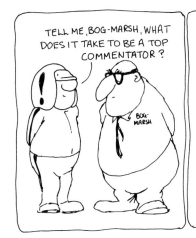

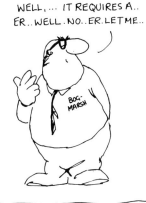

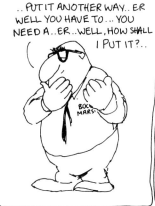

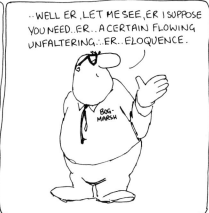

TELL ME, BOG-MARSH, WHAT DOES IT TAKE TO BE A TOP COMMENTATOR?
BOG-MARSH
WELL, ... IT REQUIRES A.. ER.. WELL. NO.. ER. LET ME..
BOG-MARSH
.. PUT IT ANOTHER WAY.. ER WELL YOU HAVE TO... YOU NEED A.. ER.. WELL, HOW SHALL I PUT IT?..
.. WELL ER, LET ME SEE, ER I SUPPOSE YOU NEED.. ER.. A CERTAIN FLOWING UNFALTERING.:.ER.. ELOQUENCE.
BOG-MARSH

28th September 1972

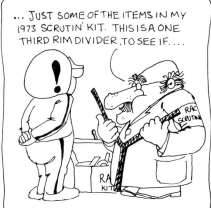

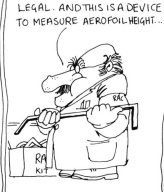

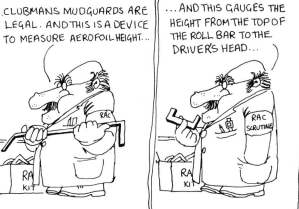

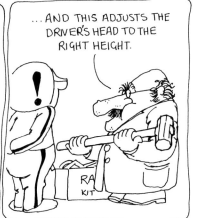

... JUST SOME OF THE ITEMS IN MY 1973 SCRUTIN' KIT. THIS IS A ONE THIRD RIM DIVIDER, TO SEE IF....
.. CLUBMANS MUDGUARDS ARE LEGAL. AND THIS IS A DEVICE TO MEASURE AEROFOIL HEIGHT...
RAC
... AND THIS GAUGES THE HEIGHT FROM THE TOP OF THE ROLL BAR TO THE DRIVER'S HEAD...
RAC SCRUTINE
... AND THIS ADJUSTS THE DRIVER'S HEAD TO THE RIGHT HEIGHT.

26th October 1972

Chapter Nine

A LETTER
HOW NICE..
IT WISHES ME EVERY SUCCESS AT SELLIN' MY OLD RACING NAIL. AND IT'S SIGNED....
...BY ALL THE SCRUTINEERS

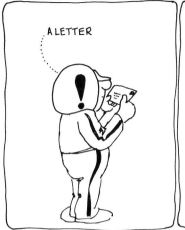

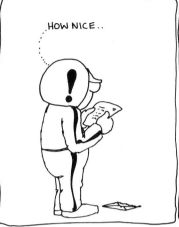

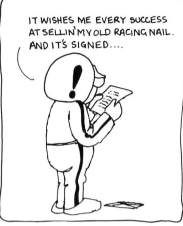

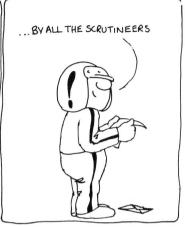

16th November 1972

I HAD A JOLLY GOOD CHRISTMAS AND I WAS NICE TO EVERY-ONE AND....
BLUE BOOK
RAC SCROOT
...EVERYONE WAS NICE TO ME. I ENJOYED MYSELF AT THE RACING CAR SHOW BECAUSE...
BLUE BOOK
RAC SCROOT
...EVERYONE WAS NICE AND FRIENDLY AND SAID KIND THINGS TO EACH OTHER...
RAC SCROOT
...NOW THE RACING SEASON IS BEGINING AND I CAN START ACTING NATURALLY AGAIN

22nd February 1973

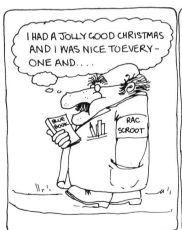

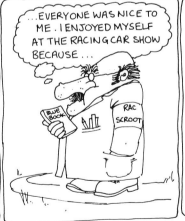

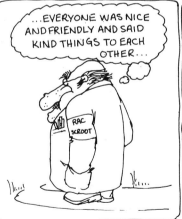

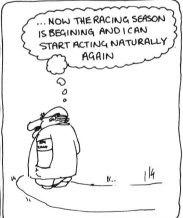

The Officials

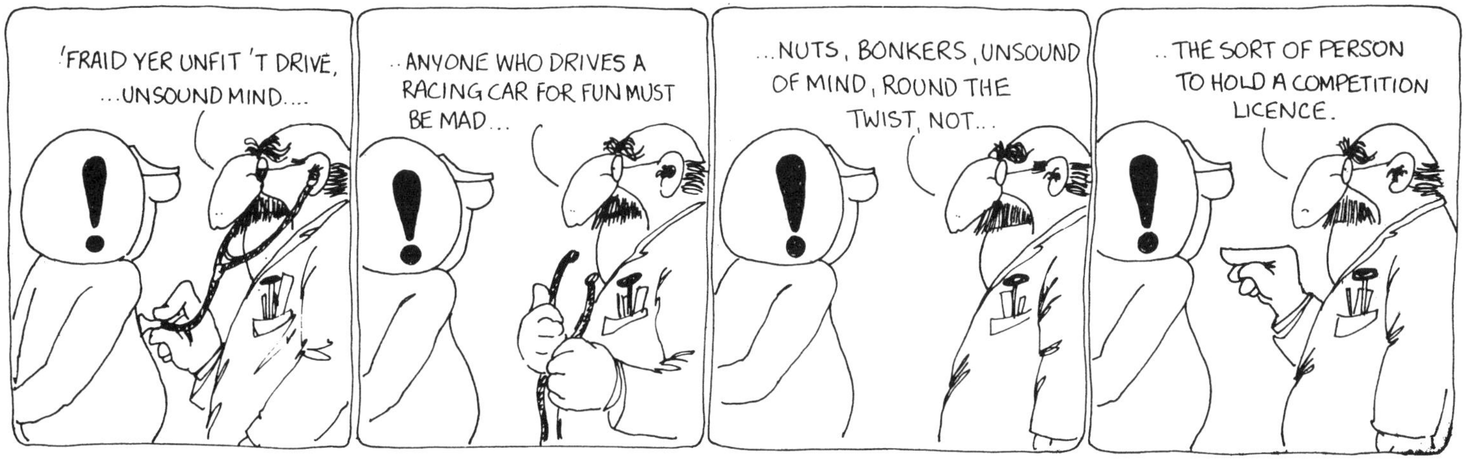
'FRAID YER UNFIT 'T DRIVE, ...UNSOUND MIND....
..ANYONE WHO DRIVES A RACING CAR FOR FUN MUST BE MAD...
...NUTS, BONKERS, UNSOUND OF MIND, ROUND THE TWIST, NOT...
..THE SORT OF PERSON TO HOLD A COMPETITION LICENCE.

26th July 1973

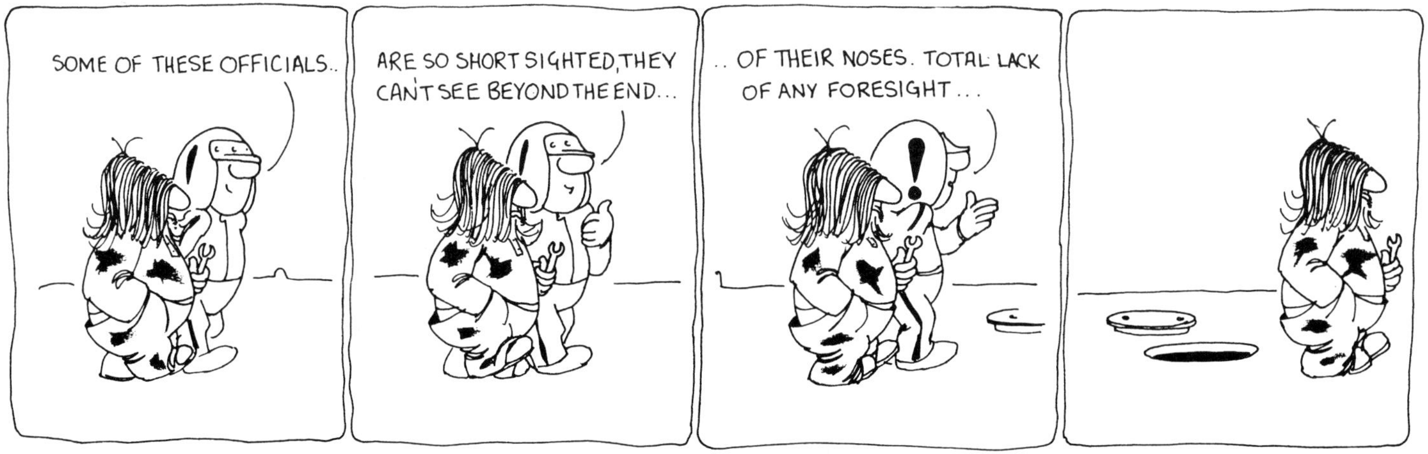
SOME OF THESE OFFICIALS..
ARE SO SHORT SIGHTED, THEY CAN'T SEE BEYOND THE END...
.. OF THEIR NOSES. TOTAL LACK OF ANY FORESIGHT...

18th October 1973

Chapter Nine

The Officials

PIG!

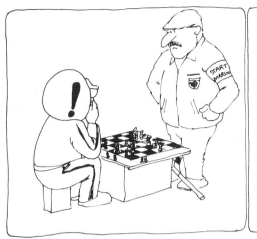

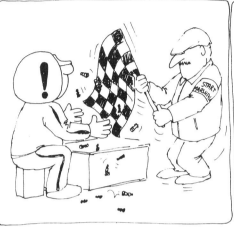

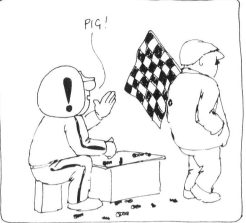

27th February 1975

THE CHOICE, GENTLEMEN, IS A SIMPLE ONE. EITHER, WE PASS A PIECE OF HIGHLY...
FIA COMMITTEE
... COMPLICATED AND VERY CONFUSING LEGISLATION IN ORDER TO CLARIFY THE SITUATION. OR WE EXPRESS THE WHOLE..
FIA COMMITTEE
... THING IN A SIMPLE STRAIGHT FORWARD MANNER THAT WILL TOTALLY CONFUSE AND MYSTIFY EVERYONE.
FIA COMMITTEE

27th March 1975

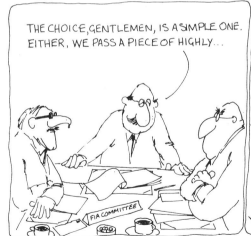

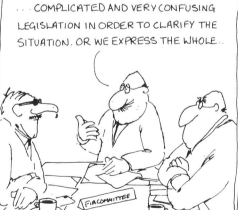

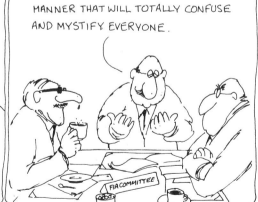

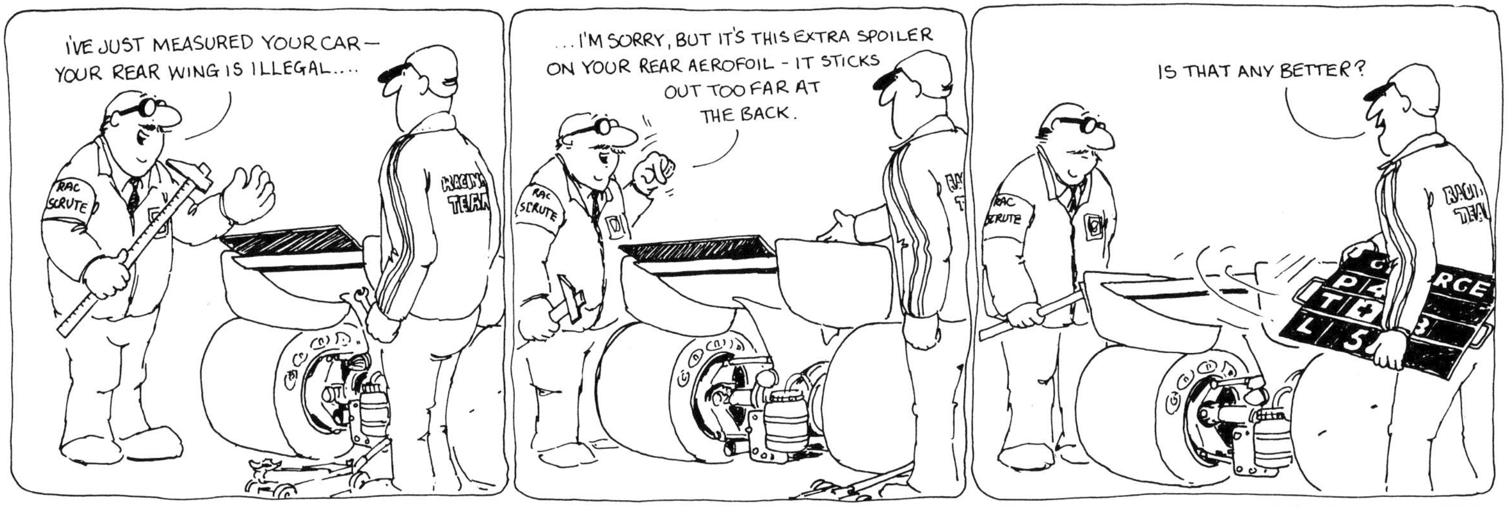
I'VE JUST MEASURED YOUR CAR—
YOUR REAR WING IS ILLEGAL....
RAC SCRUTE
...I'M SORRY, BUT IT'S THIS EXTRA SPOILER ON YOUR REAR AEROFOIL - IT STICKS OUT TOO FAR AT THE BACK.
RAC SCRUTE
IS THAT ANY BETTER?

4th November 1976

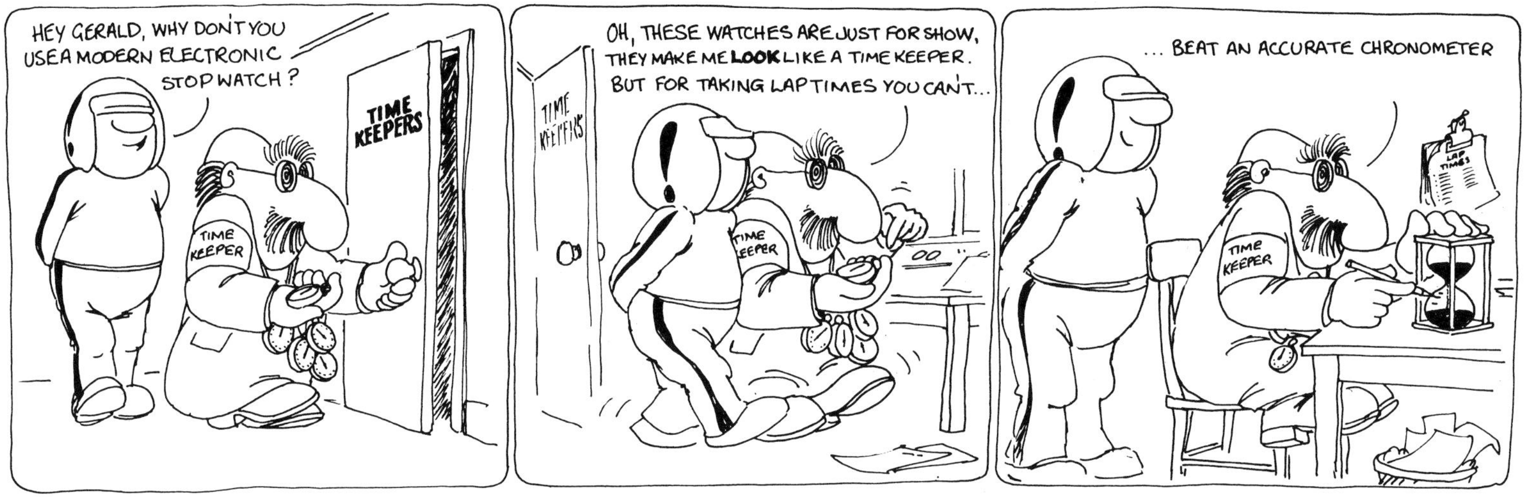
HEY GERALD, WHY DON'T YOU USE A MODERN ELECTRONIC STOP WATCH?
TIME KEEPERS
TIME KEEPER
OH, THESE WATCHES ARE JUST FOR SHOW, THEY MAKE ME LOOK LIKE A TIME KEEPER. BUT FOR TAKING LAP TIMES YOU CAN'T...
... BEAT AN ACCURATE CHRONOMETER
TIME KEEPER
LAP TIMES

6th January 1977

Chapter Nine

The Officials

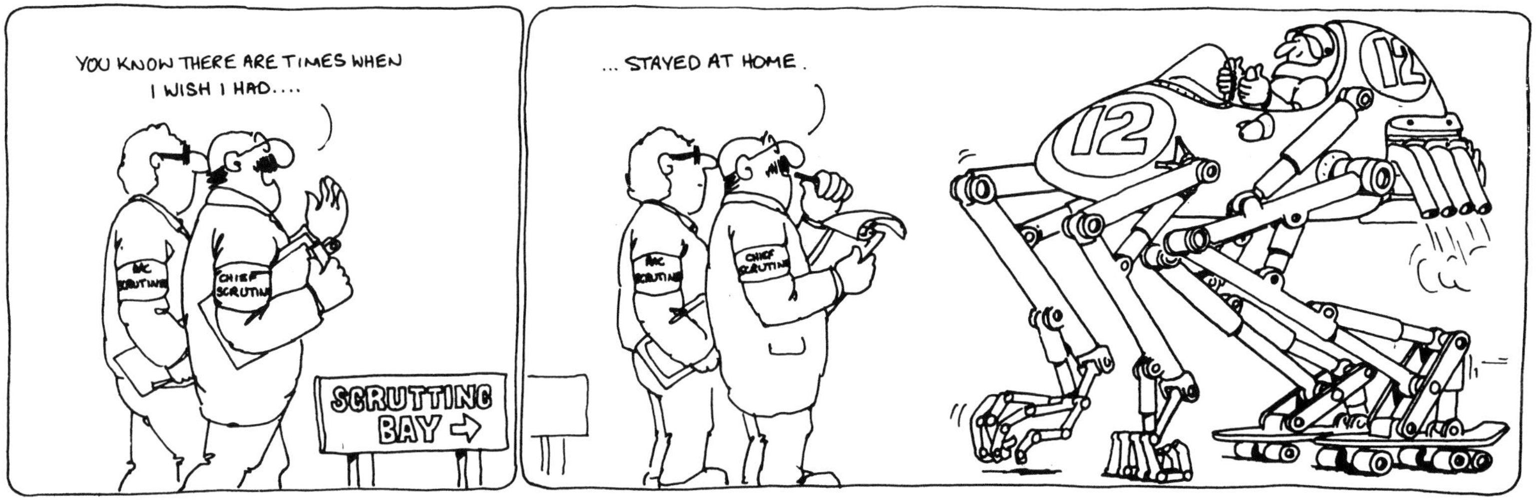

YOU KNOW THERE ARE TIMES WHEN I WISH I HAD....
SCRUTTING BAY
... STAYED AT HOME.
12

20th April 1978

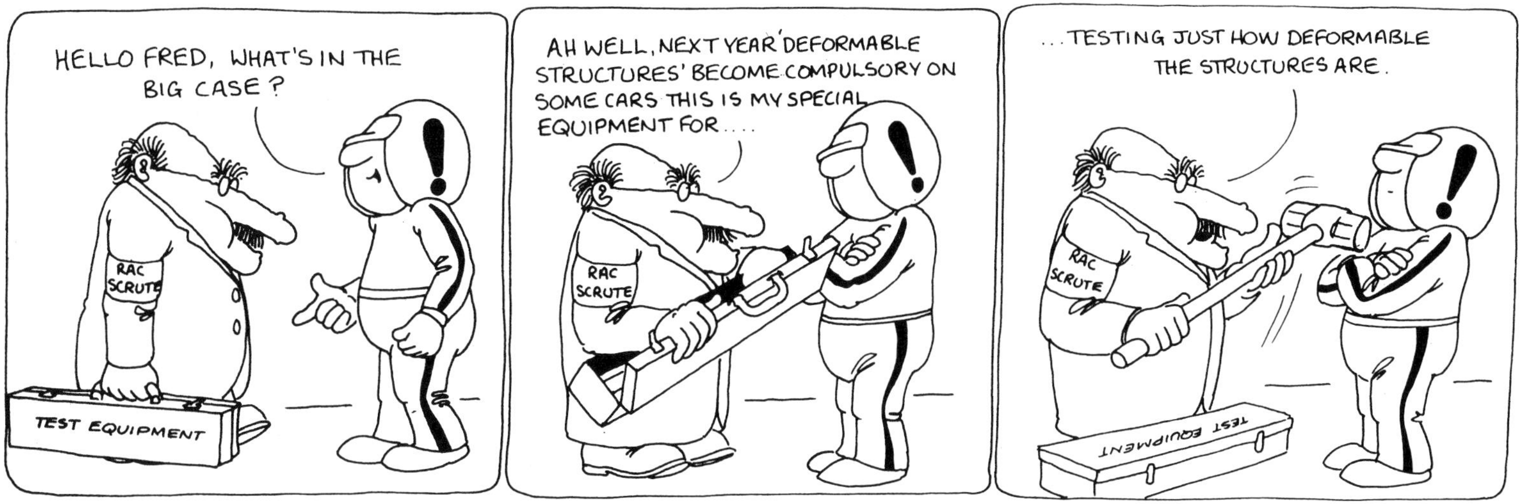

HELLO FRED, WHAT'S IN THE BIG CASE ?
RAC SCRUTE
TEST EQUIPMENT
AH WELL, NEXT YEAR 'DEFORMABLE STRUCTURES' BECOME COMPULSORY ON SOME CARS THIS IS MY SPECIAL EQUIPMENT FOR....
RAC SCRUTE
...TESTING JUST HOW DEFORMABLE THE STRUCTURES ARE.
RAC SCRUTE
TEST EQUIPMENT

14th December 1978

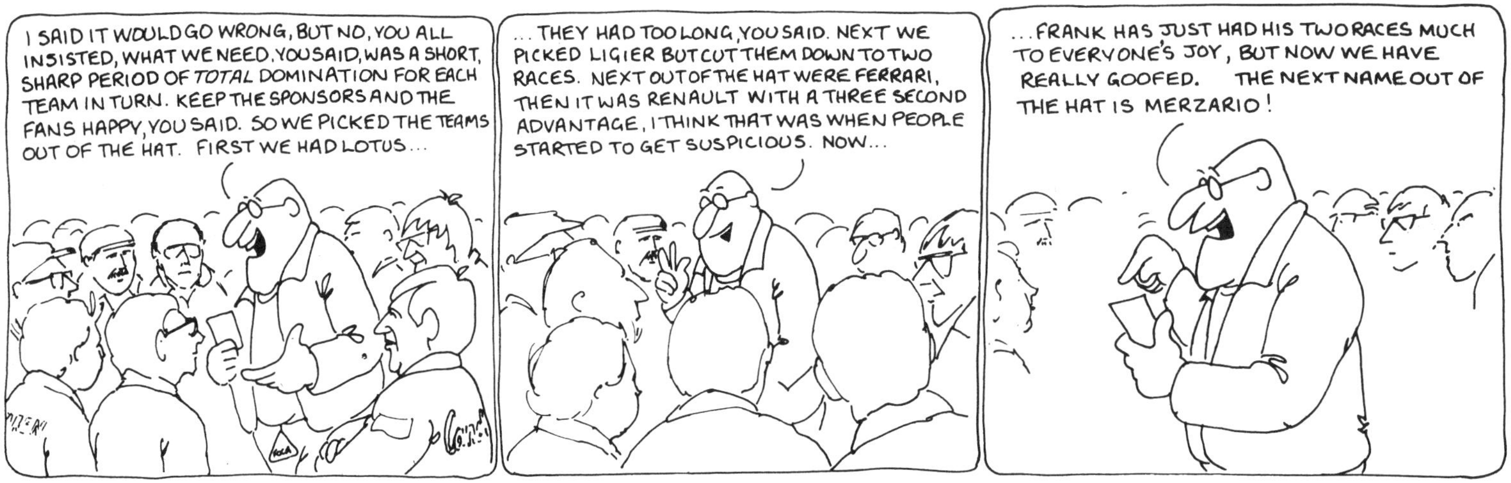
I SAID IT WOULD GO WRONG, BUT NO, YOU ALL INSISTED, WHAT WE NEED, YOU SAID, WAS A SHORT, SHARP PERIOD OF TOTAL DOMINATION FOR EACH TEAM IN TURN. KEEP THE SPONSORS AND THE FANS HAPPY, YOU SAID. SO WE PICKED THE TEAMS OUT OF THE HAT. FIRST WE HAD LOTUS...
...THEY HAD TOO LONG, YOU SAID. NEXT WE PICKED LIGIER BUT CUT THEM DOWN TO TWO RACES. NEXT OUT OF THE HAT WERE FERRARI, THEN IT WAS RENAULT WITH A THREE SECOND ADVANTAGE, I THINK THAT WAS WHEN PEOPLE STARTED TO GET SUSPICIOUS. NOW...
...FRANK HAS JUST HAD HIS TWO RACES MUCH TO EVERYONE'S JOY, BUT NOW WE HAVE REALLY GOOFED. THE NEXT NAME OUT OF THE HAT IS MERZARIO!

2nd August 1979

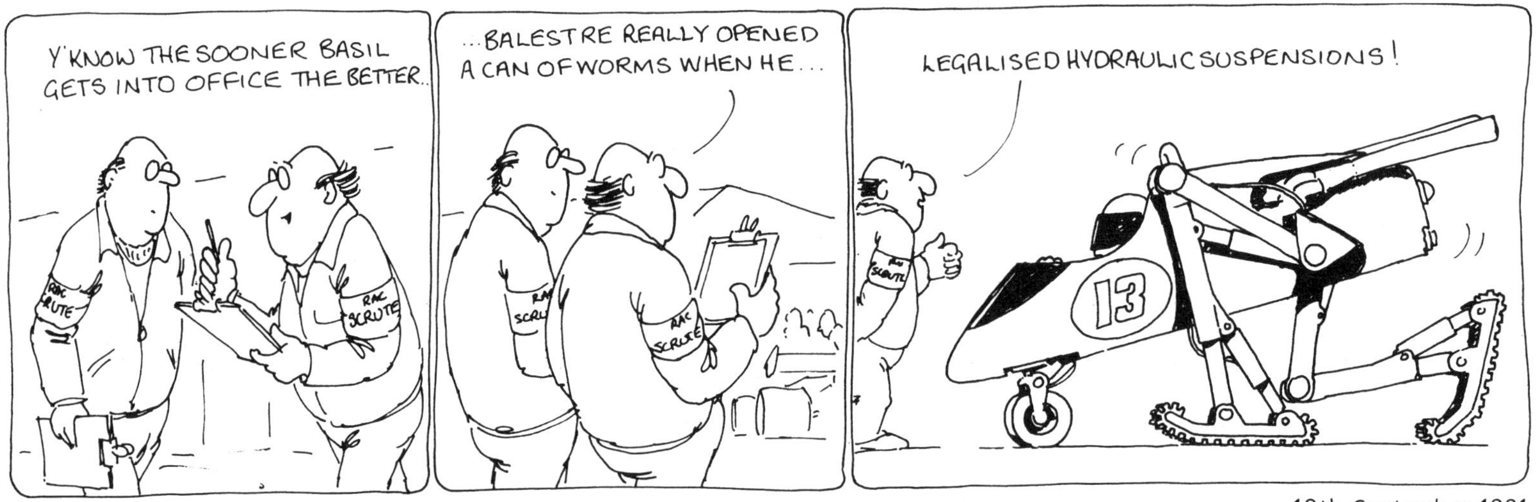
Y'KNOW THE SOONER BASIL GETS INTO OFFICE THE BETTER..
...BALESTRE REALLY OPENED A CAN OF WORMS WHEN HE...
LEGALISED HYDRAULIC SUSPENSIONS!
RAC SCRUTE
13

10th September 1981

Club Racing

Chapter Ten

Club racing is exactly like F1, but with a few minor differences. 1: Club racers are older. 2: F1 people race for the love of it. 3: People take club racing more seriously. 4: Signing on and scrutineering are earlier in the morning in club racing.
However the jokes are completely different. Catchpole is in his element in club racing. He says F1 is okay, but it's not like the real thing. If you want to watch club racing you have to go and see it, whereas you only ever see F1 on TV, so club racing is real.

LOOKS AS THOUGH WE'VE FORGOTTEN THE PETROL AGAIN
CHECK LIST
RED
BITTER
BEER
WHITE
XXX
RED
SHERRY
BROWN
FOLEY

...HE HAD MORE POWER THAN I DID, HIS CAR WAS OUTCORNERING AND OUTBRAKING MINE. INFACT HE HAD ME...
MAD DOG
...BEATEN. HE WAS OUTDRIVING ME AND HE HAD ME COMPLETELY AND UTTERLY OUT-PSYCHED. SO I DID THE ONLY HONOURABLE THING I COULD...
MAD DOG
.... I PUSHED HIM OFF AT THE NEXT BEND.
MAD DOG

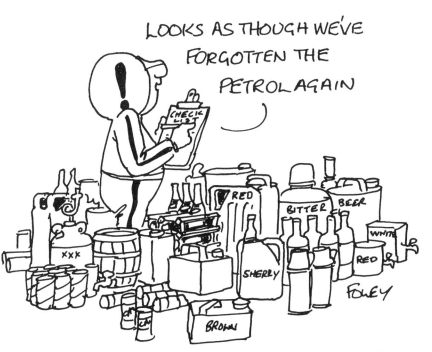

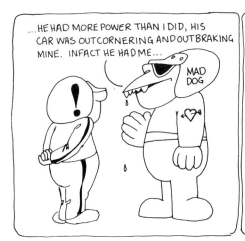

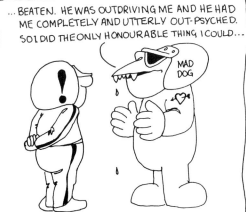

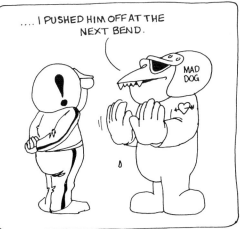

ATTENTION
ATTENTION
DRIVERS
BRIEFING
IN 10MINUTES
TIME
GOODY GOODY –
MY FAVOURITE
COMEDY SHOW

4th February 1971

WELL TWEAK, IT'S NEARLY
TIME FOR THE RACE....
.... I SUPPOSE WE HAD BETTER
SORT OUT THE OPPOSITION....
GRUNT
..... GIVE THEM SOMETHING
TO THINK ABOUT....
.... ONE LUMP OR TWO ?
GRUNT
GRUNT
SUGAR

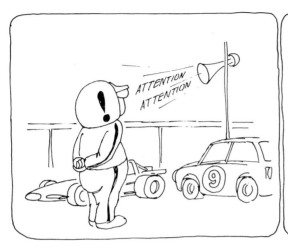

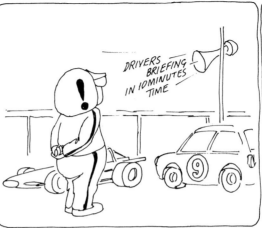

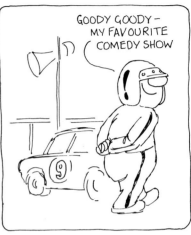

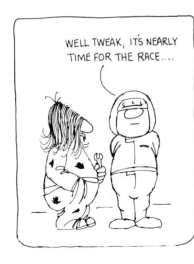

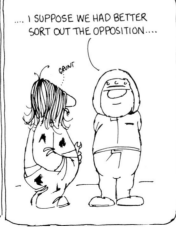

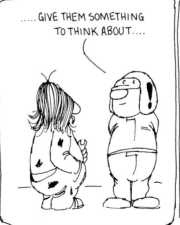

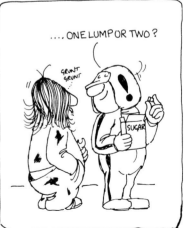

22nd April 1971

Chapter Ten

WELL TWEAK, IT'S NICE TO WIN A RACE, I SUGGEST WE GO AND CELEBRATE...
....LET'S GO REALLY MAD, LET'S BLOW THE ENTIRE WINNINGS IN ONE GLORIOUS ORGY!

11th May 1972

WHAT ON EARTH IS WRONG MAD DOG?
MAD DOG
HOW DO YOU START TO EXPLAIN TO YOUR WIFE....
MAD DOG
...JUST AS YOU ARE ABOUT TO GO ON THREE WEEKS HOLIDAY, THAT YOUR CHAMPIONSHIP IS AT STAKE?
MAD DOG

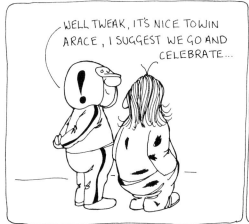

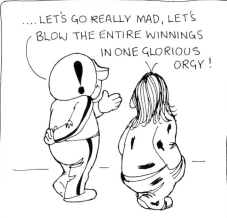

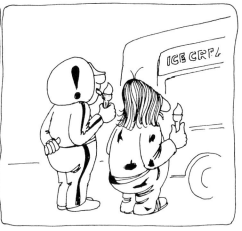

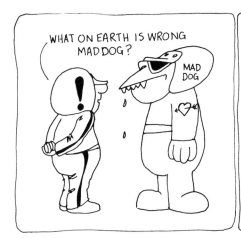

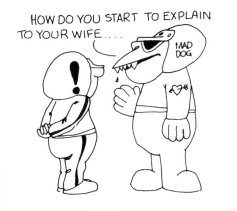

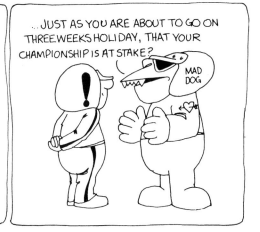

23rd May 1974

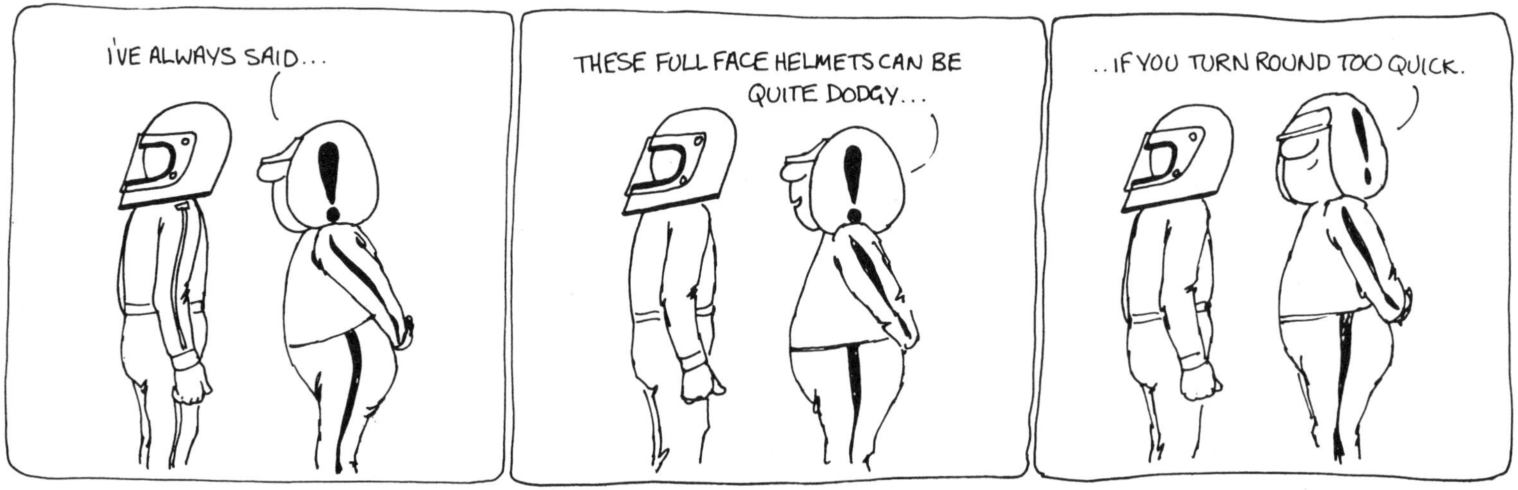
I'VE ALWAYS SAID...
THESE FULL FACE HELMETS CAN BE QUITE DODGY...
..IF YOU TURN ROUND TOO QUICK.

26th December 1974

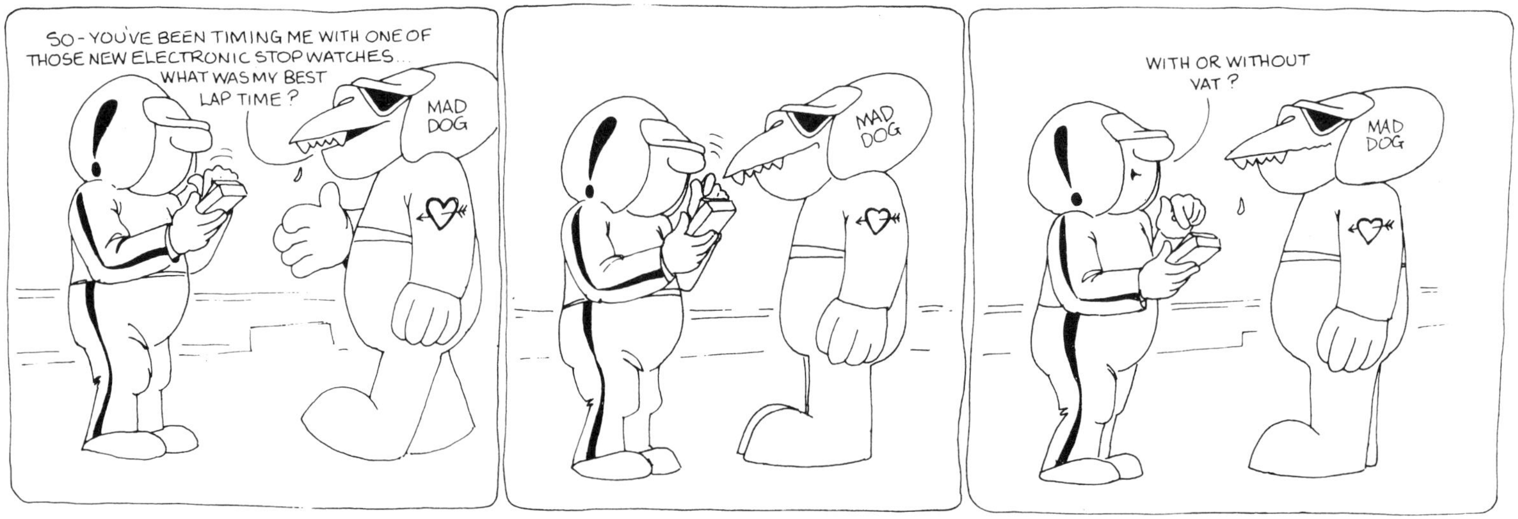
SO - YOU'VE BEEN TIMING ME WITH ONE OF THOSE NEW ELECTRONIC STOP WATCHES... WHAT WAS MY BEST LAP TIME ?
MAD DOG
MAD DOG
WITH OR WITHOUT VAT ?
MAD DOG

19th August 1976

Chapter Ten

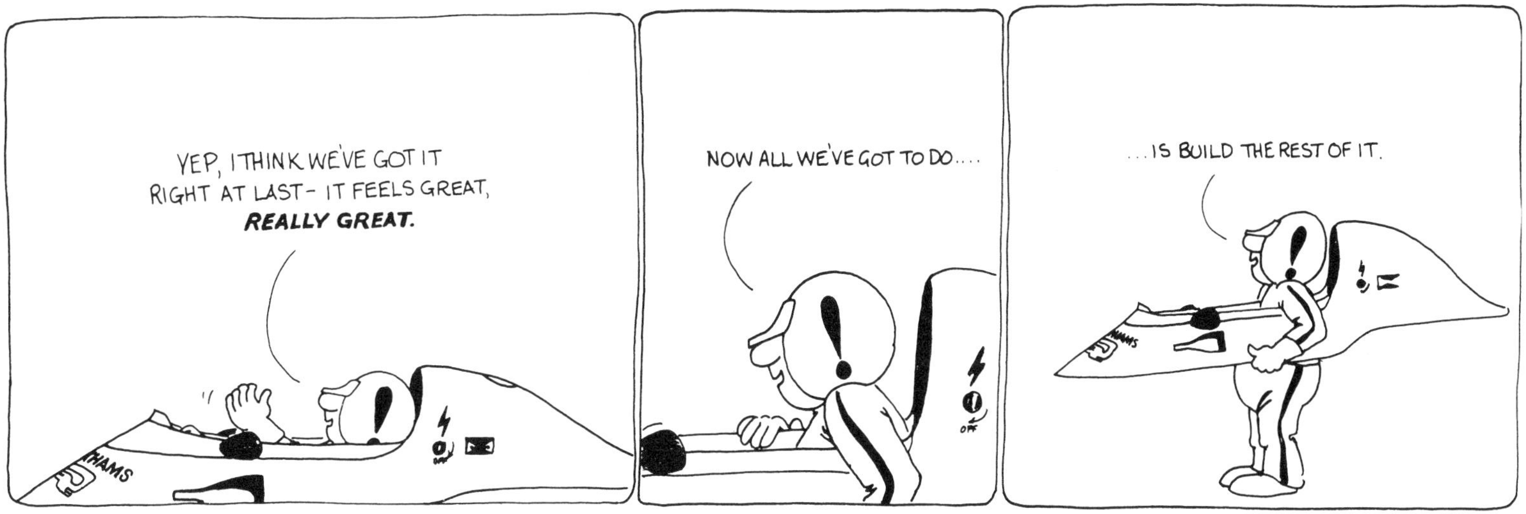
YEP, I THINK WE'VE GOT IT RIGHT AT LAST- IT FEELS GREAT, **REALLY GREAT.**
NOW ALL WE'VE GOT TO DO....
...IS BUILD THE REST OF IT.

20th January 1977

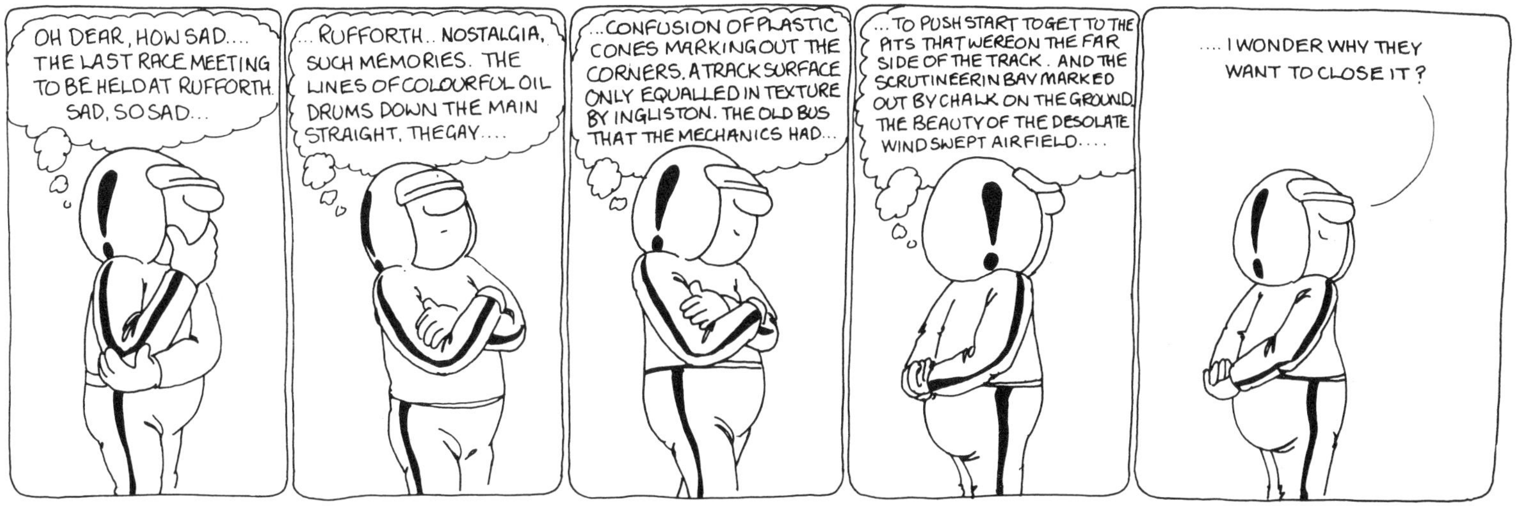
OH DEAR, HOW SAD.... THE LAST RACE MEETING TO BE HELD AT RUFFORTH. SAD, SO SAD...
...RUFFORTH.. NOSTALGIA, SUCH MEMORIES. THE LINES OF COLOURFUL OIL DRUMS DOWN THE MAIN STRAIGHT. THE GAY....
...CONFUSION OF PLASTIC CONES MARKING OUT THE CORNERS. A TRACK SURFACE ONLY EQUALLED IN TEXTURE BY INGLISTON. THE OLD BUS THAT THE MECHANICS HAD...
...TO PUSH START TO GET TO THE PITS THAT WERE ON THE FAR SIDE OF THE TRACK. AND THE SCRUTINEERING BAY MARKED OUT BY CHALK ON THE GROUND. THE BEAUTY OF THE DESOLATE WINDSWEPT AIRFIELD....
.... I WONDER WHY THEY WANT TO CLOSE IT?

8th September 1977

Club Racing

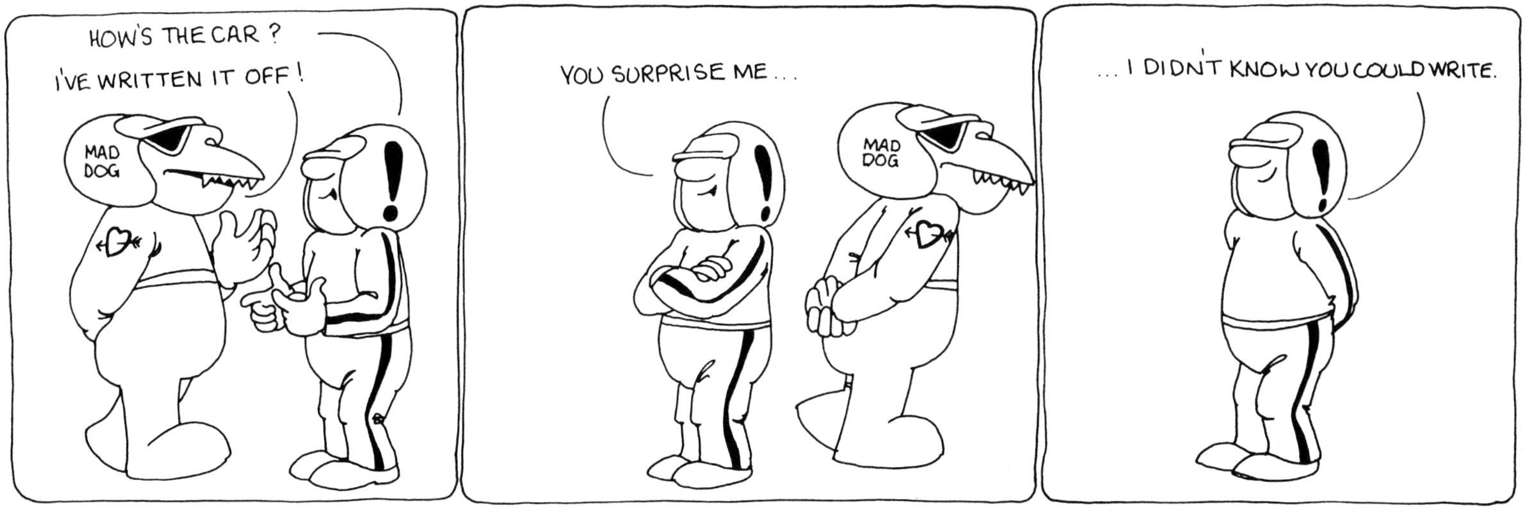
HOW'S THE CAR ?
I'VE WRITTEN IT OFF !
MAD DOG
YOU SURPRISE ME . . .
MAD DOG
. . . I DIDN'T KNOW YOU COULD WRITE.

27th July 1978

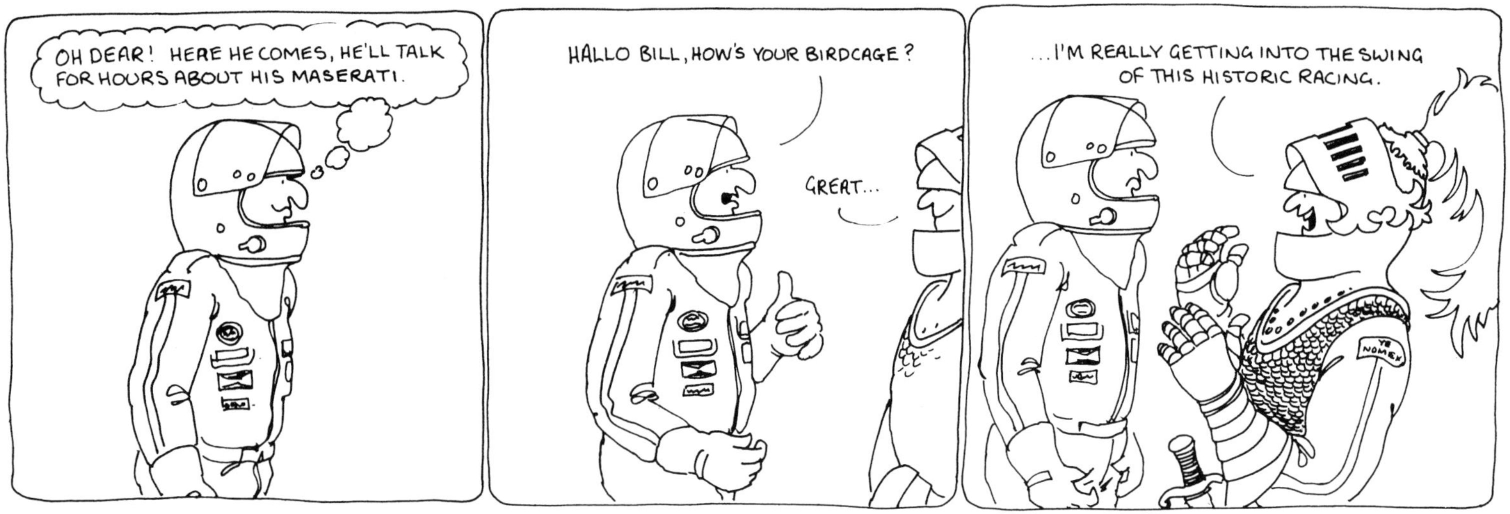
OH DEAR! HERE HE COMES, HE'LL TALK FOR HOURS ABOUT HIS MASERATI.
HALLO BILL, HOW'S YOUR BIRDCAGE ?
GREAT...
...I'M REALLY GETTING INTO THE SWING OF THIS HISTORIC RACING.

10th August 1978

Chapter Ten

Club Racing

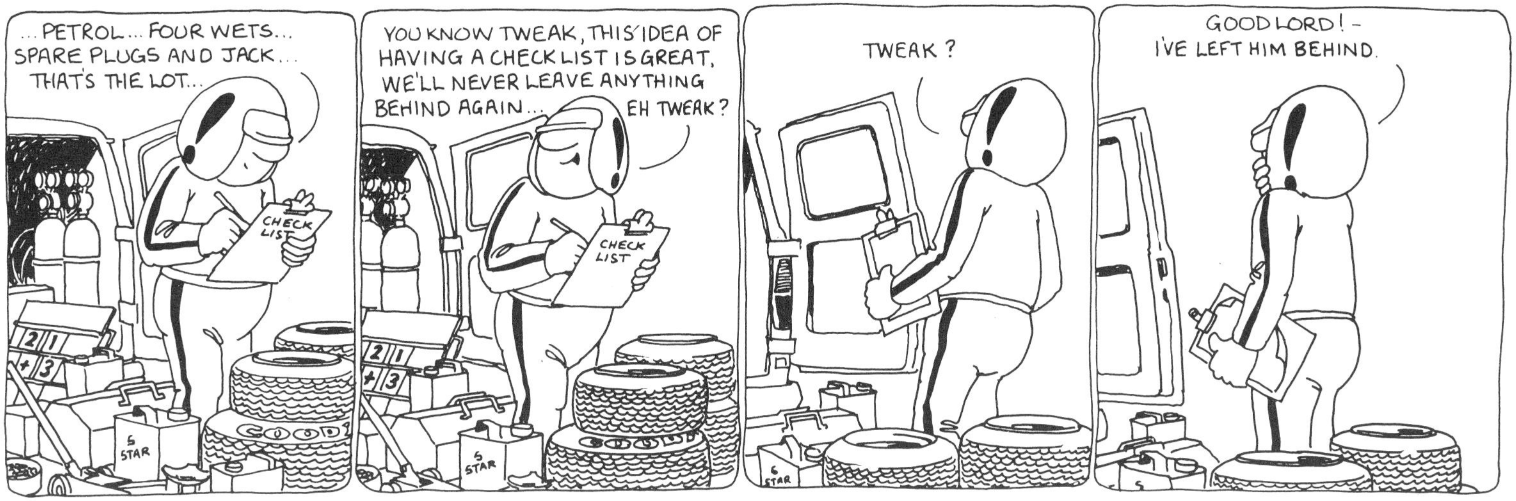

... PETROL ... FOUR WETS ... SPARE PLUGS AND JACK ... THAT'S THE LOT ...
CHECK LIST
5 STAR
YOU KNOW TWEAK, THIS IDEA OF HAVING A CHECK LIST IS GREAT, WE'LL NEVER LEAVE ANYTHING BEHIND AGAIN ...
EH TWEAK ?
CHECK LIST
5 STAR
TWEAK ?
GOOD LORD! - I'VE LEFT HIM BEHIND.

28th September 1978

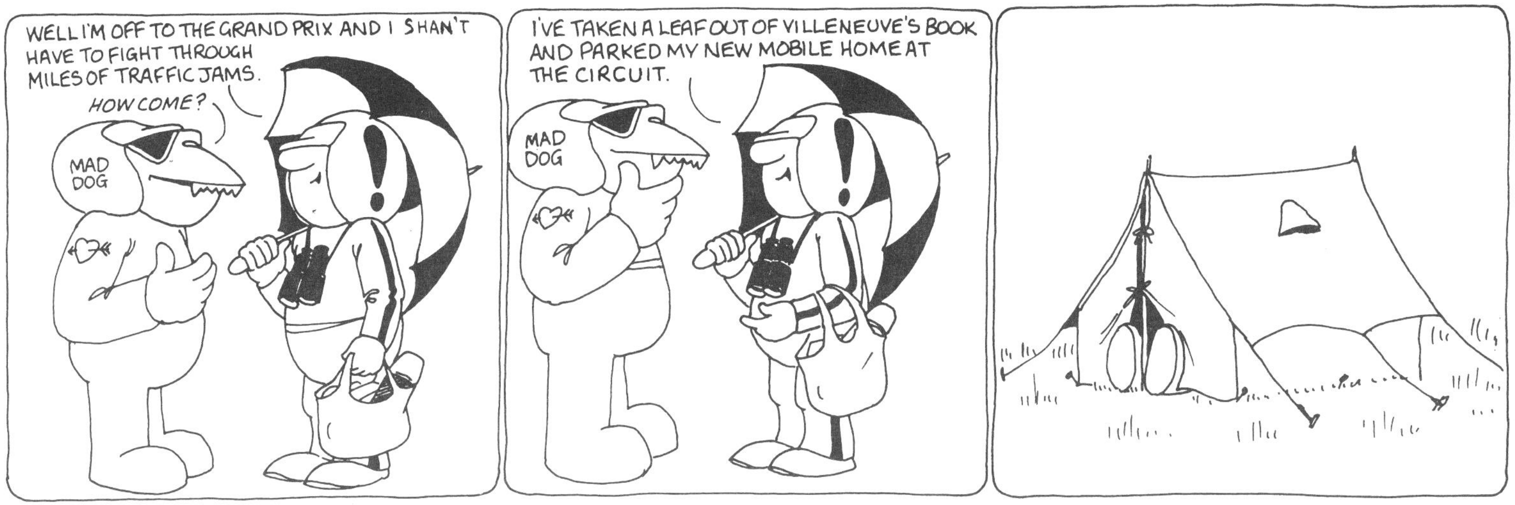

WELL I'M OFF TO THE GRAND PRIX AND I SHAN'T HAVE TO FIGHT THROUGH MILES OF TRAFFIC JAMS.
HOW COME?
MAD DOG
I'VE TAKEN A LEAF OUT OF VILLENEUVE'S BOOK AND PARKED MY NEW MOBILE HOME AT THE CIRCUIT.
MAD DOG

12th July 1979

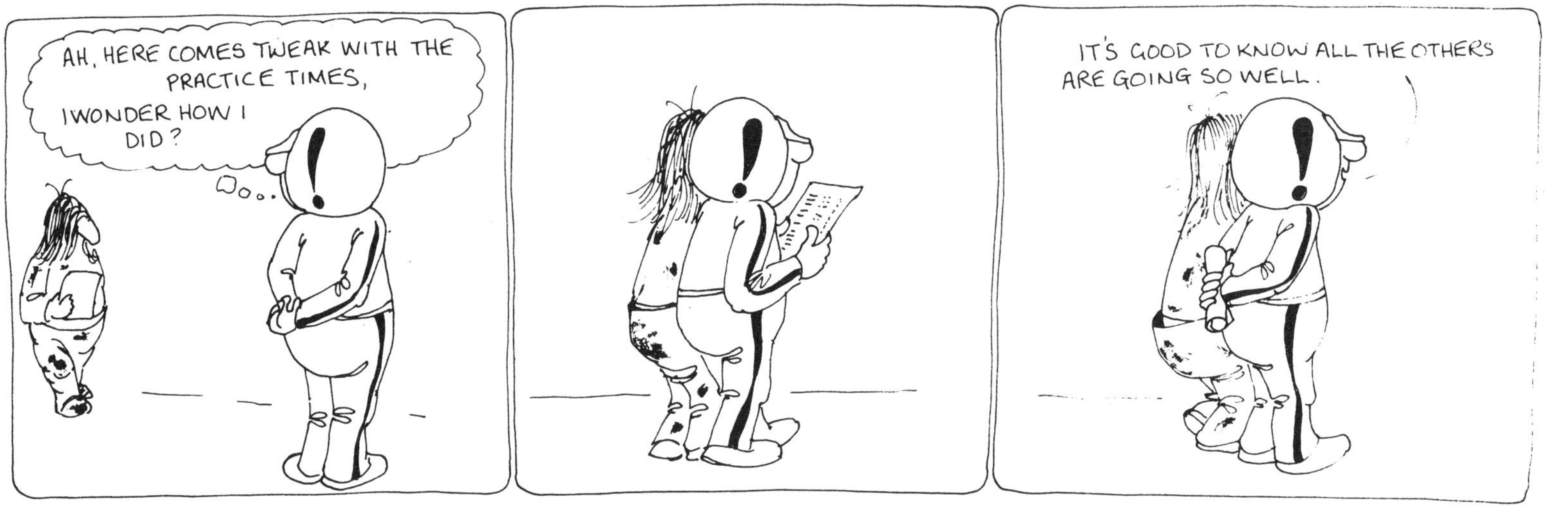
AH, HERE COMES TWEAK WITH THE PRACTICE TIMES,
I WONDER HOW I DID?
IT'S GOOD TO KNOW ALL THE OTHERS ARE GOING SO WELL.

6th September 1979

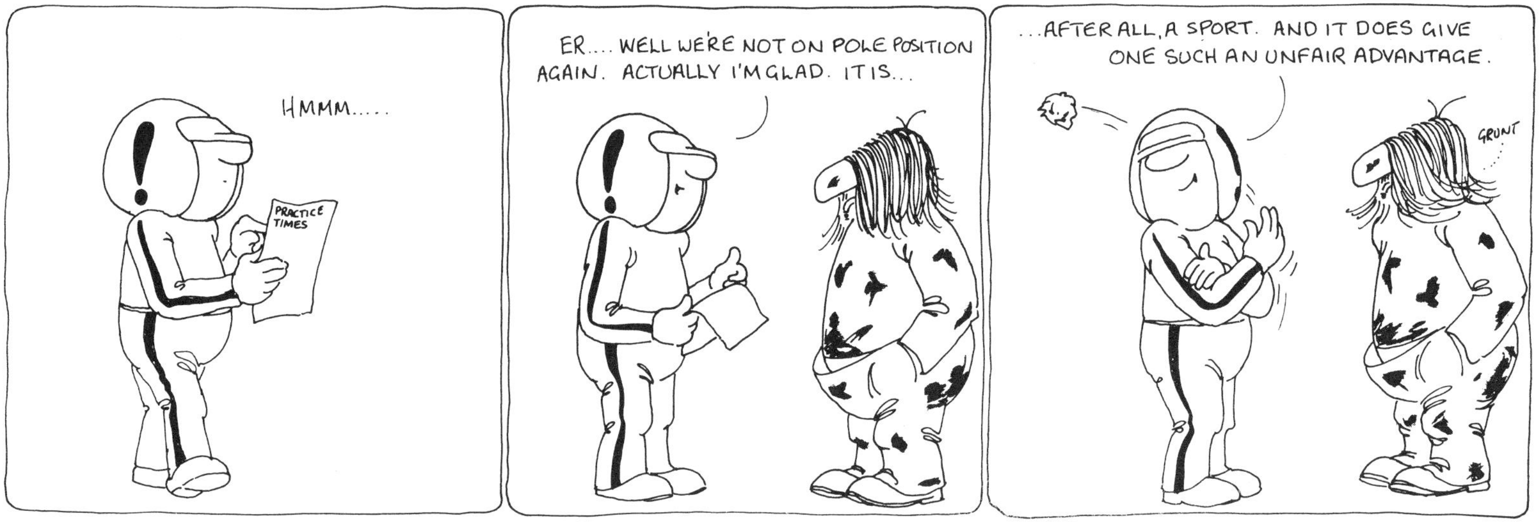
HMMM.....
PRACTICE TIMES
ER.... WELL WE'RE NOT ON POLE POSITION AGAIN. ACTUALLY I'M GLAD. IT IS...
...AFTER ALL, A SPORT. AND IT DOES GIVE ONE SUCH AN UNFAIR ADVANTAGE.
GRUNT

21st August 1980

Chapter Ten

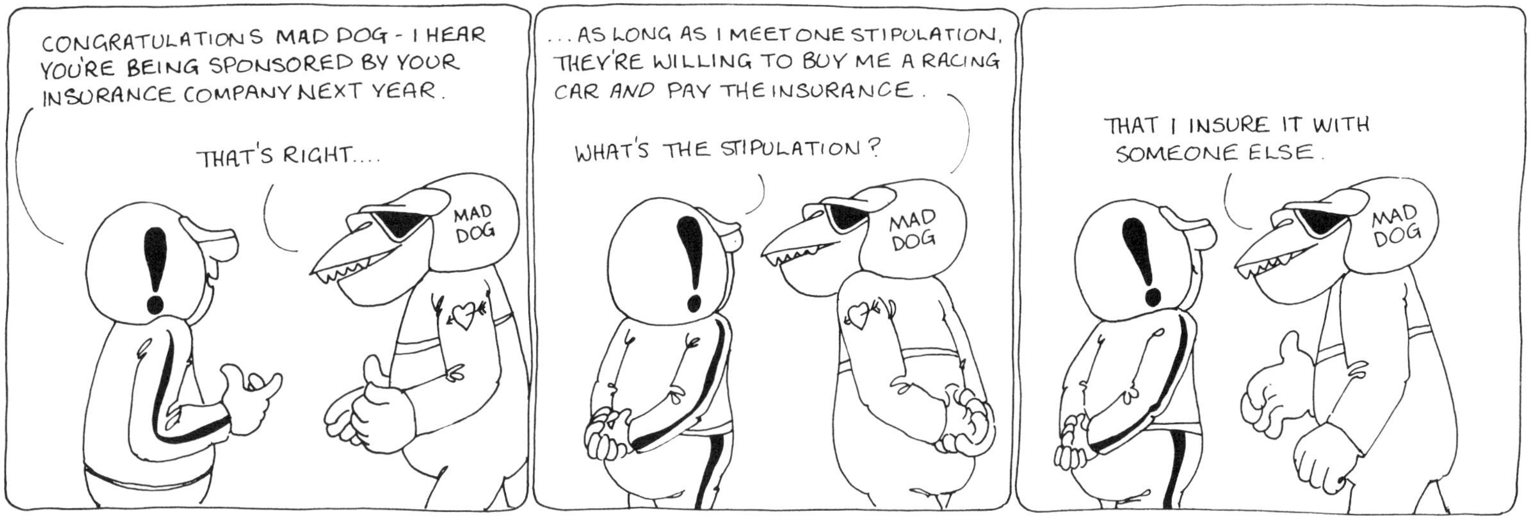
CONGRATULATIONS MAD DOG - I HEAR YOU'RE BEING SPONSORED BY YOUR INSURANCE COMPANY NEXT YEAR.
THAT'S RIGHT....
MAD DOG
...AS LONG AS I MEET ONE STIPULATION, THEY'RE WILLING TO BUY ME A RACING CAR AND PAY THE INSURANCE.
WHAT'S THE STIPULATION?
MAD DOG
THAT I INSURE IT WITH SOMEONE ELSE.
MAD DOG

8th January 1981

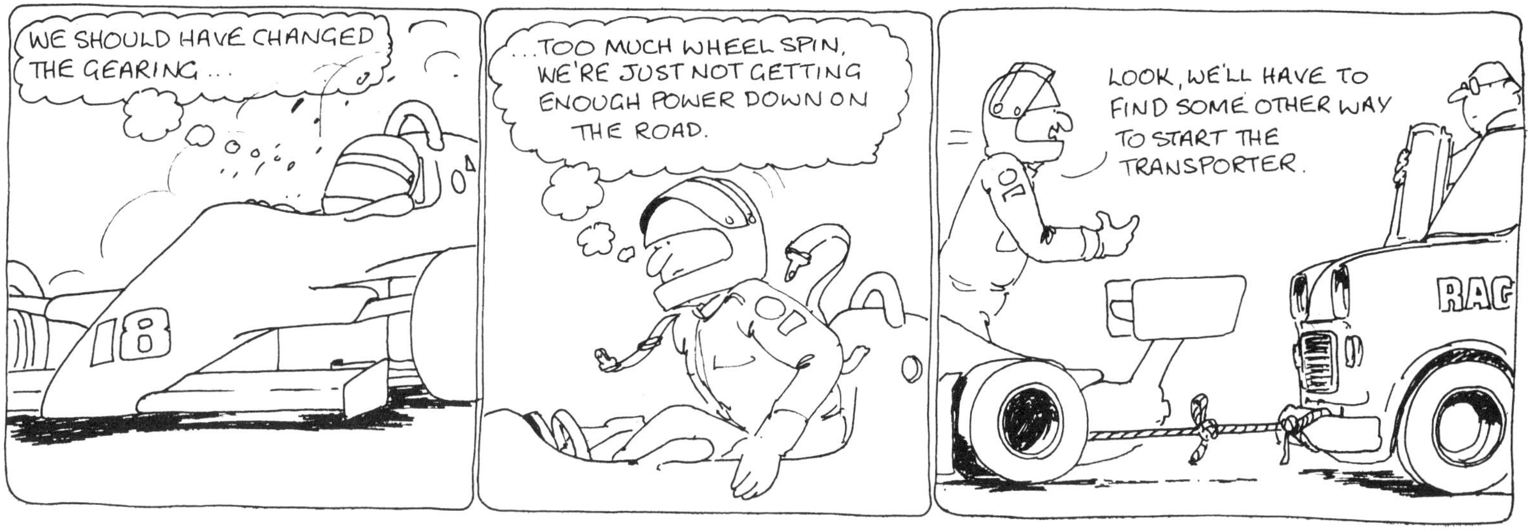
WE SHOULD HAVE CHANGED THE GEARING...
18
...TOO MUCH WHEEL SPIN, WE'RE JUST NOT GETTING ENOUGH POWER DOWN ON THE ROAD.
LOOK, WE'LL HAVE TO FIND SOME OTHER WAY TO START THE TRANSPORTER.
RAG

14th May 1981

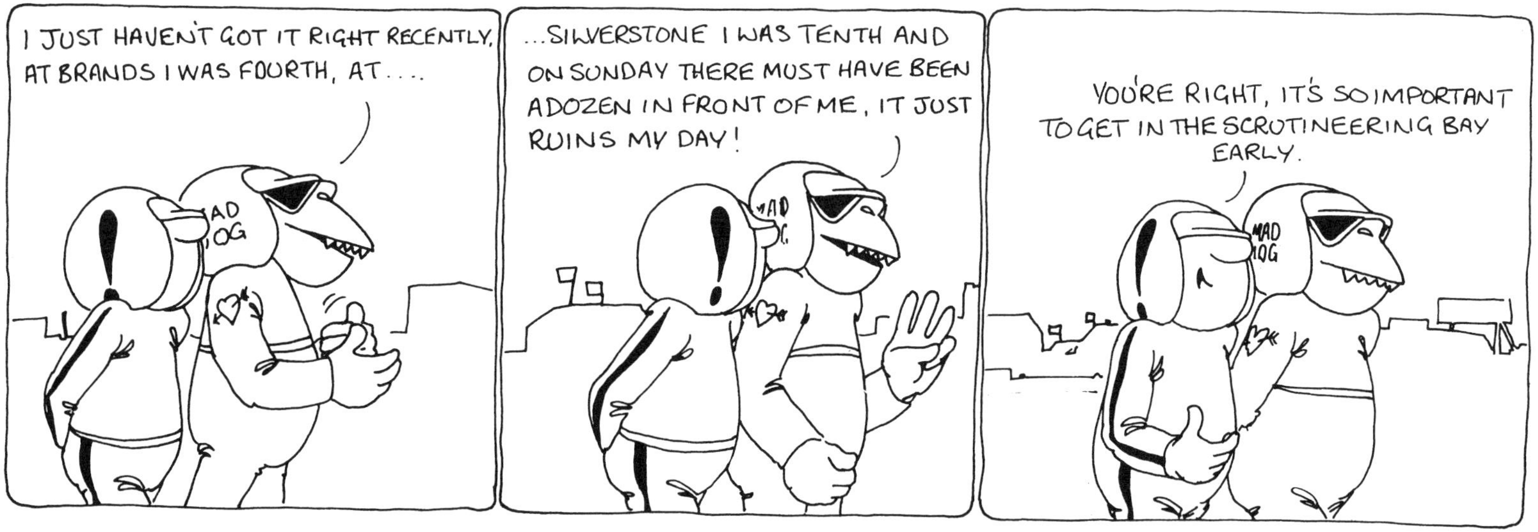
I JUST HAVEN'T GOT IT RIGHT RECENTLY, AT BRANDS I WAS FOURTH, AT....
...SILVERSTONE I WAS TENTH AND ON SUNDAY THERE MUST HAVE BEEN A DOZEN IN FRONT OF ME, IT JUST RUINS MY DAY!
MAD DOG
YOU'RE RIGHT, IT'S SO IMPORTANT TO GET IN THE SCRUTINEERING BAY EARLY.

13th August 1981

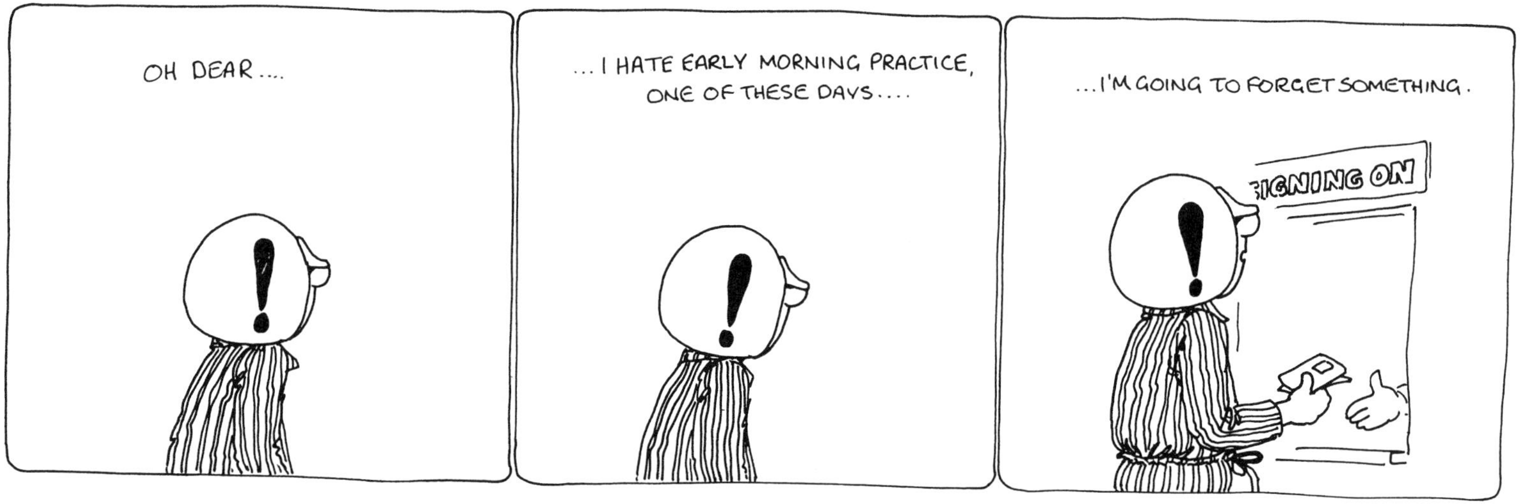
OH DEAR....
...I HATE EARLY MORNING PRACTICE, ONE OF THESE DAYS....
...I'M GOING TO FORGET SOMETHING.
SIGNING ON

1st July 1982

Chapter Ten

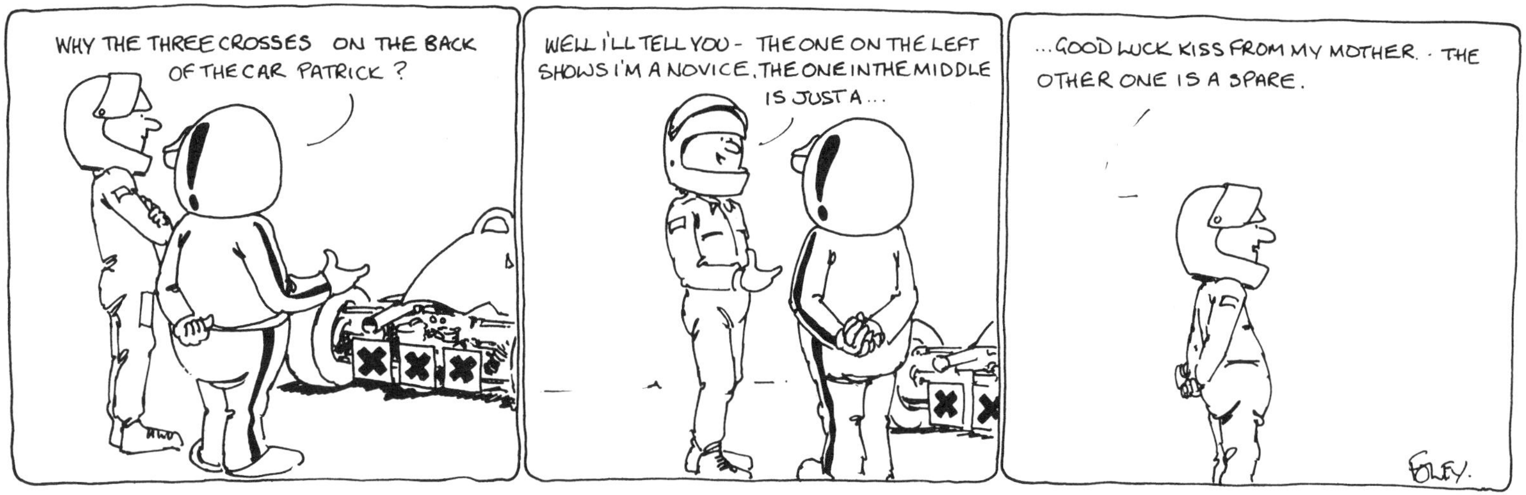
WHY THE THREE CROSSES ON THE BACK OF THE CAR PATRICK ?
WELL I'LL TELL YOU - THE ONE ON THE LEFT SHOWS I'M A NOVICE, THE ONE IN THE MIDDLE IS JUST A ...
... GOOD LUCK KISS FROM MY MOTHER. - THE OTHER ONE IS A SPARE.
FOLEY.

2nd August 1984

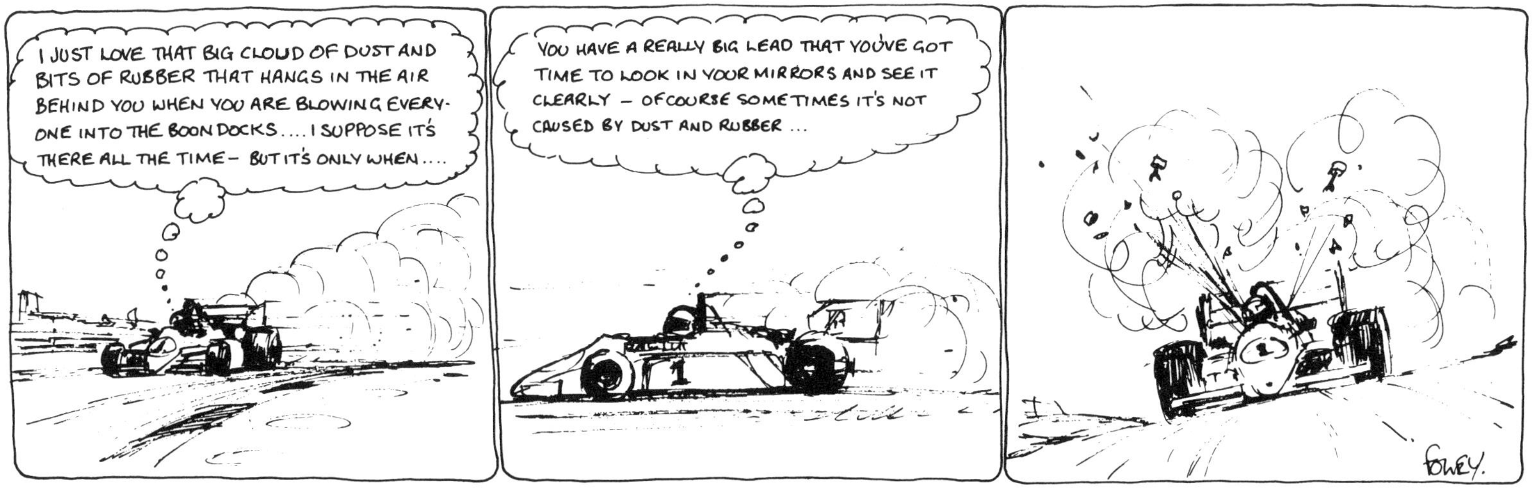
I JUST LOVE THAT BIG CLOUD OF DUST AND BITS OF RUBBER THAT HANGS IN THE AIR BEHIND YOU WHEN YOU ARE BLOWING EVERY-ONE INTO THE BOON DOCKS.... I SUPPOSE IT'S THERE ALL THE TIME - BUT IT'S ONLY WHEN....
YOU HAVE A REALLY BIG LEAD THAT YOU'VE GOT TIME TO LOOK IN YOUR MIRRORS AND SEE IT CLEARLY - OF COURSE SOMETIMES IT'S NOT CAUSED BY DUST AND RUBBER ...
FOLEY.

22nd August 1985

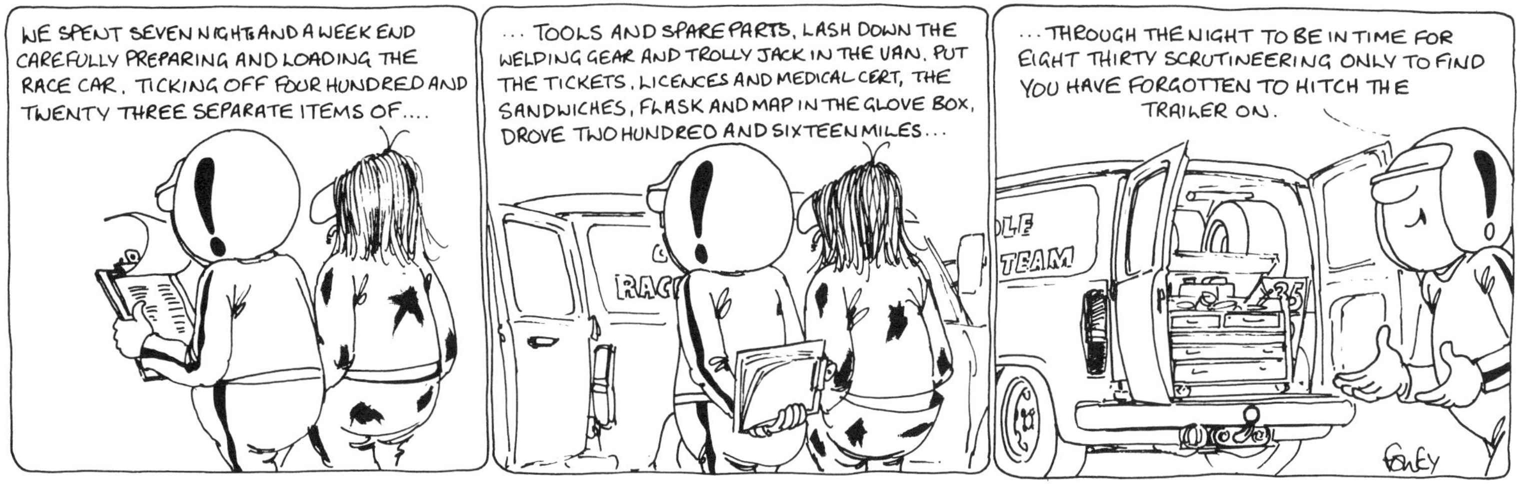
WE SPENT SEVEN NIGHTS AND A WEEK END CAREFULLY PREPARING AND LOADING THE RACE CAR. TICKING OFF FOUR HUNDRED AND TWENTY THREE SEPARATE ITEMS OF....
... TOOLS AND SPARE PARTS, LASH DOWN THE WELDING GEAR AND TROLLY JACK IN THE VAN, PUT THE TICKETS, LICENCES AND MEDICAL CERT, THE SANDWICHES, FLASK AND MAP IN THE GLOVE BOX, DROVE TWO HUNDRED AND SIXTEEN MILES...
TEAM
... THROUGH THE NIGHT TO BE IN TIME FOR EIGHT THIRTY SCRUTINEERING ONLY TO FIND YOU HAVE FORGOTTEN TO HITCH THE TRAILER ON.
FOLEY

5th September 1985

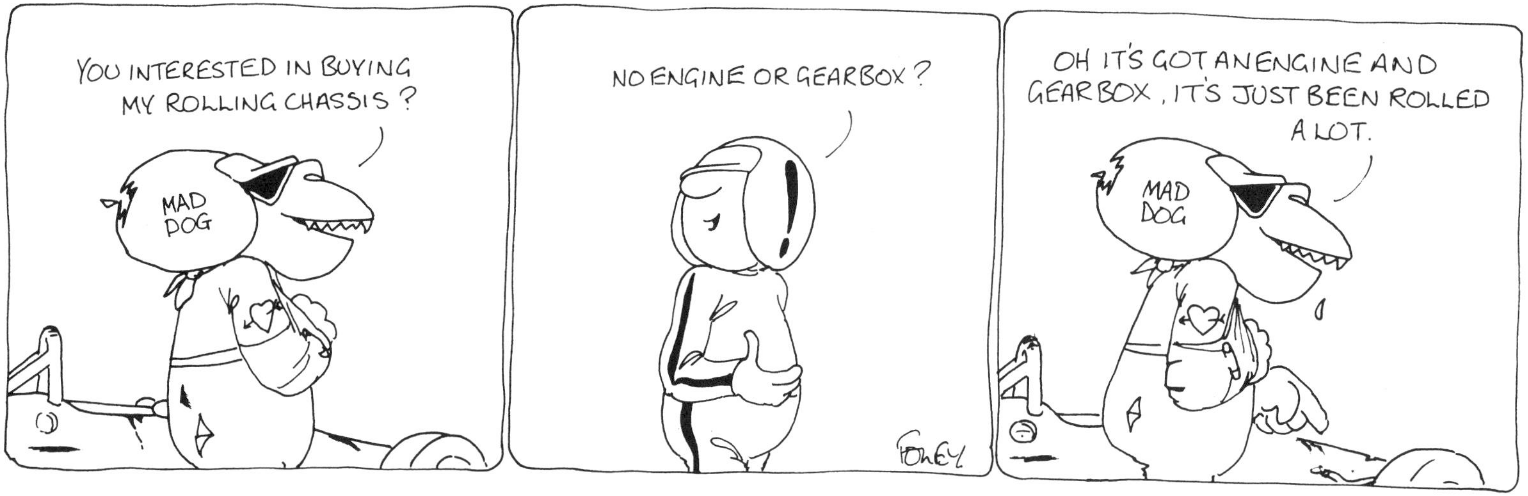
YOU INTERESTED IN BUYING MY ROLLING CHASSIS?
MAD DOG
NO ENGINE OR GEARBOX?
FOLEY
OH IT'S GOT AN ENGINE AND GEARBOX, IT'S JUST BEEN ROLLED A LOT.
MAD DOG

12th June 1986

Chapter Ten

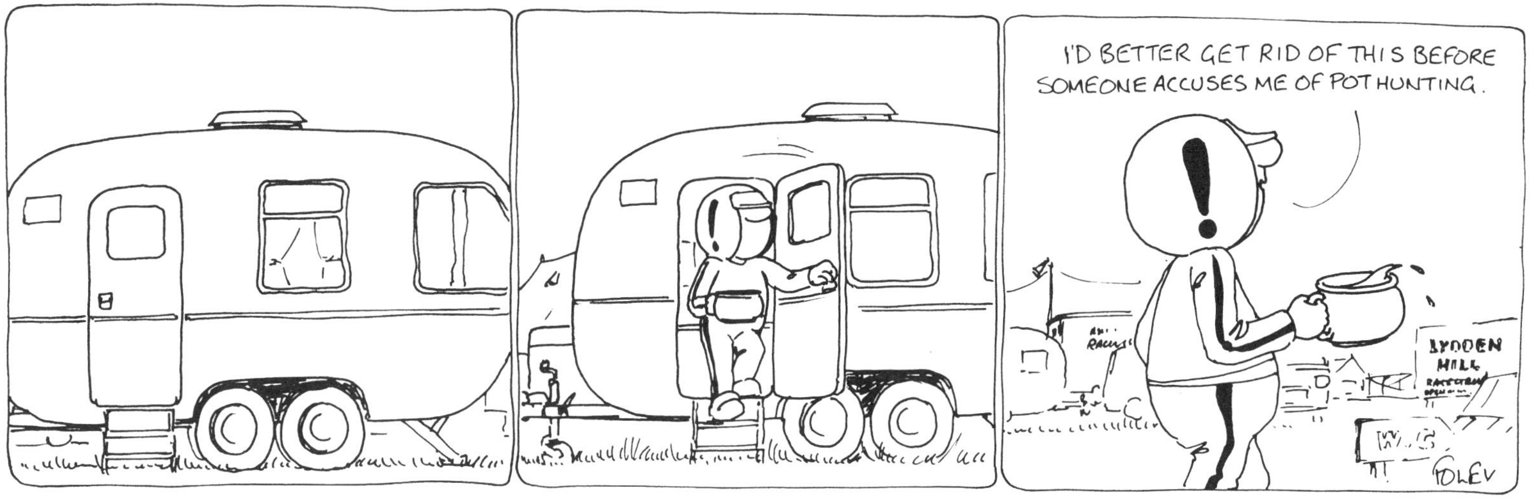
I'D BETTER GET RID OF THIS BEFORE SOMEONE ACCUSES ME OF POT HUNTING.
LYDDEN HILL
FOLEY

2nd October 1986

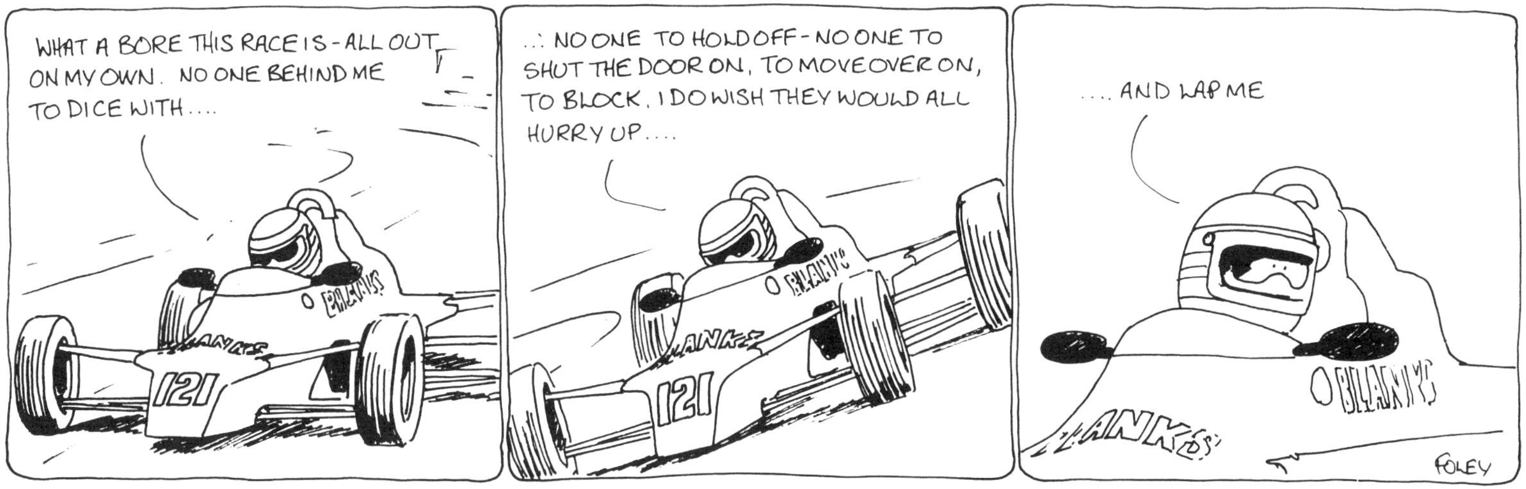
WHAT A BORE THIS RACE IS - ALL OUT ON MY OWN. NO ONE BEHIND ME TO DICE WITH....
... NO ONE TO HOLD OFF - NO ONE TO SHUT THE DOOR ON, TO MOVE OVER ON, TO BLOCK. I DO WISH THEY WOULD ALL HURRY UP....
.... AND LAP ME
121
121
FOLEY

19th February 1987

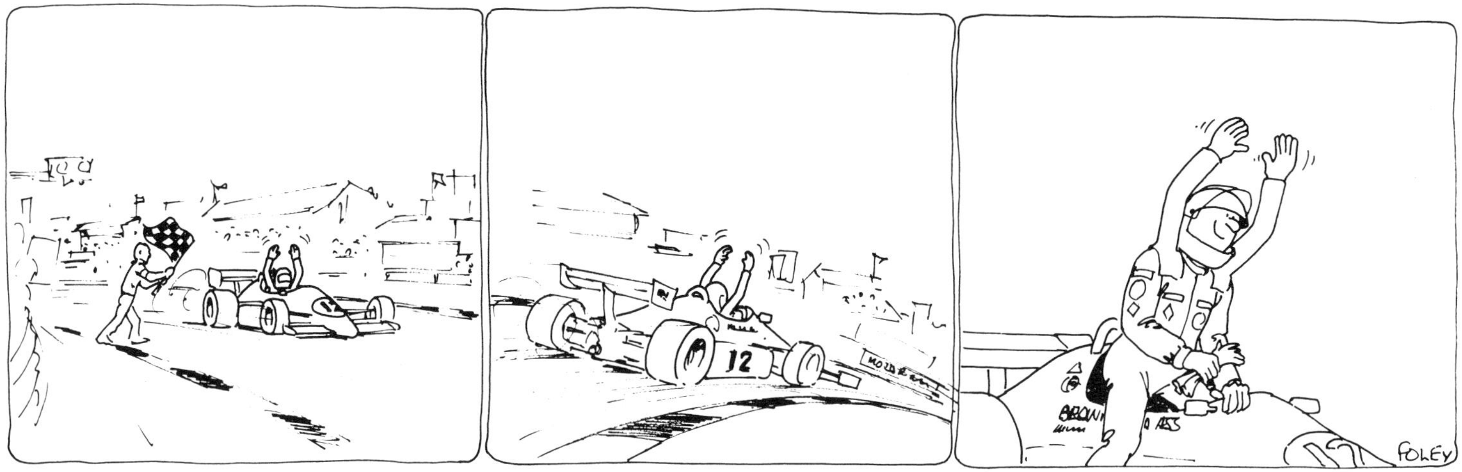
FOLEY

28th May 1987

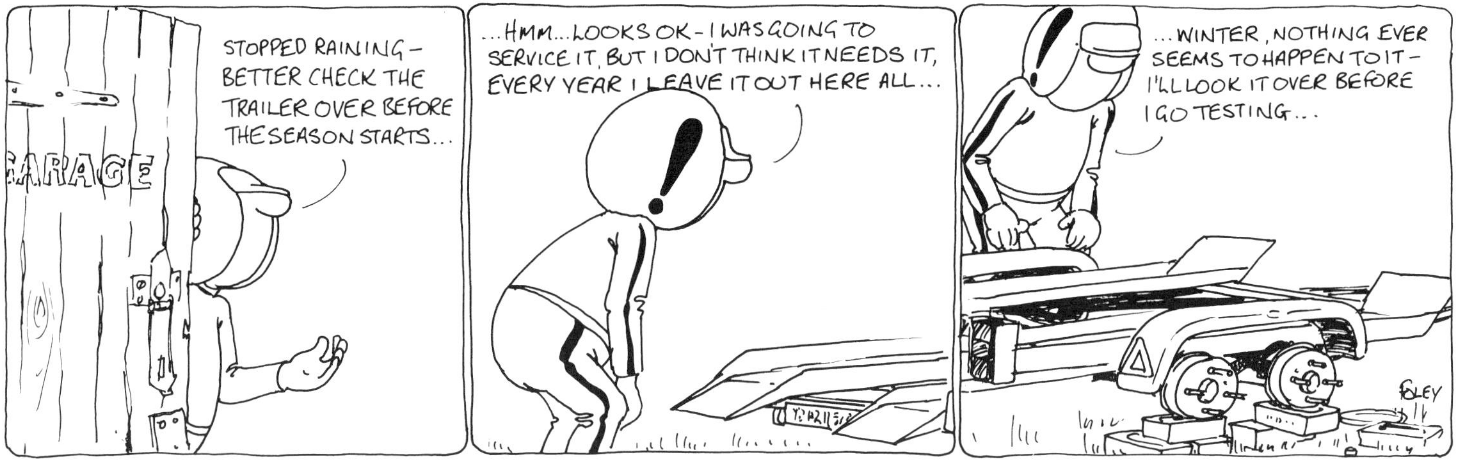
STOPPED RAINING – BETTER CHECK THE TRAILER OVER BEFORE THE SEASON STARTS...
...HMM...LOOKS OK – I WAS GOING TO SERVICE IT, BUT I DON'T THINK IT NEEDS IT, EVERY YEAR I LEAVE IT OUT HERE ALL...
...WINTER, NOTHING EVER SEEMS TO HAPPEN TO IT – I'LL LOOK IT OVER BEFORE I GO TESTING...
FOLEY

31st December 1987

Chapter Ten

RIGHT - NOW TO TRY MY NEW SEAT...
...MM... VERY COMFORTABLE - LET'S GIVE IT SOME STICK....
...DROP THE CLUTCH...
FOLEY

11th August 1988

HI 'COMPO', HOW WAS THE BRANDS F3 RACE - WAS THE TRACK VERY CROWDED?
THE TRACK? - NO, THE TRACK WAS EMPTY NOT A SOUL IN SIGHT....
COMPOSITE KID
COMPO
....THE BARRIERS, THE CATCH FENCES, THE BANKS - THEY WERE PACKED.
COMPOSITE KID
COMPO
FOLEY

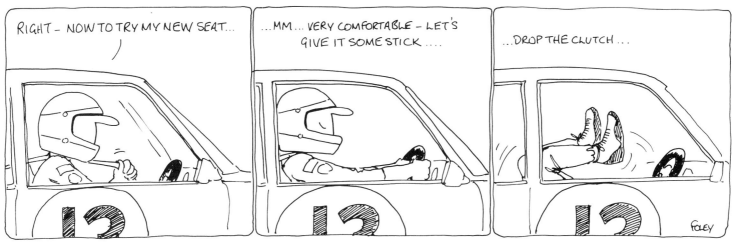

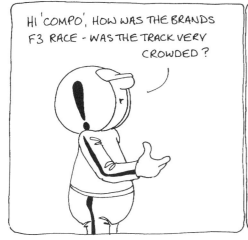

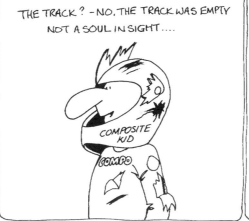

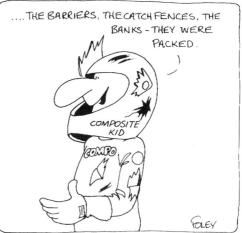

27th April 1989

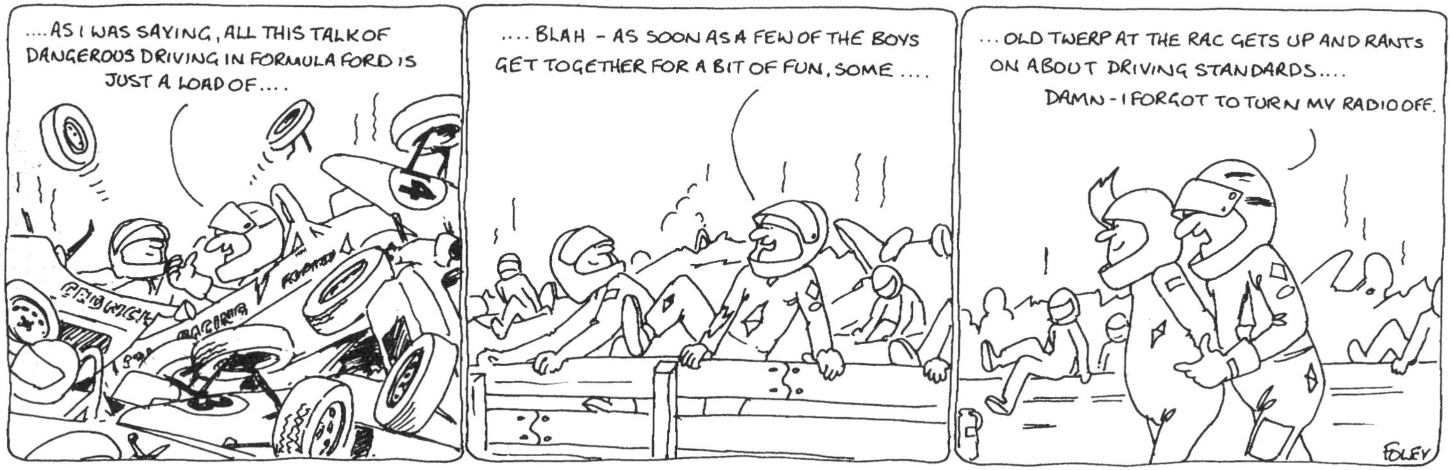
....AS I WAS SAYING, ALL THIS TALK OF DANGEROUS DRIVING IN FORMULA FORD IS JUST A LOAD OF....
.... BLAH - AS SOON AS A FEW OF THE BOYS GET TOGETHER FOR A BIT OF FUN, SOME ....
...OLD TWERP AT THE RAC GETS UP AND RANTS ON ABOUT DRIVING STANDARDS....
DAMN - I FORGOT TO TURN MY RADIO OFF.
FOLEY

7th September 1989

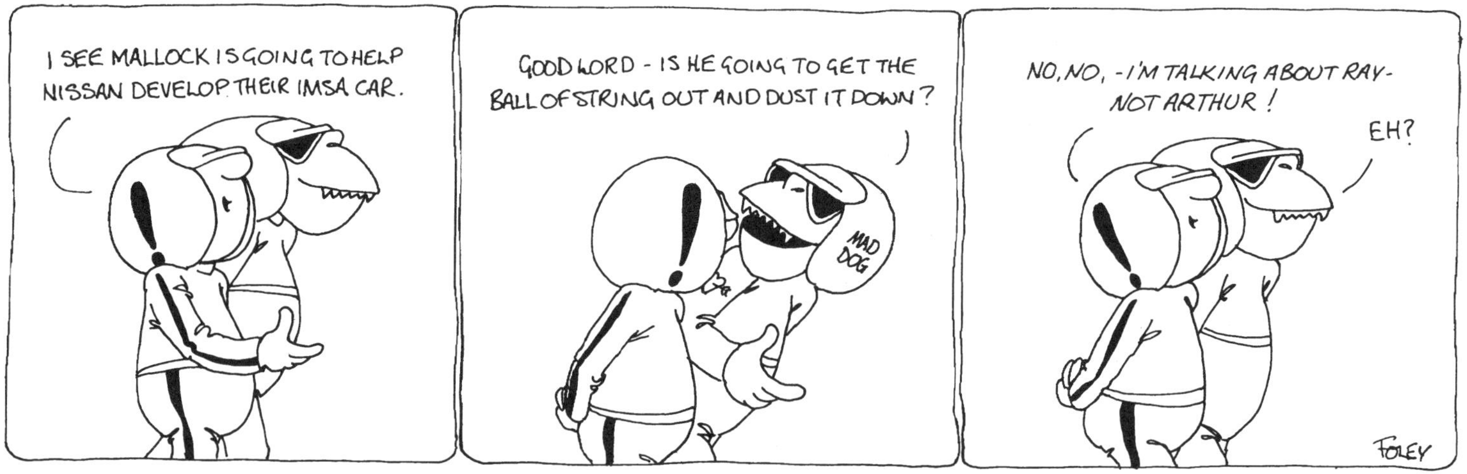
I SEE MALLOCK IS GOING TO HELP NISSAN DEVELOP THEIR IMSA CAR.
GOOD LORD - IS HE GOING TO GET THE BALL OF STRING OUT AND DUST IT DOWN?
MAD DOG
NO, NO, - I'M TALKING ABOUT RAY - NOT ARTHUR!
EH?
FOLEY

8th March 1990

Chapter Ten

OH DEAR, ALL THESE ONE MAKE RACERS SEEM TO BE GETTING OUT OF HAND...
MAD DOG
...LOOK AT THESE XR2's - PUSH, PUSH, PUSH - IF IT'S LIKE THIS IN THE....
MAD DOG
30
....SCRUTINEERING BAY, WHAT'S IT GOING TO BE LIKE IN THE RACE?
FOLEY

10th May 1990

OH. GOD....
HAPPY BIRTHDAY
....I'M TWENTY YEARS OLD...
.... AND I'M NOT EVEN IN F.3000 YET....
FOLEY

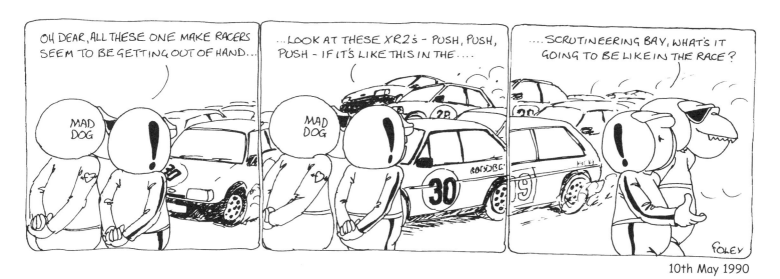

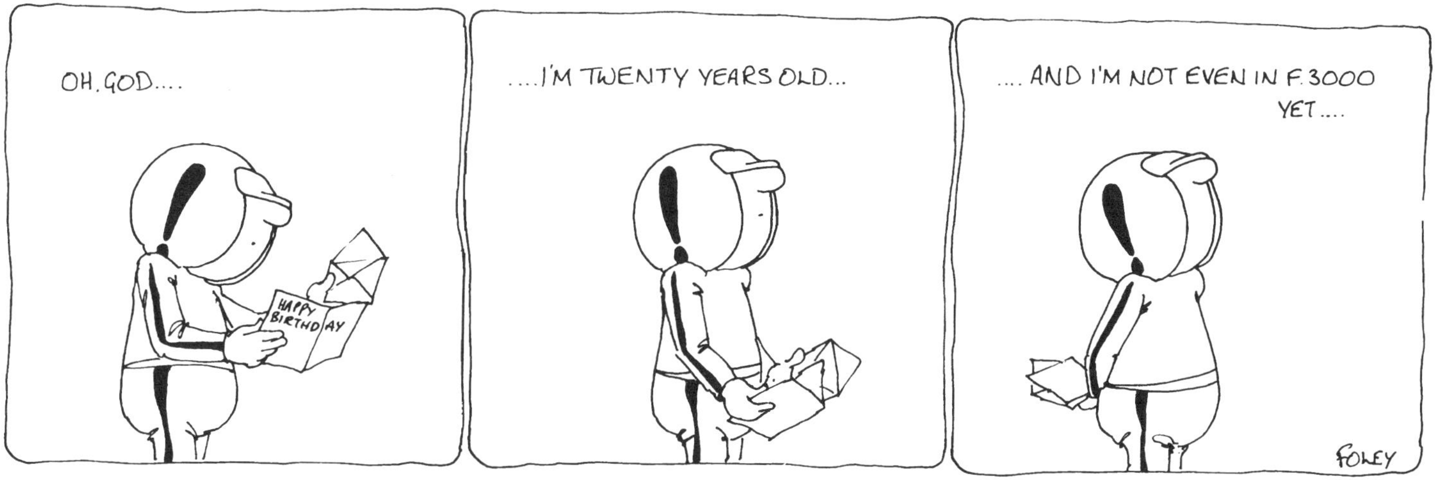

15th November 1990

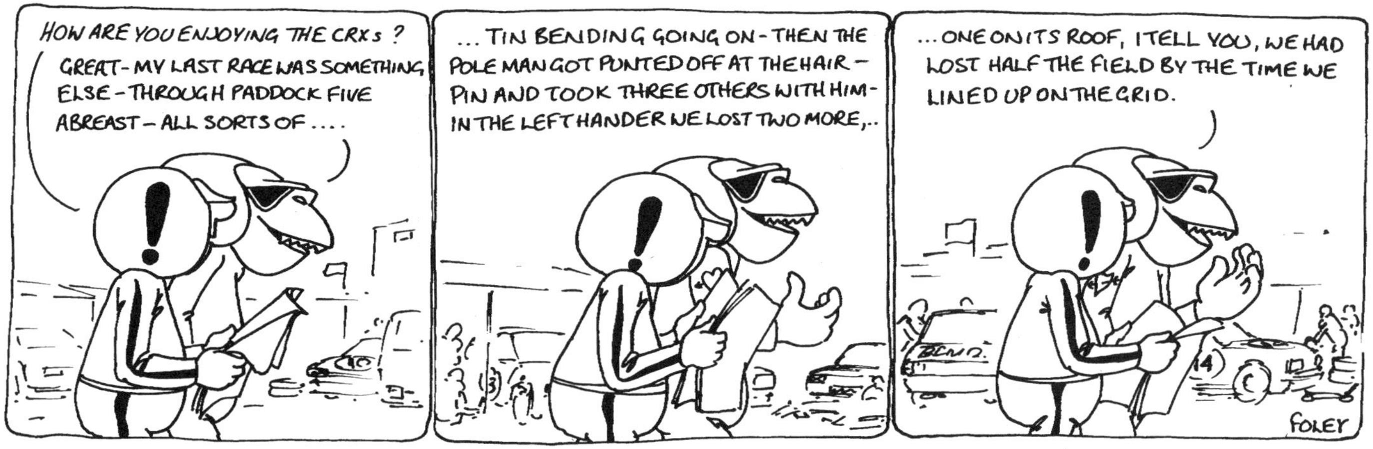
HOW ARE YOU ENJOYING THE CRXs ?
GREAT - MY LAST RACE WAS SOMETHING ELSE - THROUGH PADDOCK FIVE ABREAST - ALL SORTS OF ....
... TIN BENDING GOING ON - THEN THE POLE MAN GOT PUNTED OFF AT THE HAIR - PIN AND TOOK THREE OTHERS WITH HIM - IN THE LEFT HANDER WE LOST TWO MORE, ..
... ONE ON ITS ROOF, I TELL YOU, WE HAD LOST HALF THE FIELD BY THE TIME WE LINED UP ON THE GRID.
FOLEY

11th April 1991

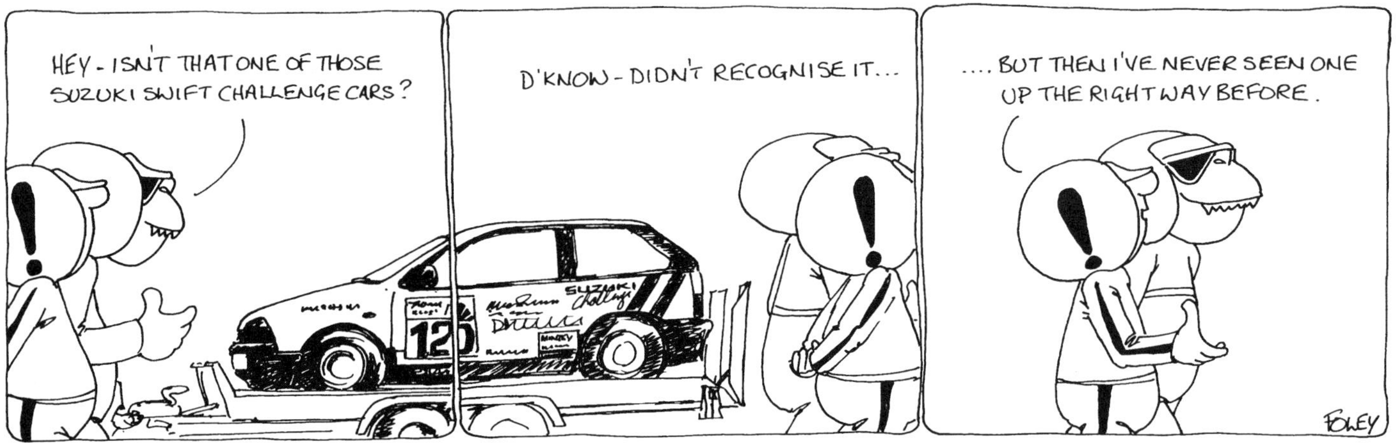
HEY - ISN'T THAT ONE OF THOSE SUZUKI SWIFT CHALLENGE CARS ?
D'KNOW - DIDN'T RECOGNISE IT...
.... BUT THEN I'VE NEVER SEEN ONE UP THE RIGHT WAY BEFORE .
FOLEY

9th May 1991

You'll Have To Explain That

YES ?

When I started looking back over old Catchpoles I was struck by two things: how many cartoons were about forgotten issues, and how many of them were issues that repeat themselves again and again. The odd one or two still seem funny, if you can figure what the hell they're about. So to help you find your way back to the event I have put in explanatory captions with each cartoon. However my memory leaves something to be desired. The issues that repeat themselves are: no tyres because a tyre manufacturer is quitting F1, the governing body is doing something silly or passing some new restrictive anti-technology rule.

I SHALL NOT BE AT ALL SORRY WHEN CHRISTMAS IS OVER....

....IT'S BEEN HELL, FIRST THERE WAS THE ECONOMIC CUTS - DOWN TO TWO REINDEER....

... INSTEAD OF SIX, THEY'RE KNACKERED POOR THINGS. BUT THE WORST THING...

.... OF ALL WAS THE TERRIBLE DRAG CAUSED BY THE INTRODUCTION OF THIS BLASTED FLAT BOTTOM CONCEPT!

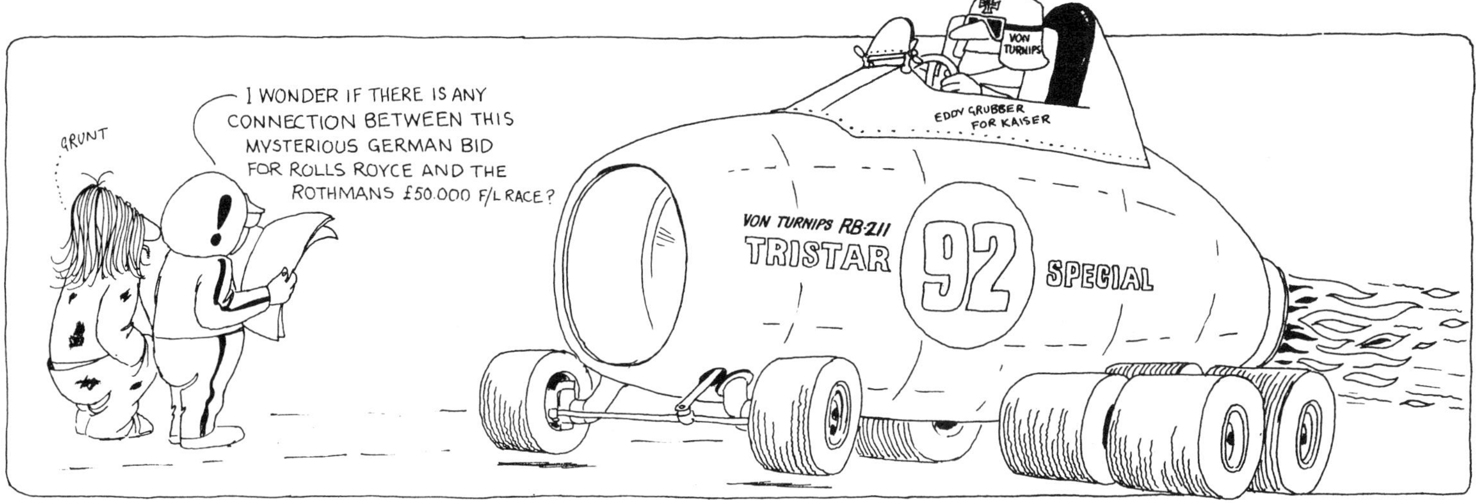
GRUNT
I WONDER IF THERE IS ANY CONNECTION BETWEEN THIS MYSTERIOUS GERMAN BID FOR ROLLS ROYCE AND THE ROTHMANS £50.000 F/L RACE?
VON TURNIPS
EDDY GRUBBER FOR KAISER
VON TURNIPS RB·211
TRISTAR
92
SPECIAL

The Rothmans 50,000 was a fantastic, anything goes, winner takes all £50,000 race at Brands. Also, an unknown German bid for Rolls Royce engines was in the news.

11th March 1971

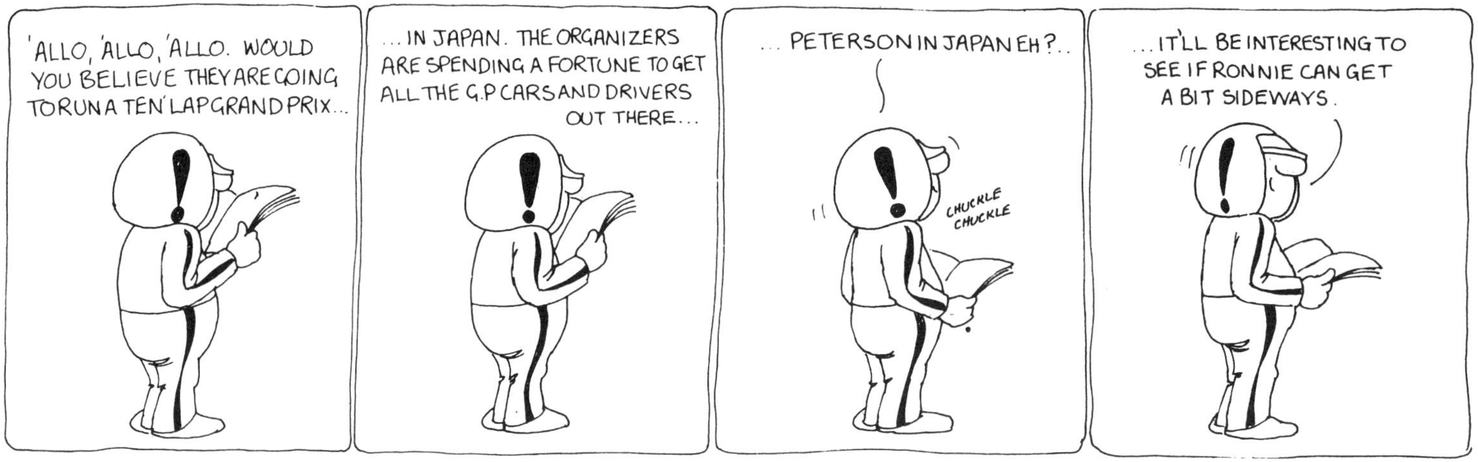
'ALLO, 'ALLO, 'ALLO. WOULD YOU BELIEVE THEY ARE GOING TO RUN A TEN LAP GRAND PRIX...
...IN JAPAN. THE ORGANIZERS ARE SPENDING A FORTUNE TO GET ALL THE G.P CARS AND DRIVERS OUT THERE...
...PETERSON IN JAPAN EH?..
CHUCKLE CHUCKLE
...IT'LL BE INTERESTING TO SEE IF RONNIE CAN GET A BIT SIDEWAYS.

Now it can be told - very naughty! This cartoon really refers to an alleged affair Ronnie had with a geisha girl.

31st October 1974

Chapter Eleven

You'll Have To Explain That

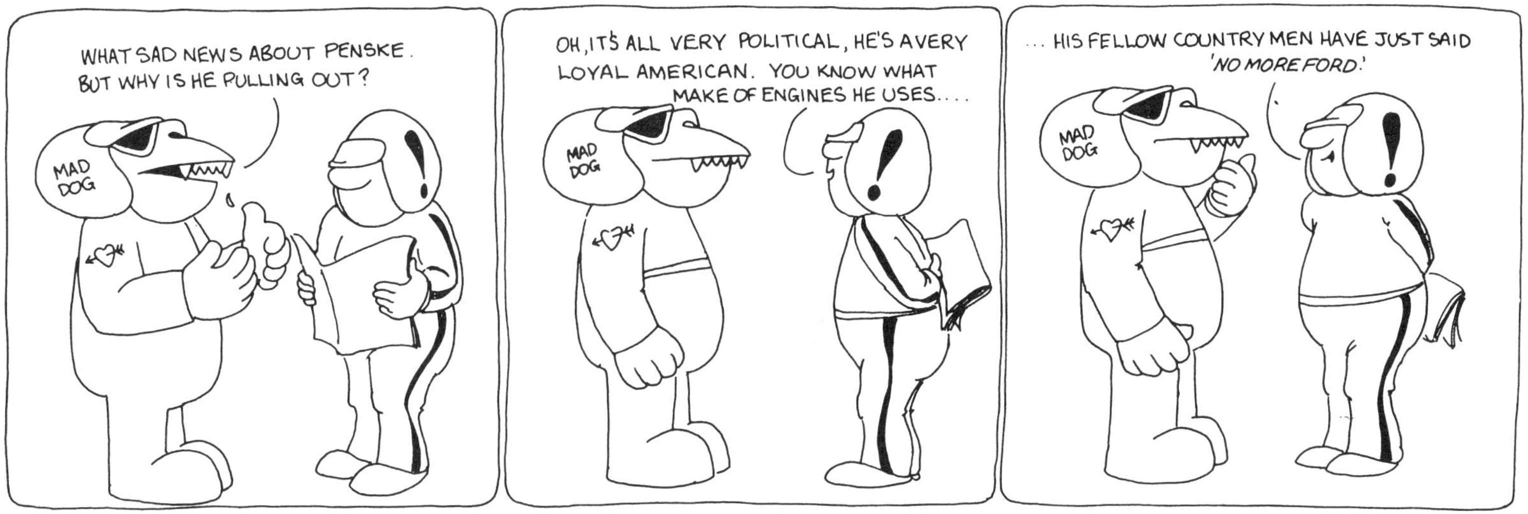
WHAT SAD NEWS ABOUT PENSKE. BUT WHY IS HE PULLING OUT?
MAD DOG
OH, IT'S ALL VERY POLITICAL, HE'S A VERY LOYAL AMERICAN. YOU KNOW WHAT MAKE OF ENGINES HE USES....
MAD DOG
... HIS FELLOW COUNTRY MEN HAVE JUST SAID 'NO MORE FORD.'
MAD DOG

In the same week Gerald Ford wasn't returned to the White House and Penske pulled out of Grand Prix racing.

11th November 1976

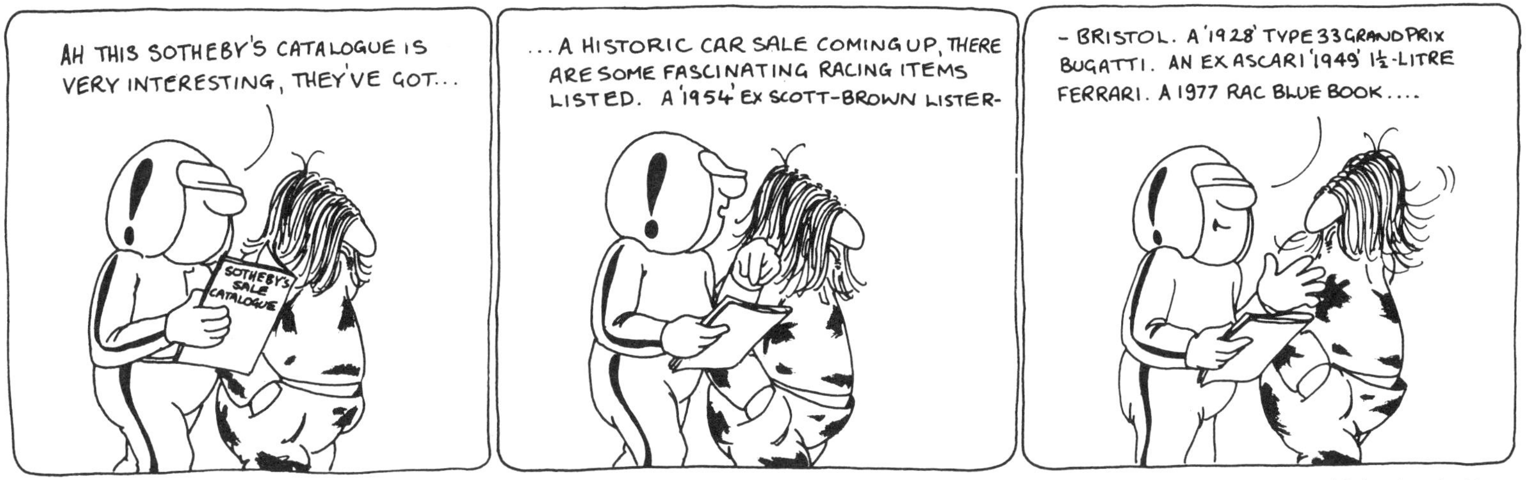
AH THIS SOTHEBY'S CATALOGUE IS VERY INTERESTING, THEY'VE GOT...
SOTHEBY'S SALE CATALOGUE
... A HISTORIC CAR SALE COMING UP, THERE ARE SOME FASCINATING RACING ITEMS LISTED. A '1954' EX SCOTT-BROWN LISTER-
- BRISTOL. A '1928' TYPE 33 GRAND PRIX BUGATTI. AN EX ASCARI '1949' 1½-LITRE FERRARI. A 1977 RAC BLUE BOOK....

Mid-March and still the RAC Blue Book wasn't out!

10th March 1977

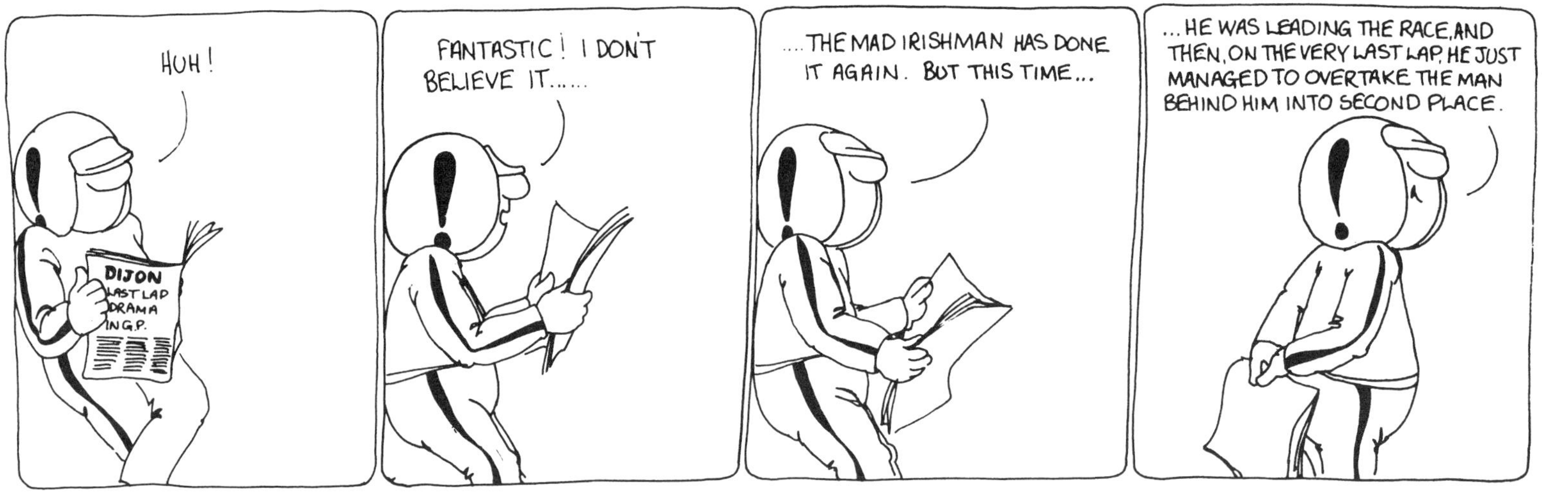
HUH!
FANTASTIC! I DON'T BELIEVE IT......
....THE MAD IRISHMAN HAS DONE IT AGAIN. BUT THIS TIME...
...HE WAS LEADING THE RACE, AND THEN, ON THE VERY LAST LAP, HE JUST MANAGED TO OVERTAKE THE MAN BEHIND HIM INTO SECOND PLACE.
DIJON LAST LAP DRAMA IN G.P.

Poor old John Watson manages to lose the lead on the last lap again.

7th July 1977

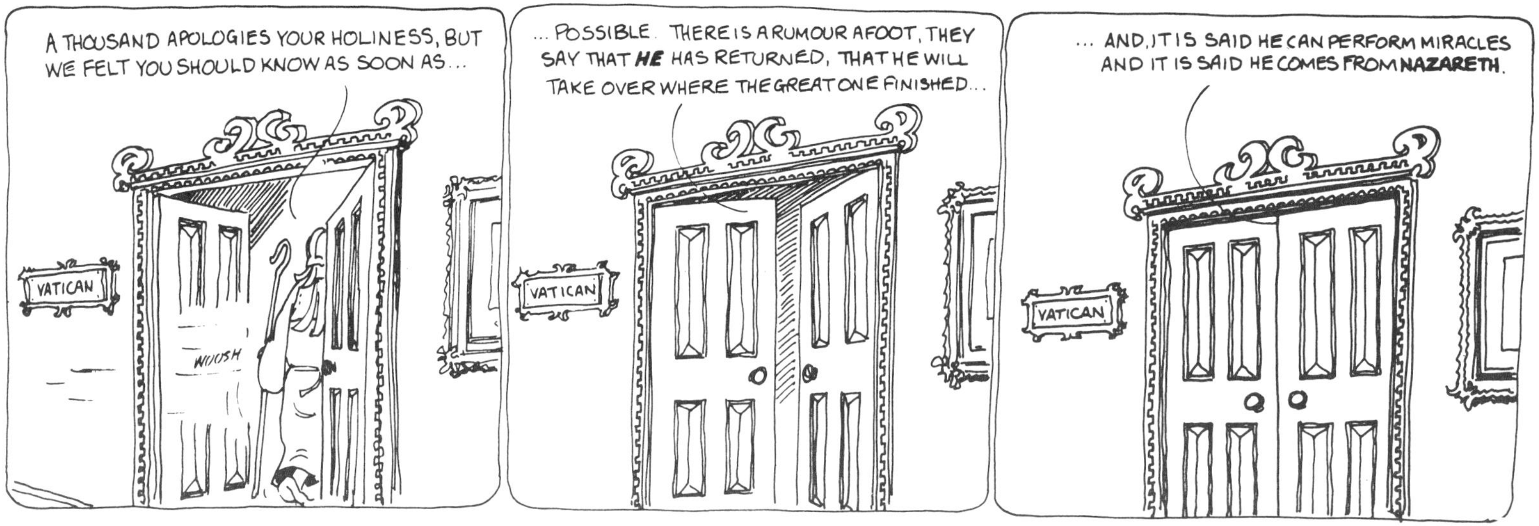
A THOUSAND APOLOGIES YOUR HOLINESS, BUT WE FELT YOU SHOULD KNOW AS SOON AS...
VATICAN
WOOSH
...POSSIBLE. THERE IS A RUMOUR AFOOT, THEY SAY THAT **HE** HAS RETURNED, THAT HE WILL TAKE OVER WHERE THE GREAT ONE FINISHED...
VATICAN
... AND, IT IS SAID HE CAN PERFORM MIRACLES AND IT IS SAID HE COMES FROM **NAZARETH**.
VATICAN

Mario Andretti returns to Ferrari.

22nd September 1977

Chapter Eleven

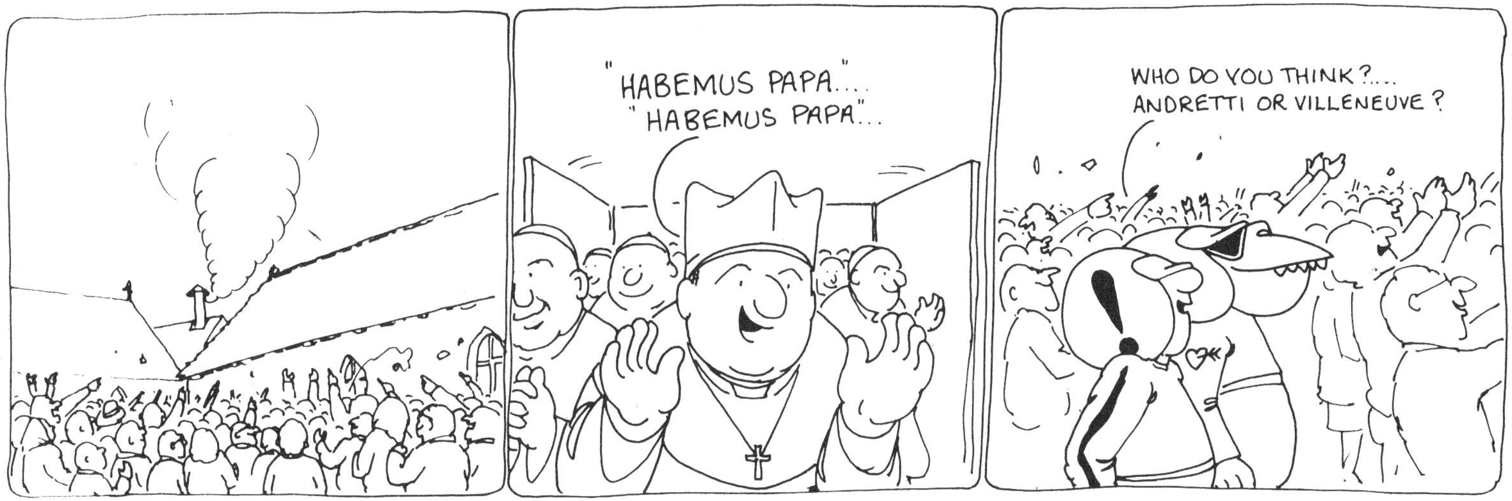
"HABEMUS PAPA"....
"HABEMUS PAPA"...
WHO DO YOU THINK?....
ANDRETTI OR VILLENEUVE?

After long deliberations a new Pope was announced and Gilles Villeneuve was signed by Ferrari.

19th October 1978

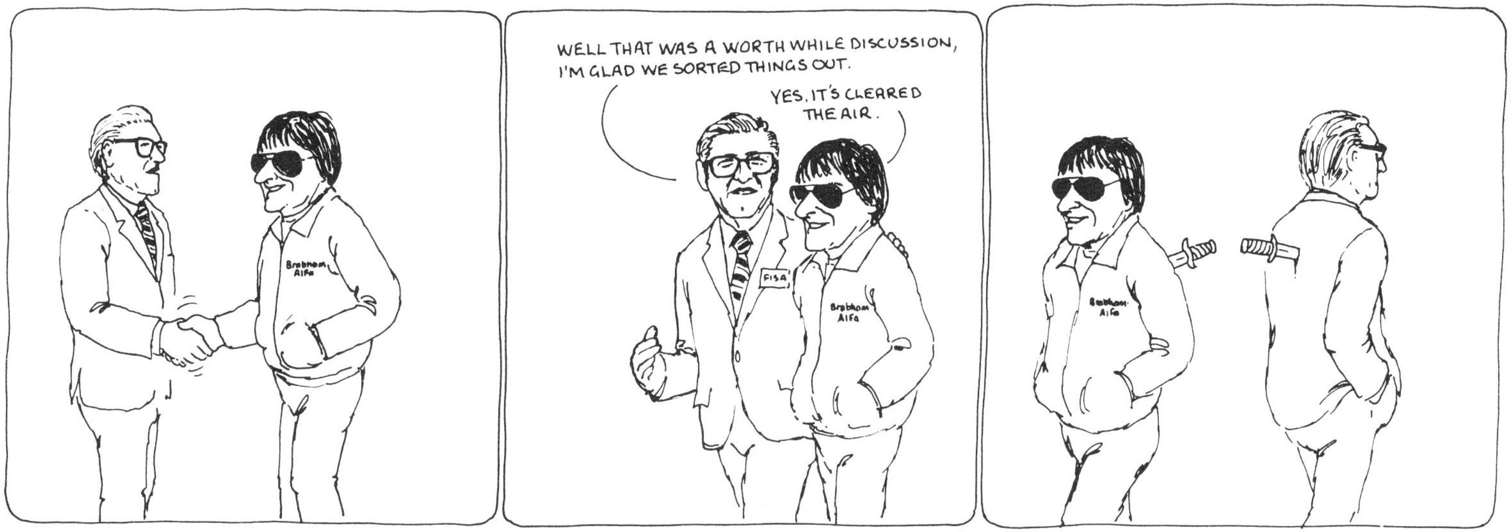
Brabham Alfa
WELL THAT WAS A WORTH WHILE DISCUSSION,
I'M GLAD WE SORTED THINGS OUT.
YES, IT'S CLEARED THE AIR.
FISA
Brabham Alfa
Brabham Alfa

F1 was split apart by the FISA-FOCA battle for control. After a bloody battle, Bernie and Balestre declared a truce.

5th April 1979

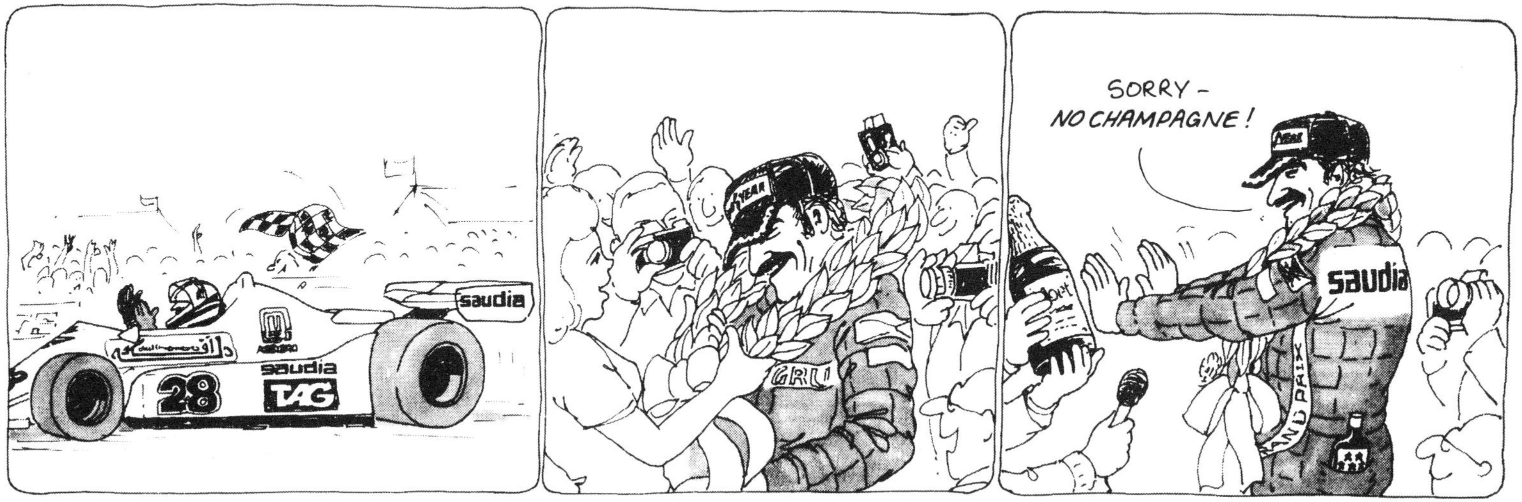
saudia
28
TAG
SORRY -
NO CHAMPAGNE!
saudia

Alcohol was banned in Saudi Arabia, Williams' new sponsor.

9th August 1979

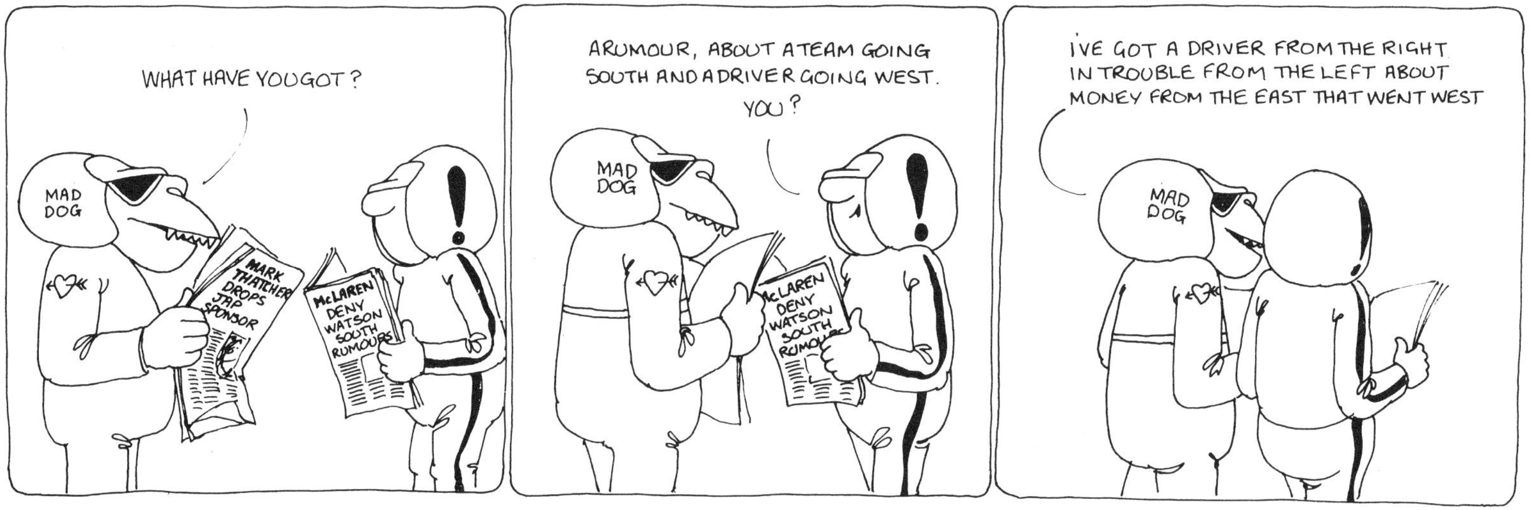
WHAT HAVE YOU GOT?
MAD DOG
MARK THATCHER DROPS JAP SPONSOR
McLAREN DENY WATSON SOUTH RUMOURS
A RUMOUR, ABOUT A TEAM GOING SOUTH AND A DRIVER GOING WEST.
YOU?
MAD DOG
McLAREN DENY WATSON SOUTH
I'VE GOT A DRIVER FROM THE RIGHT IN TROUBLE FROM THE LEFT ABOUT MONEY FROM THE EAST THAT WENT WEST
MAD DOG

You'll have to think about it. McLaren was going to dump Watson and sign Steven South. Funny to think that McLaren did go 'West' eventually.

21st February 1980

Chapter Eleven

You'll Have To Explain That

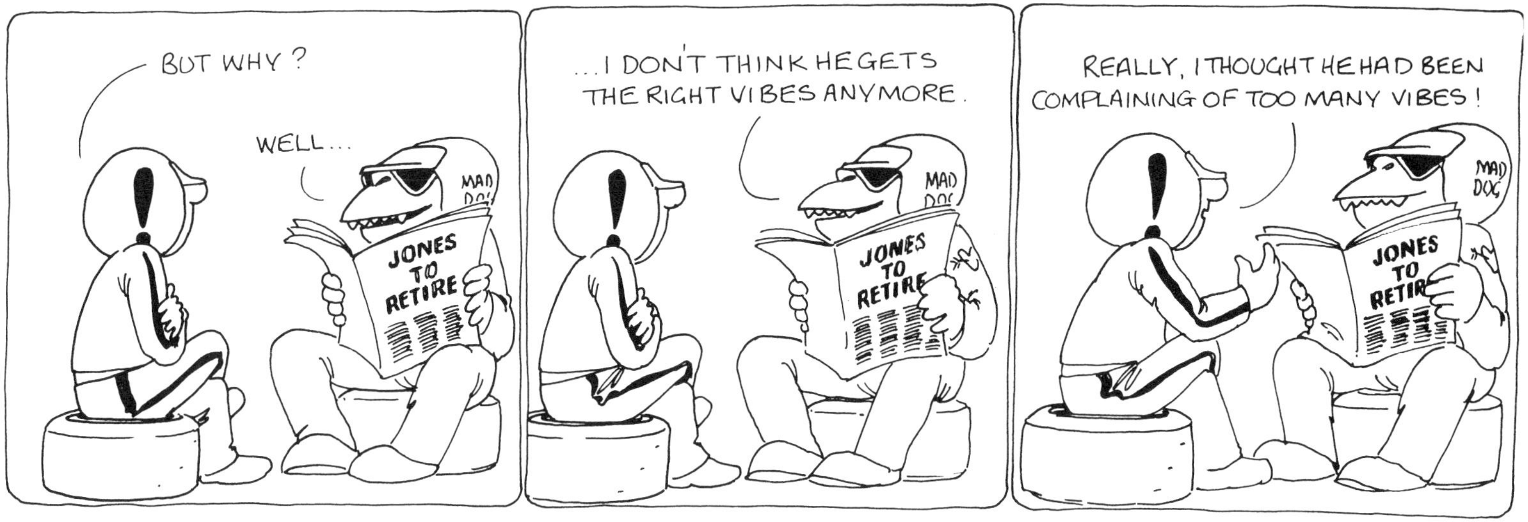
BUT WHY ?
WELL...
JONES TO RETIRE
MAD DOG
...I DON'T THINK HE GETS THE RIGHT VIBES ANYMORE.
REALLY, I THOUGHT HE HAD BEEN COMPLAINING OF TOO MANY VIBES!

Alan complained loudly about the pounding a driver took in a skirted F1 car.

24th September 1981

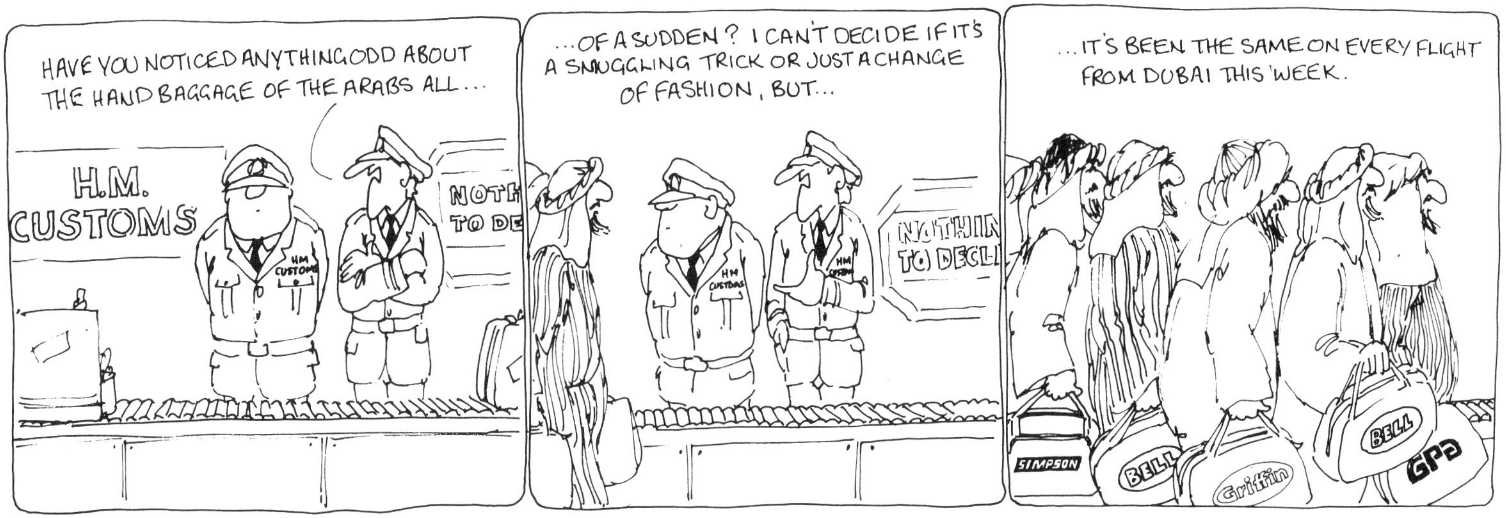
HAVE YOU NOTICED ANYTHING ODD ABOUT THE HAND BAGGAGE OF THE ARABS ALL...
H.M. CUSTOMS
...OF A SUDDEN? I CAN'T DECIDE IF IT'S A SMUGGLING TRICK OR JUST A CHANGE OF FASHION, BUT...
...IT'S BEEN THE SAME ON EVERY FLIGHT FROM DUBAI THIS WEEK.
SIMPSON
BELL
Griffin
BELL

Rumours were strong about a Dubai Grand Prix.

10th December 1981

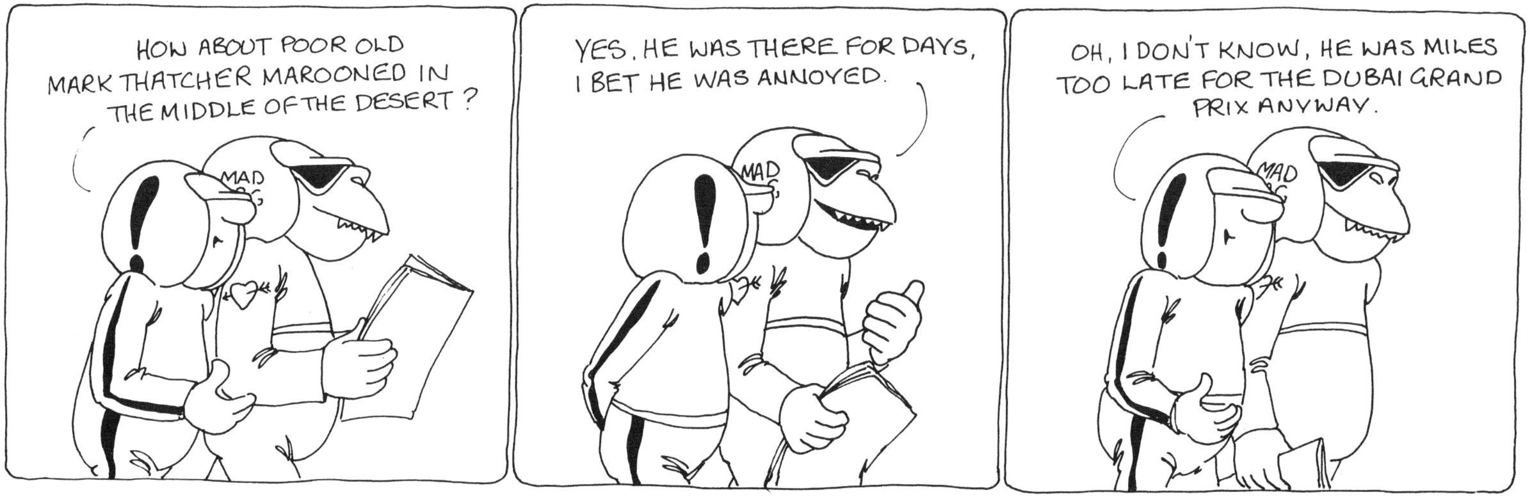
HOW ABOUT POOR OLD MARK THATCHER MAROONED IN THE MIDDLE OF THE DESERT ?
MAD DOG
YES. HE WAS THERE FOR DAYS, I BET HE WAS ANNOYED.
MAD
OH, I DON'T KNOW, HE WAS MILES TOO LATE FOR THE DUBAI GRAND PRIX ANYWAY.
MAD

This one really caused trouble. Everyone thought he was dead, lost in the desert. I had to apologise to Margaret Thatcher (see the intro).

13th January 1982

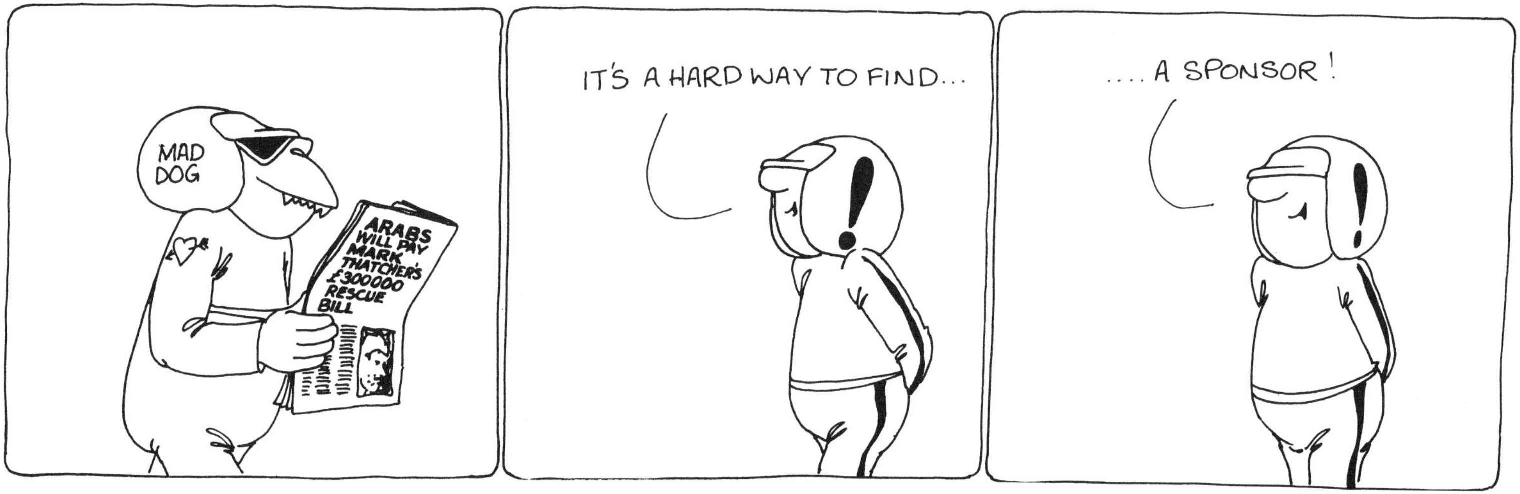
MAD DOG
ARABS WILL PAY MARK THATCHER'S £300000 RESCUE BILL
IT'S A HARD WAY TO FIND...
.... A SPONSOR !

More of the same.

21st January 1982

Chapter Eleven

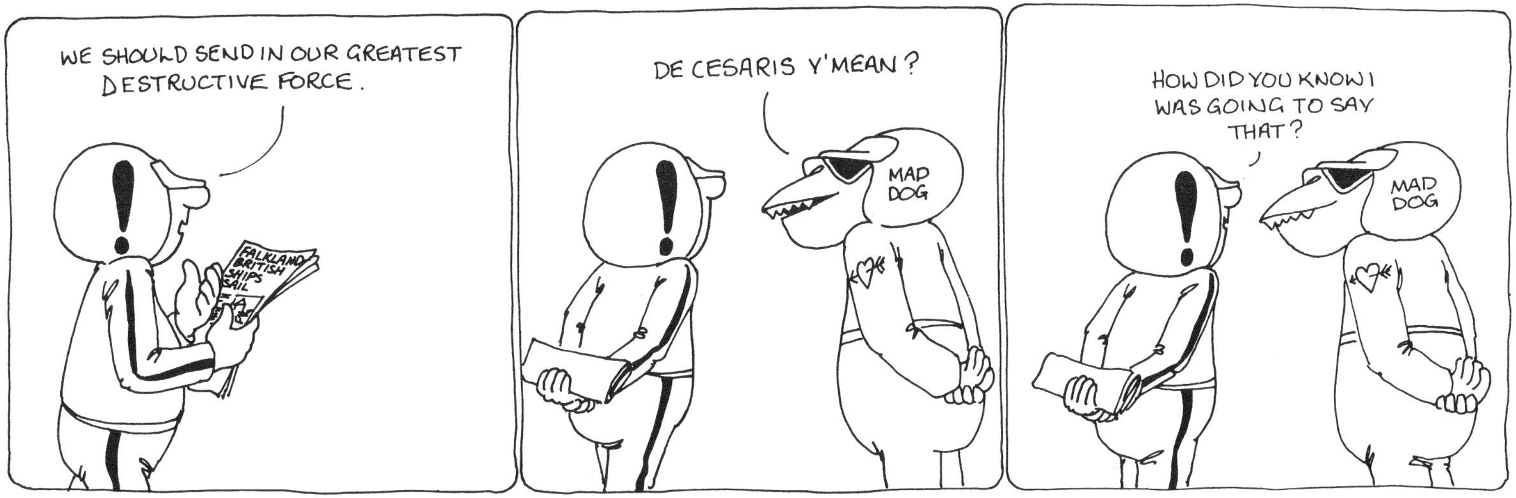
WE SHOULD SEND IN OUR GREATEST DESTRUCTIVE FORCE.
DE CESARIS Y'MEAN?
MAD DOG
HOW DID YOU KNOW I WAS GOING TO SAY THAT?
MAD DOG

The British armada sails for the Falklands.

8th April 1982

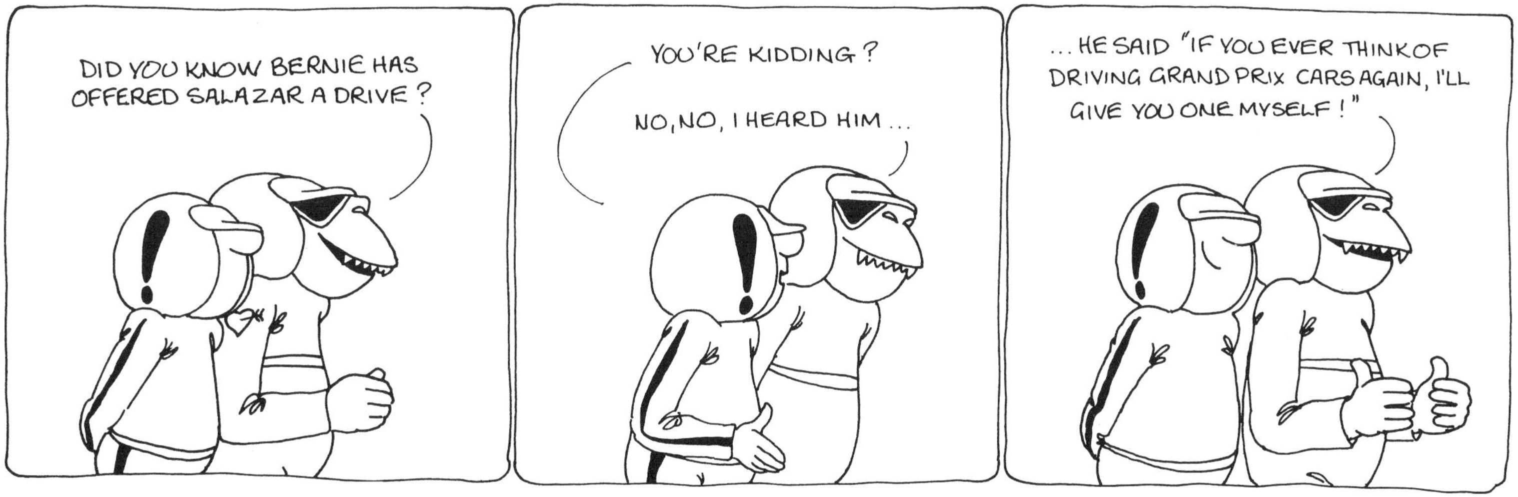
DID YOU KNOW BERNIE HAS OFFERED SALAZAR A DRIVE?
YOU'RE KIDDING?
NO, NO, I HEARD HIM...
...HE SAID "IF YOU EVER THINK OF DRIVING GRAND PRIX CARS AGAIN, I'LL GIVE YOU ONE MYSELF!"

This was when Piquet famously punched Salazar after he had been taken out of the lead of the German GP.

12th August 1982

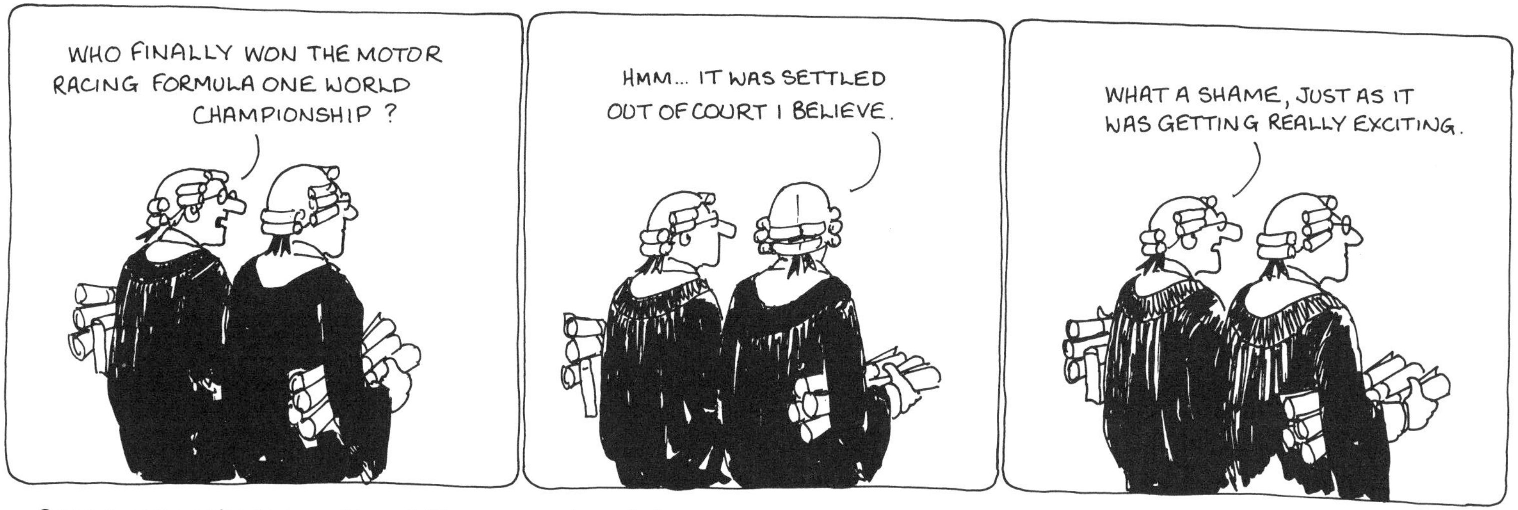
WHO FINALLY WON THE MOTOR RACING FORMULA ONE WORLD CHAMPIONSHIP ?
HMM... IT WAS SETTLED OUT OF COURT I BELIEVE.
WHAT A SHAME, JUST AS IT WAS GETTING REALLY EXCITING.

Someone was going to sue - blowed if I can remember who!

30th September 1982

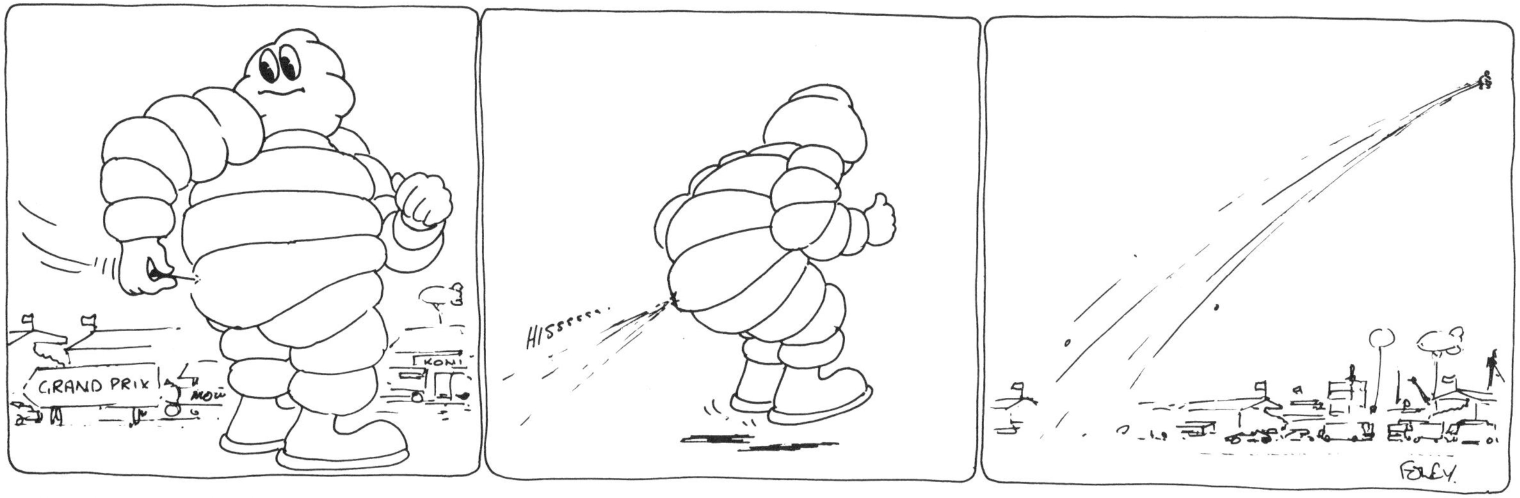
GRAND PRIX
KONI
FOLEY.

Michelin pulls out of F1.

4th October 1984

Chapter Eleven

You'll Have To Explain That

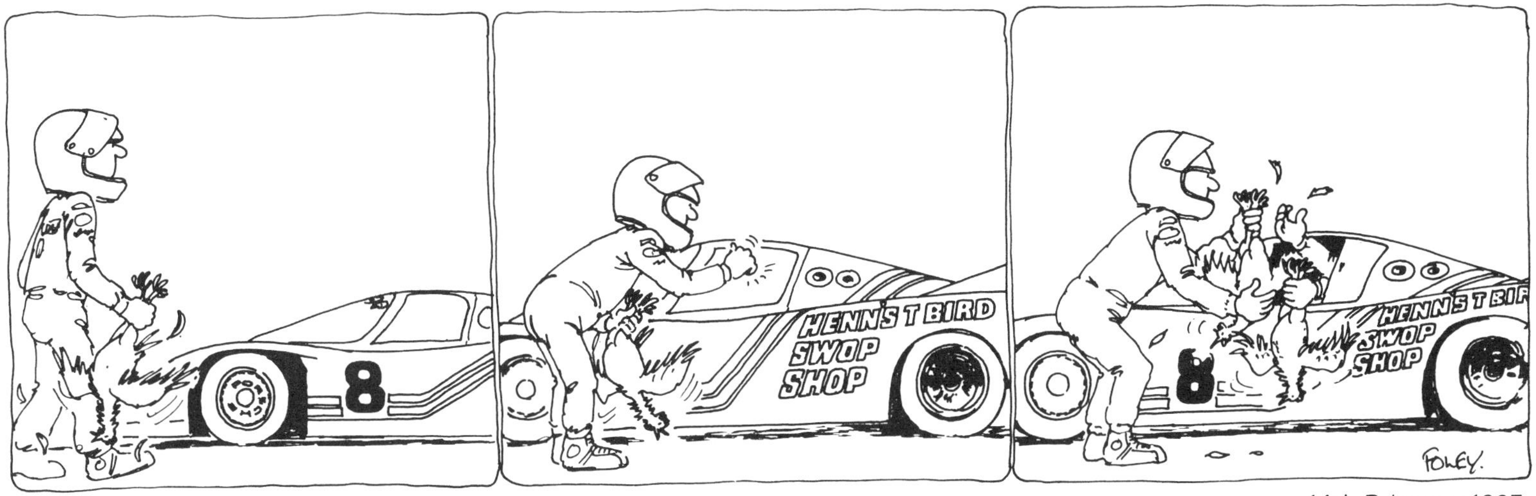
HENN'S T BIRD
SWOP
SHOP
8
FOLEY

The T-Bird Swop Shop sponsors a sports car.

14th February 1985

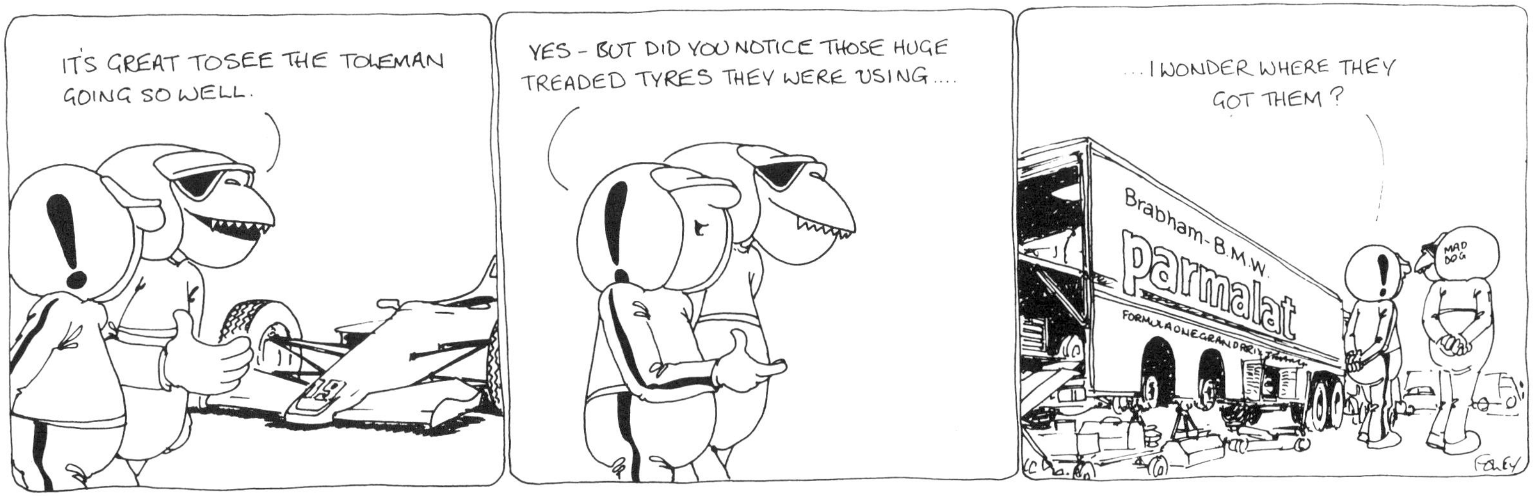
IT'S GREAT TO SEE THE TOLEMAN GOING SO WELL.
YES – BUT DID YOU NOTICE THOSE HUGE TREADED TYRES THEY WERE USING....
...I WONDER WHERE THEY GOT THEM?
Brabham-B.M.W.
parmalat
MAD DOG
FOLEY

Another tyre crisis in F1.

21st February 1985

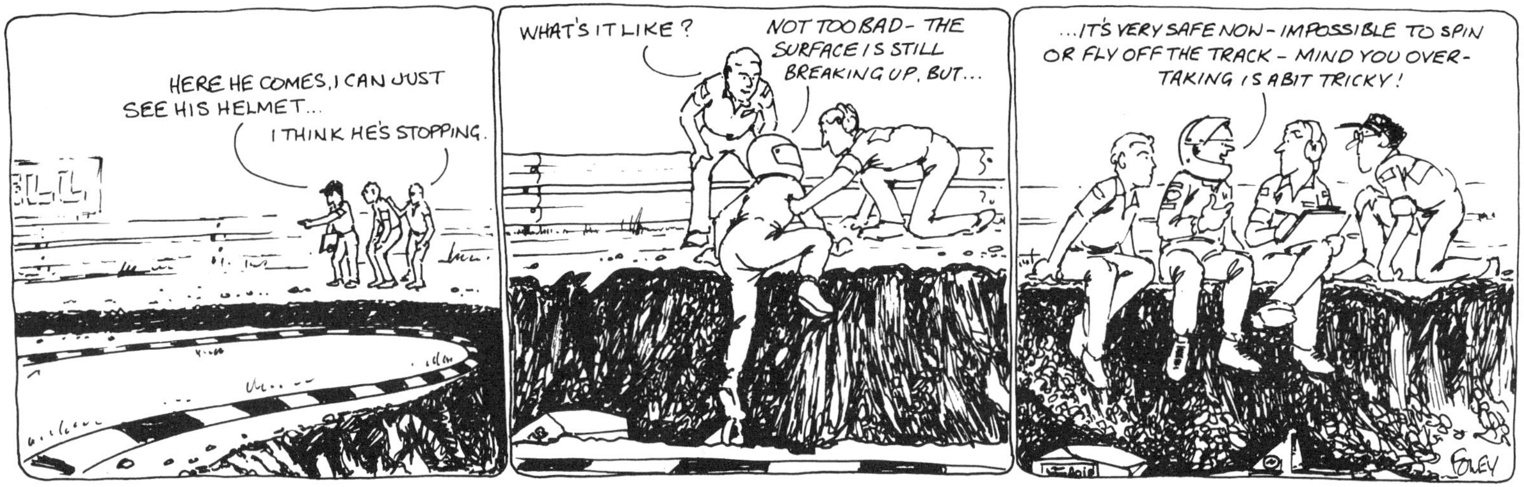
HERE HE COMES, I CAN JUST SEE HIS HELMET...
I THINK HE'S STOPPING.
WHAT'S IT LIKE?
NOT TOO BAD - THE SURFACE IS STILL BREAKING UP, BUT...
...IT'S VERY SAFE NOW - IMPOSSIBLE TO SPIN OR FLY OFF THE TRACK - MIND YOU OVER-TAKING IS A BIT TRICKY!
FOLEY

Silverstone resurfaces the track just before the Grand Prix.

6th June 1985

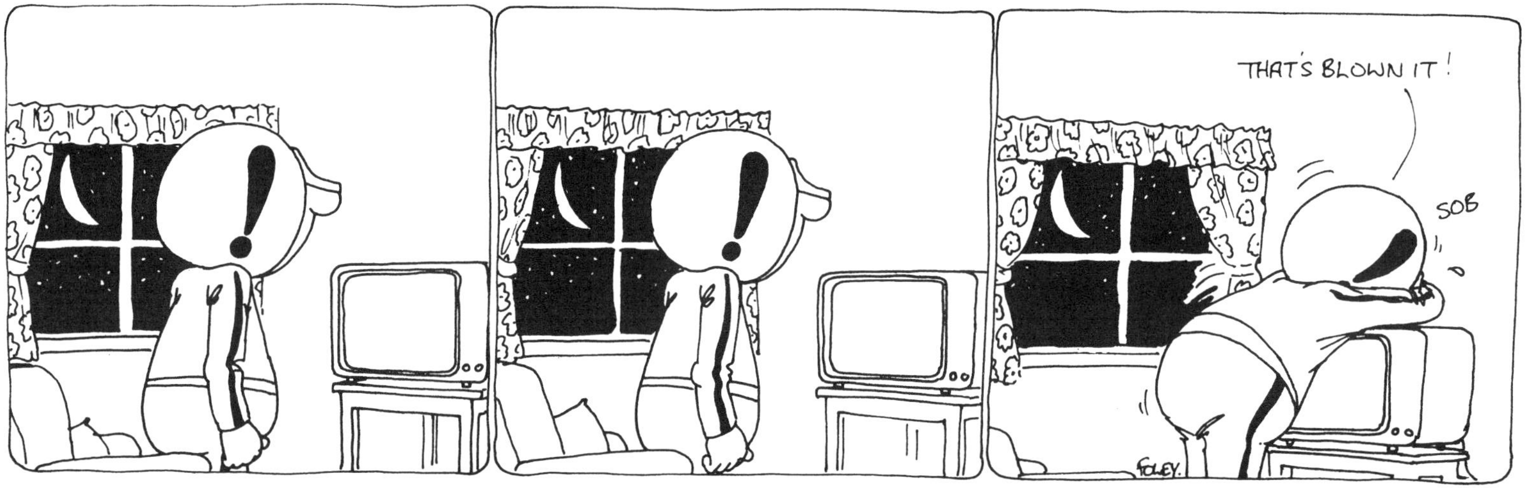
THAT'S BLOWN IT!
SOB
FOLEY.

Mansell's rear tyre blows in Australia, losing him the championship.

30th October 1986

Chapter Eleven

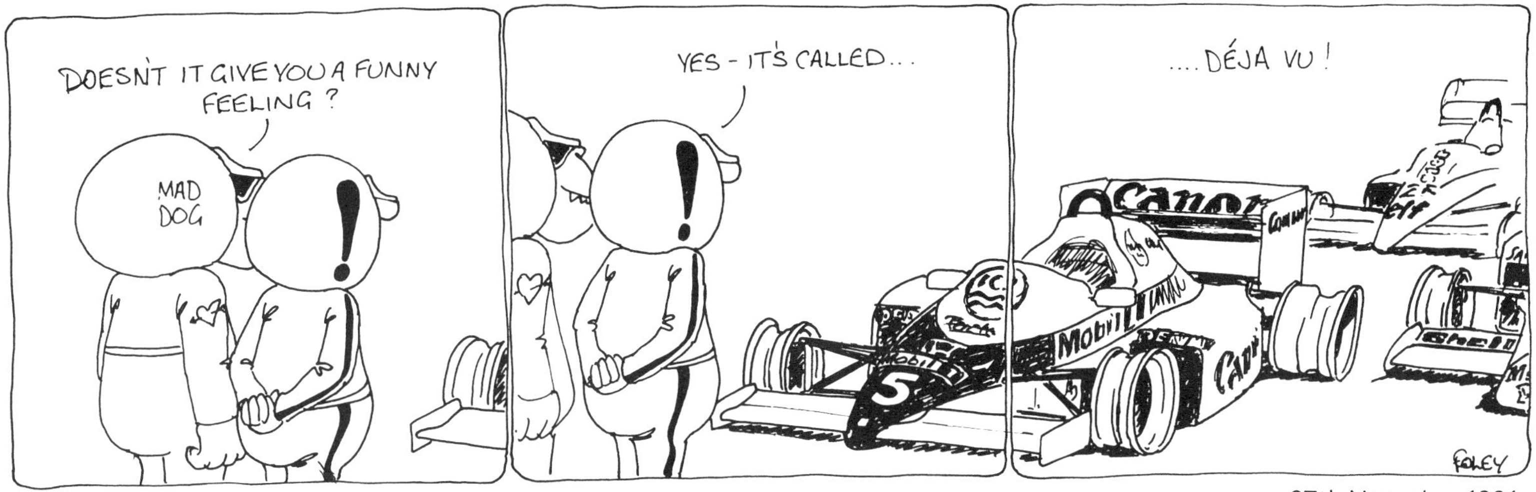
DOESN'T IT GIVE YOU A FUNNY FEELING ?
MAD DOG
YES - IT'S CALLED...
....DÉJA VU !
FOLEY

No tyres for GP racing again.

27th November 1986

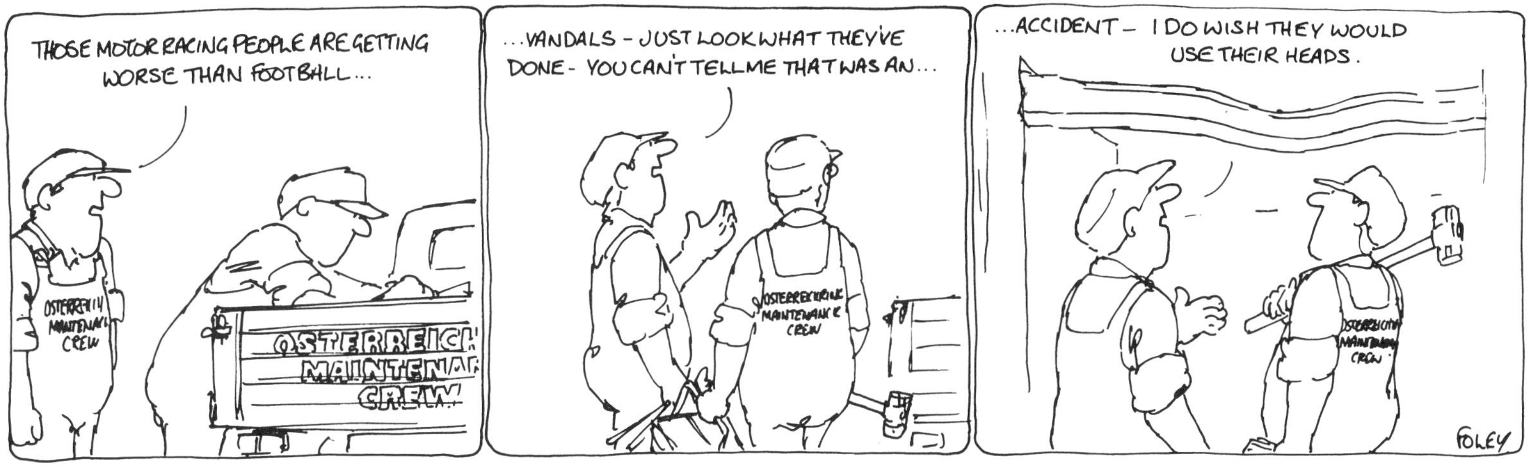
THOSE MOTOR RACING PEOPLE ARE GETTING WORSE THAN FOOTBALL...
...VANDALS - JUST LOOK WHAT THEY'VE DONE - YOU CAN'T TELL ME THAT WAS AN...
...ACCIDENT - I DO WISH THEY WOULD USE THEIR HEADS.
FOLEY

Mansell hits his head on an RSJ while on the winner's car.

27th August 1987

GREAT – 5·3 SECONDS – THAT'S 1·7 SECS. FASTER THAN HERBERT...
CLICK!
...I THINK IT WOULD HAVE BEEN EVEN FASTER IF YOU HAD...
...UNDONE THE SEAT BELTS.
MAD DOG
FOLEY

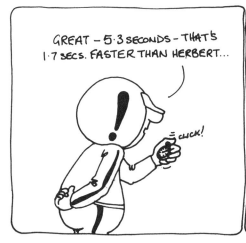

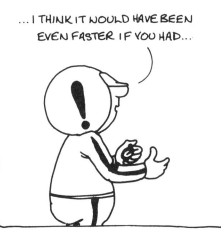

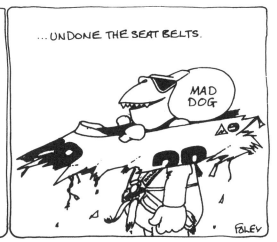

After Johnny broke his legs, they timed how quickly he could exit a racing car.

9th February 1989

GOOD, IT LOOKS AS THOUGH THERE IS SOME F1 TESTING GOING ON.
MAD DOG
YES, HELLO – I WONDER WHAT THIS BUTTON...
MAD DOG
DAMON
.....IS ?
THUD
DAMON
FOLEY

22nd July 1993

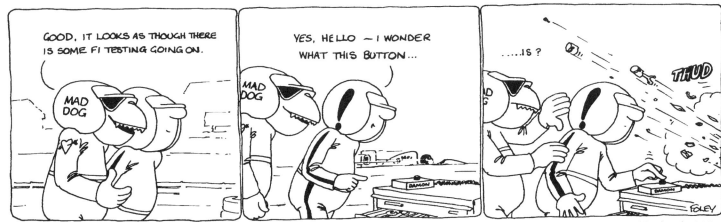

Damon Hill's engines kept blowing whenever he led Prost.

Technical

I'd like to explain this chapter to you, however if it was something the ordinary man in the street could understand I wouldn't have called it Technical. These are cartoons that concern matters that only designers talk about and I'm afraid they might go clean over your head. On the other hand you wouldn't have bought this book unless you were of above average intelligence, so perhaps you'll be okay.
It seems ironic that now, when all F1 cars look exactly the same, we should start paying designers vast sums. Adrian Newey now earns more than Colin Chapman, Jim Hall and Harvey Postlethwaite put together.

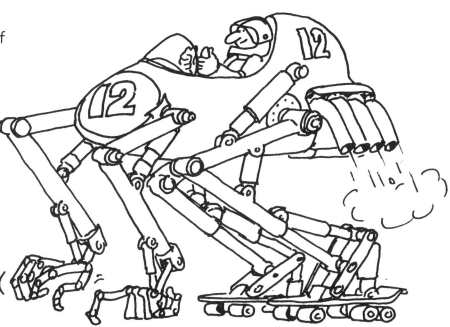

I HEAR YOU HAVE BEEN TESTING THE NEW F3....
MAD DOG MALONE
WHAT DID YOU FIND OUT ?
MAD DOG MALONE
WELL, BRIEFLY, WE PROVED CONCLUSIVELY THAT THE CHASSIS BENDS WHEN HIT BY AN EARTH BANK.
MAD DOG MALONE

21st October 1971

THUMP!
12
GRUNT
WHACK!
12
IT'S CALLED 'TOE IN' ADJUSTMENT
BIFF!
THUMP!
12

16th December 1971

Chapter Twelve

Technical

WHAT DO YOU DO IN THE WINTER TO EARN A CRUST ?
MAD DOG
WELL, I DRIVE FOR THE ARTISTS, THE CHAPS WHO DO THE CUTAWAY DRAWINGS.
MAD DOG
YOU DON'T MEAN THOSE ILLUSTRATIONS WITH BIG HOLES IN THEM SO THAT YOU CAN SEE WHAT'S INSIDE ?
MAD DOG
THAT'S THEM, BUT WHO DO YOU THINK PUTS THE BIG HOLES IN THEM ?
MAD DOG

18th January 1973

....HE WAS SHOWING ME THE DAMAGE TO THE...
... FRONT CORNER THAT HE HAD KNOCKED OFF.
SO I SAID THAT'S...
...WHY THEY CALL IT A 'WISH BONE'....
...YOU JUST HAVE TO HOPE IT HOLDS THE WHEEL ON.

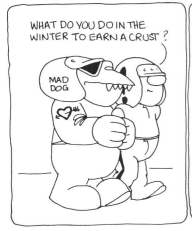

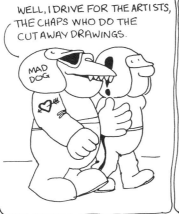

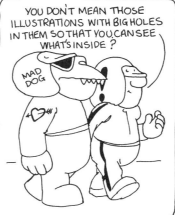

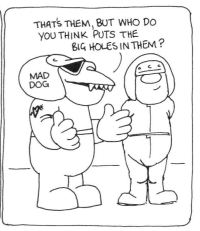

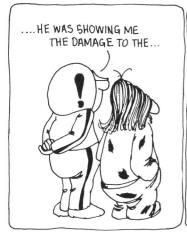

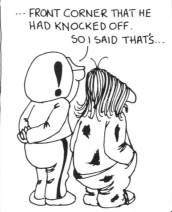

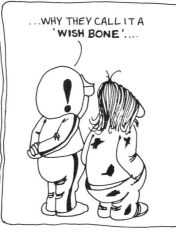

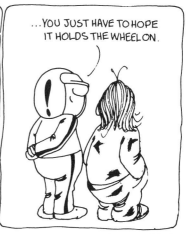

7th June 1973

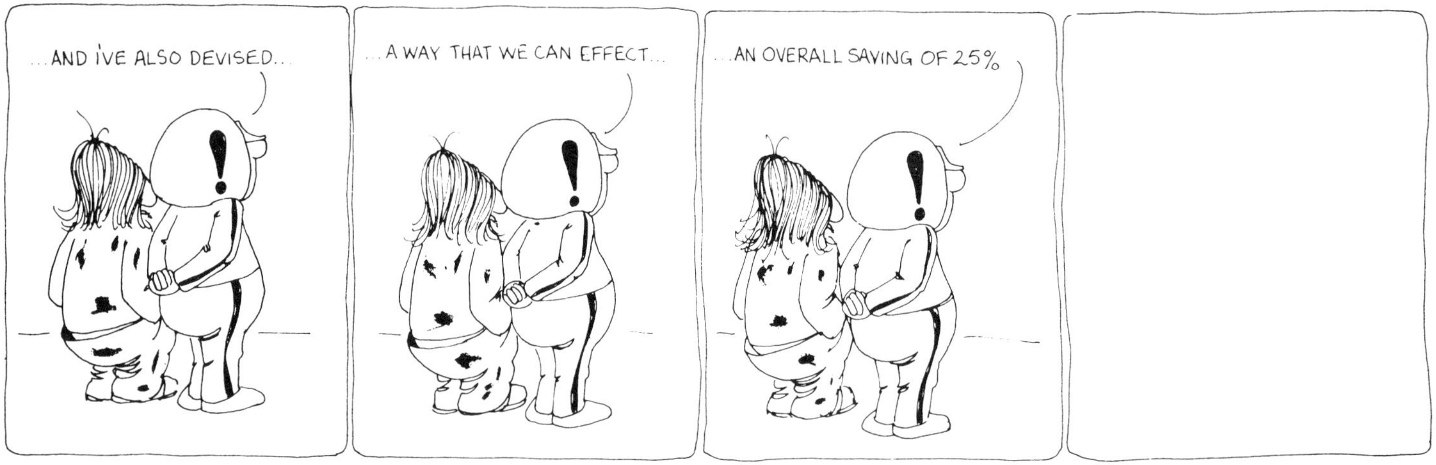
...AND I'VE ALSO DEVISED...
...A WAY THAT WE CAN EFFECT...
...AN OVERALL SAVING OF 25%

14th February 1974

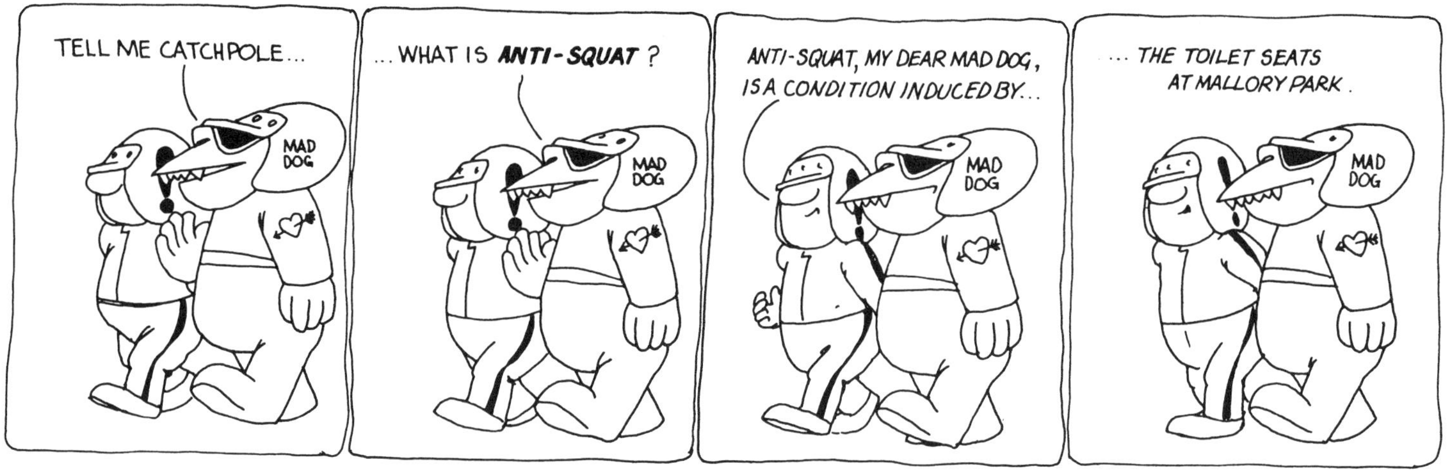
TELL ME CATCHPOLE...
MAD DOG
...WHAT IS **ANTI-SQUAT** ?
MAD DOG
ANTI-SQUAT, MY DEAR MAD DOG, IS A CONDITION INDUCED BY...
MAD DOG
...THE TOILET SEATS AT MALLORY PARK.
MAD DOG

7th March 1974

Chapter Twelve

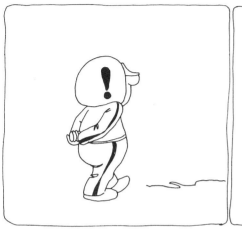

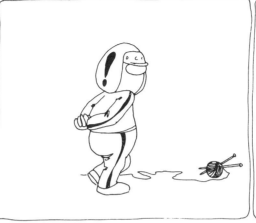

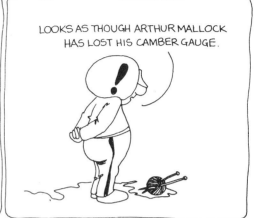

LOOKS AS THOUGH ARTHUR MALLOCK HAS LOST HIS CAMBER GAUGE.

21st March 1974

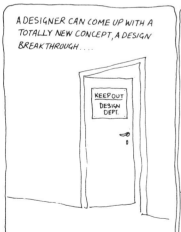

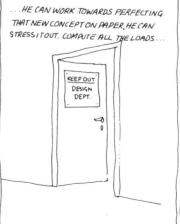

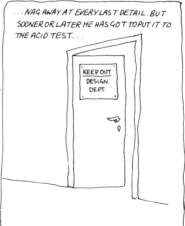

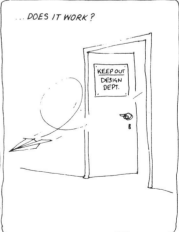

A DESIGNER CAN COME UP WITH A TOTALLY NEW CONCEPT, A DESIGN BREAKTHROUGH....
KEEP OUT
DESIGN DEPT.
...HE CAN WORK TOWARDS PERFECTING THAT NEW CONCEPT ON PAPER, HE CAN STRESS IT OUT. COMPUTE ALL THE LOADS...
KEEP OUT
DESIGN DEPT.
...NAG AWAY AT EVERY LAST DETAIL. BUT SOONER OR LATER HE HAS GOT TO PUT IT TO THE ACID TEST...
KEEP OUT
DESIGN DEPT.
...DOES IT WORK?
KEEP OUT
DESIGN DEPT.

4th July 1974

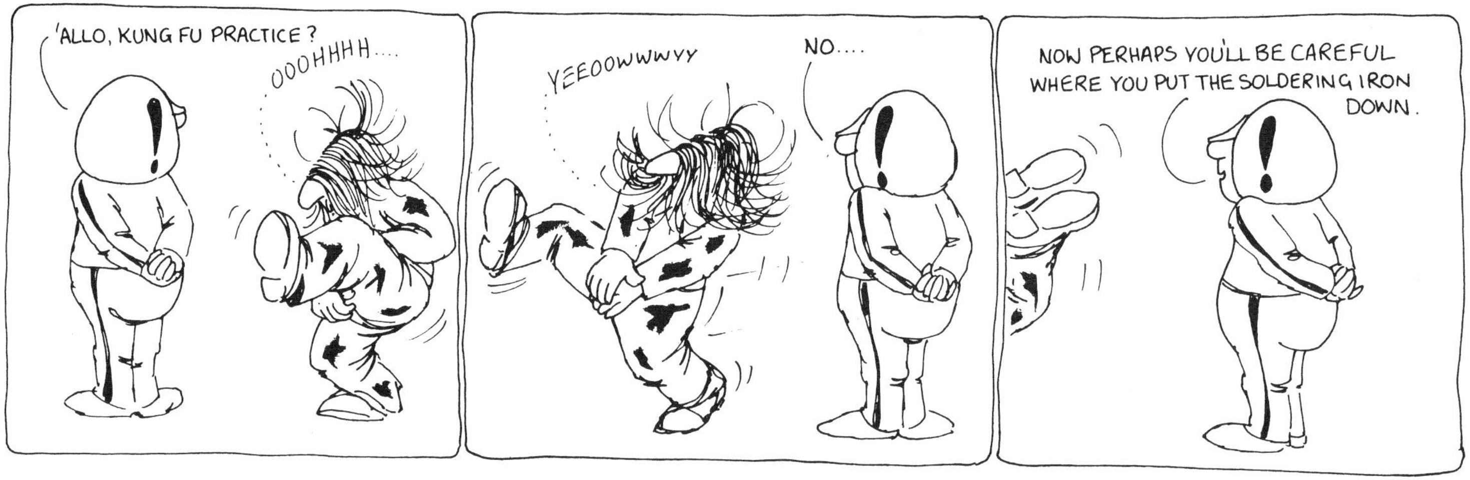
'ALLO, KUNG FU PRACTICE?
OOOHHHH....
YEEOOWWWYY
NO....
NOW PERHAPS YOU'LL BE CAREFUL WHERE YOU PUT THE SOLDERING IRON DOWN.

12th September 1974

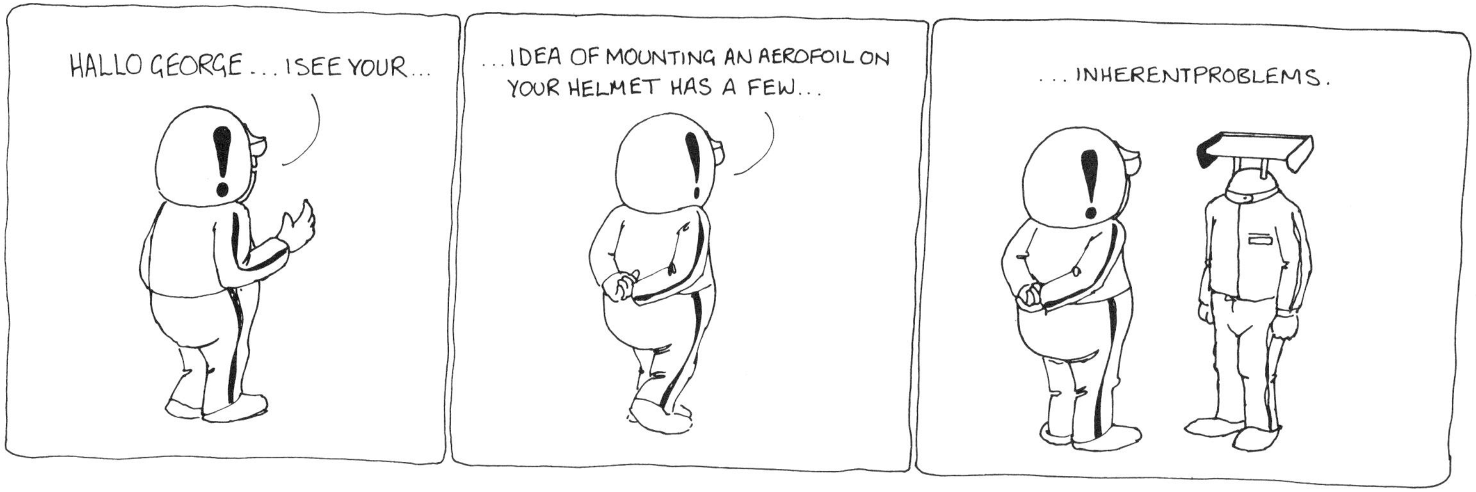
HALLO GEORGE... I SEE YOUR...
...IDEA OF MOUNTING AN AEROFOIL ON YOUR HELMET HAS A FEW...
...INHERENT PROBLEMS.

20th February 1975

Chapter Twelve

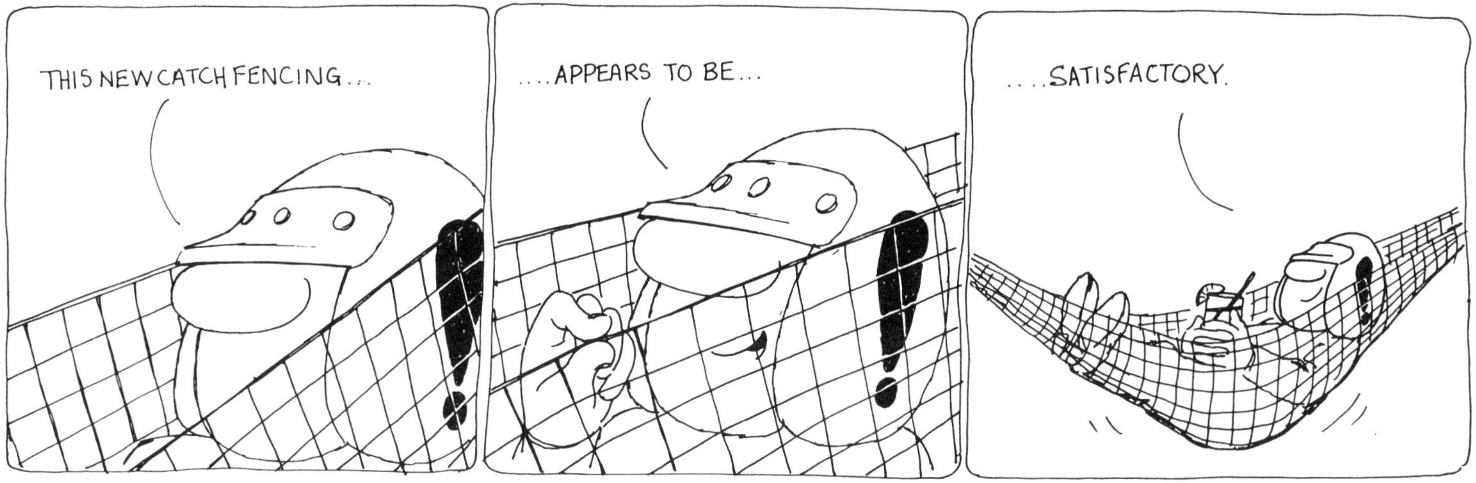
THIS NEW CATCH FENCING...
....APPEARS TO BE...
....SATISFACTORY.

8th May 1975

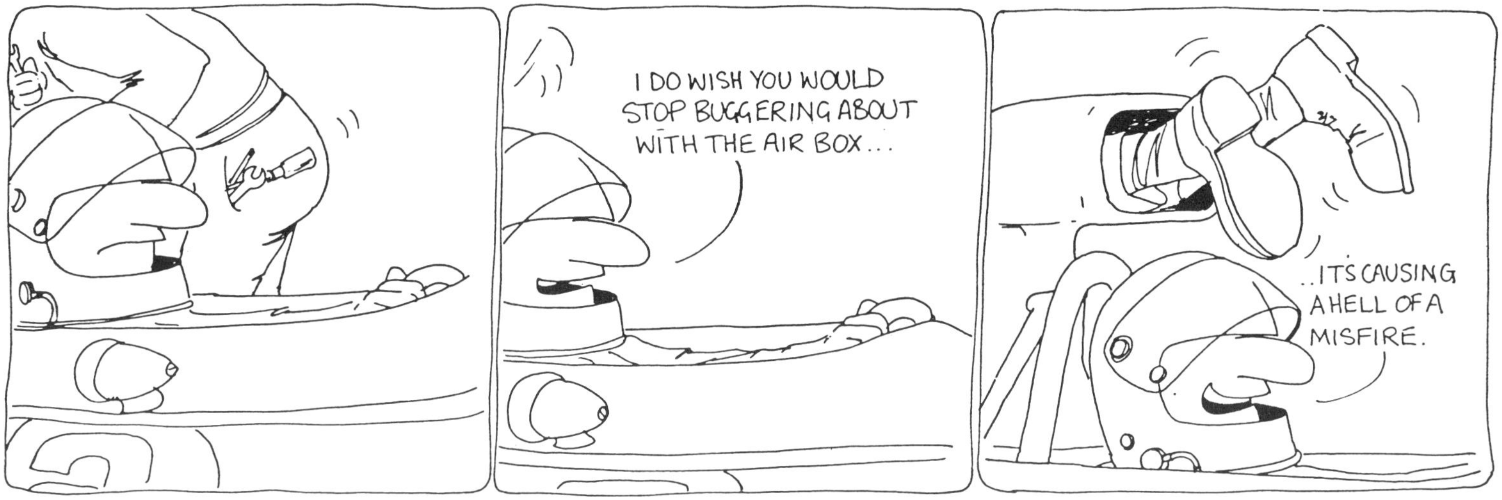
I DO WISH YOU WOULD STOP BUGGERING ABOUT WITH THE AIR BOX...
..IT'S CAUSING A HELL OF A MISFIRE.

31st July 1975

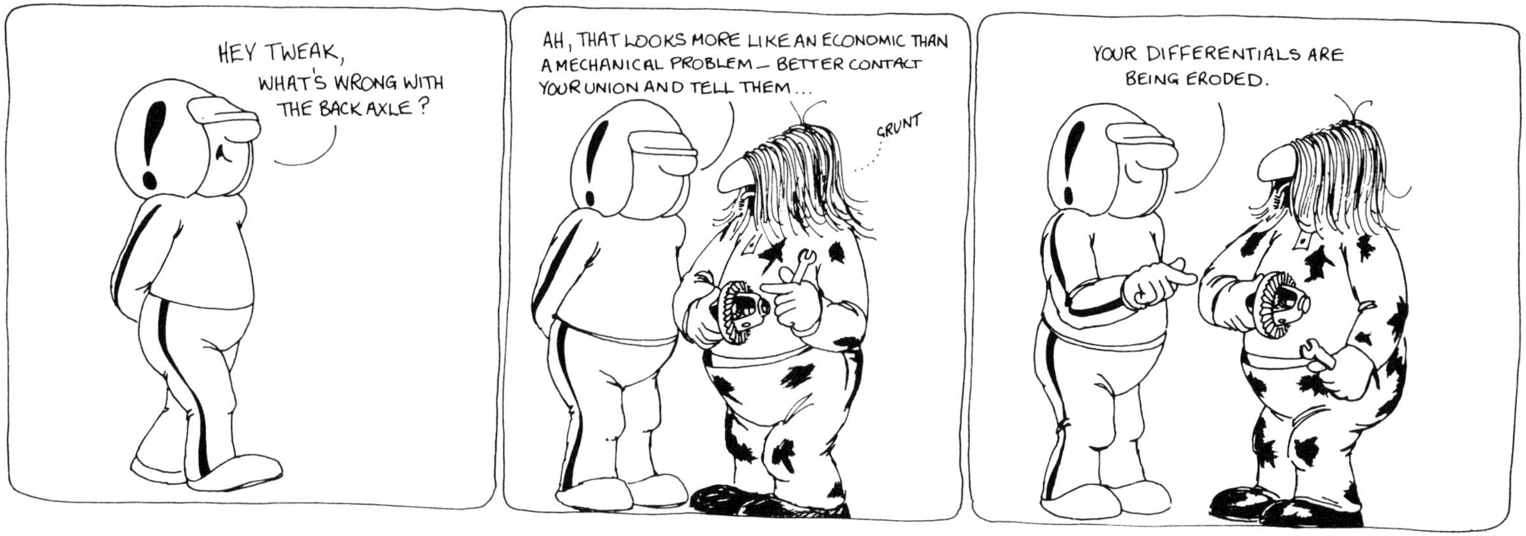
HEY TWEAK,
WHAT'S WRONG WITH THE BACK AXLE?
AH, THAT LOOKS MORE LIKE AN ECONOMIC THAN A MECHANICAL PROBLEM – BETTER CONTACT YOUR UNION AND TELL THEM...
GRUNT
YOUR DIFFERENTIALS ARE BEING ERODED.

24th February 1977

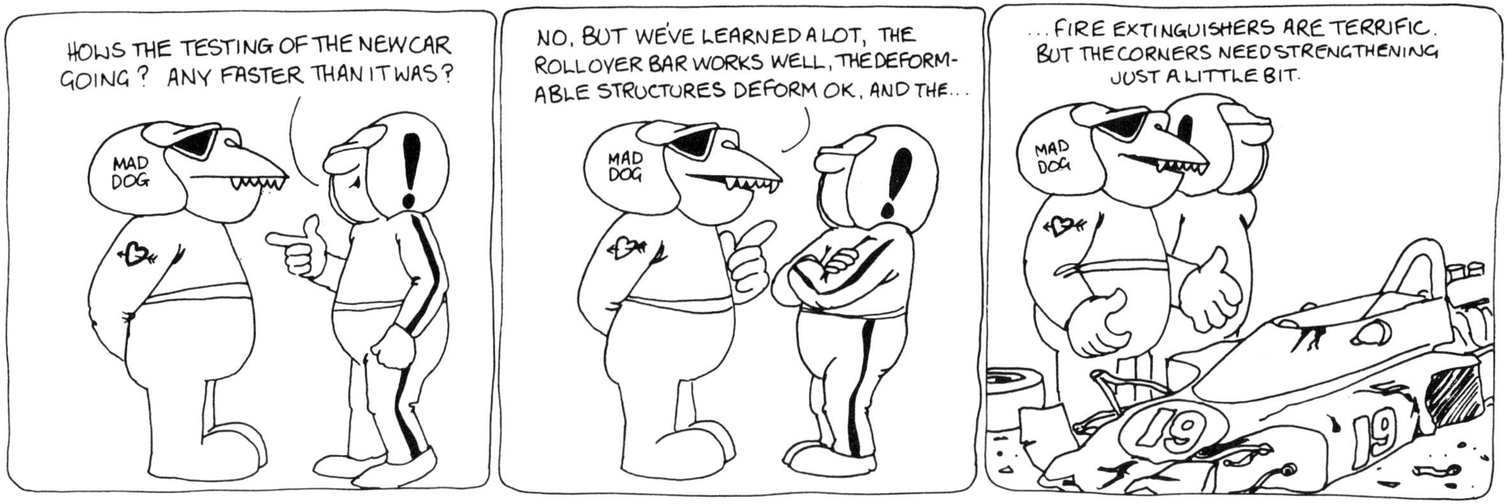
HOWS THE TESTING OF THE NEW CAR GOING? ANY FASTER THAN IT WAS?
MAD DOG
NO, BUT WE'VE LEARNED A LOT, THE ROLL OVER BAR WORKS WELL, THE DEFORMABLE STRUCTURES DEFORM OK, AND THE...
MAD DOG
...FIRE EXTINGUISHERS ARE TERRIFIC. BUT THE CORNERS NEED STRENGTHENING JUST A LITTLE BIT.
MAD DOG
19
19

29th September 1977

Chapter Twelve

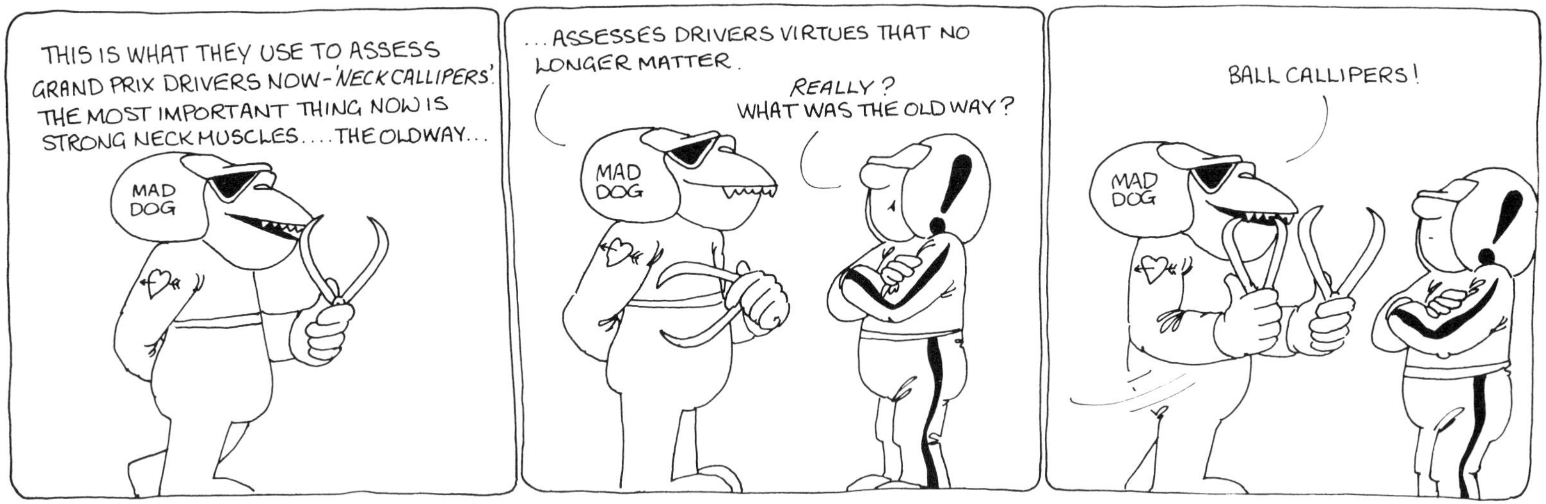
THIS IS WHAT THEY USE TO ASSESS GRAND PRIX DRIVERS NOW - 'NECK CALLIPERS'. THE MOST IMPORTANT THING NOW IS STRONG NECK MUSCLES.... THE OLD WAY...
MAD DOG
...ASSESSES DRIVERS VIRTUES THAT NO LONGER MATTER.
REALLY? WHAT WAS THE OLD WAY?
MAD DOG
BALL CALLIPERS!
MAD DOG

30th October 1980

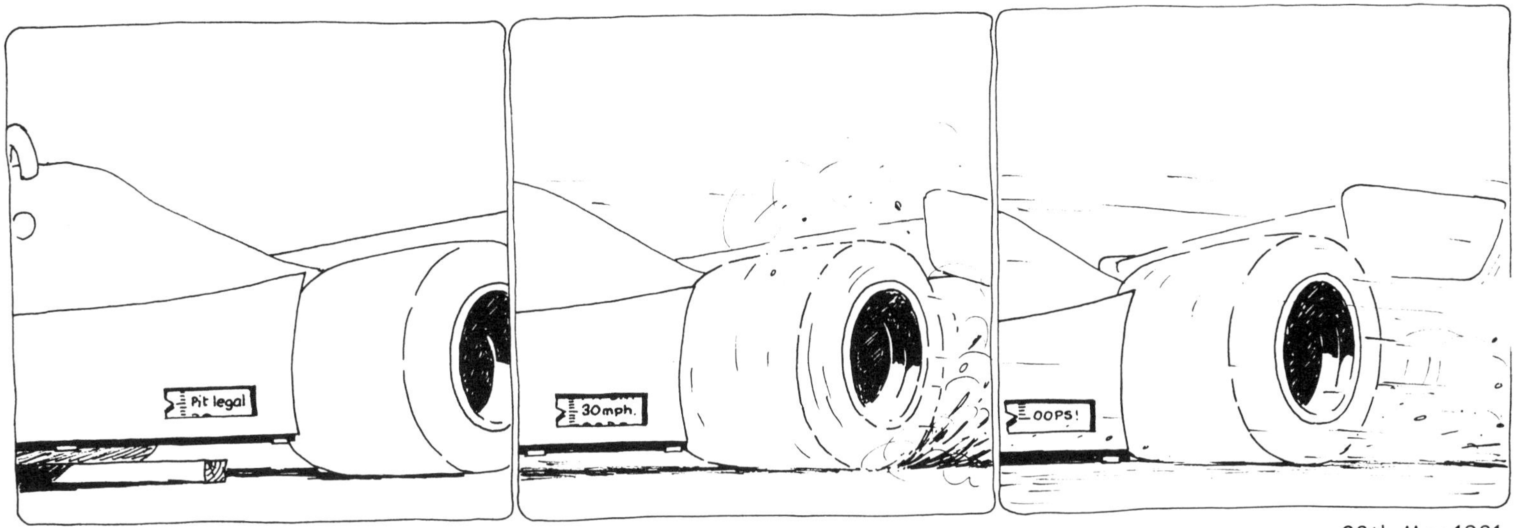
Pit legal
30mph.
OOPS!

28th May 1981

Technical

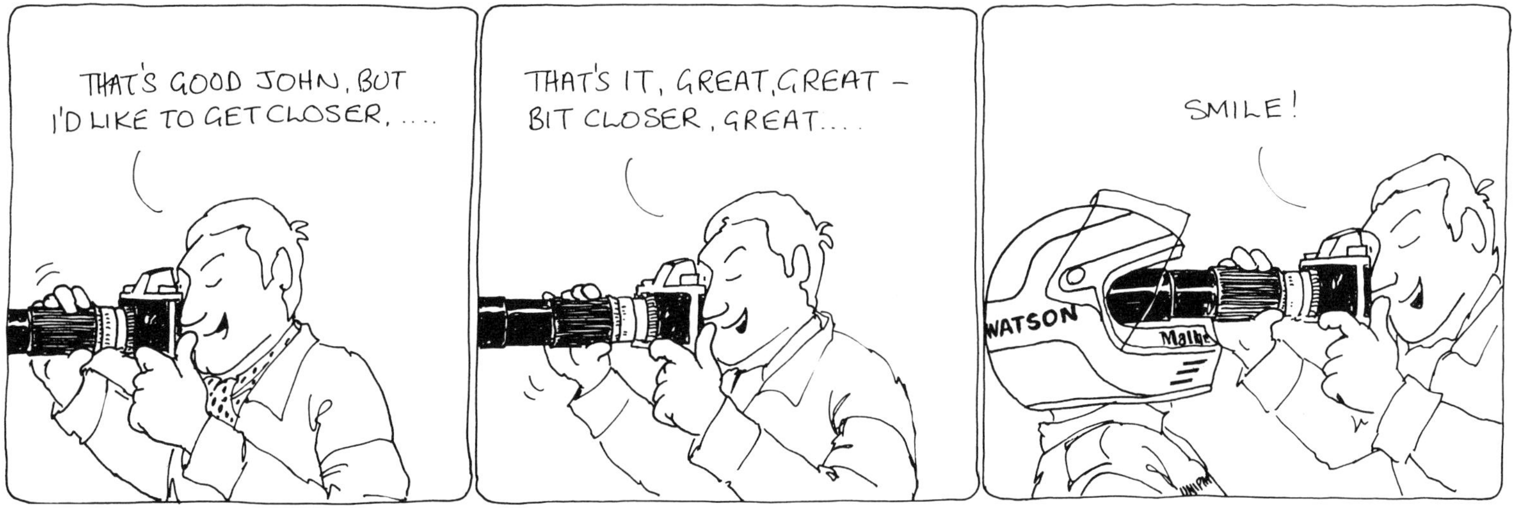

THAT'S GOOD JOHN, BUT I'D LIKE TO GET CLOSER, ...
THAT'S IT, GREAT, GREAT – BIT CLOSER, GREAT....
SMILE!
WATSON

6th August 1981

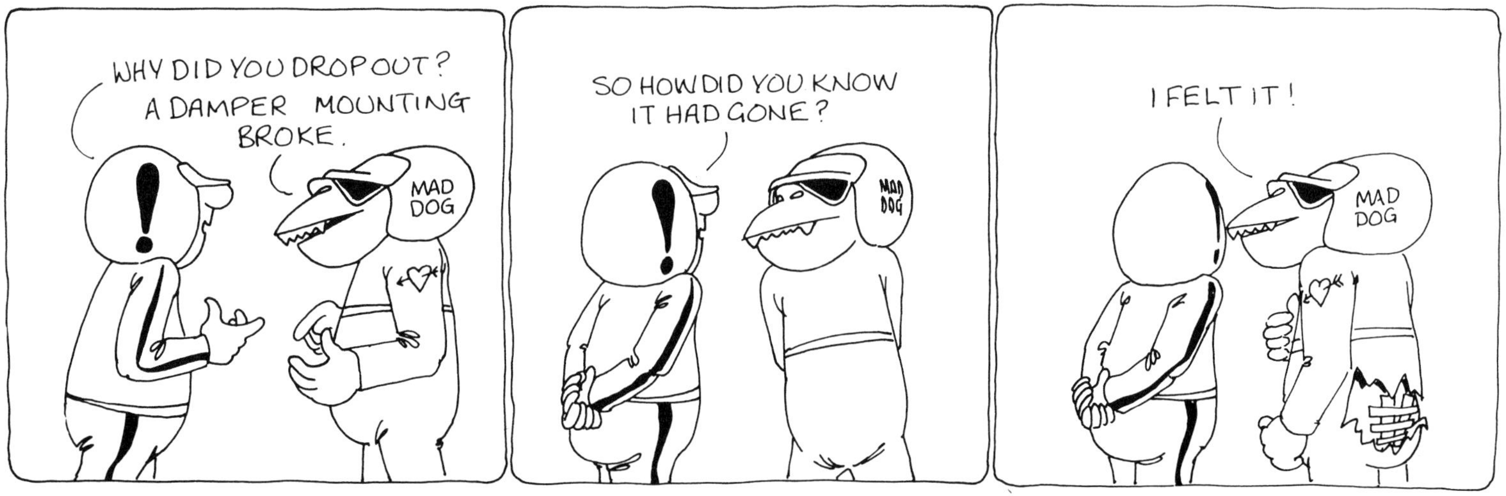

WHY DID YOU DROP OUT?
A DAMPER MOUNTING BROKE.
MAD DOG
SO HOW DID YOU KNOW IT HAD GONE?
MAD DOG
I FELT IT!
MAD DOG

3rd September 1981

Chapter Twelve

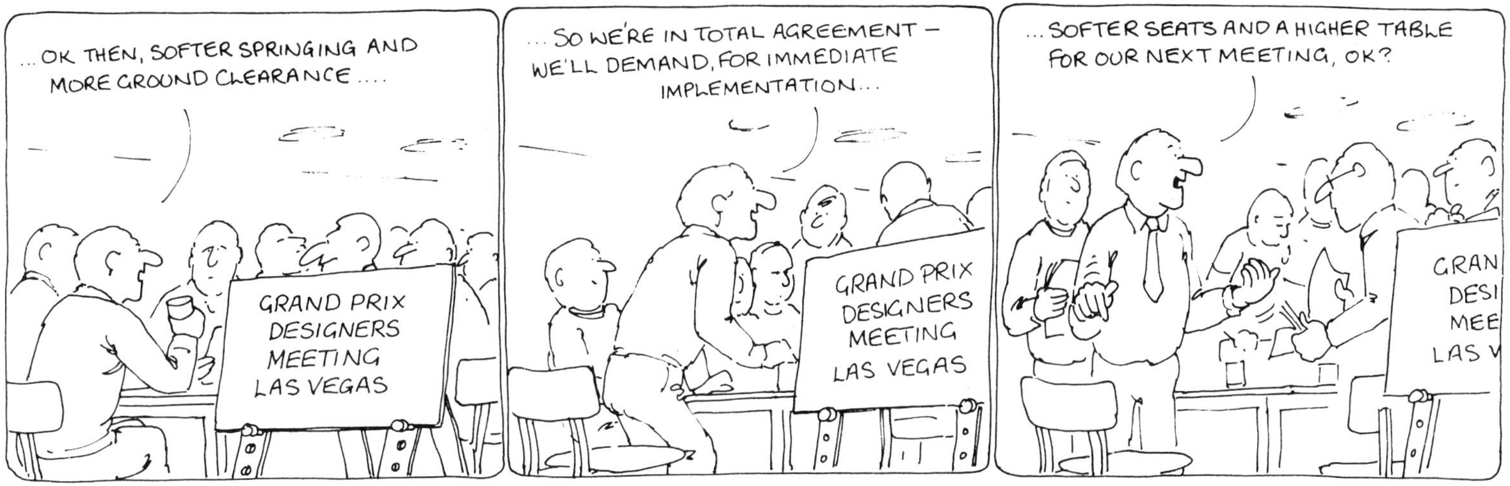
...OK THEN, SOFTER SPRINGING AND MORE GROUND CLEARANCE....
GRAND PRIX DESIGNERS MEETING LAS VEGAS
...SO WE'RE IN TOTAL AGREEMENT – WE'LL DEMAND, FOR IMMEDIATE IMPLEMENTATION...
GRAND PRIX DESIGNERS MEETING LAS VEGAS
...SOFTER SEATS AND A HIGHER TABLE FOR OUR NEXT MEETING, OK?

29th October 1981

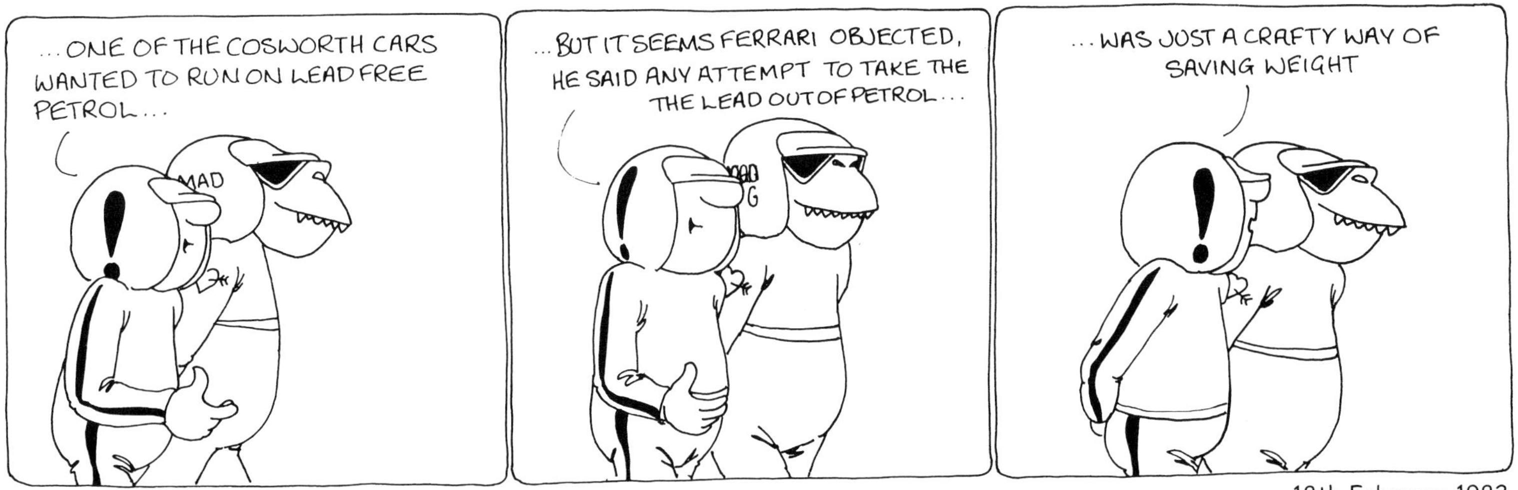
...ONE OF THE COSWORTH CARS WANTED TO RUN ON LEAD FREE PETROL...
...BUT IT SEEMS FERRARI OBJECTED, HE SAID ANY ATTEMPT TO TAKE THE THE LEAD OUT OF PETROL...
...WAS JUST A CRAFTY WAY OF SAVING WEIGHT

18th February 1982

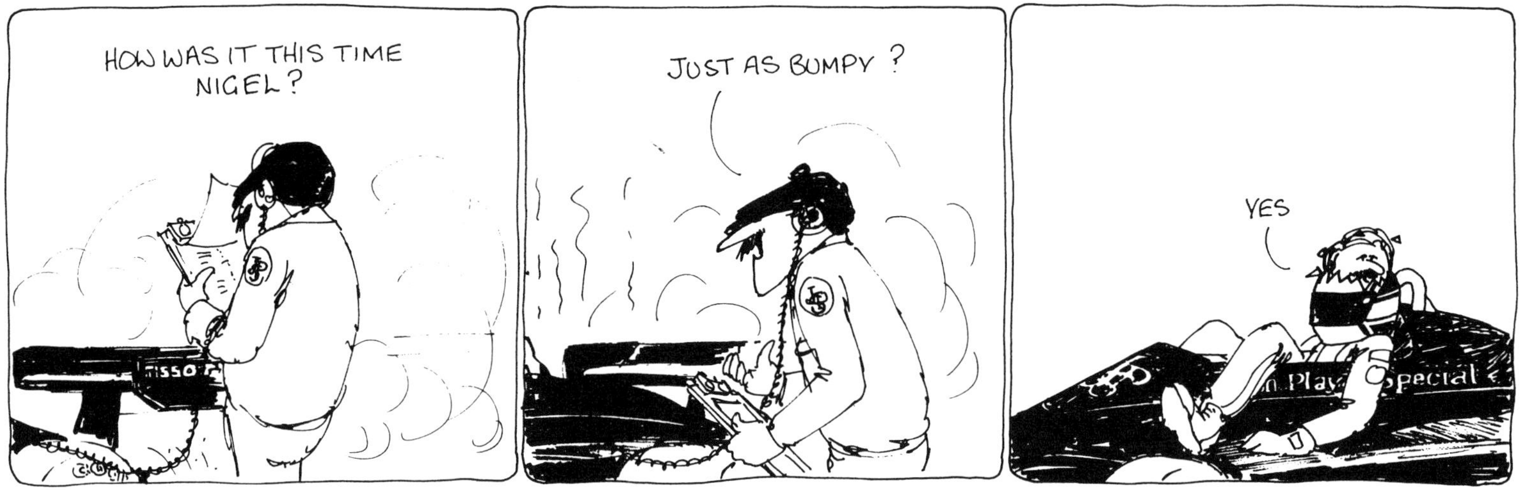
HOW WAS IT THIS TIME NIGEL?
JUST AS BUMPY?
YES

22nd April 1982

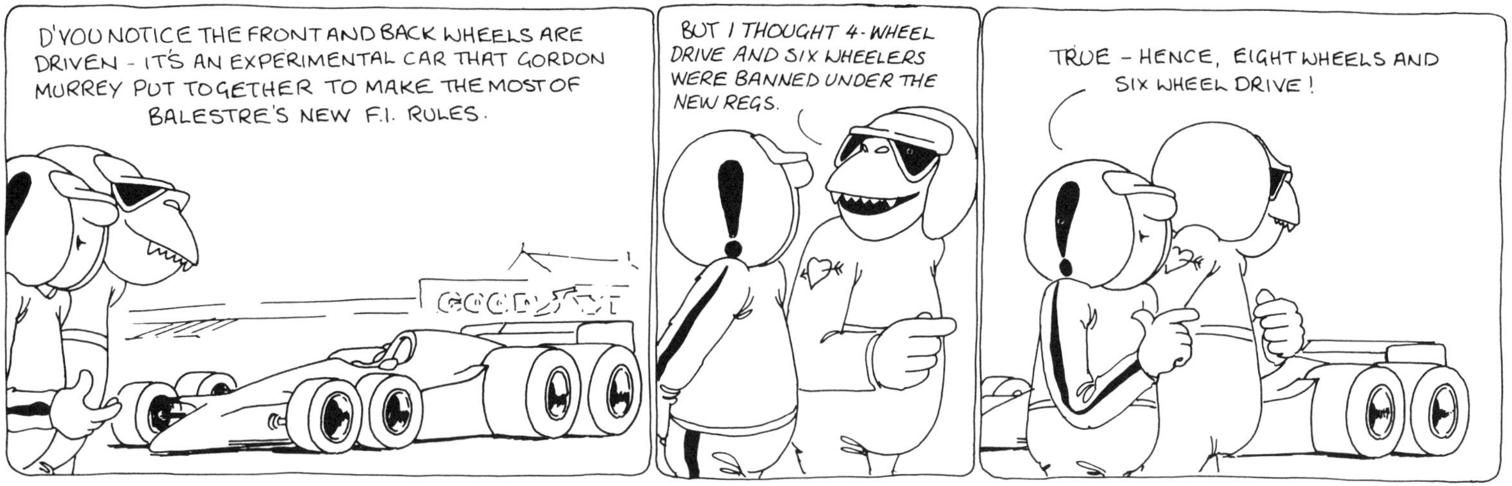
D'YOU NOTICE THE FRONT AND BACK WHEELS ARE DRIVEN - IT'S AN EXPERIMENTAL CAR THAT GORDON MURREY PUT TOGETHER TO MAKE THE MOST OF BALESTRE'S NEW F.I. RULES.
BUT I THOUGHT 4-WHEEL DRIVE AND SIX WHEELERS WERE BANNED UNDER THE NEW REGS.
TRUE - HENCE, EIGHT WHEELS AND SIX WHEEL DRIVE!

3rd June 1982

Chapter Thirteen

F1 Through The Years

FARTZ SPECIAL

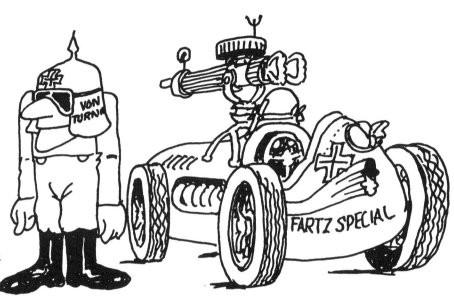

Grand Prix racing only goes back a short way, which is strange when you consider how old Bernie is. It makes you wonder what he did before motor racing was invented.

When Catchpole started names like Hill, Brabham, Stewart, Villeneuve, Lauda, Prost, Fittipaldi, Unser and Andretti were on everyone's lips. Now thirty years later they have all retired and it's Hill, Brabham, Stewart, Villeneuve, Lauda, Prost, Fittipaldi, Unser and Andretti who are current. But not all of them have the same christian names of course, and even some of the second lot like Hill 2 and Stewart 2 have now retired.

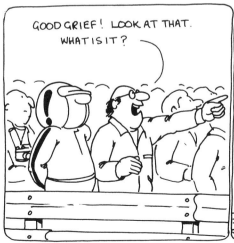

GOOD GRIEF! LOOK AT THAT. WHAT IS IT?
AH, THAT'S CHAPMAN'S ANSWER TO THE BRABHAM - IT FLIES AROUND INSTEAD OF SUCKING...
... HE SAYS IT'S LEGAL BECAUSE THE PROPELLER'S *PRIMARY FUNCTION* IS TO REDUCE TYRE WEAR, **NOT** TO FLY.

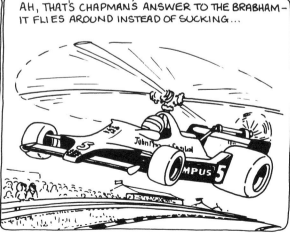

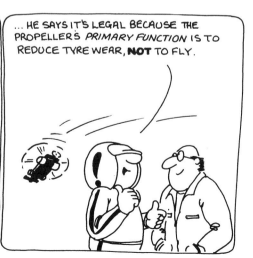

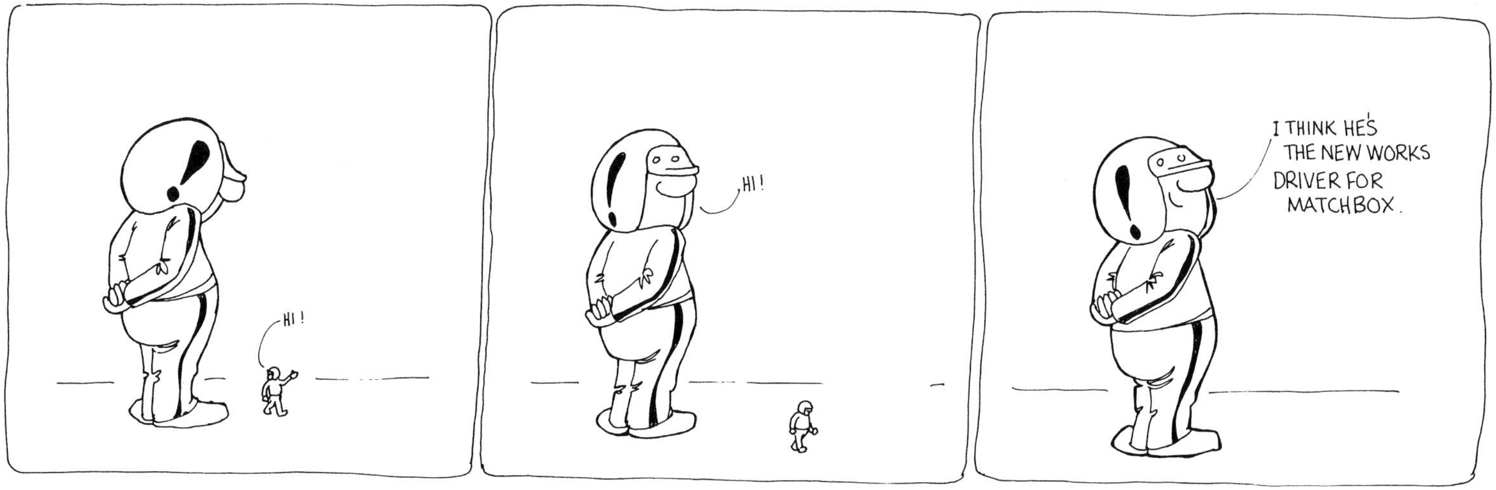
HI !
HI !
I THINK HE'S THE NEW WORKS DRIVER FOR MATCHBOX.

13th April 1972

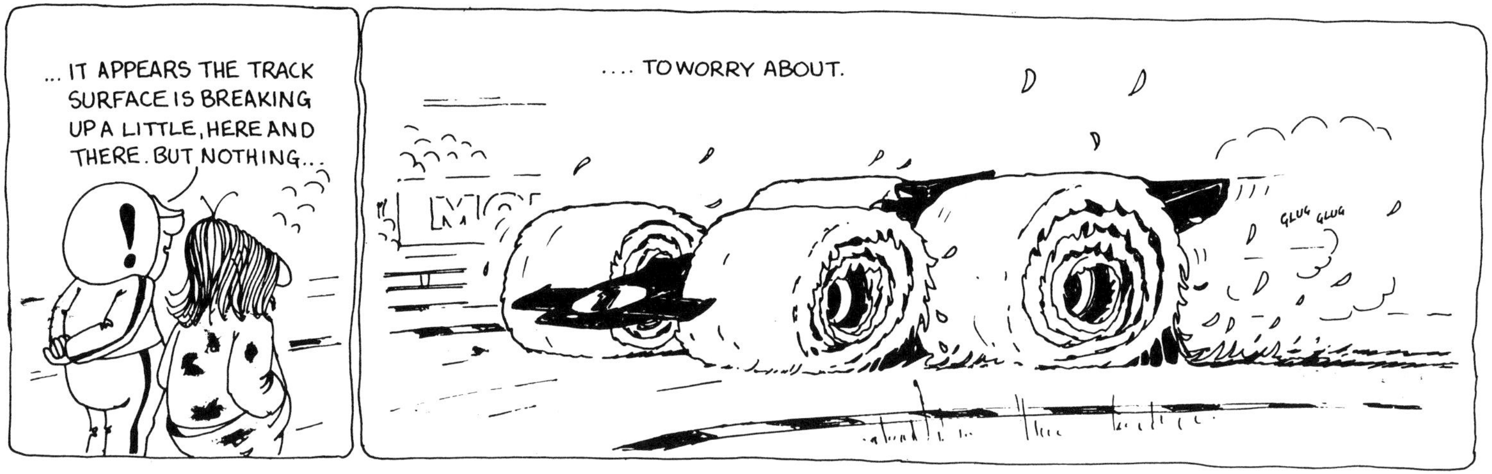
... IT APPEARS THE TRACK SURFACE IS BREAKING UP A LITTLE, HERE AND THERE. BUT NOTHING...
.... TO WORRY ABOUT.
GLUG GLUG

24th May 1973

Chapter Thirteen

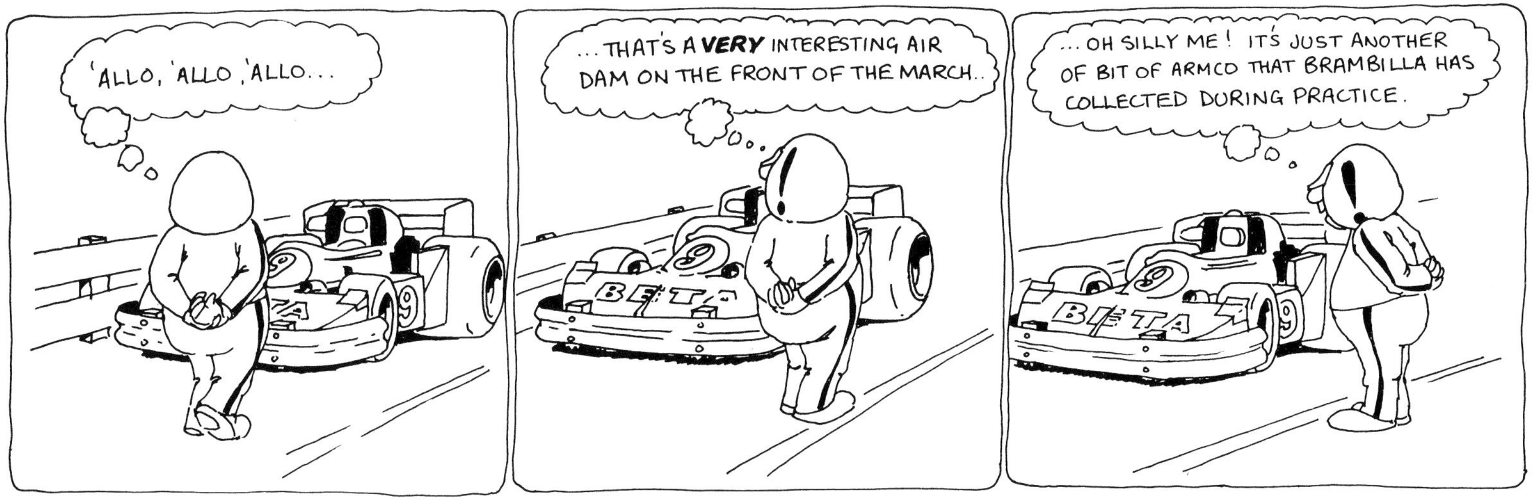
'ALLO, 'ALLO, 'ALLO...
...THAT'S A VERY INTERESTING AIR DAM ON THE FRONT OF THE MARCH..
...OH SILLY ME! IT'S JUST ANOTHER OF BIT OF ARMCO THAT BRAMBILLA HAS COLLECTED DURING PRACTICE.
BETA
9

27th May 1976

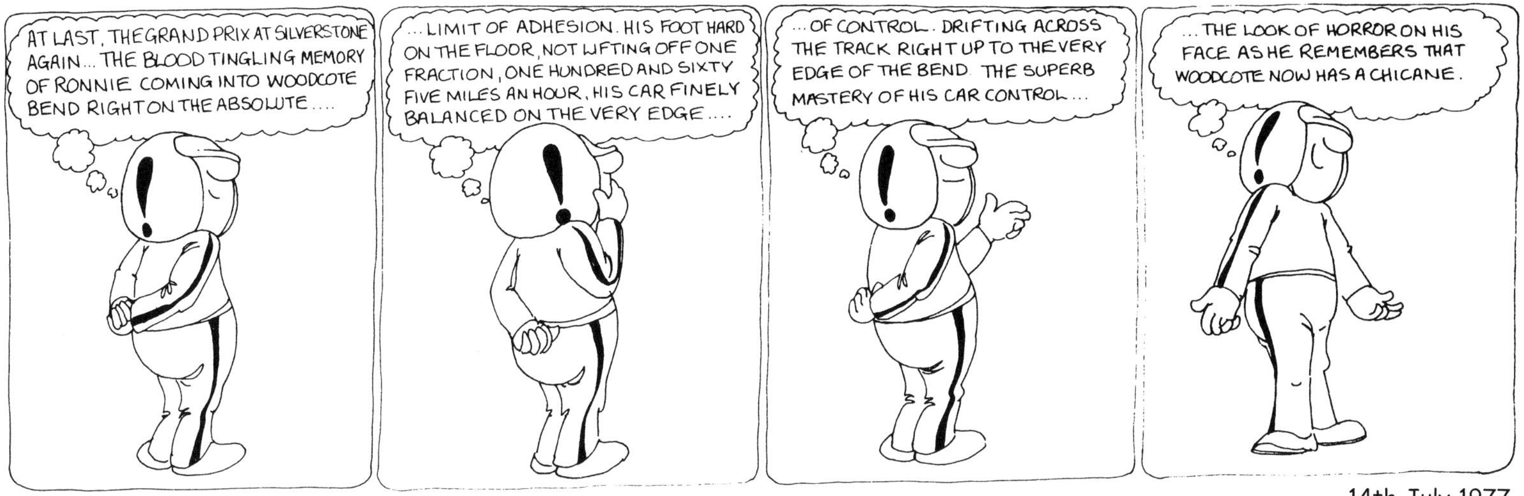
AT LAST, THE GRAND PRIX AT SILVERSTONE AGAIN... THE BLOOD TINGLING MEMORY OF RONNIE COMING INTO WOODCOTE BEND RIGHT ON THE ABSOLUTE....
...LIMIT OF ADHESION. HIS FOOT HARD ON THE FLOOR, NOT LIFTING OFF ONE FRACTION, ONE HUNDRED AND SIXTY FIVE MILES AN HOUR, HIS CAR FINELY BALANCED ON THE VERY EDGE....
...OF CONTROL. DRIFTING ACROSS THE TRACK RIGHT UP TO THE VERY EDGE OF THE BEND. THE SUPERB MASTERY OF HIS CAR CONTROL...
...THE LOOK OF HORROR ON HIS FACE AS HE REMEMBERS THAT WOODCOTE NOW HAS A CHICANE.

14th July 1977

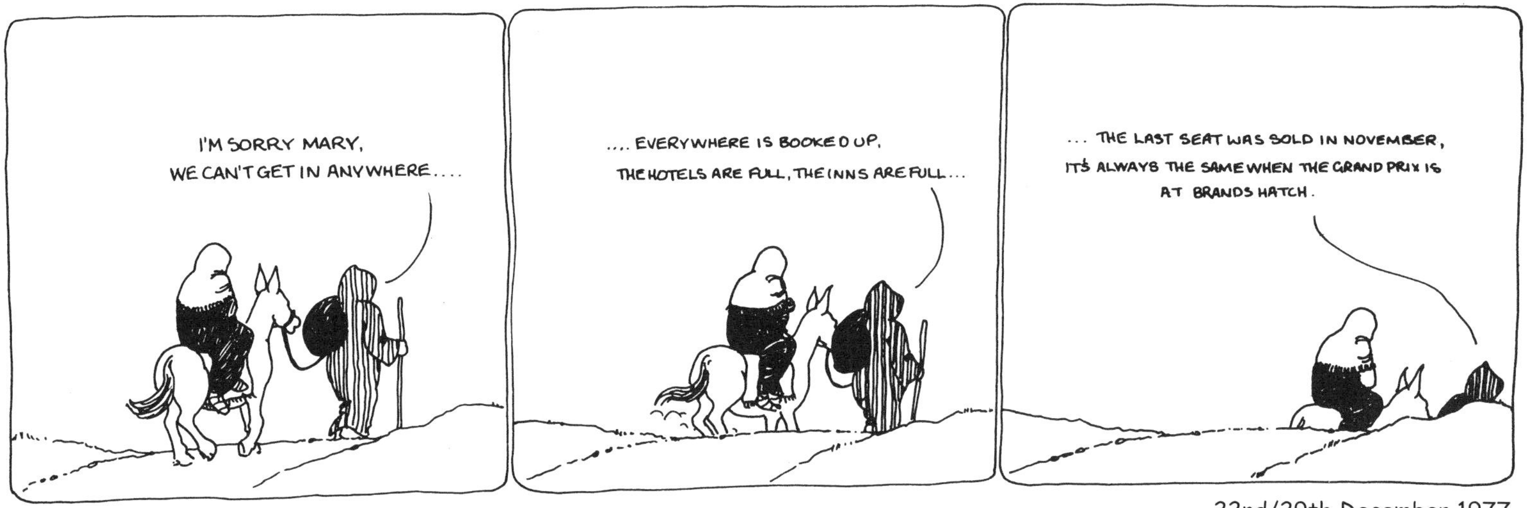
I'M SORRY MARY,
WE CAN'T GET IN ANYWHERE....
....EVERYWHERE IS BOOKED UP,
THE HOTELS ARE FULL, THE INNS ARE FULL...
... THE LAST SEAT WAS SOLD IN NOVEMBER,
IT'S ALWAYS THE SAME WHEN THE GRAND PRIX IS
AT BRANDS HATCH.

22nd/29th December 1977

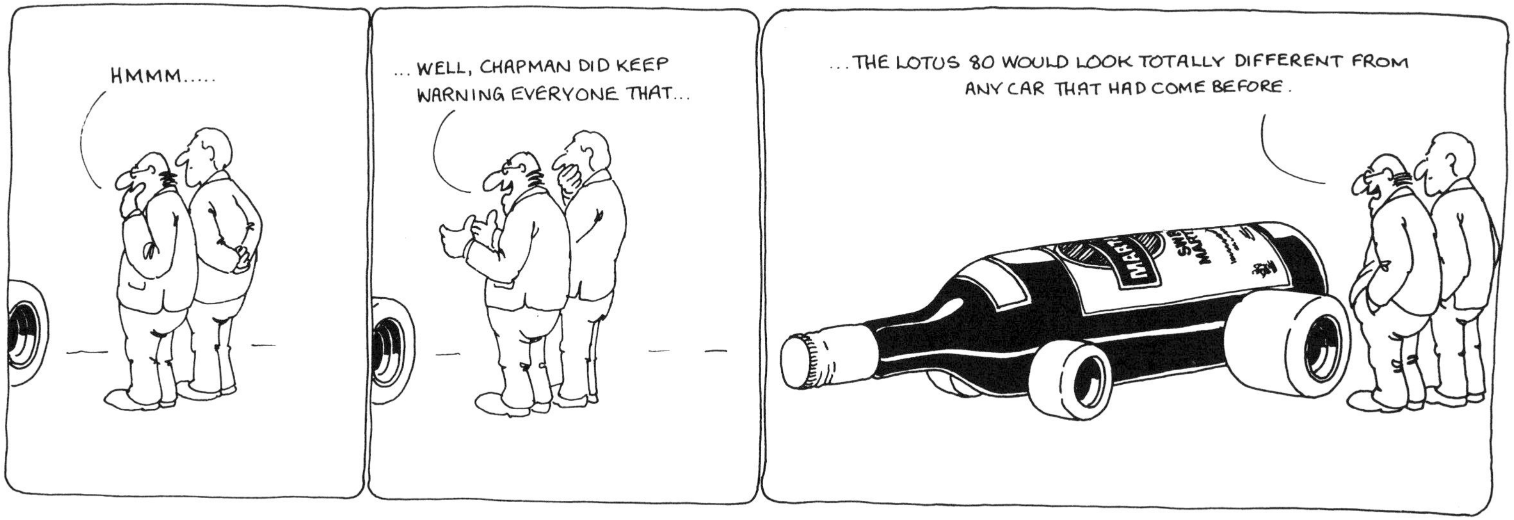
HMMM.....
...WELL, CHAPMAN DID KEEP
WARNING EVERYONE THAT...
...THE LOTUS 80 WOULD LOOK TOTALLY DIFFERENT FROM
ANY CAR THAT HAD COME BEFORE.

1st March 1979

Chapter Thirteen

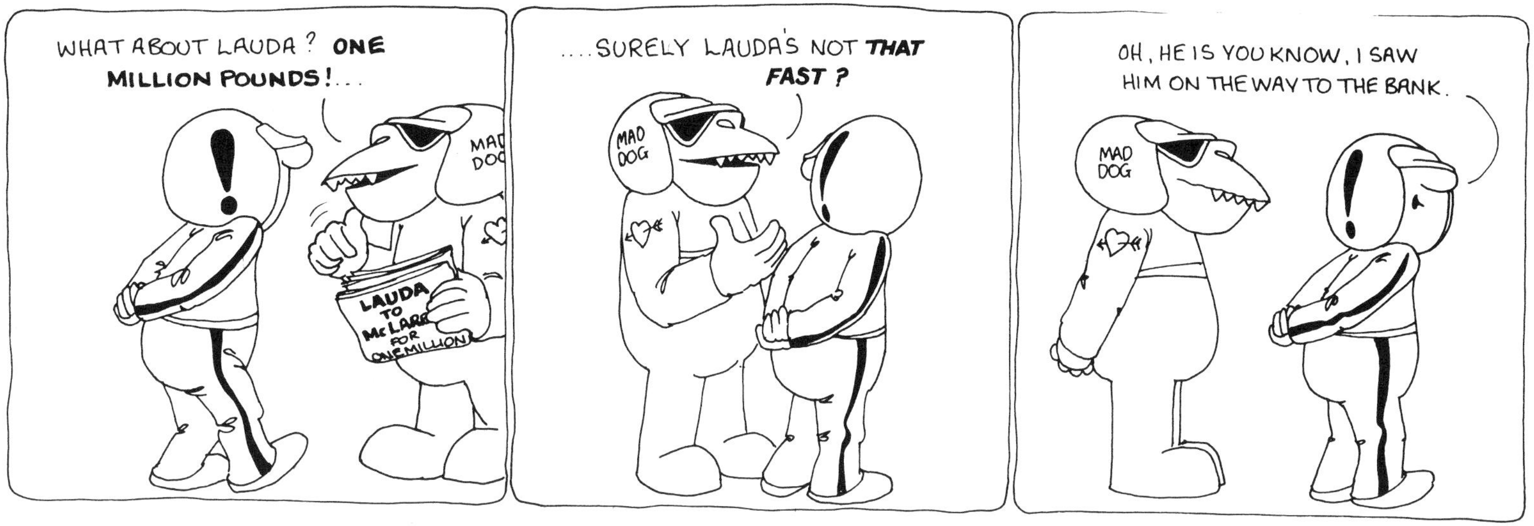
WHAT ABOUT LAUDA? ONE MILLION POUNDS!...
....SURELY LAUDA'S NOT THAT FAST?
MAD DOG
OH, HE IS YOU KNOW, I SAW HIM ON THE WAY TO THE BANK.
MAD DOG

16th August 1979

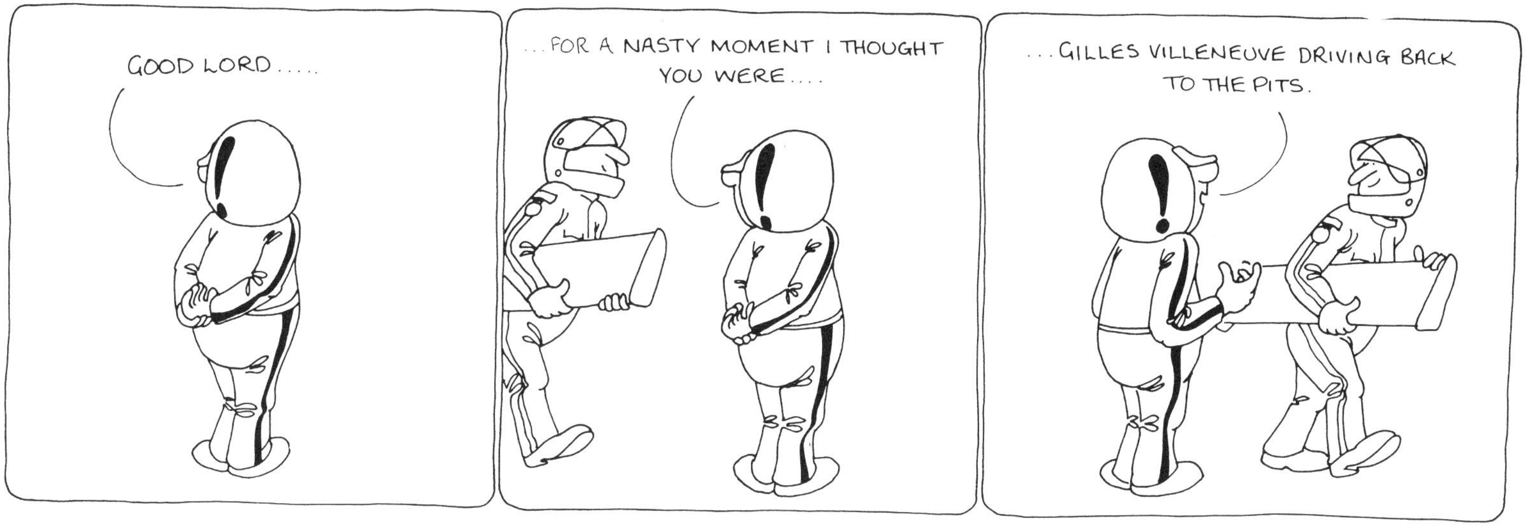
GOOD LORD.....
...FOR A NASTY MOMENT I THOUGHT YOU WERE....
...GILLES VILLENEUVE DRIVING BACK TO THE PITS.

30th August 1979

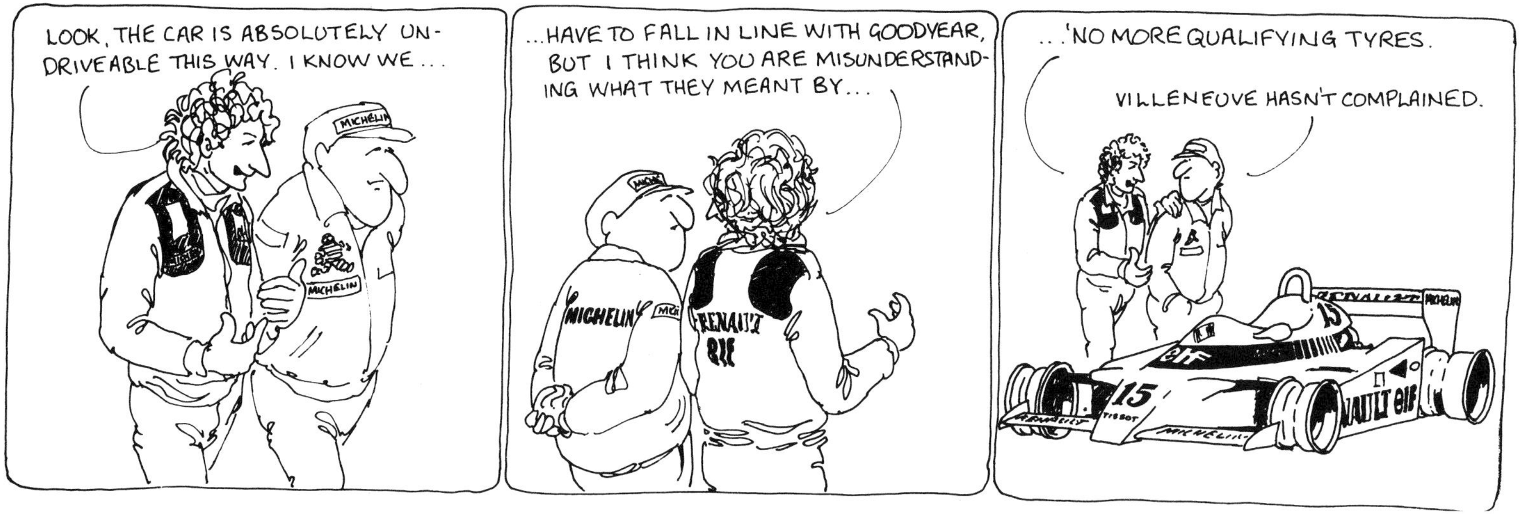
LOOK, THE CAR IS ABSOLUTELY UN-DRIVEABLE THIS WAY. I KNOW WE...
...HAVE TO FALL IN LINE WITH GOODYEAR, BUT I THINK YOU ARE MISUNDERSTANDING WHAT THEY MEANT BY...
...'NO MORE QUALIFYING TYRES.
VILLENEUVE HASN'T COMPLAINED.

14th February 1980

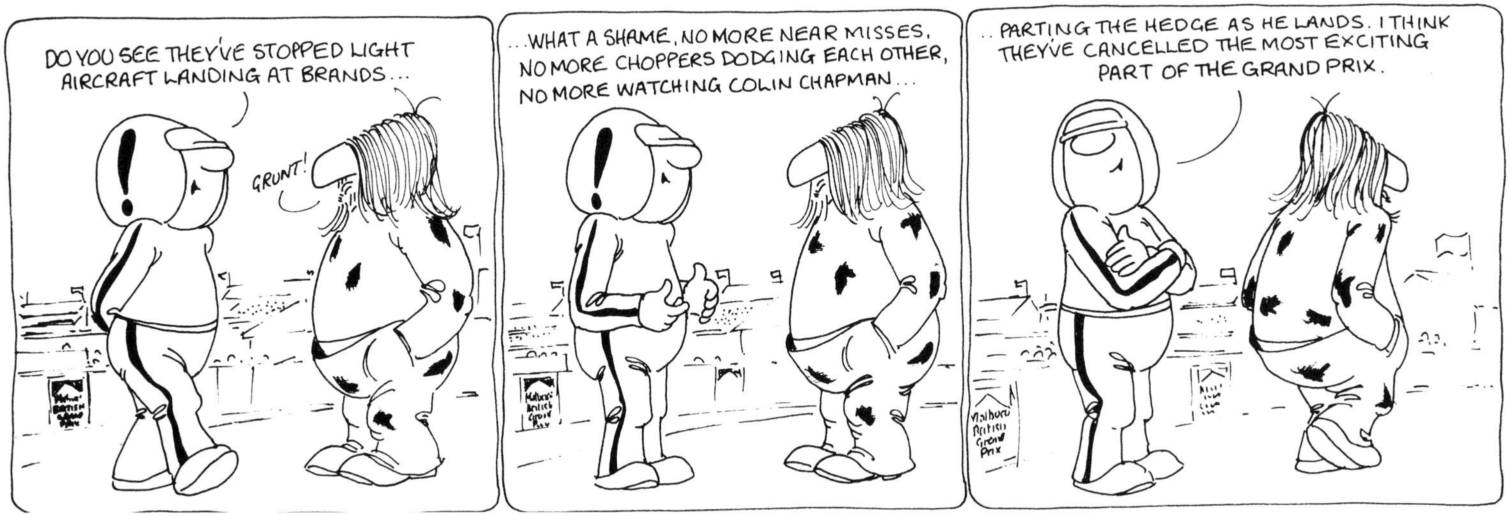
DO YOU SEE THEY'VE STOPPED LIGHT AIRCRAFT LANDING AT BRANDS...
GRUNT!
...WHAT A SHAME, NO MORE NEAR MISSES, NO MORE CHOPPERS DODGING EACH OTHER, NO MORE WATCHING COLIN CHAPMAN...
...PARTING THE HEDGE AS HE LANDS. I THINK THEY'VE CANCELLED THE MOST EXCITING PART OF THE GRAND PRIX.

10th June 1980

Chapter Thirteen

HEY - WHAT'S NIGELS HANDICAP AT THE MOMENT ?
MANSELL ENTERS AUSTRALIAN OPEN GOLF TOURNAMENT
EGO ?
FOLEY

24th September 1987

DID YOU SEE THIS BIT ABOUT THE PEOPLE OF MARANELLO CHANGING THE NAME OF THE TOWN TO FERRARI ?
MAD DOG
YES - COME TO THINK OF IT...
MAD DOG
...I SUPPOSE THAT'S HOW SILVERSTONE VILLAGE GOT ITS NAME.
MAD DOG
FOLEY

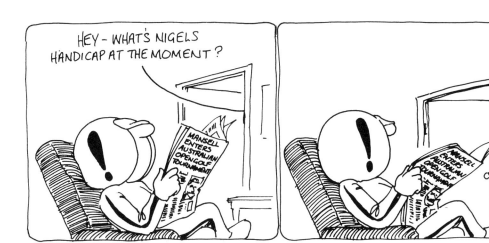

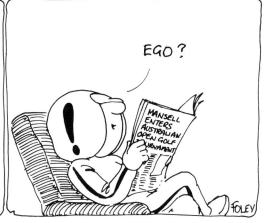

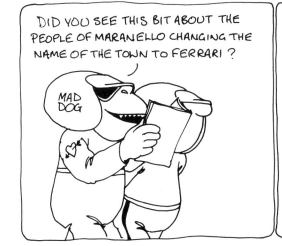

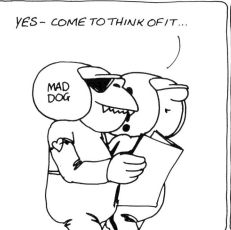

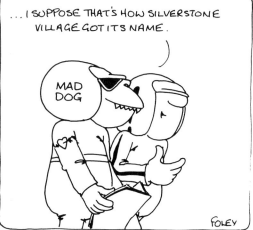

12th January 1989

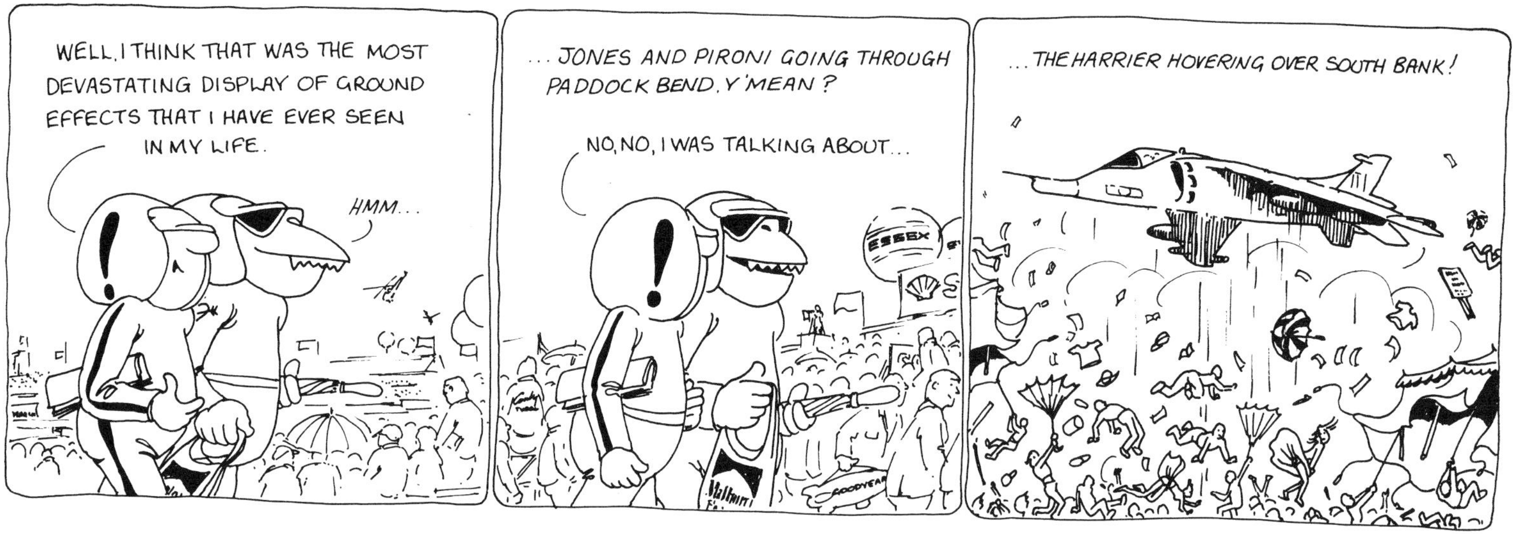
WELL, I THINK THAT WAS THE MOST DEVASTATING DISPLAY OF GROUND EFFECTS THAT I HAVE EVER SEEN IN MY LIFE.
HMM...
... JONES AND PIRONI GOING THROUGH PADDOCK BEND, Y'MEAN?
NO, NO, I WAS TALKING ABOUT...
ESSEX
... THE HARRIER HOVERING OVER SOUTH BANK!

17th July 1980

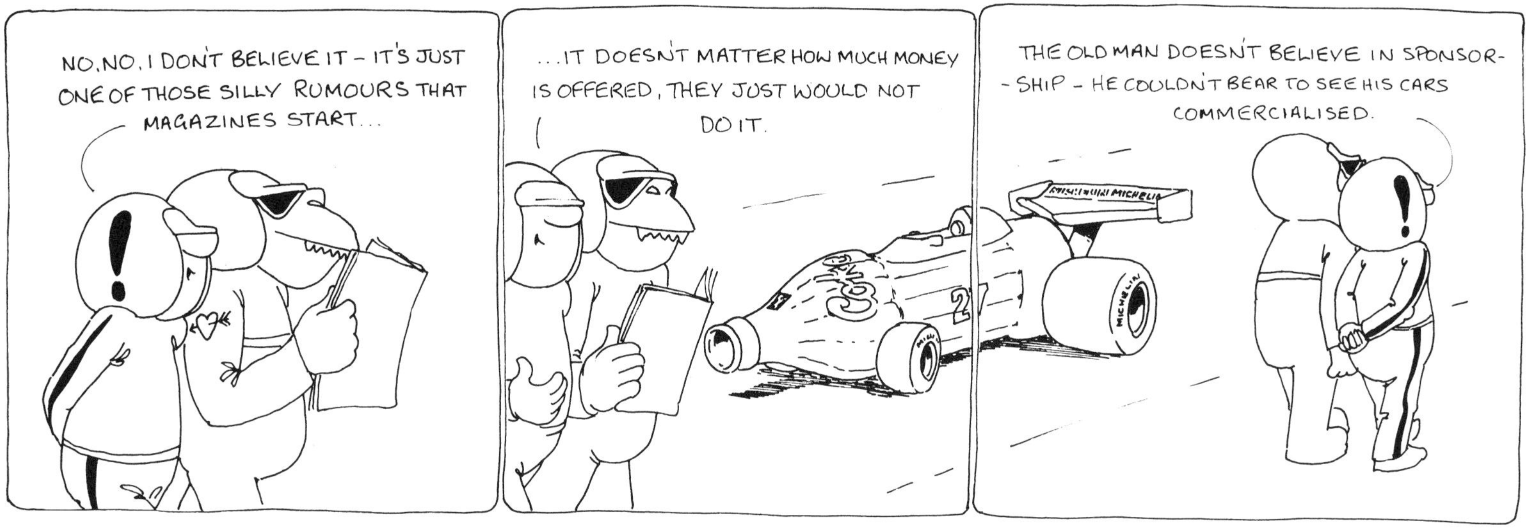
NO, NO, I DON'T BELIEVE IT – IT'S JUST ONE OF THOSE SILLY RUMOURS THAT MAGAZINES START...
... IT DOESN'T MATTER HOW MUCH MONEY IS OFFERED, THEY JUST WOULD NOT DO IT.
THE OLD MAN DOESN'T BELIEVE IN SPONSOR-SHIP – HE COULDN'T BEAR TO SEE HIS CARS COMMERCIALISED.

9th October 1980

Chapter Thirteen

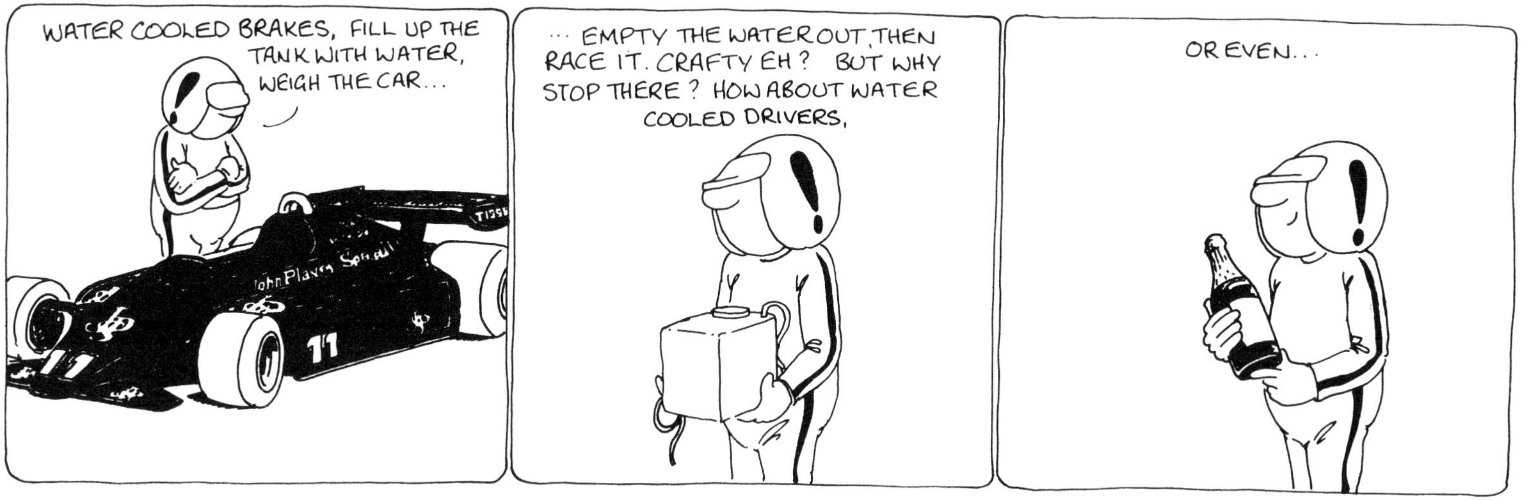
WATER COOLED BRAKES, FILL UP THE TANK WITH WATER, WEIGH THE CAR...
... EMPTY THE WATER OUT, THEN RACE IT. CRAFTY EH? BUT WHY STOP THERE? HOW ABOUT WATER COOLED DRIVERS,
OR EVEN...

25th February 1982

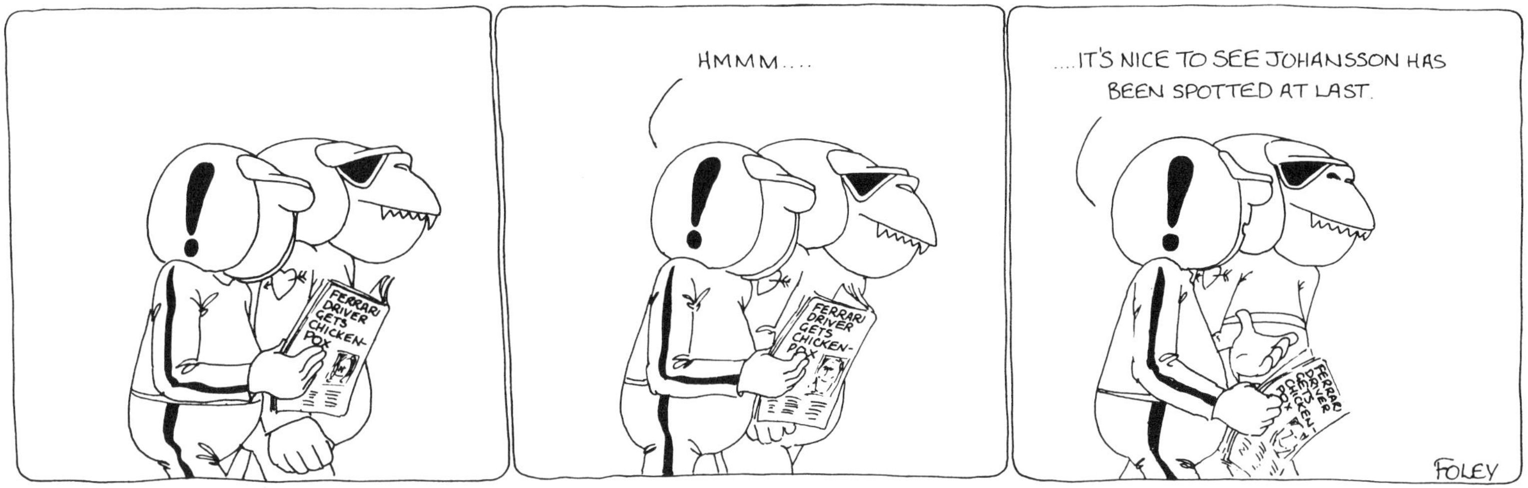
FERRARI DRIVER GETS CHICKEN-POX
HMMM....
....IT'S NICE TO SEE JOHANSSON HAS BEEN SPOTTED AT LAST.
FOLEY

11th July 1985

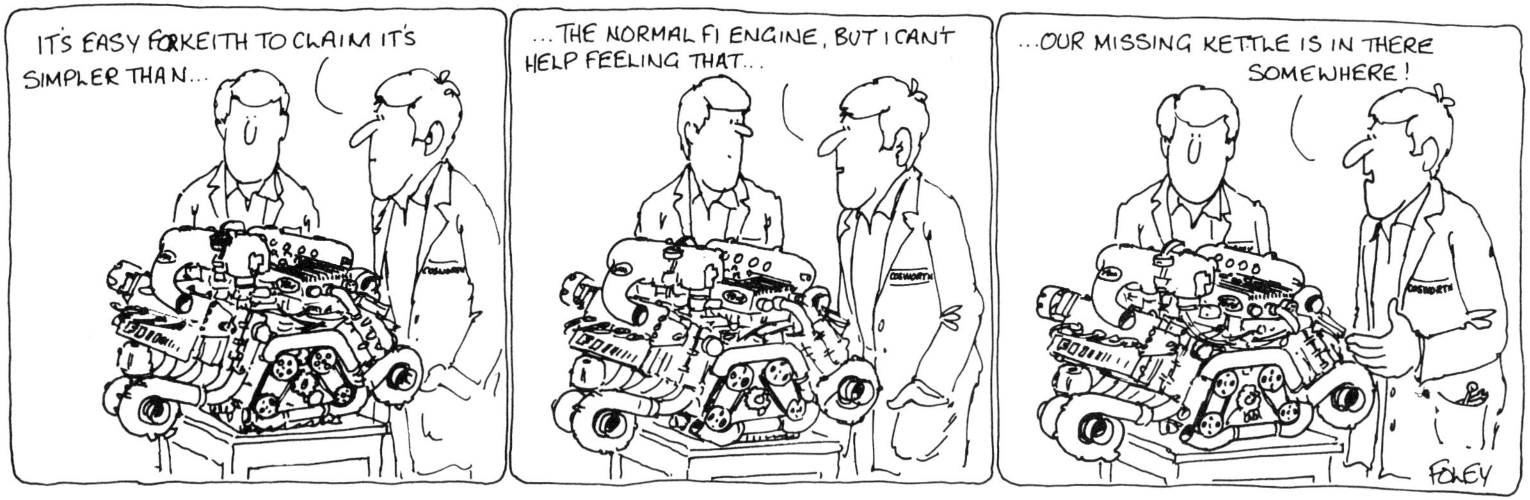
IT'S EASY FOR KEITH TO CLAIM IT'S SIMPLER THAN...
...THE NORMAL F1 ENGINE, BUT I CAN'T HELP FEELING THAT...
...OUR MISSING KETTLE IS IN THERE SOMEWHERE!
FOLEY

13th March 1986

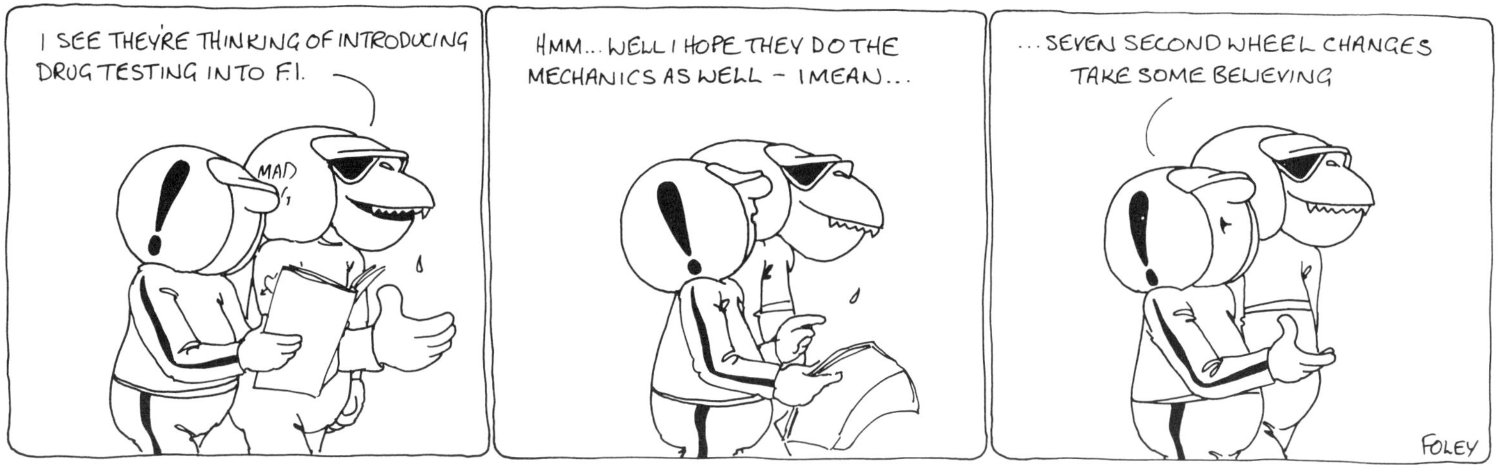
I SEE THEY'RE THINKING OF INTRODUCING DRUG TESTING INTO F.1.
MAD
HMM... WELL I HOPE THEY DO THE MECHANICS AS WELL - I MEAN...
...SEVEN SECOND WHEEL CHANGES TAKE SOME BELIEVING
FOLEY

10th September 1987

Chapter Thirteen

WHAT WENT WRONG NIGEL?
NIGEL
WELL, IT WAS GOING NICELY - I HAD IT FLAT IN TOP GEAR, WHEN I PUSHED THE WRONG BUTTON AND...
NIGEL
...IT CHANGED DOWN INTO FIRST!
FOLEY

26th January 1989

WHO DO YOU THINK WILL GET THE CAMEL SPONSORSHIP NEXT YEAR? - THEY SAY IT'S WORTH FIVE MILLION.
MAD DOG
PROST!
PROST?
MAD DOG
YEH, - I HEARD RON DENNIS SAYING THAT BY THE END OF THE SEASON PROST WILL HAVE THE HUMP.
MAD DOG
FOLEY

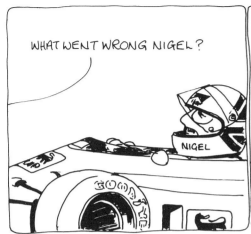

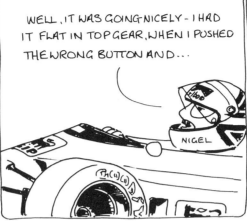

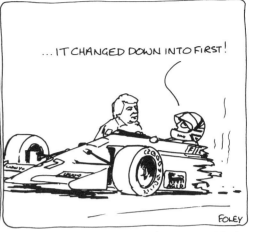

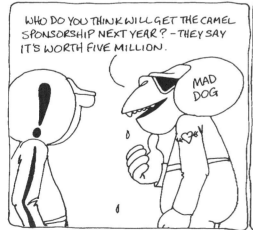

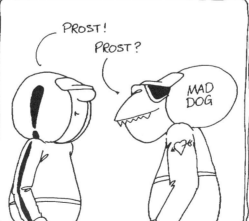

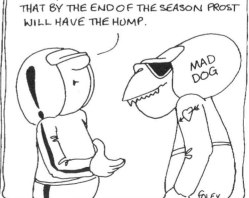

31st August 1989

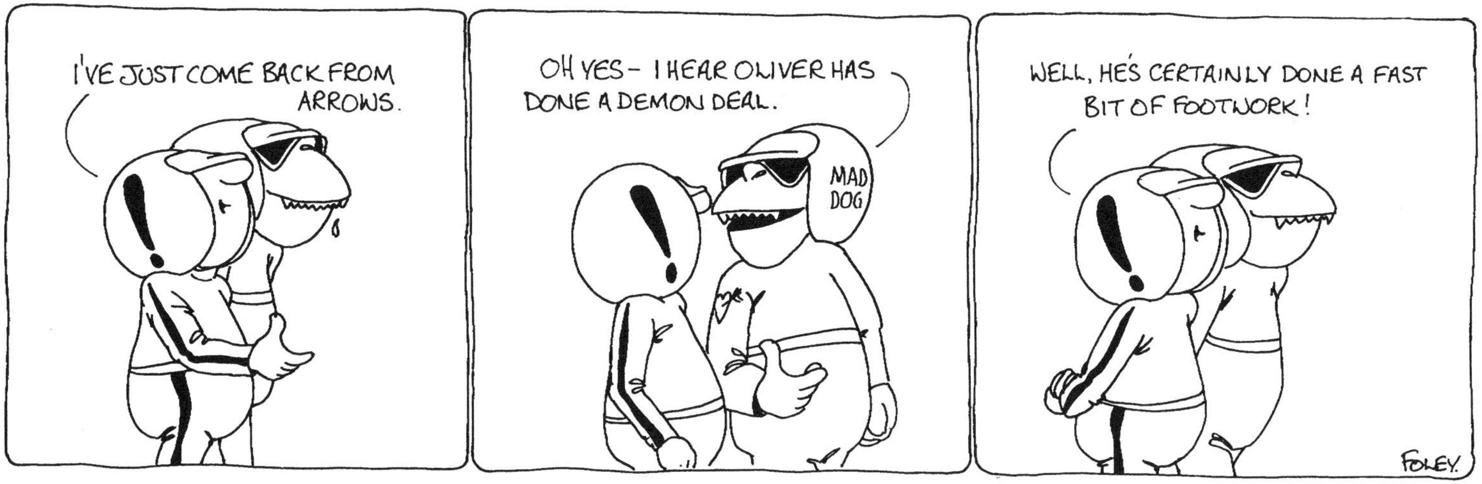
I'VE JUST COME BACK FROM ARROWS.
OH YES - I HEAR OLIVER HAS DONE A DEMON DEAL.
MAD DOG
WELL, HE'S CERTAINLY DONE A FAST BIT OF FOOTWORK!
FOLEY

2nd November 1989

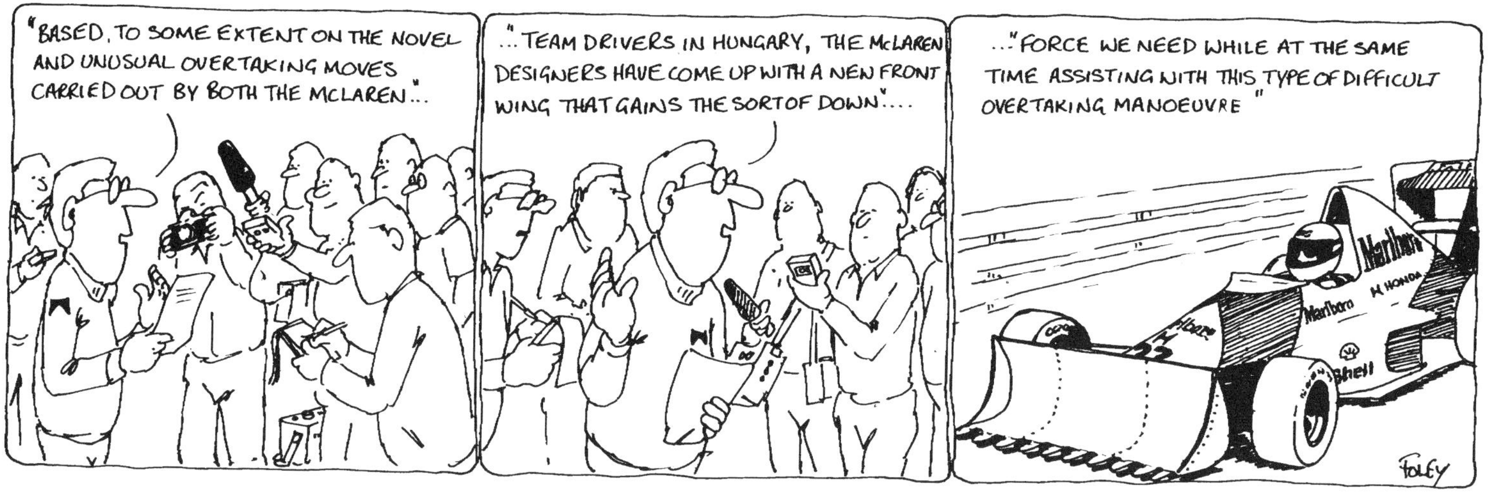
"BASED, TO SOME EXTENT ON THE NOVEL AND UNUSUAL OVERTAKING MOVES CARRIED OUT BY BOTH THE MCLAREN"...
..."TEAM DRIVERS IN HUNGARY, THE McLAREN DESIGNERS HAVE COME UP WITH A NEW FRONT WING THAT GAINS THE SORT OF DOWN"...
..."FORCE WE NEED WHILE AT THE SAME TIME ASSISTING WITH THIS TYPE OF DIFFICULT OVERTAKING MANOEUVRE"
Marlboro
HONDA
Shell
FOLEY

16th August 1990

Chapter Thirteen

LOOK JEAN, YOU'VE GOT TO DECIDE, WHY DON'T YOU JUST SPIN A COIN IF YOU CAN'T MAKE UP YOUR MIND...
EDDIE JORDAN DRIVER MANAGEMENT
...JUST FLIP THE COIN IN THE AIR, IF IT LANDS HEADS UP - YOU DRIVE FOR FERRARI, IF IT LANDS TAILS UP, ITS WILLIAMS...
....AND IF IT STANDS ON IT'S EDGE - YOU STAY AT TYRRELL !
FOLEY

13th September 1990

I DON'T THINK IT WOULD NEED A LOT MORE TO MAKE HIM CHANGE HIS MIND - HE'S NOT WORRIED ABOUT FINANCIAL SECURITY, BUT HE IS AFFECTED BY WHAT PEOPLE THINK - HE'S VERY SWAYED BY ALL THE THOUSANDS OF FANS PLEADING FOR HIM TO CARRY ON RACING....
MANSELL RETIREMENT
... HE'S ALSO SWAYED BY THE HUGE MEDIA SUPPORT AND AFFECTION HE'S GETTING, AND HE'S BEING SEDUCED BY OFFERS OF A REALLY GOOD SINGLEMINDED SHOT AT THE WORLD CHAMPIONSHIP - ALL IT NEEDS NOW IS FOR SOME SMALL, INSIGNIFICANT FACTOR TO TIP THE SCALES, JUST SOME TINY LITTLE THING TO CHANGE HIS MIND.
HMM, DO YOU FEEL THAT SEVEN MILLION COULD POSSIBLY BE **SMALL** ENOUGH TO DO IT ?
FOLEY

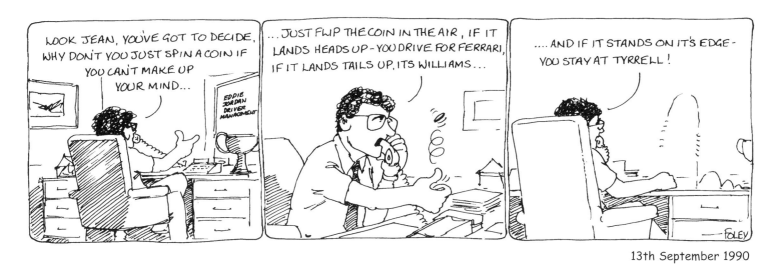

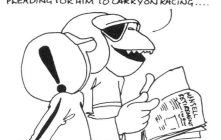

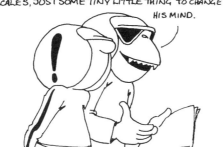

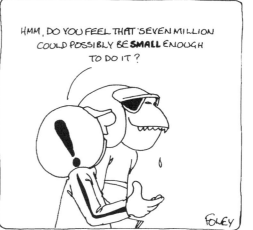

27th September 1990

I JUST PUT A FIVER INTO THE COLLECTION THE GRANDPRIX PEOPLE ARE TAKING UP FOR DE CESARIS'S LEAVING PRESENT.
GOOD LORD - IS HE RETIRING AT LAST?
NO - BUT THEY LIVE IN HOPE.
FOLEY

11th October 1990

WHAT'S ALL THIS I HEAR ABOUT FUJI COMING INTO F1?
YES - EVERYONES ZOOMING IN ON THEM - THEY'RE ALL HAVING A SHOT AT IT.
HMM... I CAN JUST PICTURE IT - AND I BET EDDIE'S CLICKED WITH THEM.
MAD DOG
YER - I'M SURE HE'LL SNAP IT UP!
MAD DOG
FOLEY

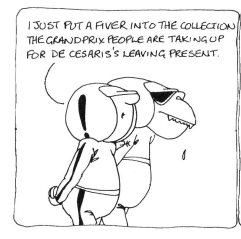

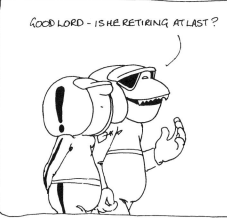

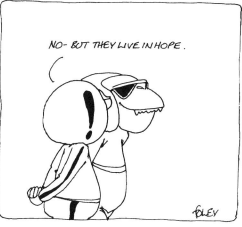

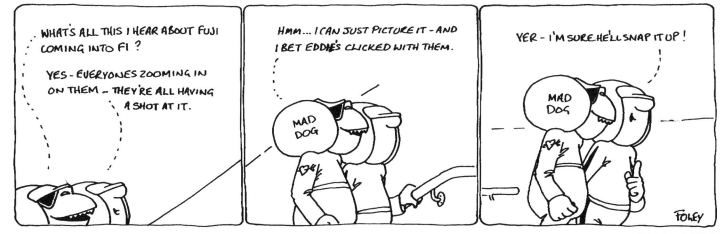

4th April 1991

Chapter Thirteen

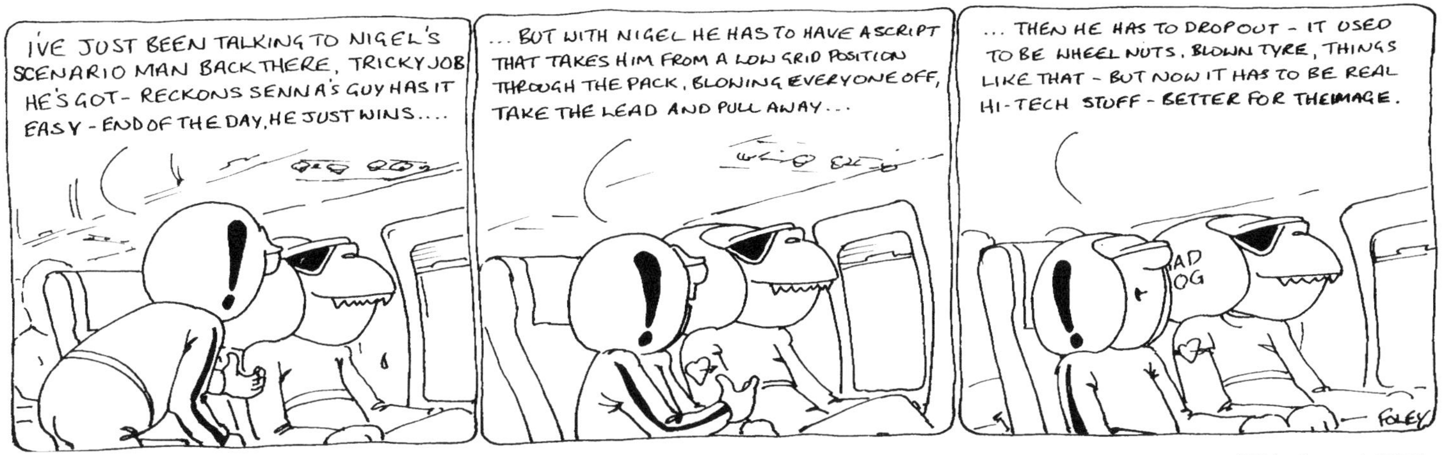
I'VE JUST BEEN TALKING TO NIGEL'S SCENARIO MAN BACK THERE, TRICKY JOB HE'S GOT - RECKONS SENNA'S GUY HAS IT EASY - END OF THE DAY, HE JUST WINS....
... BUT WITH NIGEL HE HAS TO HAVE A SCRIPT THAT TAKES HIM FROM A LOW GRID POSITION THROUGH THE PACK, BLOWING EVERYONE OFF, TAKE THE LEAD AND PULL AWAY...
... THEN HE HAS TO DROPOUT - IT USED TO BE WHEEL NUTS, BLOWN TYRE, THINGS LIKE THAT - BUT NOW IT HAS TO BE REAL HI-TECH STUFF - BETTER FOR THE IMAGE.
FOLEY

15th August 1991

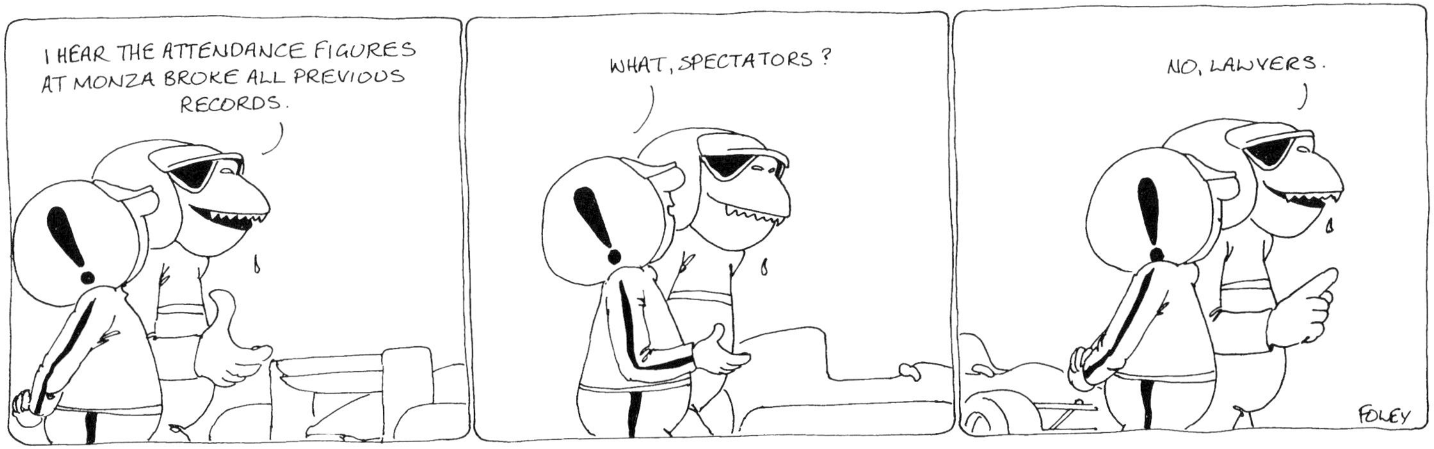
I HEAR THE ATTENDANCE FIGURES AT MONZA BROKE ALL PREVIOUS RECORDS.
WHAT, SPECTATORS?
NO, LAWYERS.
FOLEY

12th September 1991

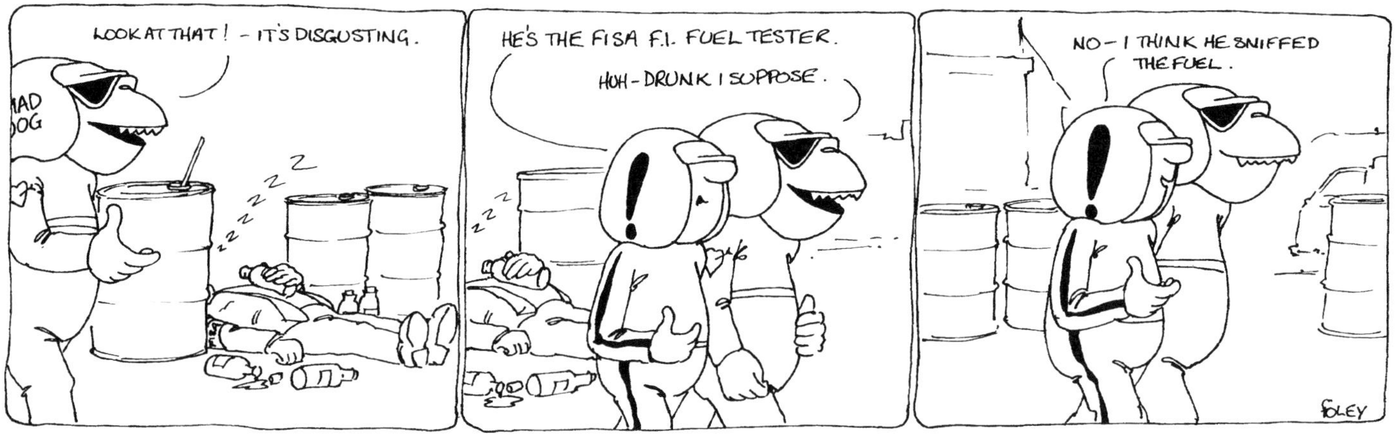
LOOK AT THAT! - IT'S DISGUSTING.
MAD DOG
HE'S THE FISA F.1. FUEL TESTER.
HUH - DRUNK I SUPPOSE.
NO - I THINK HE SNIFFED THE FUEL.
FOLEY

13th August 1992

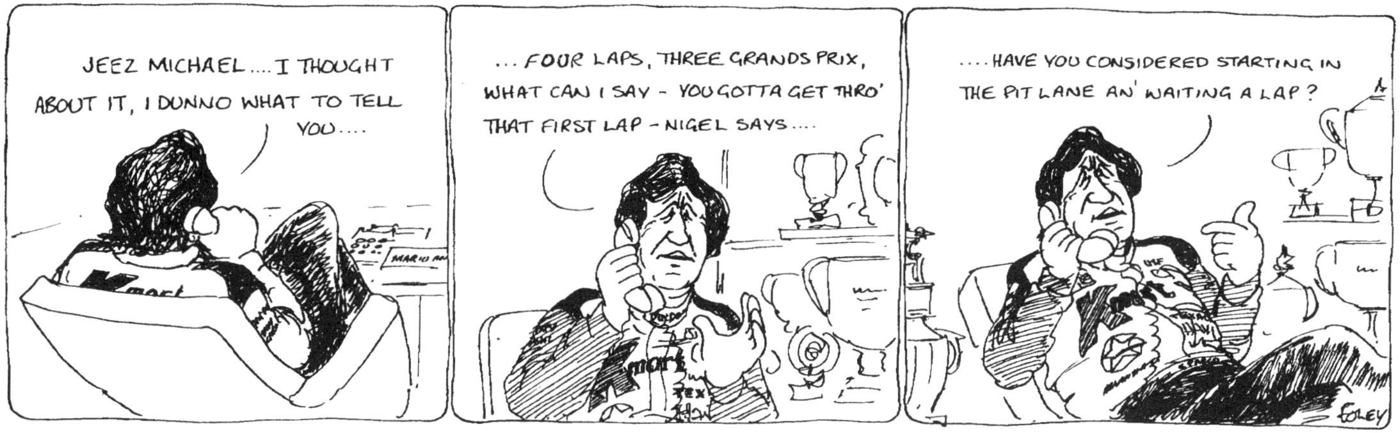
JEEZ MICHAEL.... I THOUGHT ABOUT IT, I DUNNO WHAT TO TELL YOU....
... FOUR LAPS, THREE GRANDS PRIX, WHAT CAN I SAY - YOU GOTTA GET THRO' THAT FIRST LAP - NIGEL SAYS....
.... HAVE YOU CONSIDERED STARTING IN THE PIT LANE AN' WAITING A LAP?
FOLEY

15th April 1993

Chapter Thirteen

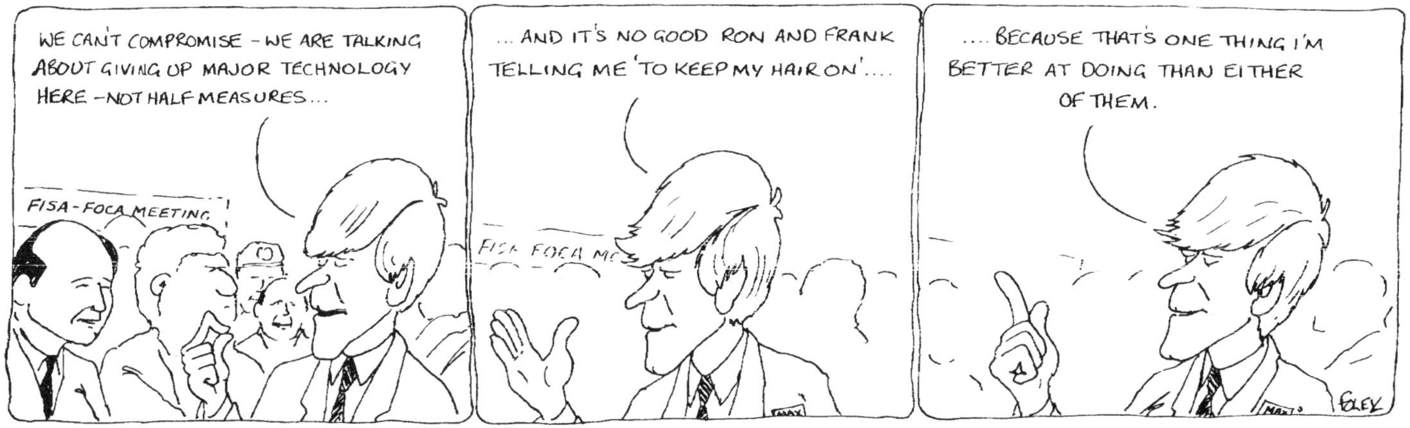
WE CAN'T COMPROMISE – WE ARE TALKING ABOUT GIVING UP MAJOR TECHNOLOGY HERE – NOT HALF MEASURES...
FISA-FOCA MEETING
... AND IT'S NO GOOD RON AND FRANK TELLING ME 'TO KEEP MY HAIR ON'....
.... BECAUSE THAT'S ONE THING I'M BETTER AT DOING THAN EITHER OF THEM.
FOLEY

13th May 1993

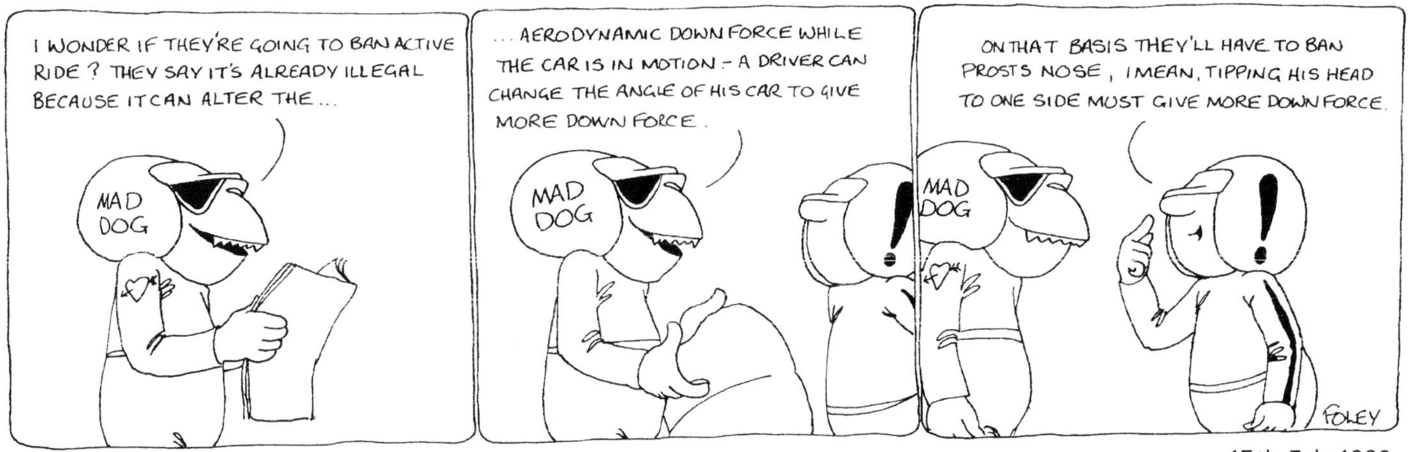
I WONDER IF THEY'RE GOING TO BAN ACTIVE RIDE? THEY SAY IT'S ALREADY ILLEGAL BECAUSE IT CAN ALTER THE...
MAD DOG
... AERODYNAMIC DOWN FORCE WHILE THE CAR IS IN MOTION – A DRIVER CAN CHANGE THE ANGLE OF HIS CAR TO GIVE MORE DOWN FORCE.
ON THAT BASIS THEY'LL HAVE TO BAN PROST'S NOSE, I MEAN, TIPPING HIS HEAD TO ONE SIDE MUST GIVE MORE DOWN FORCE.
FOLEY

15th July 1993

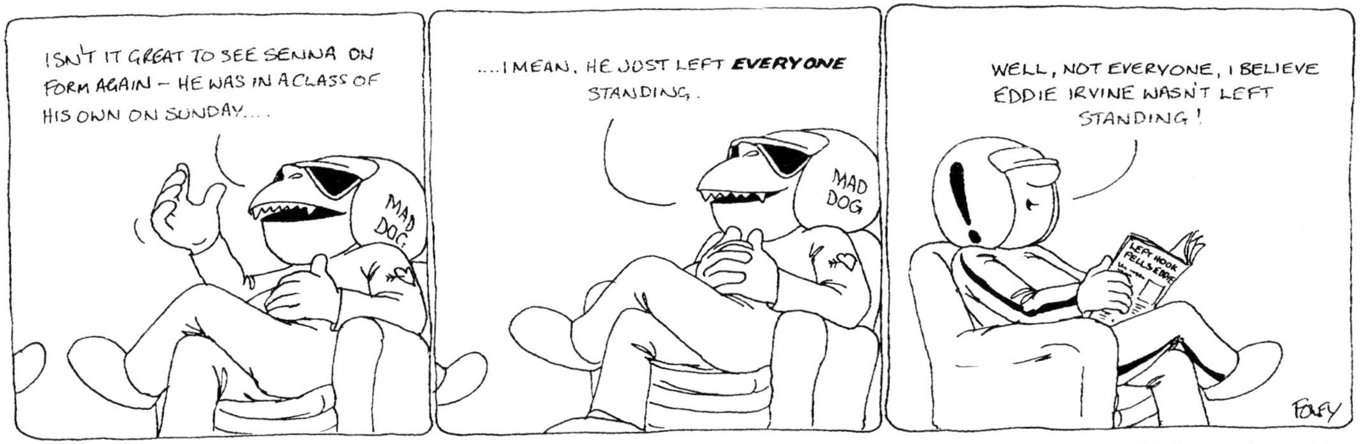
ISN'T IT GREAT TO SEE SENNA ON FORM AGAIN – HE WAS IN A CLASS OF HIS OWN ON SUNDAY....
MAD DOG
...I MEAN, HE JUST LEFT **EVERYONE** STANDING.
MAD DOG
WELL, NOT EVERYONE, I BELIEVE EDDIE IRVINE WASN'T LEFT STANDING!
LEFT HOOK FELLS EDDIE
FOLEY

28th October 1993

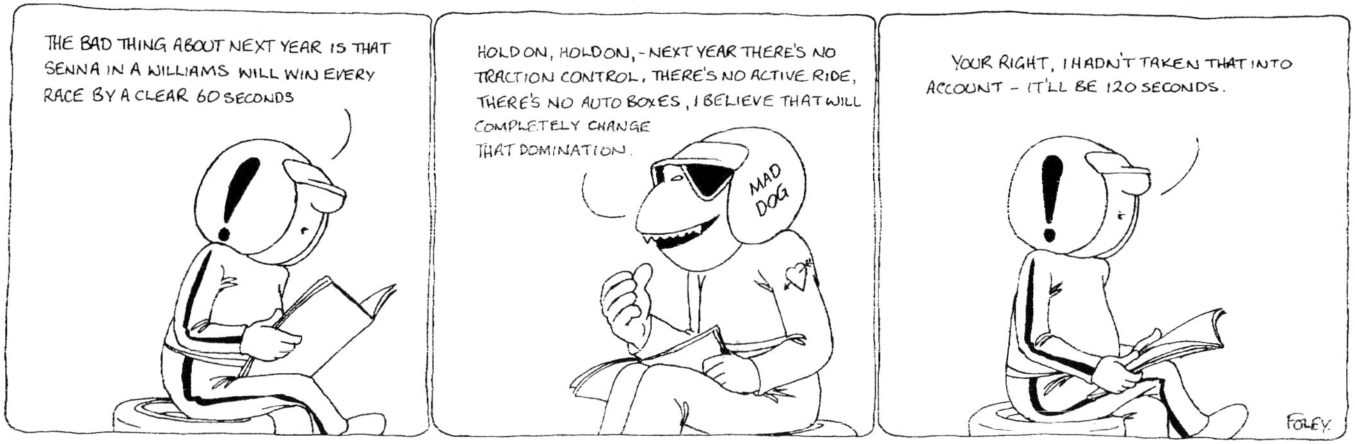
THE BAD THING ABOUT NEXT YEAR IS THAT SENNA IN A WILLIAMS WILL WIN EVERY RACE BY A CLEAR 60 SECONDS
HOLD ON, HOLD ON, - NEXT YEAR THERE'S NO TRACTION CONTROL, THERE'S NO ACTIVE RIDE, THERE'S NO AUTO BOXES, I BELIEVE THAT WILL COMPLETELY CHANGE THAT DOMINATION.
MAD DOG
YOUR RIGHT, I HADN'T TAKEN THAT INTO ACCOUNT – IT'LL BE 120 SECONDS.
FOLEY

18th November 1993

TV Stuff

TV has changed things. The funny thing about television is that F1 and rallying are only any good on TV, whereas other forms of motor racing are only any good if they're not. Club racing tends to be stiff and boring when televised. That of course doesn't matter - no one watches it. It's only there to please the sponsors. In fact they wouldn't have sponsors if it wasn't televised. The racers need the sponsors to pay for their racing. The TV people need the sponsors to pay for the filming. The sponsors need the TV to justify the expenditure.

BOOM-BOOM!

AH. HELLO BERNIE - I'M SORRY, WE BLEW IT. AS YOU KNOW WE HAD THIS NEW CHAP WRITING THE SCREEN PLAY - WE FIRED THE LAST GUY -

B.B.C. PROGRAMME PLANNING

BECAUSE HE KEPT USING THAT OLD MCLAREN SCRIPT OVER AND OVER AGAIN - SO WE TRIED OUT THIS NEW CHAP IN ESTORIL AND EVERY ONE SEEMED TO LIKE HIS 'SENNA IN THE ...

.. RAIN' SCRIPT, SO WE GAVE HIM HIS HEAD IN ITALY, BUT I'D NO IDEA HE WAS GOING TO PULL ALL OF THIS RUNNING OUT OF PETROL RUBBISH AND HE'D HAVE BEEN BACK IN THE PROST RUT IF WE HADN'T STEPPED IN AND ...

FOLEY.

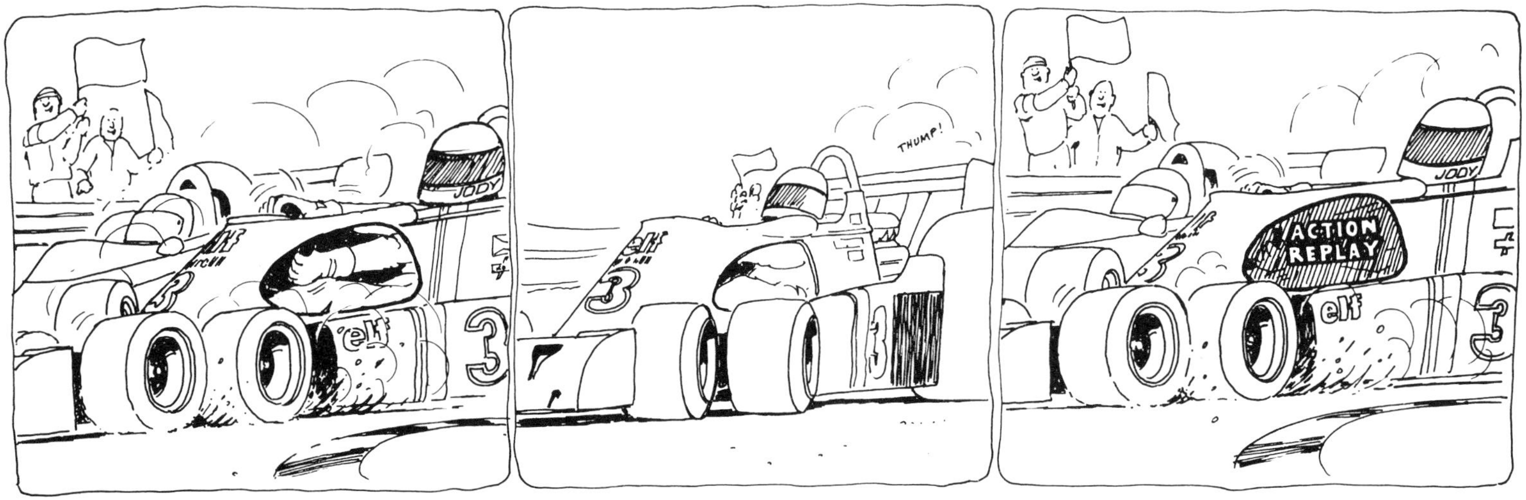
JODY
THUMP!
ACTION REPLAY

29th July 1976

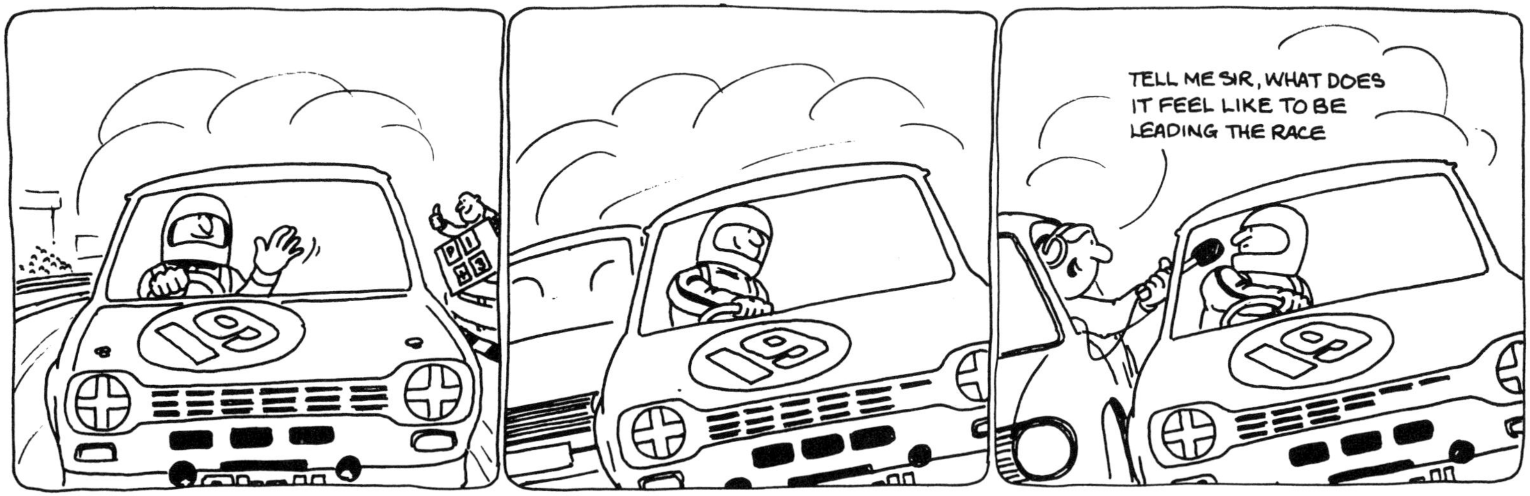
TELL ME SIR, WHAT DOES IT FEEL LIKE TO BE LEADING THE RACE

12th January 1978

Chapter Fourteen

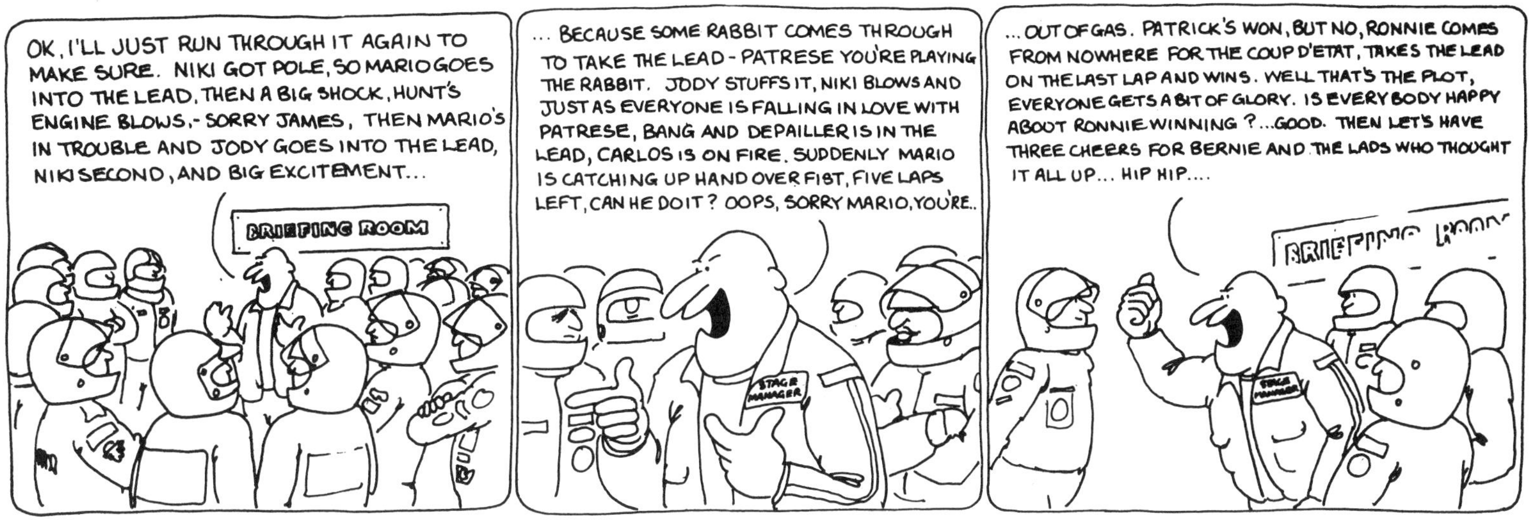
OK, I'LL JUST RUN THROUGH IT AGAIN TO MAKE SURE. NIKI GOT POLE, SO MARIO GOES INTO THE LEAD, THEN A BIG SHOCK, HUNT'S ENGINE BLOWS, - SORRY JAMES, THEN MARIO'S IN TROUBLE AND JODY GOES INTO THE LEAD, NIKI SECOND, AND BIG EXCITEMENT...
BRIEFING ROOM
... BECAUSE SOME RABBIT COMES THROUGH TO TAKE THE LEAD - PATRESE YOU'RE PLAYING THE RABBIT. JODY STUFFS IT, NIKI BLOWS AND JUST AS EVERYONE IS FALLING IN LOVE WITH PATRESE, BANG AND DEPAILLER IS IN THE LEAD, CARLOS IS ON FIRE. SUDDENLY MARIO IS CATCHING UP HAND OVER FIST, FIVE LAPS LEFT, CAN HE DO IT? OOPS, SORRY MARIO, YOU'RE..
... OUT OF GAS. PATRICK'S WON, BUT NO, RONNIE COMES FROM NOWHERE FOR THE COUP D'ETAT, TAKES THE LEAD ON THE LAST LAP AND WINS. WELL THAT'S THE PLOT, EVERYONE GETS A BIT OF GLORY. IS EVERYBODY HAPPY ABOUT RONNIE WINNING ?...GOOD. THEN LET'S HAVE THREE CHEERS FOR BERNIE AND THE LADS WHO THOUGHT IT ALL UP... HIP HIP....

8th March 1978

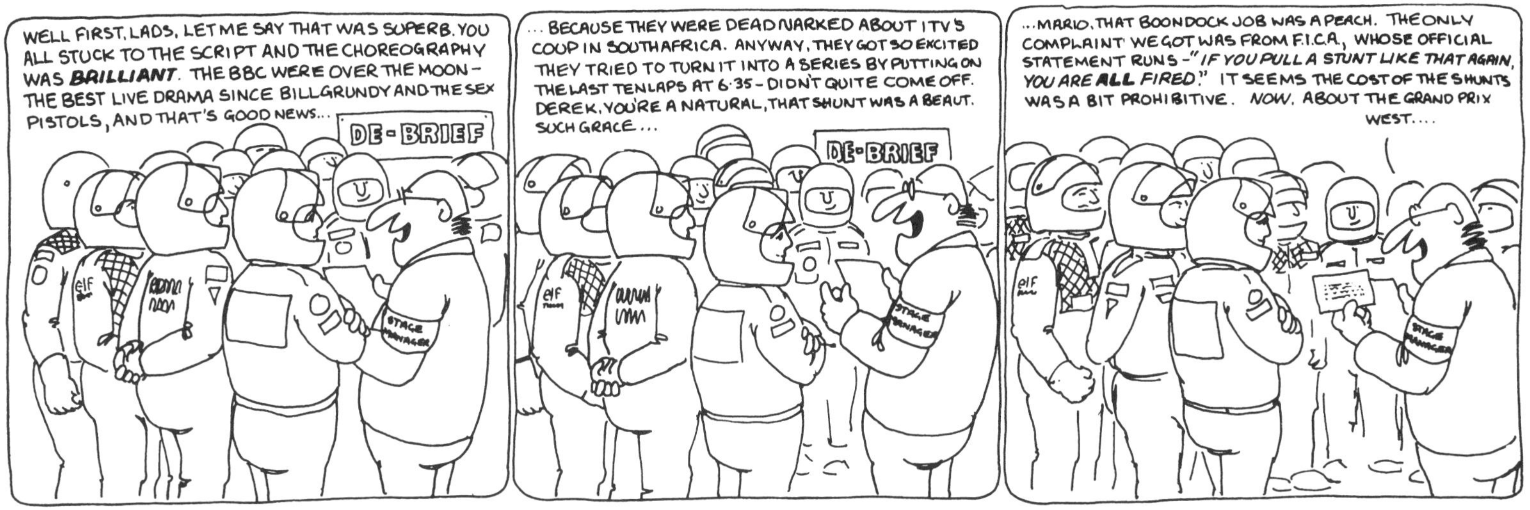
WELL FIRST, LADS, LET ME SAY THAT WAS SUPERB. YOU ALL STUCK TO THE SCRIPT AND THE CHOREOGRAPHY WAS **BRILLIANT**. THE BBC WERE OVER THE MOON - THE BEST LIVE DRAMA SINCE BILL GRUNDY AND THE SEX PISTOLS, AND THAT'S GOOD NEWS...
DE-BRIEF
... BECAUSE THEY WERE DEAD NARKED ABOUT ITV'S COUP IN SOUTH AFRICA. ANYWAY, THEY GOT SO EXCITED THEY TRIED TO TURN IT INTO A SERIES BY PUTTING ON THE LAST TEN LAPS AT 6:35 - DIDN'T QUITE COME OFF. DEREK, YOU'RE A NATURAL, THAT SHUNT WAS A BEAUT. SUCH GRACE...
DE-BRIEF
...MARIO, THAT BOONDOCK JOB WAS A PEACH. THE ONLY COMPLAINT WE GOT WAS FROM F.I.C.A., WHOSE OFFICIAL STATEMENT RUNS - "*IF YOU PULL A STUNT LIKE THAT AGAIN, YOU ARE **ALL** FIRED.*" IT SEEMS THE COST OF THE SHUNTS WAS A BIT PROHIBITIVE. *NOW*, ABOUT THE GRAND PRIX WEST....

23rd March 1978

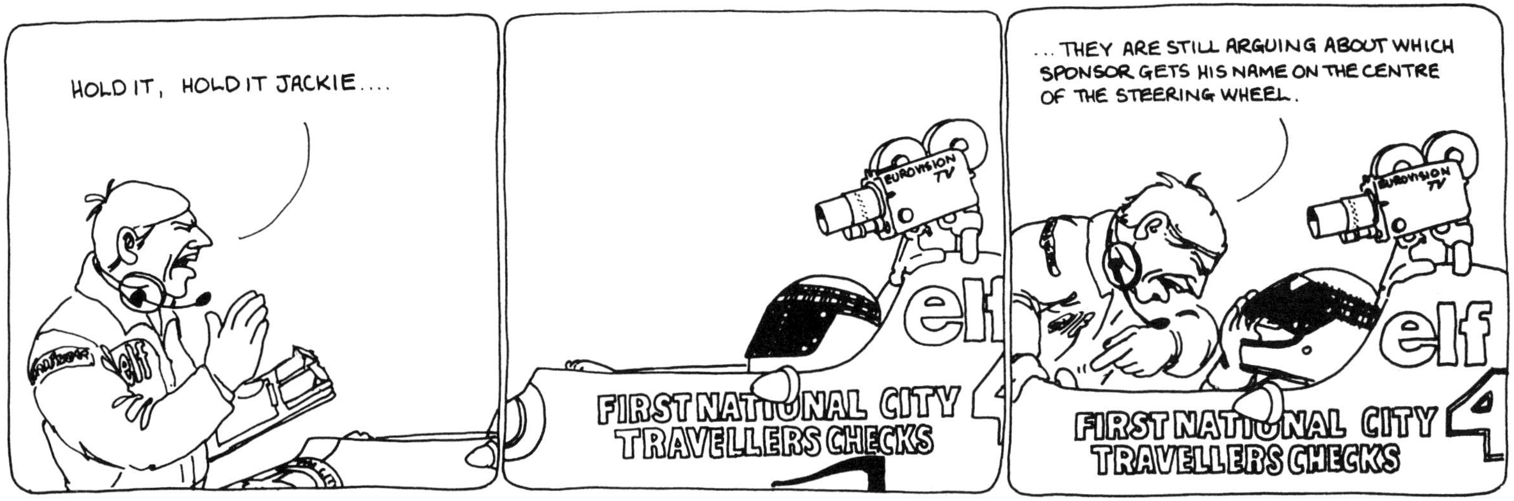
HOLD IT, HOLD IT JACKIE....
EUROVISION TV
elf
FIRST NATIONAL CITY TRAVELLERS CHECKS
...THEY ARE STILL ARGUING ABOUT WHICH SPONSOR GETS HIS NAME ON THE CENTRE OF THE STEERING WHEEL.
EUROVISION TV
elf
FIRST NATIONAL CITY TRAVELLERS CHECKS

18th May 1978

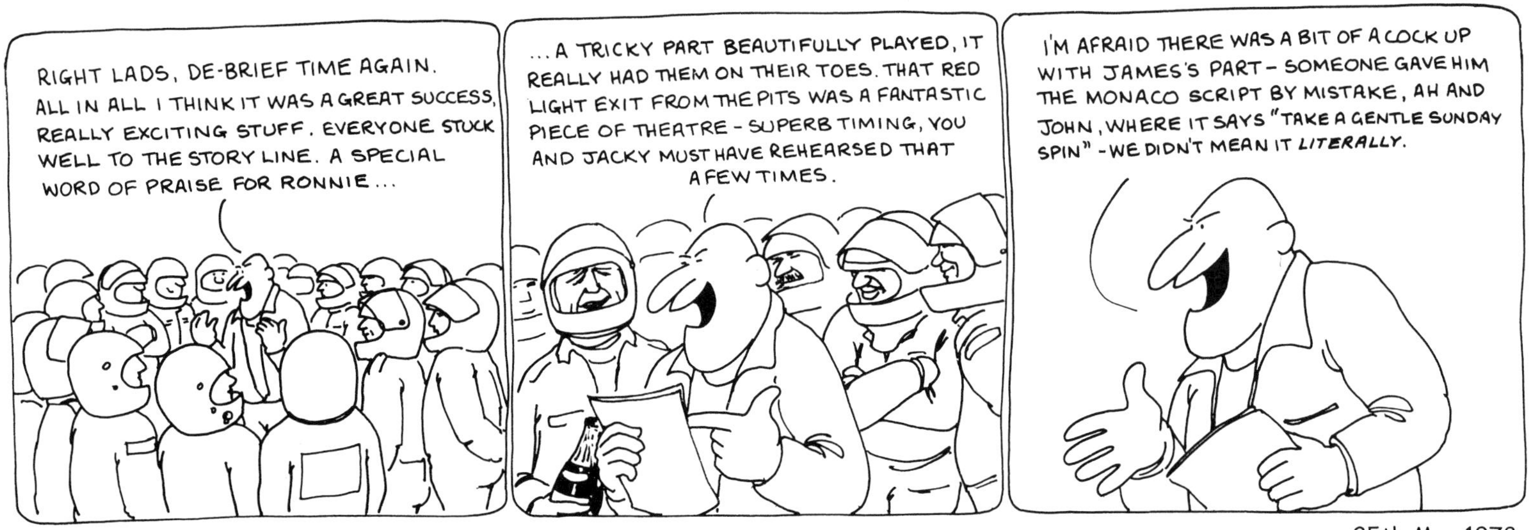
RIGHT LADS, DE-BRIEF TIME AGAIN. ALL IN ALL I THINK IT WAS A GREAT SUCCESS, REALLY EXCITING STUFF. EVERYONE STUCK WELL TO THE STORY LINE. A SPECIAL WORD OF PRAISE FOR RONNIE...
...A TRICKY PART BEAUTIFULLY PLAYED, IT REALLY HAD THEM ON THEIR TOES. THAT RED LIGHT EXIT FROM THE PITS WAS A FANTASTIC PIECE OF THEATRE - SUPERB TIMING, YOU AND JACKY MUST HAVE REHEARSED THAT A FEW TIMES.
I'M AFRAID THERE WAS A BIT OF A COCK UP WITH JAMES'S PART - SOMEONE GAVE HIM THE MONACO SCRIPT BY MISTAKE, AH AND JOHN, WHERE IT SAYS "TAKE A GENTLE SUNDAY SPIN" - WE DIDN'T MEAN IT *LITERALLY*.

25th May 1978

Chapter Fourteen

TV Stuff

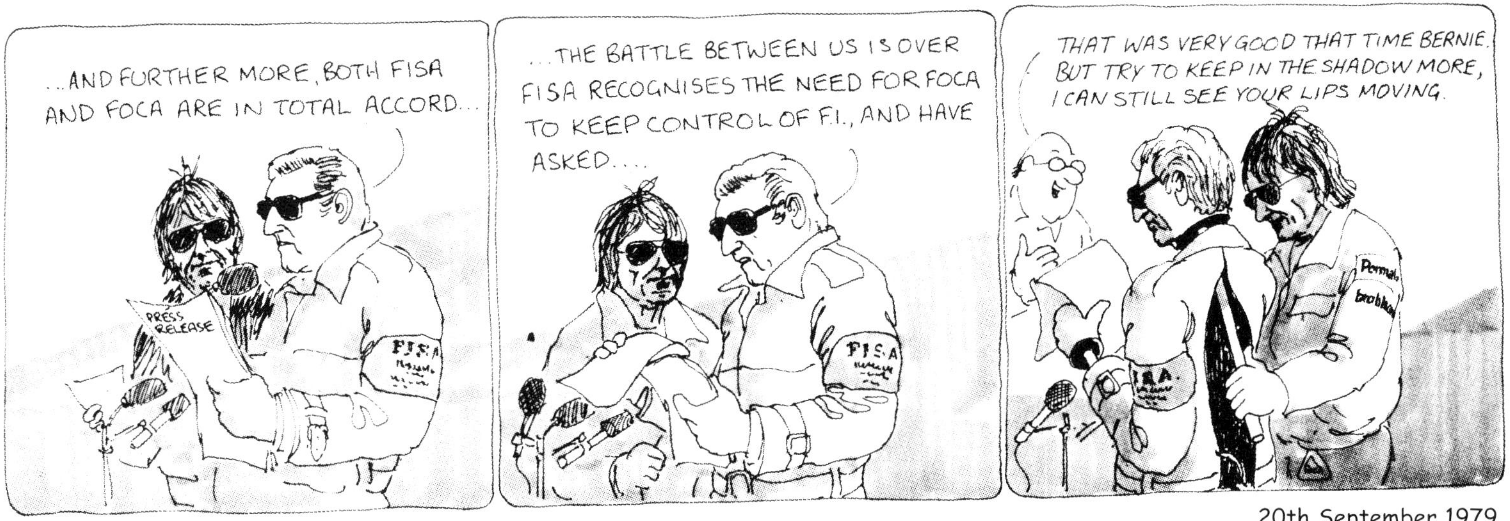
...AND FURTHER MORE, BOTH FISA AND FOCA ARE IN TOTAL ACCORD...
PRESS RELEASE
FISA
...THE BATTLE BETWEEN US IS OVER FISA RECOGNISES THE NEED FOR FOCA TO KEEP CONTROL OF F.1., AND HAVE ASKED....
FISA
THAT WAS VERY GOOD THAT TIME BERNIE. BUT TRY TO KEEP IN THE SHADOW MORE, I CAN STILL SEE YOUR LIPS MOVING.

20th September 1979

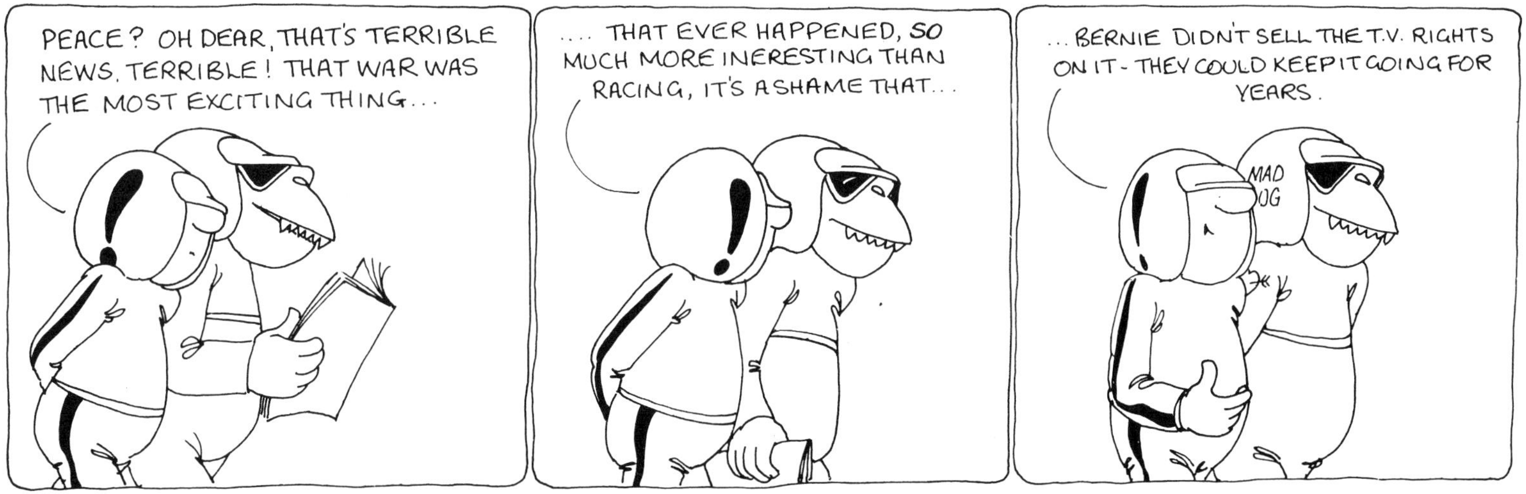
PEACE? OH DEAR, THAT'S TERRIBLE NEWS, TERRIBLE! THAT WAR WAS THE MOST EXCITING THING...
.... THAT EVER HAPPENED, SO MUCH MORE INERESTING THAN RACING, IT'S A SHAME THAT...
...BERNIE DIDN'T SELL THE T.V. RIGHTS ON IT - THEY COULD KEEP IT GOING FOR YEARS.

26th February 1981

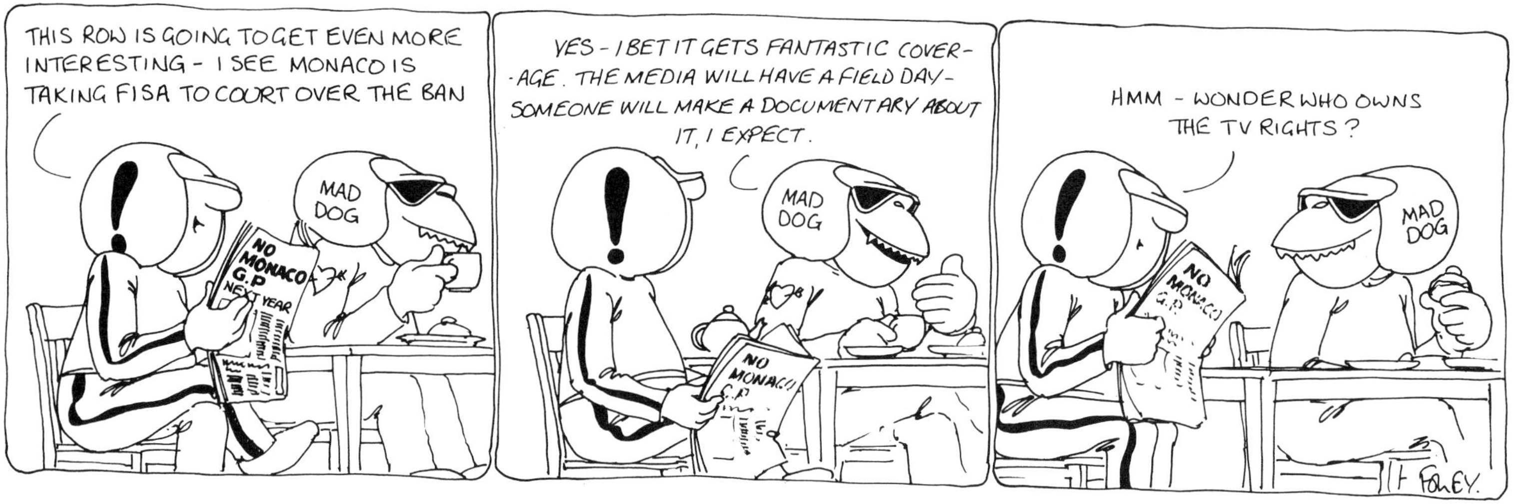
THIS ROW IS GOING TO GET EVEN MORE INTERESTING - I SEE MONACO IS TAKING FISA TO COURT OVER THE BAN
MAD DOG
NO MONACO G.P NEXT YEAR
YES - I BET IT GETS FANTASTIC COVER-AGE. THE MEDIA WILL HAVE A FIELD DAY - SOMEONE WILL MAKE A DOCUMENTARY ABOUT IT, I EXPECT.
MAD DOG
NO MONACO G.P
HMM - WONDER WHO OWNS THE TV RIGHTS?
MAD DOG
NO MONACO G.P
FOLEY.

18th October 1984

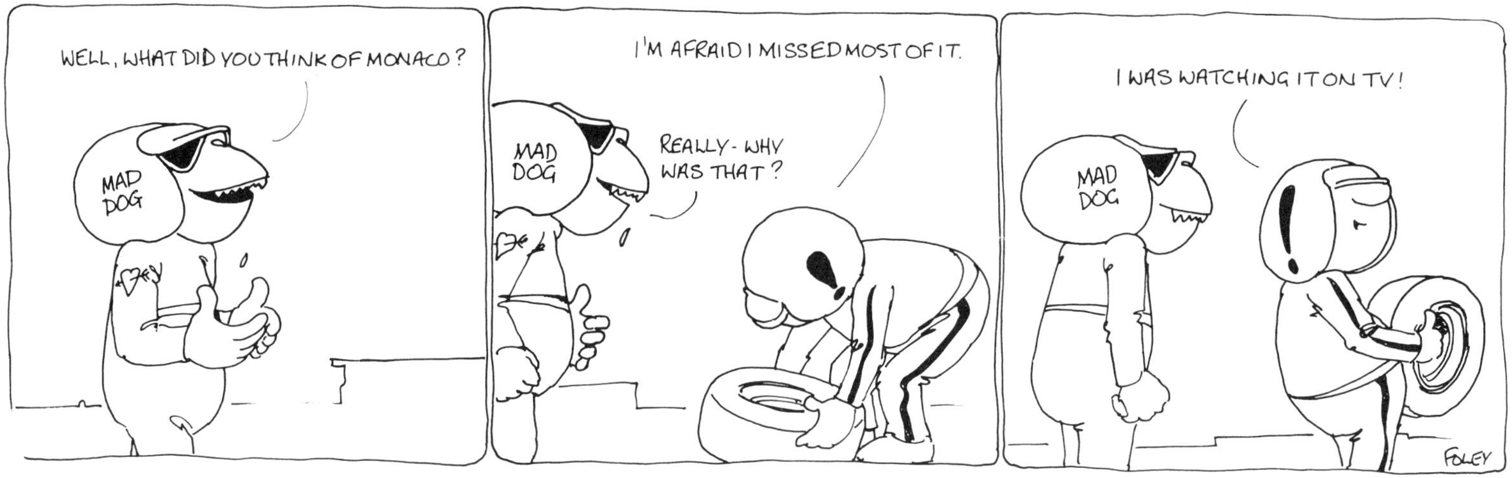
WELL, WHAT DID YOU THINK OF MONACO?
MAD DOG
I'M AFRAID I MISSED MOST OF IT.
MAD DOG
REALLY - WHY WAS THAT?
I WAS WATCHING IT ON TV!
MAD DOG
FOLEY

19th May 1988

Chapter Fifteen

Indy Cars

The new stuff is Indy racing - Indycars, Champcars, Cart, what have you. It's all watchable if rather quaint. They've invented a few new things such as 'wicker bills', (an invoice for having your baskets re-woven) pushing, (nothing like shoving) drafting, (nothing to do with the Army) and overtaking (cars passing each other). I don't think this latter one will catch on, after all you don't see it in real racing.

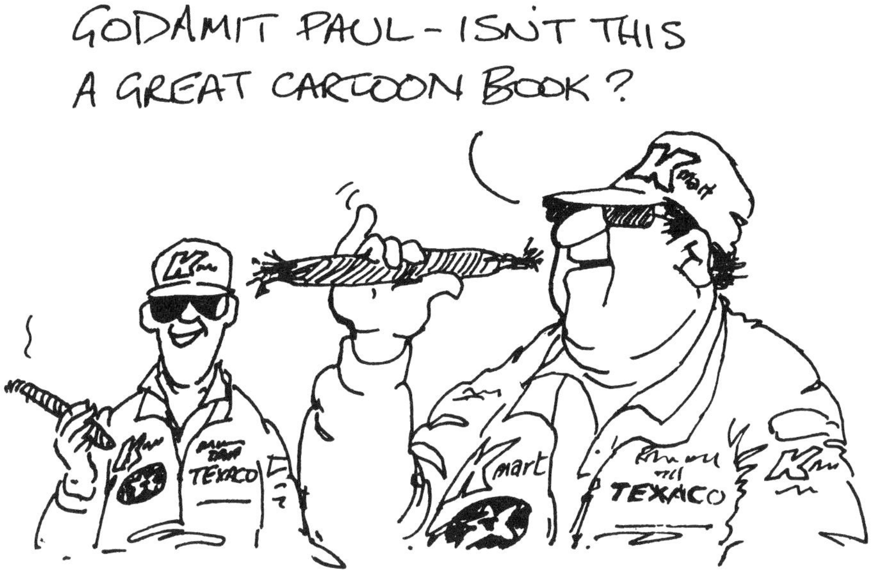
GODAMIT PAUL - ISN'T THIS A GREAT CARTOON BOOK?
TEXACO
Kmart
TEXACO

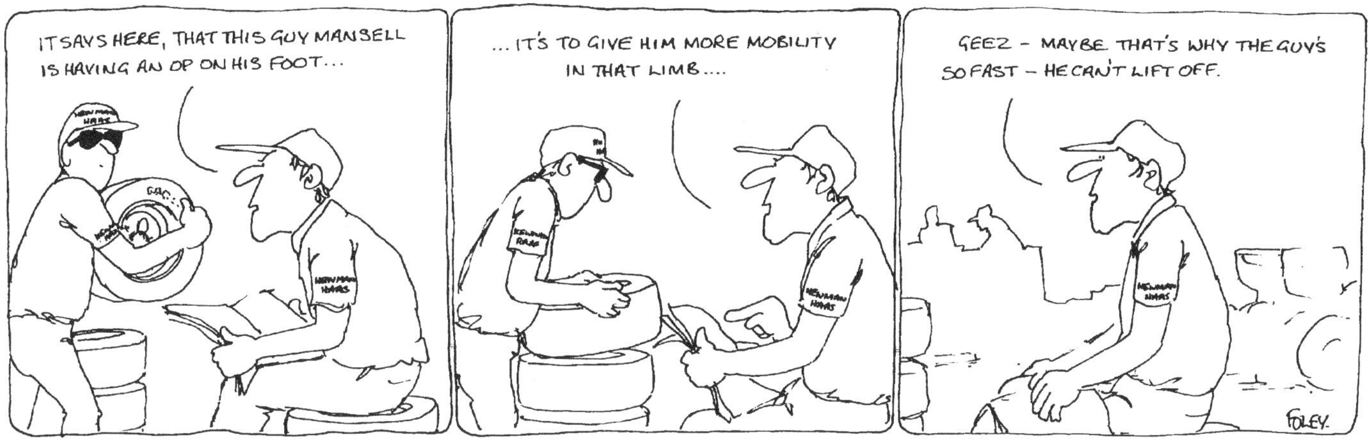
ITSAYS HERE, THAT THIS GUY MANSELL IS HAVING AN OP ON HIS FOOT...
...IT'S TO GIVE HIM MORE MOBILITY IN THAT LIMB....
GEEZ - MAYBE THAT'S WHY THE GUY'S SO FAST - HE CAN'T LIFT OFF.
FOLEY.

Indy Cars

WELL, WELL, MARCHES FIRST, SECOND, THIRD, FOURTH, SIXTH, SEVENTH, EIGHTH, NINTH, TENTH AND SO ON....
... BUT, A LOLA WAS FIFTH...
.... TELL ME ROBIN, WHAT WENT WRONG?
FOLEY

5th June 1986

WANNAT GREAT CARL?
YEP - JUST HOPE IT DON' GO TO HIS HEAD....
....GODAMIT - I SUPPOSE MARIO IS GONNA ASK FOR A BIGGER PENSION.
FOLEY

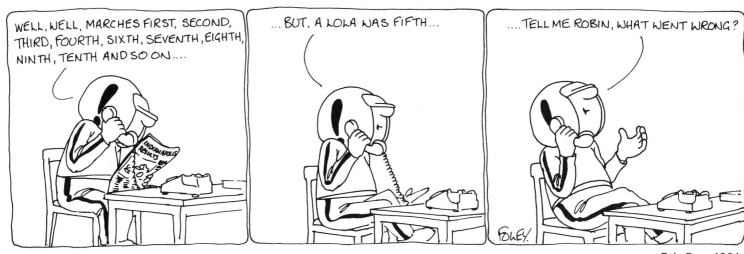

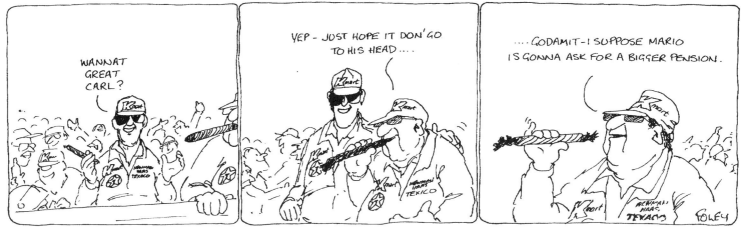

8th April 1993

Chapter Fifteen

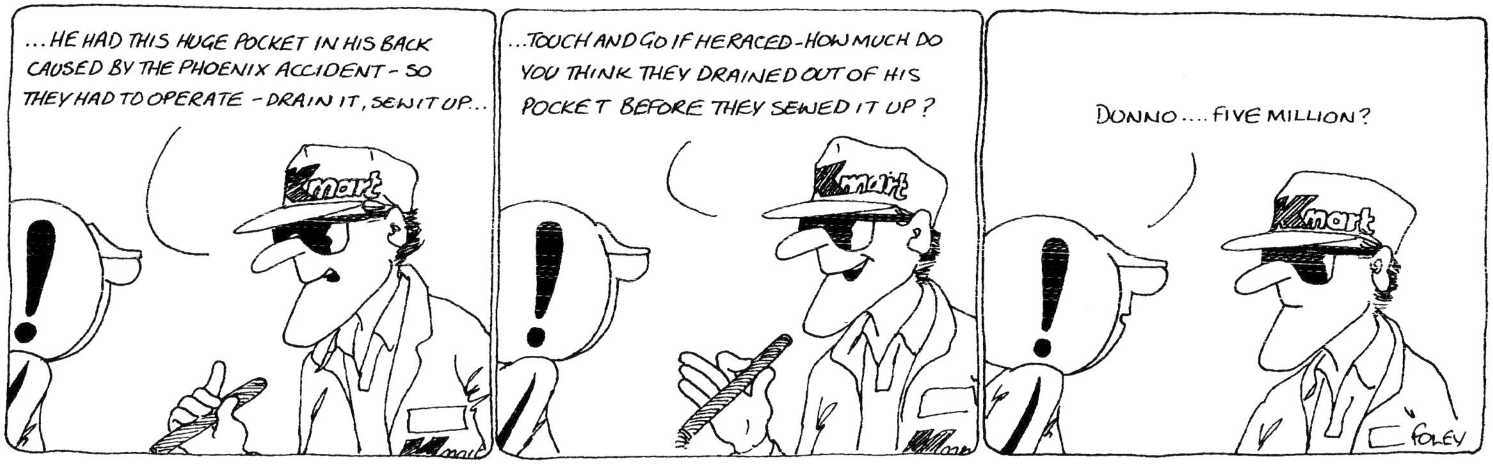
...HE HAD THIS HUGE POCKET IN HIS BACK CAUSED BY THE PHOENIX ACCIDENT - SO THEY HAD TO OPERATE - DRAIN IT, SEW IT UP...
...TOUCH AND GO IF HE RACED - HOW MUCH DO YOU THINK THEY DRAINED OUT OF HIS POCKET BEFORE THEY SEWED IT UP?
DONNO.... FIVE MILLION?
FOLEY

20th May 1993

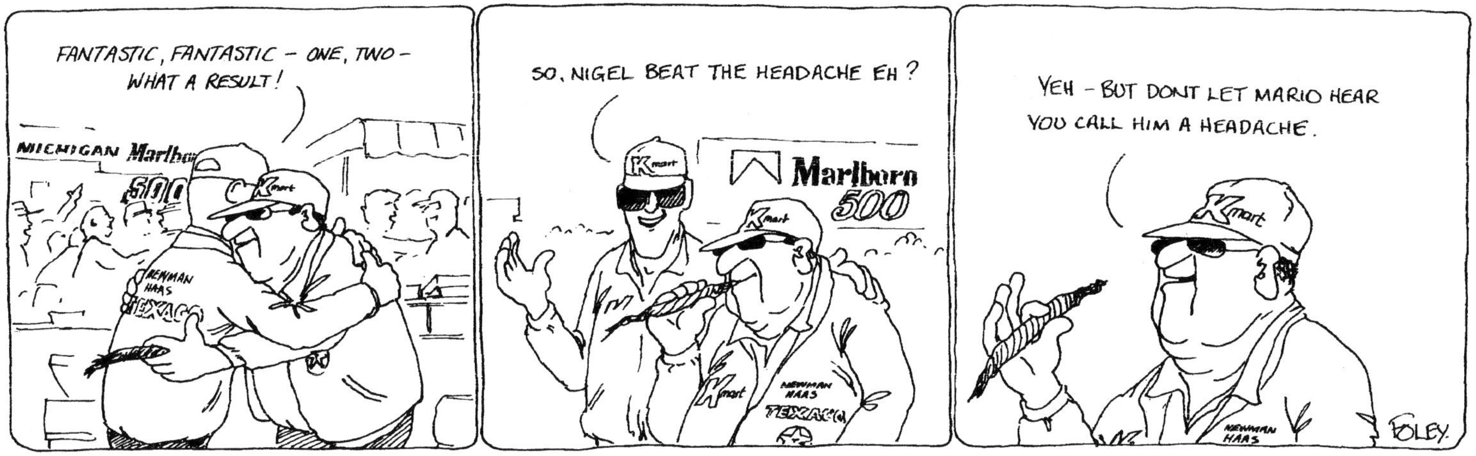
FANTASTIC, FANTASTIC - ONE, TWO - WHAT A RESULT!
SO, NIGEL BEAT THE HEADACHE EH?
Marlboro 500
YEH - BUT DONT LET MARIO HEAR YOU CALL HIM A HEADACHE.
FOLEY

5th August 1993

Indy Cars

Things Don't Change

Chapter Sixteen

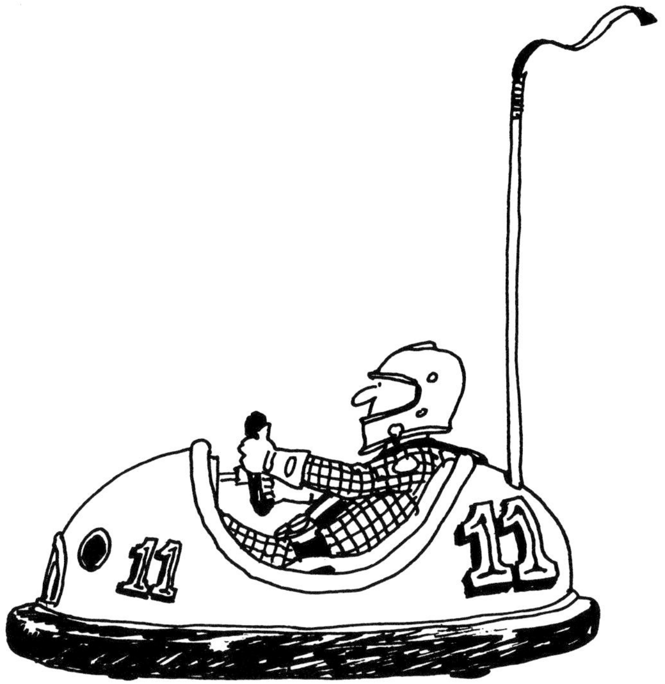

I suppose this is another way of saying these are just tired old jokes. But that is after all what you have bought - a book of old jokes! (sorry). However, it is true that things don't change. People still mount aerofoils upside down, forget to put petrol in cars, leave their licences at home, put diesel in the petrol van, and forget to bring the wets. So join Catchpole laughing at himself doing all the usual silly things.

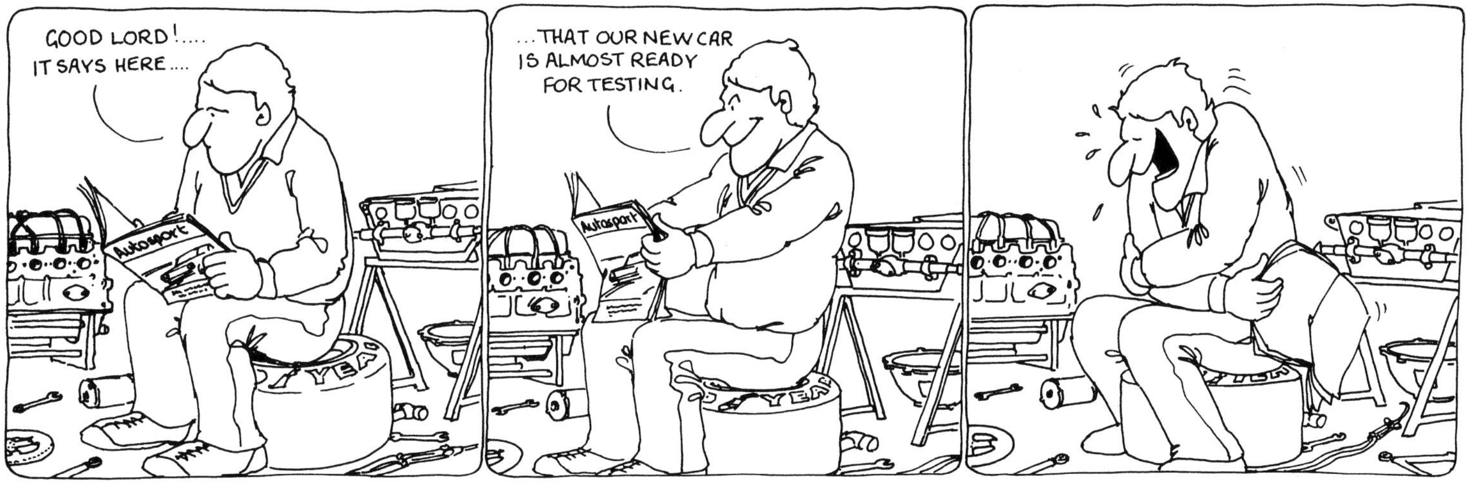
GOOD LORD!.... IT SAYS HERE....
...THAT OUR NEW CAR IS ALMOST READY FOR TESTING.
Autosport
Autosport

Things Don't Change

.....AND IT'S GOT AN ALL FIBREGLASS BODY OVER A TUBE SPACE FRAME AND BIG SLICKS ON WIDE MAG ALLOY WHEELS, FULLY ROSE JOINTED SUSPENSION, FULL ROLL CAGE, DS11 PADS VARLEY BATTERY.....
ELBOW
....PERSPEX WINDOWS, BENDIX PUMP, STEEL CRANK TITANIUM RODS, DRY SUMP FUEL INJECTION AND A MAG COG SWOP.
FORD ENGINE?
ELBOW
OF COURSE IT HAS. WE HAVE TO KEEP THE CAR AUTHENTIC

9th December 1971

IT'S A GOOD JOB I'VE GOT MY DARK VISOR ON OTHERWISE EVERYBODY WOULD RECOGNIZE ME...
...BUT SUPPOSING NOBODY AT ALL RECOGNIZES ME... THAT WOULD BE AWFUL...
...JUST AWFUL. I HAD BETTER GO AND STAND BESIDE MY CAR, SO...
...THEY WILL REALIZE, THAT IT'S ME, IN DISGUISE.

1st June 1972

Chapter Sixteen

IF THIS CARRIES ON FOR ANOTHER THREE LAPS, THEY'LL HAVE TO STOP THE RACE

26th April 1973

... PRODSPORTS, AT LEAST THEY LOOK LIKE REAL CARS, REAL SPORTS....
...CARS. ROAD CARS THAT WE CAN IDENTIFY WITH, NONE OF YOUR HYBRID SINGLE SEATER SPECIALS, BUT...
... GOOD HONEST EVERY DAY ROAD CARS, THE SORT OF CAR THE MAN IN THE STREET DRIVES, ORDINARY..
...BREAD AND BUTTER PANTERAS DICING WITH BOG STANDARD SHOPPING CARRERAS

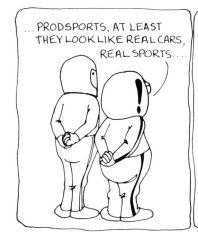

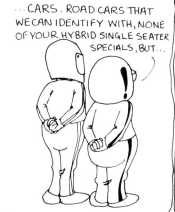

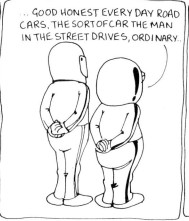

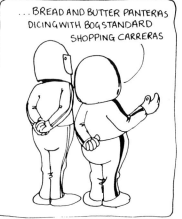

5th July 1973

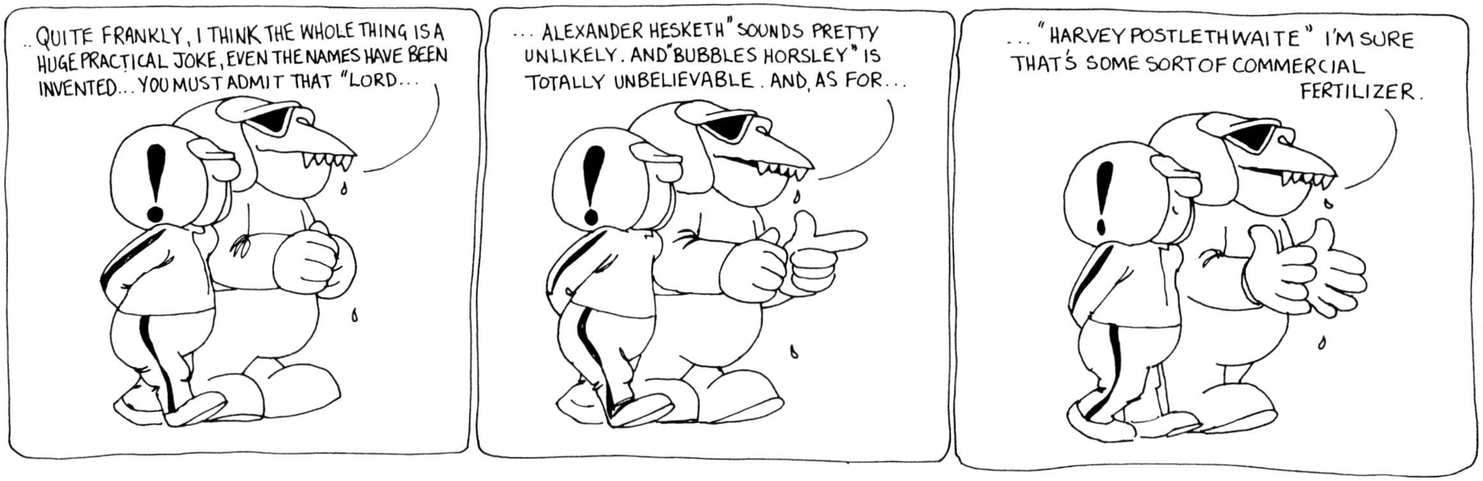
..QUITE FRANKLY, I THINK THE WHOLE THING IS A HUGE PRACTICAL JOKE, EVEN THE NAMES HAVE BEEN INVENTED... YOU MUST ADMIT THAT "LORD...
... ALEXANDER HESKETH" SOUNDS PRETTY UNLIKELY. AND "BUBBLES HORSLEY" IS TOTALLY UNBELIEVABLE. AND, AS FOR...
... "HARVEY POSTLETHWAITE" I'M SURE THAT'S SOME SORT OF COMMERCIAL FERTILIZER.

20th September 1970

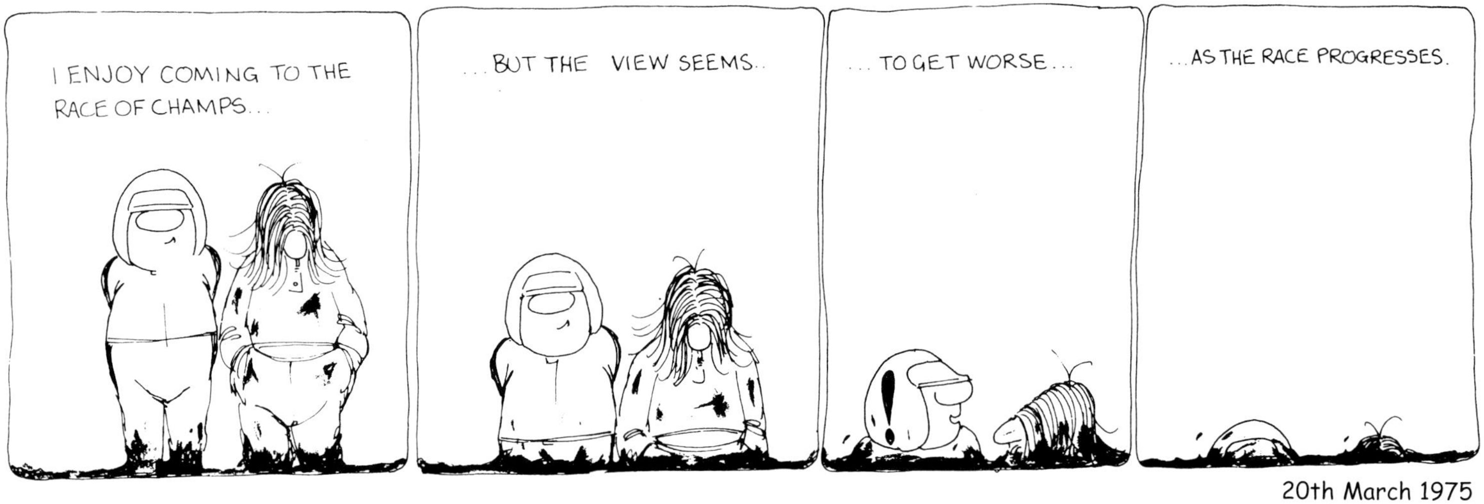
I ENJOY COMING TO THE RACE OF CHAMPS...
... BUT THE VIEW SEEMS..
... TO GET WORSE...
... AS THE RACE PROGRESSES.

20th March 1975

Chapter Sixteen

Things Don't Change

'EXCUSE ME ... 'ALLO .. ER ..
... I SAY, I SAY .... EXCUSE ME ..
... CAN YOU TELL ME PLEASE .. AM I ON THE RIGHT ROAD FOR SILVERSTONE ?

17th April 1975

23 LITRE, 1,840 BHP, SINGLE SUPERCHARGER DOUBLE TURBOCHARGED, FUEL INJECTED SEVEN VALVES PER CYLINDER ...
... DOUBLE OVERHEAD CAM ZEPPELIN ENGINED ESCORT. NOW THERE IS A SUPER SALOON ...
... THAT THE MAN IN THE STREET CAN REALLY IDENTIFY WITH HIS BREAD AND BUTTER ROAD CAR.

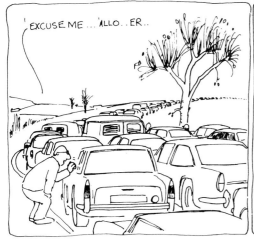

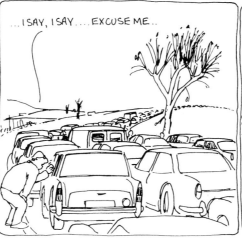

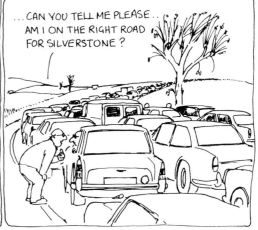

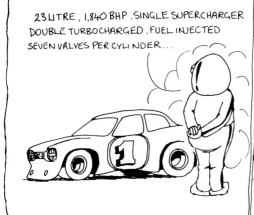

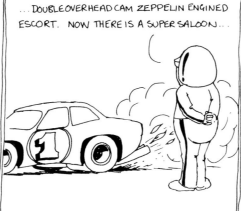

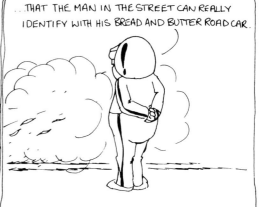

12th June 1975

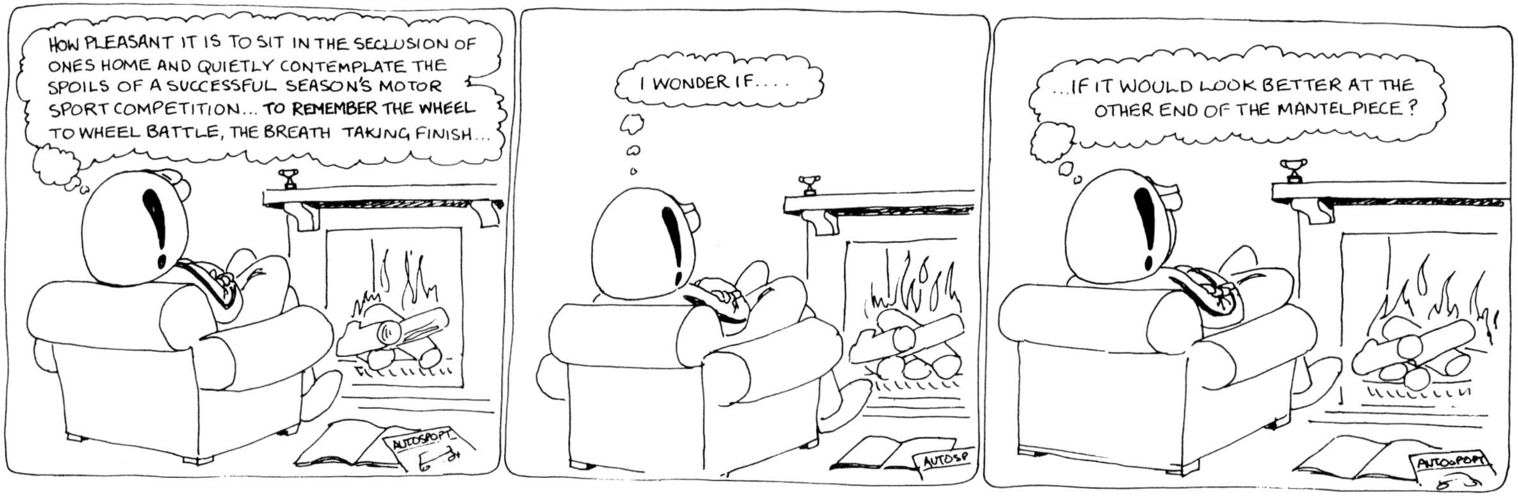
HOW PLEASANT IT IS TO SIT IN THE SECLUSION OF ONES HOME AND QUIETLY CONTEMPLATE THE SPOILS OF A SUCCESSFUL SEASON'S MOTOR SPORT COMPETITION... TO REMEMBER THE WHEEL TO WHEEL BATTLE, THE BREATH TAKING FINISH...
AUTOSPORT
I WONDER IF....
AUTOSP
...IF IT WOULD LOOK BETTER AT THE OTHER END OF THE MANTELPIECE?
AUTOSPORT

29th January 1976

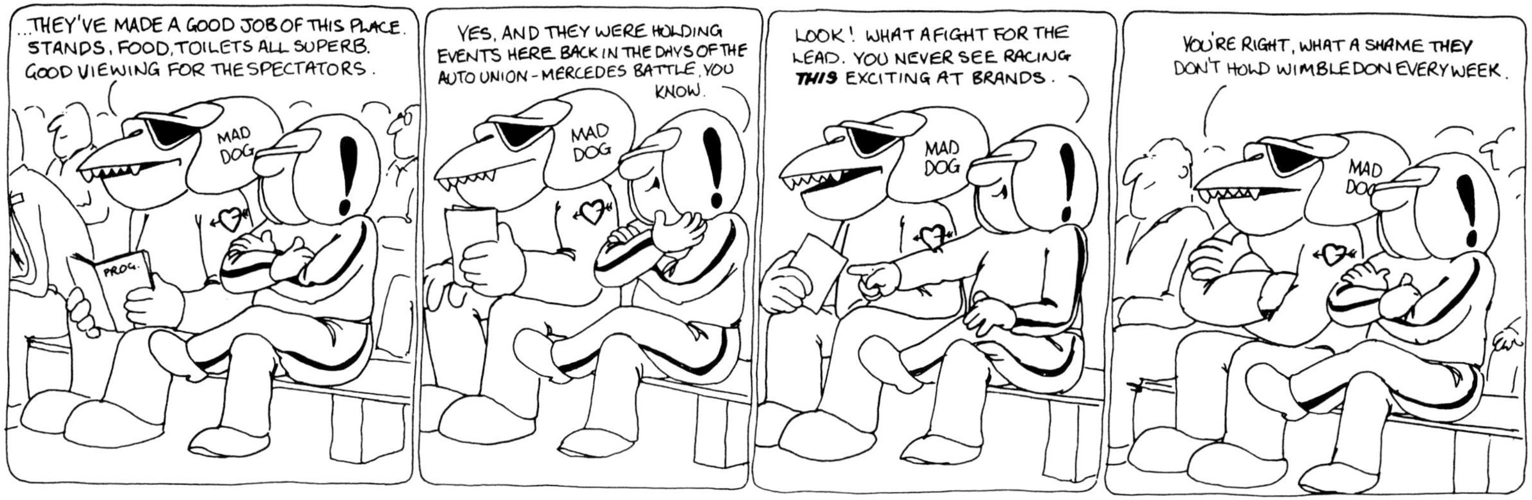
...THEY'VE MADE A GOOD JOB OF THIS PLACE. STANDS, FOOD, TOILETS ALL SUPERB. GOOD VIEWING FOR THE SPECTATORS.
MAD DOG
PROG.
YES, AND THEY WERE HOLDING EVENTS HERE BACK IN THE DAYS OF THE AUTO UNION - MERCEDES BATTLE, YOU KNOW.
MAD DOG
LOOK! WHAT A FIGHT FOR THE LEAD. YOU NEVER SEE RACING THIS EXCITING AT BRANDS.
MAD DOG
YOU'RE RIGHT, WHAT A SHAME THEY DON'T HOLD WIMBLEDON EVERY WEEK.
MAD DOG

30th June 1977

Chapter Sixteen

Things Don't Change

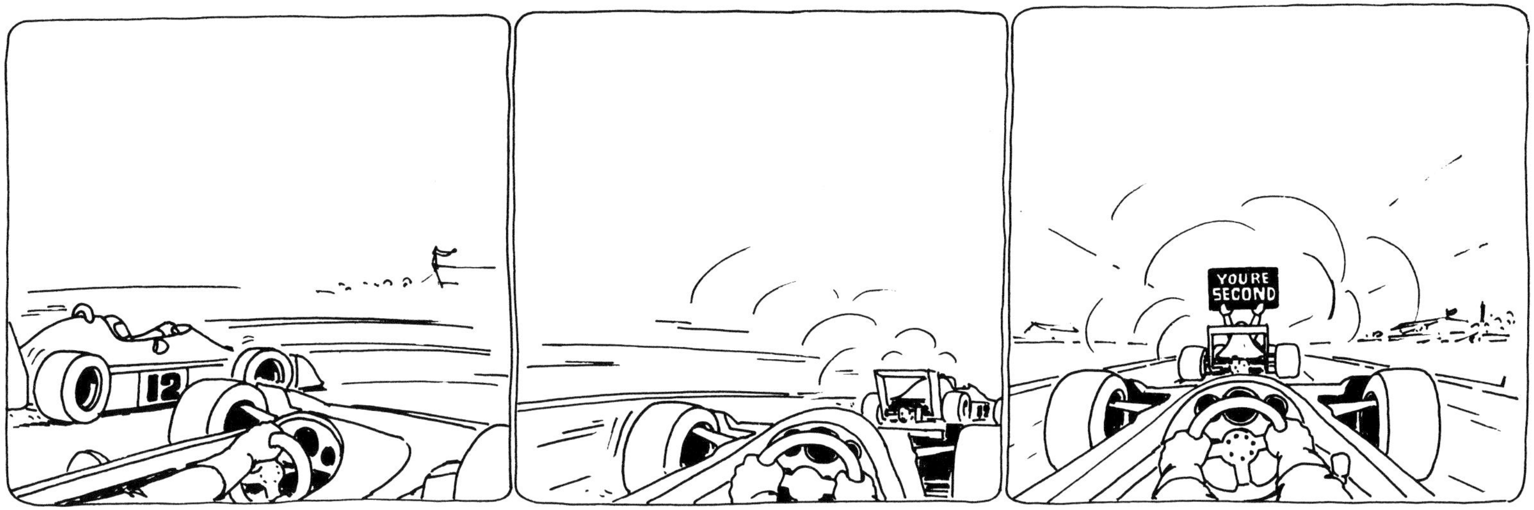
12
YOU'RE SECOND

27th April 1978

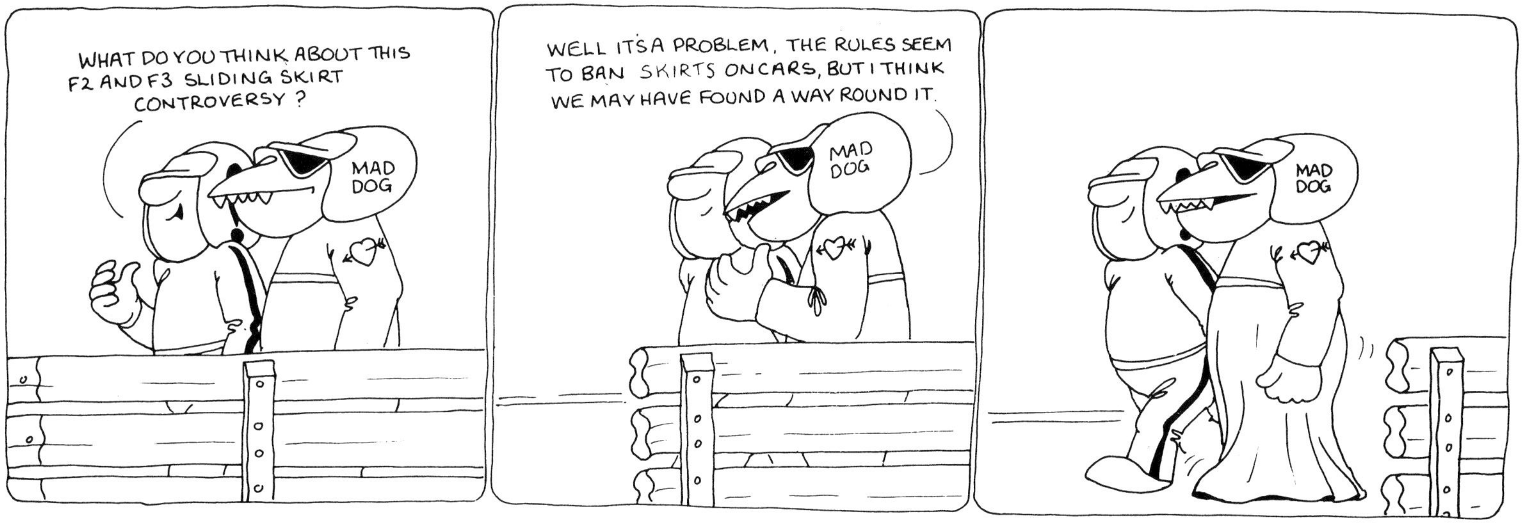
WHAT DO YOU THINK ABOUT THIS F2 AND F3 SLIDING SKIRT CONTROVERSY ?
MAD DOG
WELL ITS A PROBLEM, THE RULES SEEM TO BAN SKIRTS ON CARS, BUT I THINK WE MAY HAVE FOUND A WAY ROUND IT.
MAD DOG
MAD DOG

8th March 1979

Things Don't Change

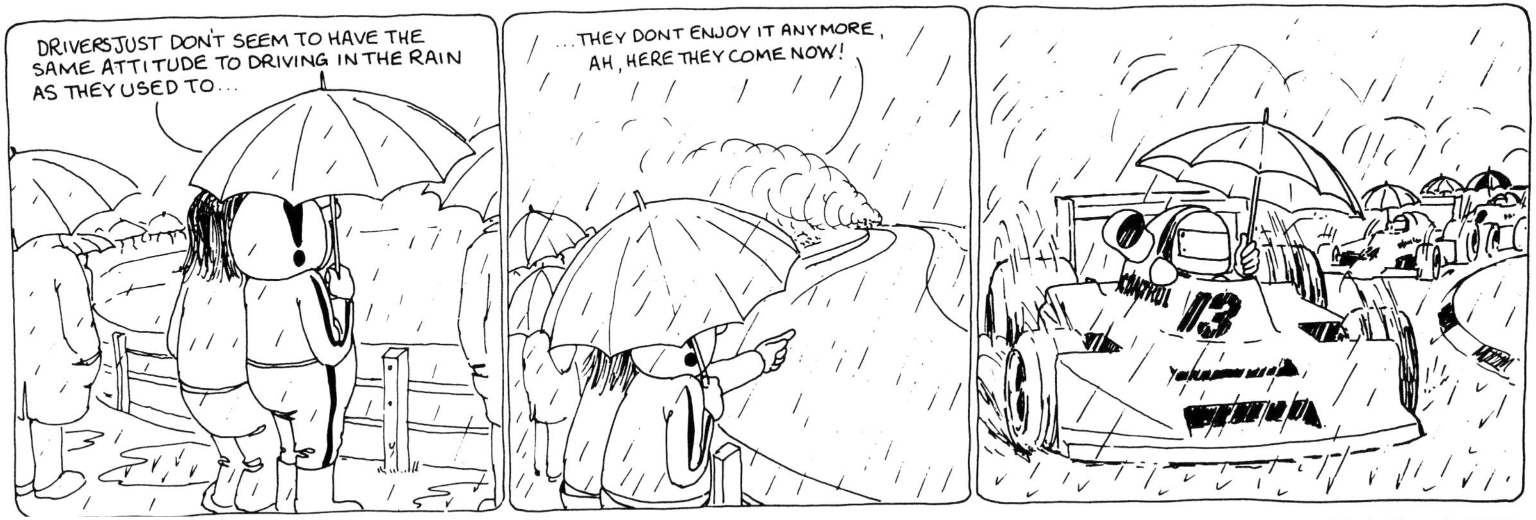
DRIVERS JUST DON'T SEEM TO HAVE THE SAME ATTITUDE TO DRIVING IN THE RAIN AS THEY USED TO...
...THEY DONT ENJOY IT ANYMORE, AH, HERE THEY COME NOW!
13

29th March 1979

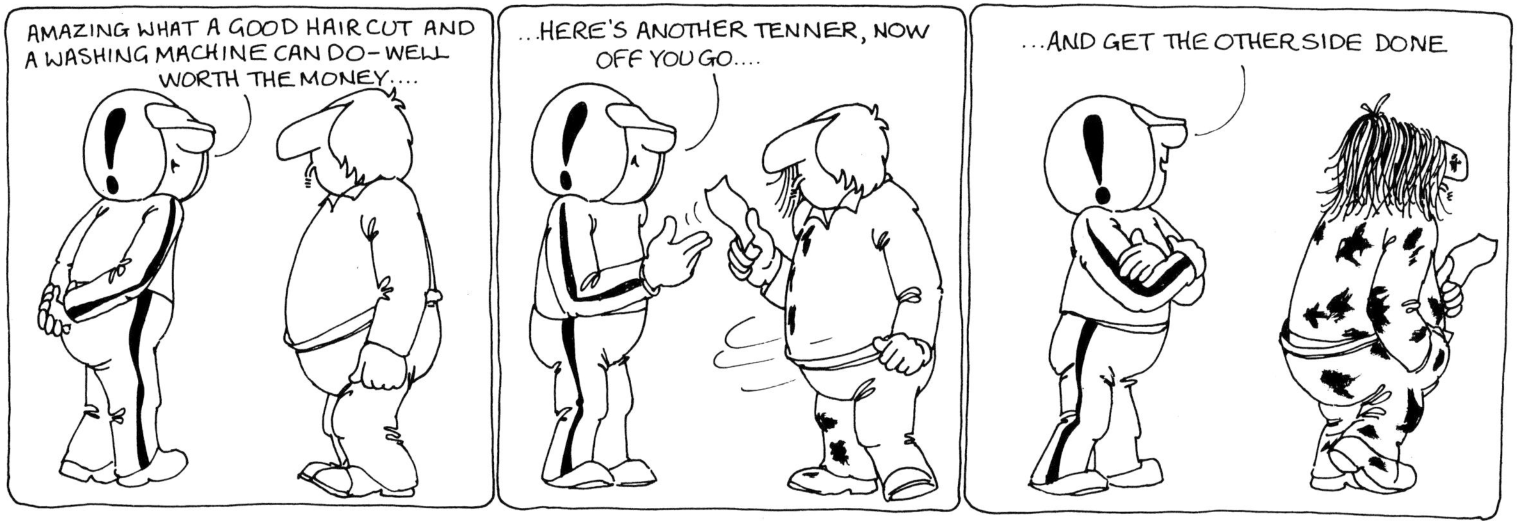
AMAZING WHAT A GOOD HAIR CUT AND A WASHING MACHINE CAN DO-WELL WORTH THE MONEY....
...HERE'S ANOTHER TENNER, NOW OFF YOU GO....
...AND GET THE OTHER SIDE DONE

29th January 1981

Chapter Sixteen

Things Don't Change

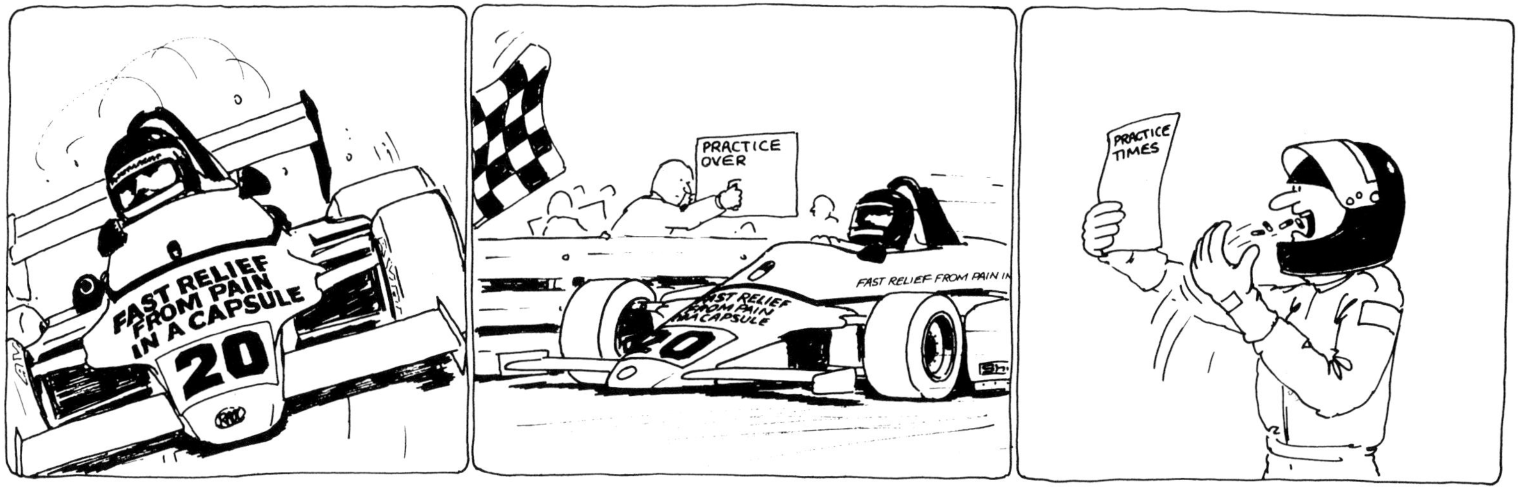
FAST RELIEF FROM PAIN IN A CAPSULE
20
PRACTICE OVER
FAST RELIEF FROM PAIN IN
PRACTICE TIMES

11th March 1982

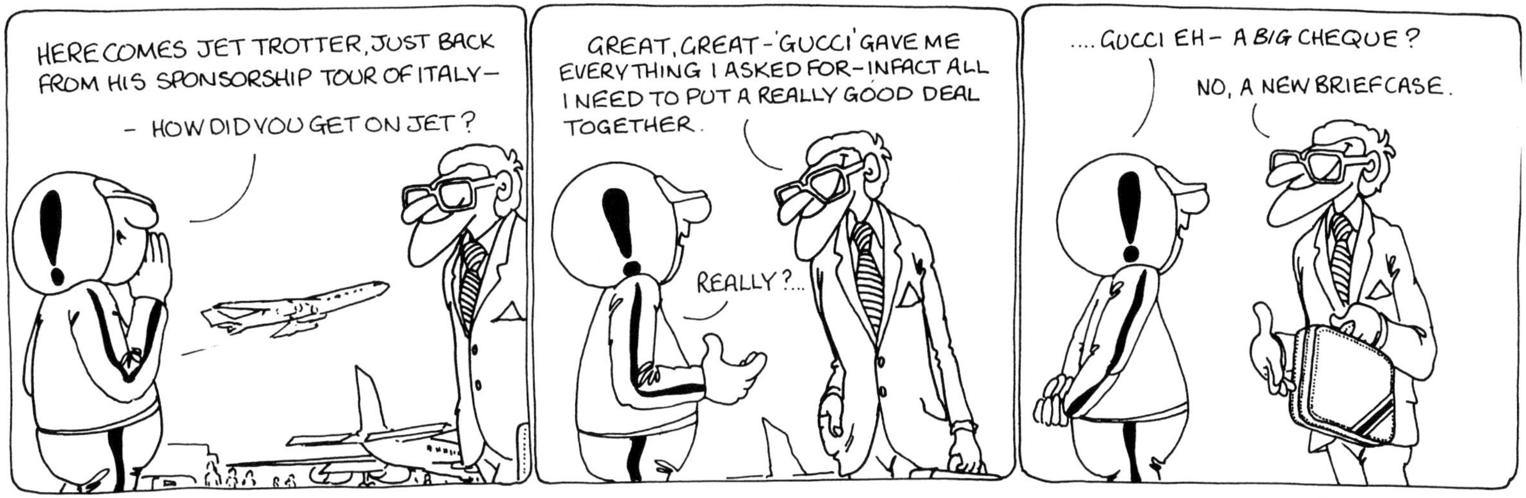
HERE COMES JET TROTTER, JUST BACK FROM HIS SPONSORSHIP TOUR OF ITALY–
– HOW DID YOU GET ON JET?
GREAT, GREAT – 'GUCCI' GAVE ME EVERYTHING I ASKED FOR – INFACT ALL I NEED TO PUT A REALLY GOOD DEAL TOGETHER.
REALLY?...
....GUCCI EH – A BIG CHEQUE?
NO, A NEW BRIEFCASE.

23rd September 1982

Things Don't Change

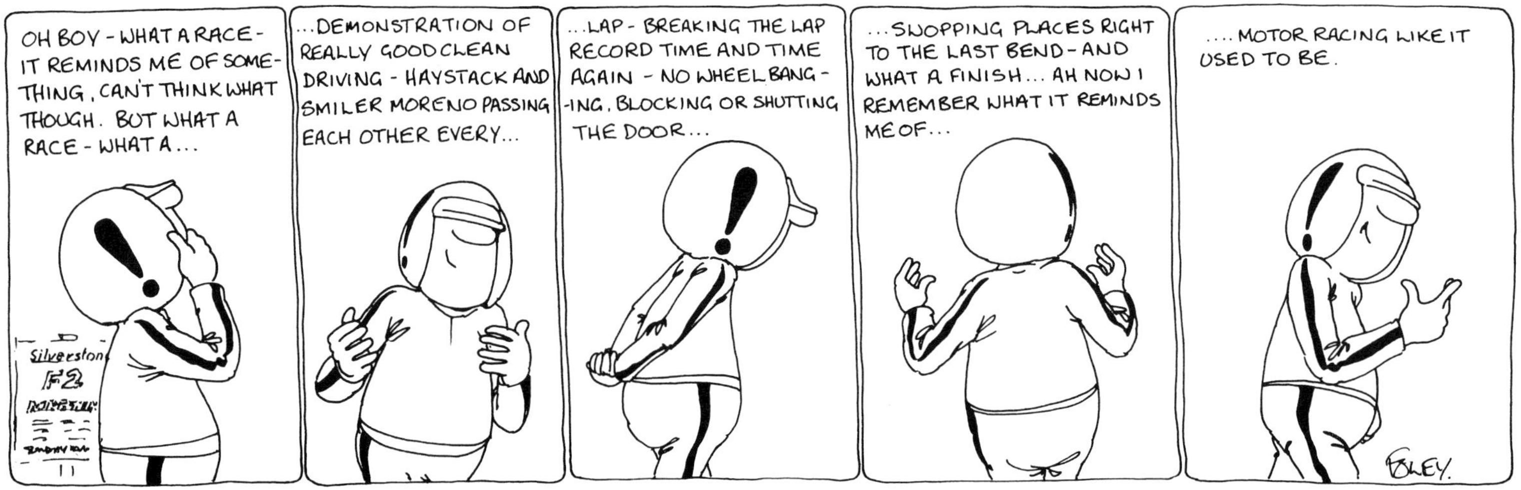

OH BOY - WHAT A RACE - IT REMINDS ME OF SOMETHING, CAN'T THINK WHAT THOUGH. BUT WHAT A RACE - WHAT A...
Silverstone
F2
...DEMONSTRATION OF REALLY GOOD CLEAN DRIVING - HAYSTACK AND SMILER MORENO PASSING EACH OTHER EVERY...
...LAP - BREAKING THE LAP RECORD TIME AND TIME AGAIN - NO WHEEL BANGING, BLOCKING OR SHUTTING THE DOOR...
...SWOPPING PLACES RIGHT TO THE LAST BEND - AND WHAT A FINISH... AH NOW I REMEMBER WHAT IT REMINDS ME OF...
....MOTOR RACING LIKE IT USED TO BE.
FOLEY.

5th April 1984

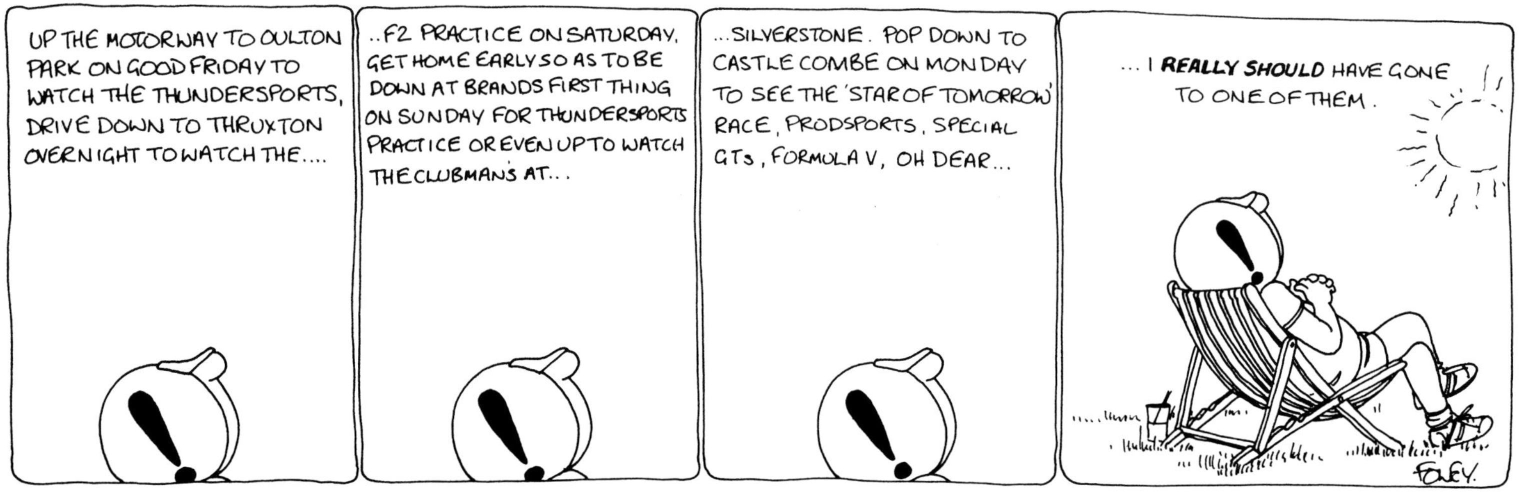

UP THE MOTORWAY TO OULTON PARK ON GOOD FRIDAY TO WATCH THE THUNDERSPORTS, DRIVE DOWN TO THRUXTON OVERNIGHT TO WATCH THE....
..F2 PRACTICE ON SATURDAY, GET HOME EARLY SO AS TO BE DOWN AT BRANDS FIRST THING ON SUNDAY FOR THUNDERSPORTS PRACTICE OR EVEN UP TO WATCH THE CLUBMANS AT...
...SILVERSTONE. POP DOWN TO CASTLE COMBE ON MONDAY TO SEE THE 'STAR OF TOMORROW' RACE, PRODSPORTS, SPECIAL GTs, FORMULA V, OH DEAR...
... I **REALLY SHOULD** HAVE GONE TO ONE OF THEM.
FOLEY.

26th April 1984

Chapter Sixteen

Things Don't Change

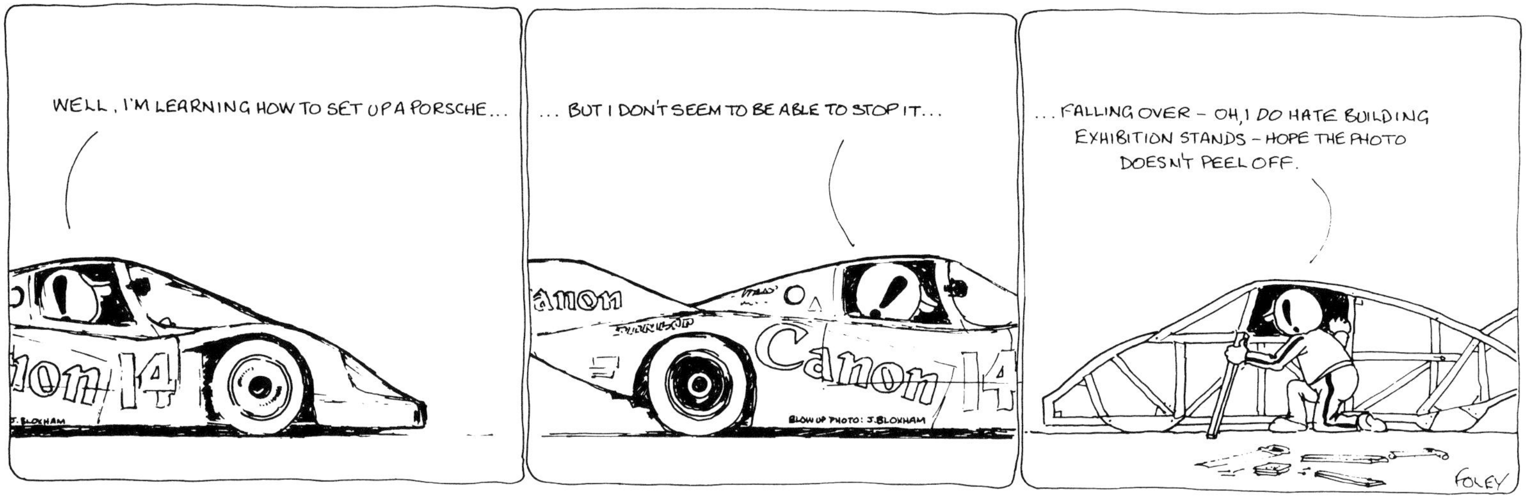

WELL, I'M LEARNING HOW TO SET UP A PORSCHE...
... BUT I DON'T SEEM TO BE ABLE TO STOP IT...
... FALLING OVER – OH, I DO HATE BUILDING EXHIBITION STANDS – HOPE THE PHOTO DOESN'T PEEL OFF.
BLOW UP PHOTO: J. BLOXHAM
FOLEY

24th January 1985

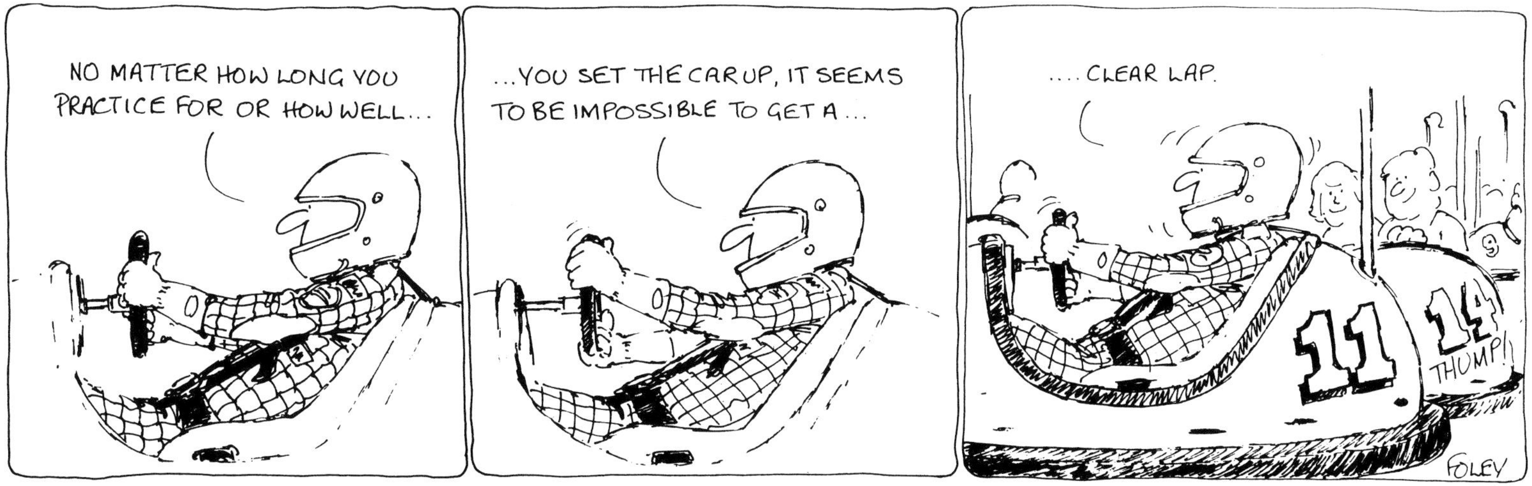

NO MATTER HOW LONG YOU PRACTICE FOR OR HOW WELL...
...YOU SET THE CAR UP, IT SEEMS TO BE IMPOSSIBLE TO GET A...
....CLEAR LAP.
11
14
THUMP!
FOLEY

28th February 1985

Things Don't Change

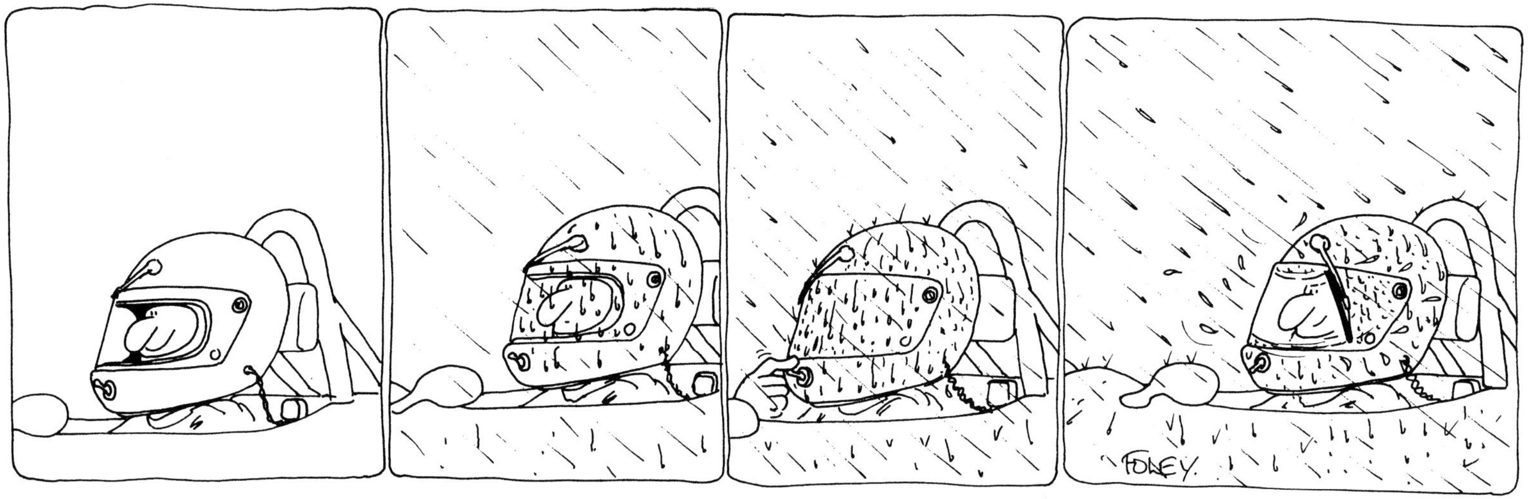
FOLEY.

24th April 1986

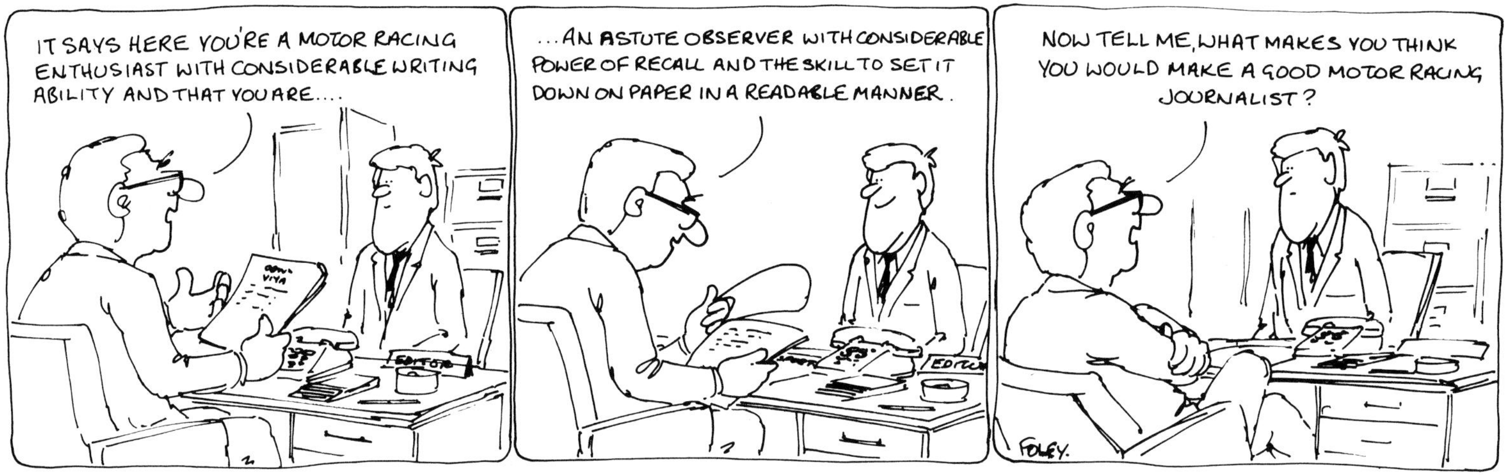
IT SAYS HERE YOU'RE A MOTOR RACING ENTHUSIAST WITH CONSIDERABLE WRITING ABILITY AND THAT YOU ARE....
...AN ASTUTE OBSERVER WITH CONSIDERABLE POWER OF RECALL AND THE SKILL TO SET IT DOWN ON PAPER IN A READABLE MANNER.
NOW TELL ME, WHAT MAKES YOU THINK YOU WOULD MAKE A GOOD MOTOR RACING JOURNALIST?
FOLEY.

2nd February 1989

At The Track

Chapter Seventeen

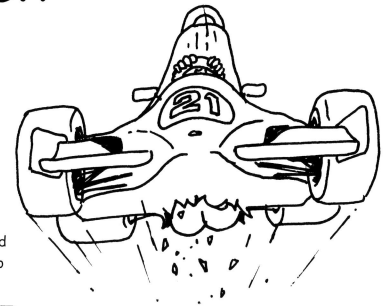

These are the funnies that happen at the track, the banana skins of racing. I remember a true story about a driver called Jack Hugh at Ingliston. It was a foggy day, they shouldn't have started the race, but it was getting late and everyone wanted to go home. On the first lap Jack spun. He made a snap decision about which direction he faced and set off into the growing murk only to meet another car coming towards him. He managed to miss the car, braked to a halt, turned around and set off again only to meet the entire pack coming the other way.

21

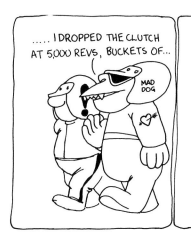

..... I DROPPED THE CLUTCH AT 5,000 REVS, BUCKETS OF...
MAD DOG
... WHEEL SPIN, 7000 IN FIRST 8,500 IN SECOND, EYE BALLED THE MIRRORS INCASE ANYONE...
MAD DOG
WAS GETTING A TOW, HIT THE BRAKES REAL LATE AND THERE I WAS....
MAD DOG
.... IN THE SCRUTINEERING BAY.... EARLY.
MAD DOG

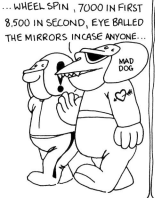

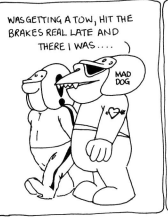

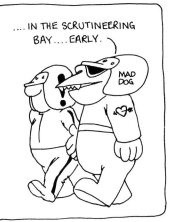

At The Track

I KNOW THAT FIRST IMPRESSIONS ARE...
...ARE VERY DECEPTIVE,..
...BUT, OFF HAND I'D SAY THAT YOU HAVE HAD...
A BIT OF A 'MOMENT'.

20th July 1972

VROOM VVRROOM
MAD DOG
VROOM
VROOM...
MAD DOG
THE DEDICATED PROFESSIONAL, NOTHING BUT PRACTICE, PRACTICE, PRACTICE.
MAD DOG

7th September 1972

Chapter Seventeen

At The Track

I'VE BEEN TRYING OUT ONE OF THESE NEW VISORS.
NOT THE NEW **TOUGH ONE**, THE ONE THEY FIRE AT WITH A 12 BORE SHOTGUN?
YES
HOW DO YOU LIKE IT?
I DON'T.

21st June 1973

Firestone
PESSSSSSSSSSSSS

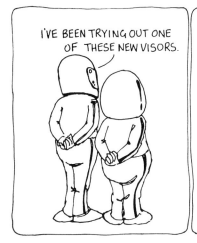

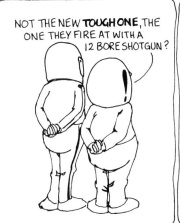

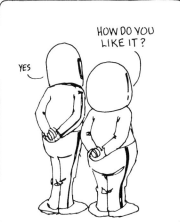

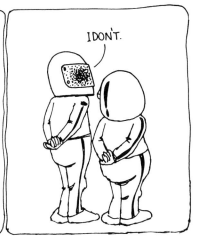

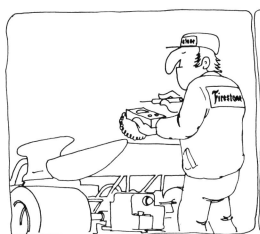

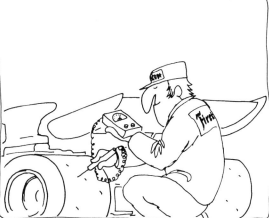

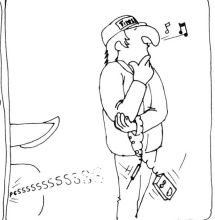

25th October 1973

At The Track

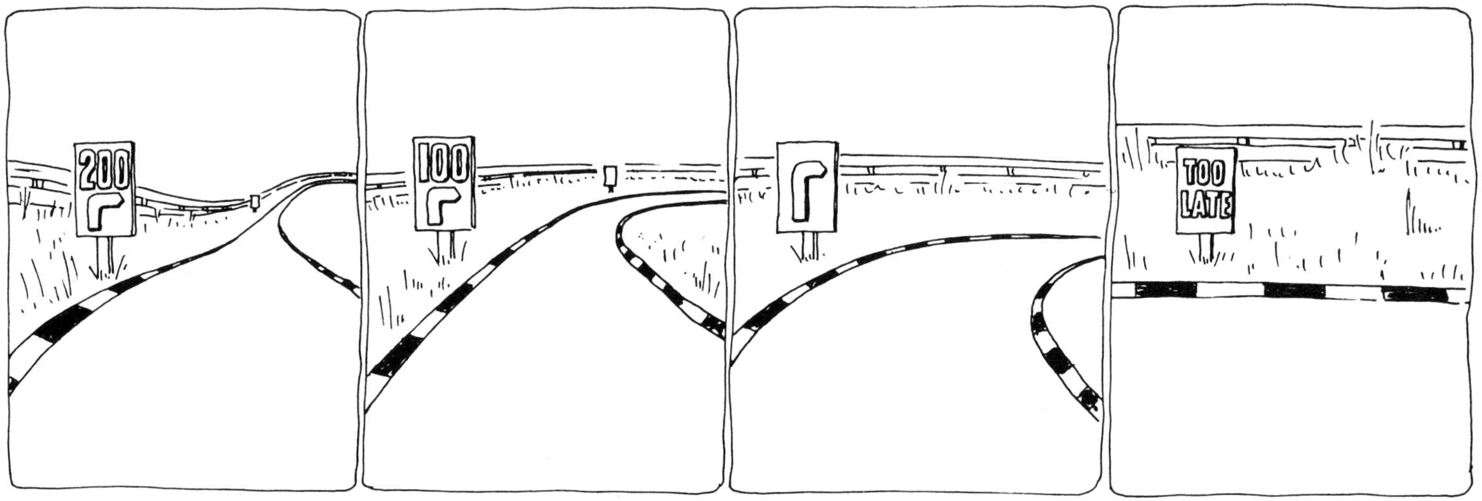
200
100
TOO LATE

29th August 1974

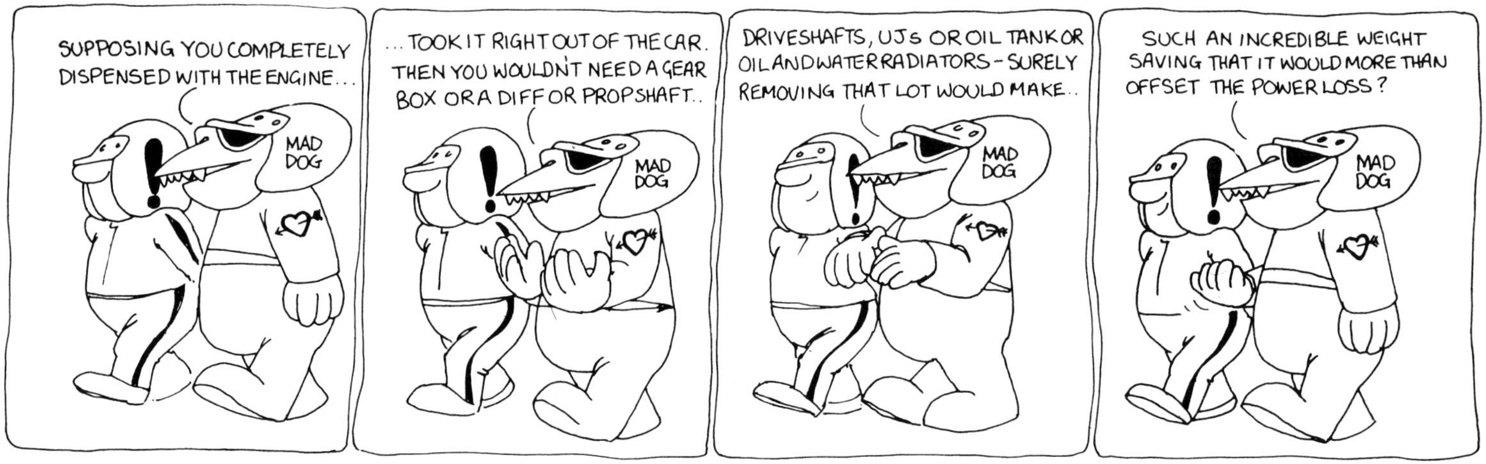
SUPPOSING YOU COMPLETELY DISPENSED WITH THE ENGINE...
MAD DOG
...TOOK IT RIGHT OUT OF THE CAR. THEN YOU WOULDN'T NEED A GEAR BOX OR A DIFF OR PROPSHAFT..
MAD DOG
DRIVESHAFTS, UJs OR OIL TANK OR OIL AND WATER RADIATORS - SURELY REMOVING THAT LOT WOULD MAKE..
MAD DOG
SUCH AN INCREDIBLE WEIGHT SAVING THAT IT WOULD MORE THAN OFFSET THE POWER LOSS?
MAD DOG

21st November 1974

Chapter Seventeen

At The Track

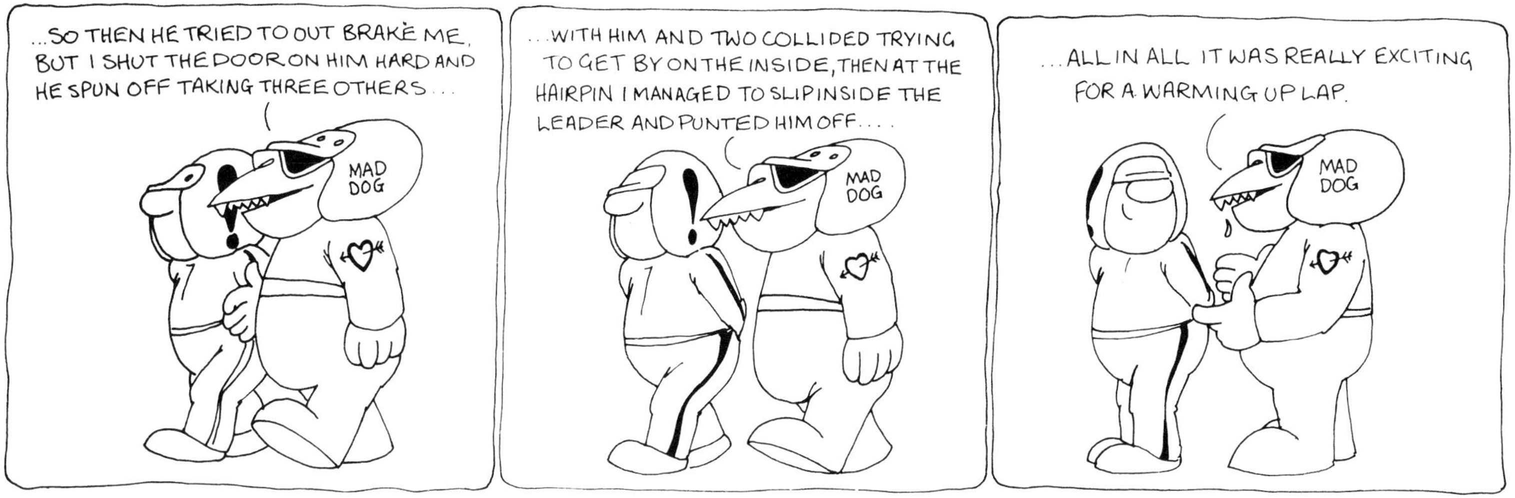

...SO THEN HE TRIED TO OUT BRAKE ME, BUT I SHUT THE DOOR ON HIM HARD AND HE SPUN OFF TAKING THREE OTHERS...
MAD DOG
...WITH HIM AND TWO COLLIDED TRYING TO GET BY ON THE INSIDE, THEN AT THE HAIRPIN I MANAGED TO SLIP INSIDE THE LEADER AND PUNTED HIM OFF....
MAD DOG
...ALL IN ALL IT WAS REALLY EXCITING FOR A WARMING UP LAP.
MAD DOG

10th June 1976

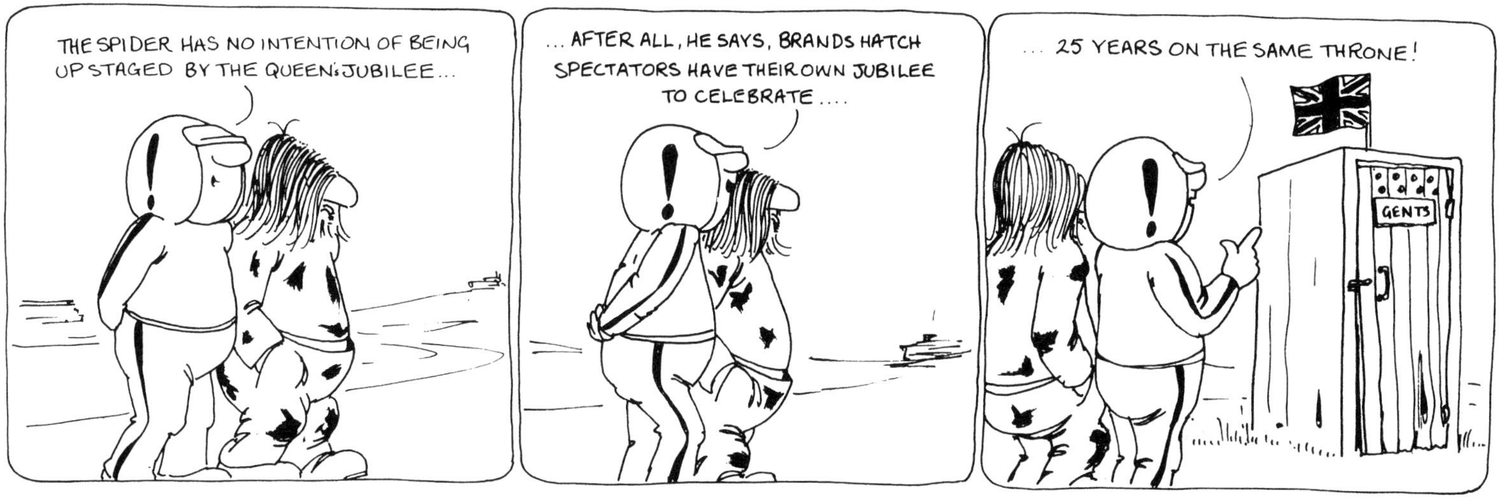

THE SPIDER HAS NO INTENTION OF BEING UPSTAGED BY THE QUEEN'S JUBILEE...
...AFTER ALL, HE SAYS, BRANDS HATCH SPECTATORS HAVE THEIR OWN JUBILEE TO CELEBRATE....
...25 YEARS ON THE SAME THRONE!
GENTS

2nd June 1977

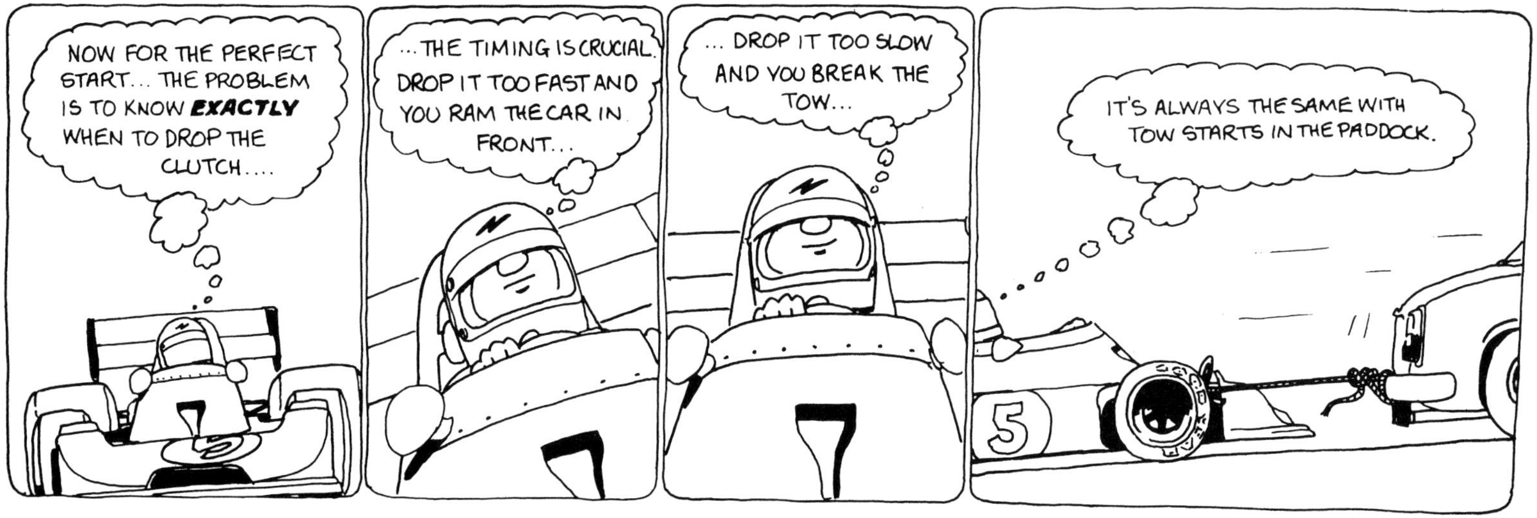
NOW FOR THE PERFECT START... THE PROBLEM IS TO KNOW **EXACTLY** WHEN TO DROP THE CLUTCH....
...THE TIMING IS CRUCIAL. DROP IT TOO FAST AND YOU RAM THE CAR IN FRONT...
... DROP IT TOO SLOW AND YOU BREAK THE TOW...
IT'S ALWAYS THE SAME WITH TOW STARTS IN THE PADDOCK.

4th August 1977

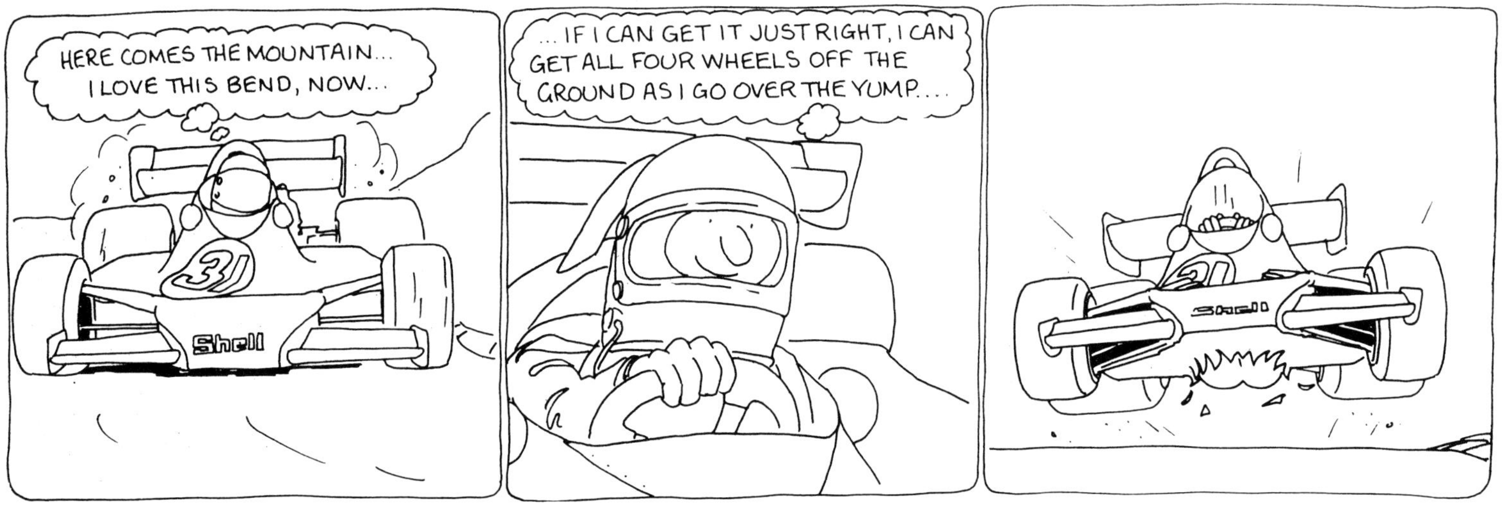
HERE COMES THE MOUNTAIN... I LOVE THIS BEND, NOW...
... IF I CAN GET IT JUST RIGHT, I CAN GET ALL FOUR WHEELS OFF THE GROUND AS I GO OVER THE YUMP....

26th October 1978

Chapter Seventeen

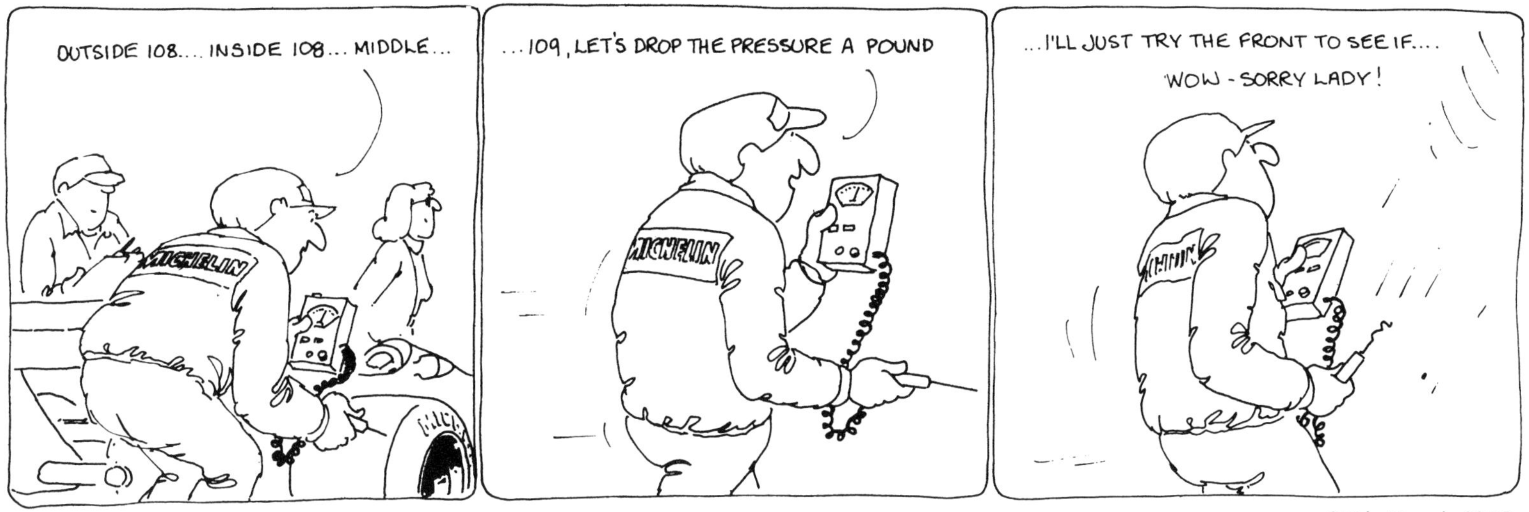

OUTSIDE 108.... INSIDE 108... MIDDLE...
...109, LET'S DROP THE PRESSURE A POUND
...I'LL JUST TRY THE FRONT TO SEE IF....
WOW - SORRY LADY!

27th March 1980

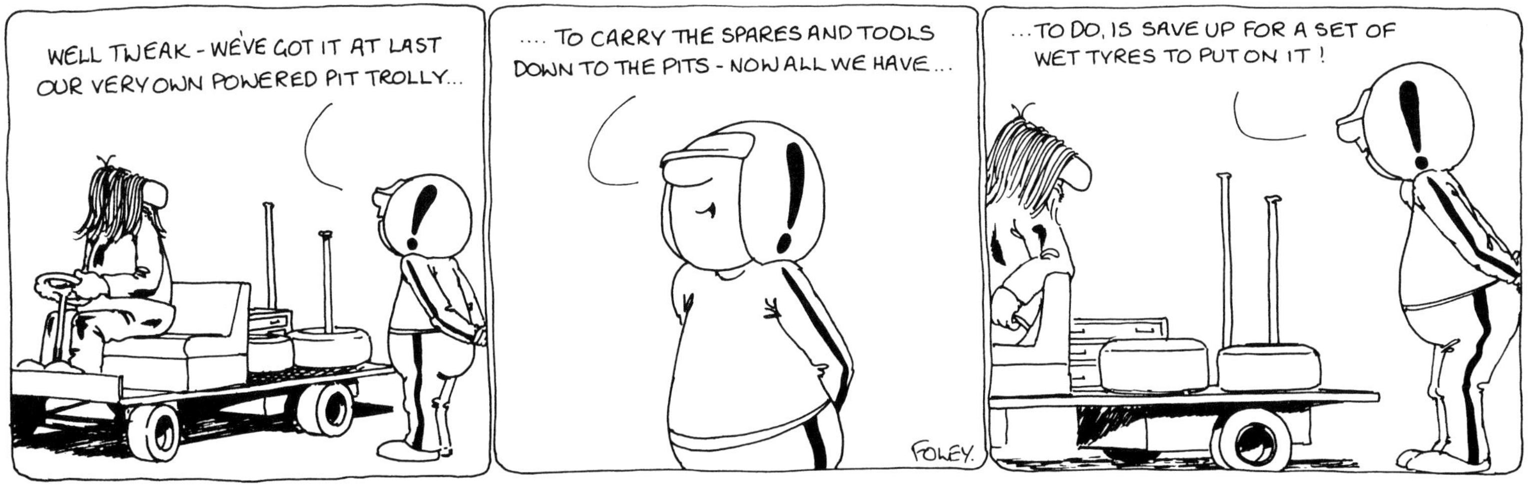

WELL TWEAK - WE'VE GOT IT AT LAST OUR VERY OWN POWERED PIT TROLLY...
.... TO CARRY THE SPARES AND TOOLS DOWN TO THE PITS - NOW ALL WE HAVE...
...TO DO, IS SAVE UP FOR A SET OF WET TYRES TO PUT ON IT!
FOLEY

28th March 1985

At The Track

POOR LITTLE SOULS....
...UNDERNOURISHED, UNDERPRIVILEGED, COLD, WET, HUNGRY...
WHO ARE YOU TALKING ABOUT THE CHILDREN OR THE SPECTATORS?

3rd December 1987

WHAT DID THE MAKERS SAY ABOUT THE STATE OF YOUR NEW SINGLE SEATER?
THEY SAID IT WAS A GOOD THING — DISSIPATION OF ENERGY IN A CRASH ETC... AFTER ALL, I WASN'T HURT.
I SAID "NO, I WASN'T HURT, AND I DIDN'T CRASH — IT WAS LIKE THAT WHEN WE OPENED THE TRANSPORTER!"
FOLEY

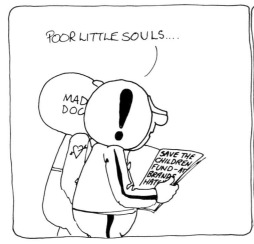

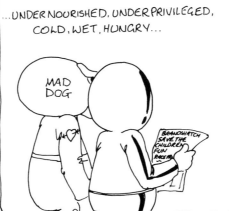

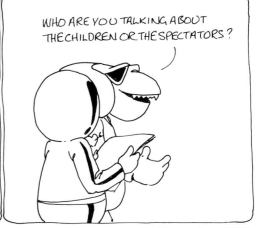

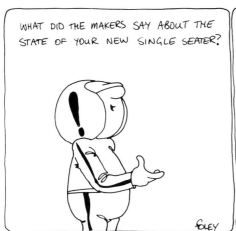

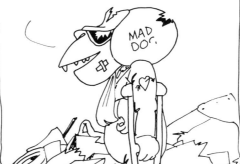

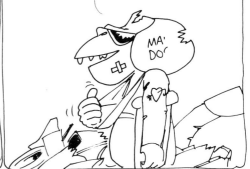

3rd March 1988

Chapter Eighteen

In The Pits

Everything happens in the pits. This is where raw amateurism meets incompetence. It's a shame signal boards don't boast full alphabets. We would really get some interesting messages then. No longer the simple 'OUT' or 'IN' or 'FUEL ON', instead we could have things like 'SLOUCH' or 'GET YOUR FINGER OUT'. In '98 when I drove in Phil Lane's 2CV with Tom Commander and Chris Hart in the Mondello 24-hour race, I drew up lots of special signal boards with things like 'ARSEHOLE' and 'PIG' and 'CRAP' on them. We caused a fair bit of consternation.

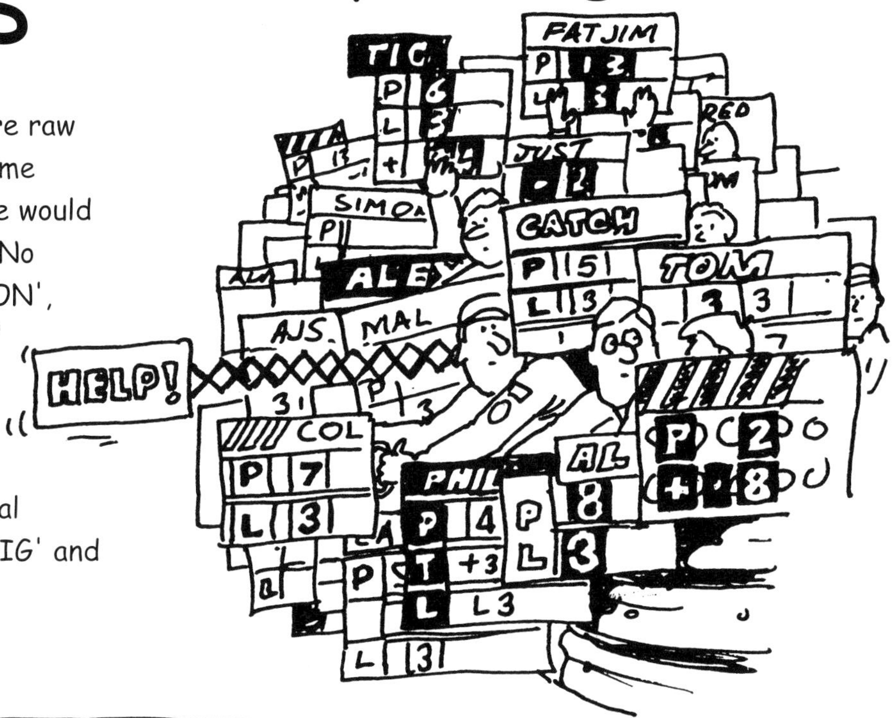
FATJIM
TIC
CATCH
TOM
ALEX
HELP!
AUS
MAL
COL
PHIL
AL

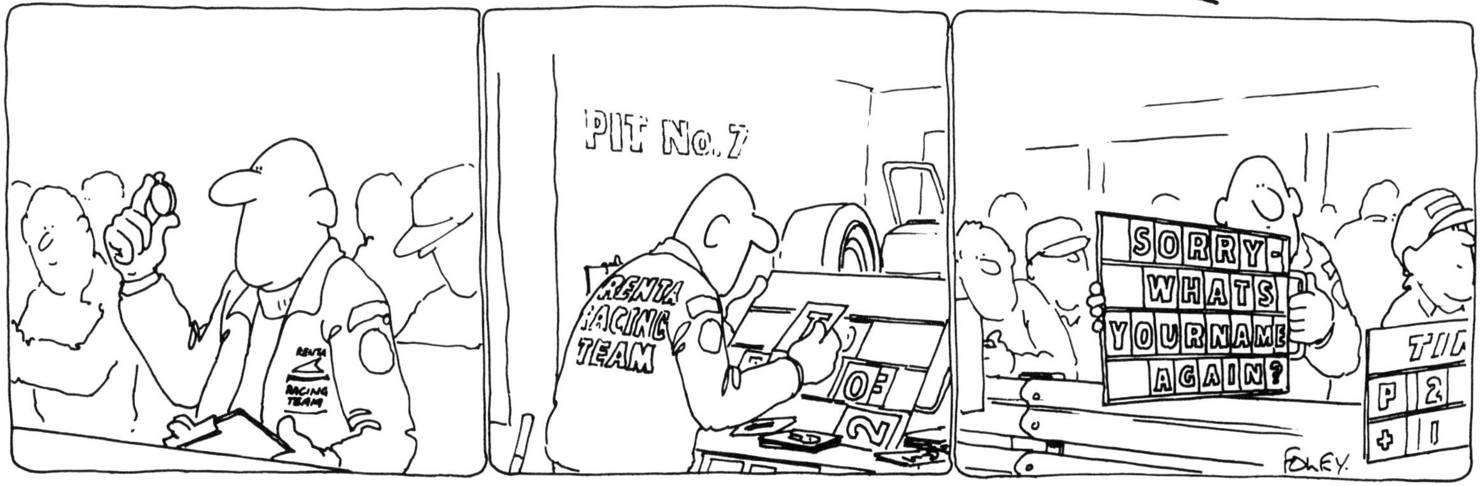
PIT No. 7
RENTA RACING TEAM
SORRY-
WHATS
YOURNAME
AGAIN?
FOLEY

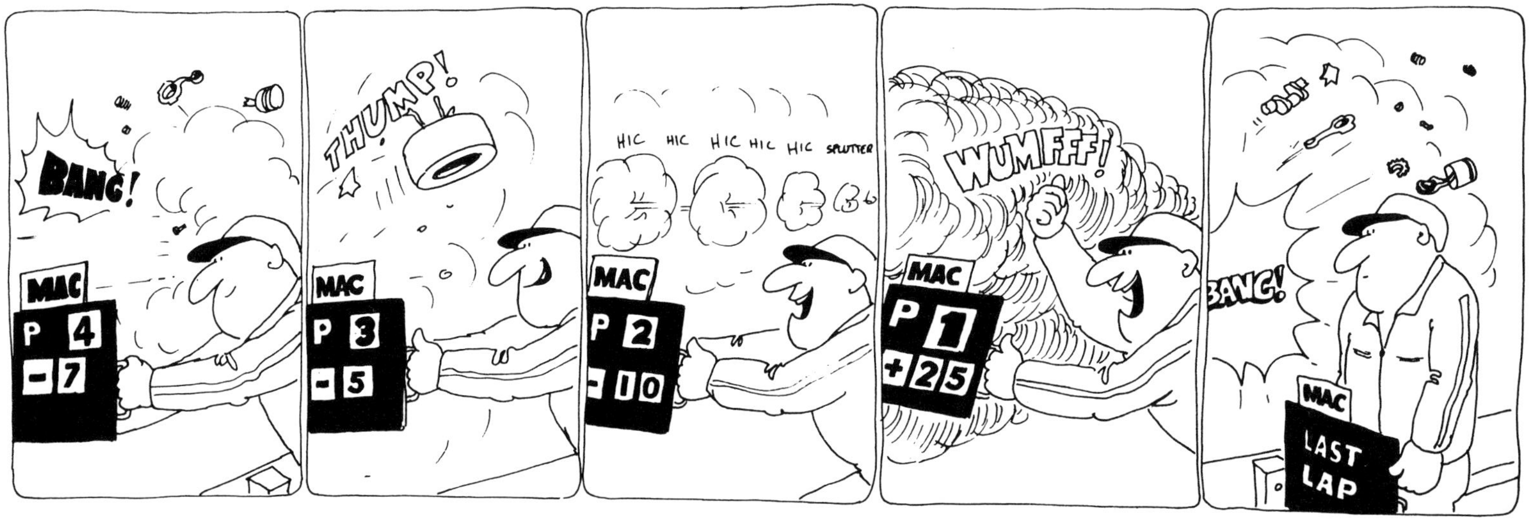
BANG!
MAC
P 4
-7
THUMP!
MAC
P 3
-5
HIC HIC HIC HIC HIC SPLUTTER
MAC
P 2
-10
WUMFFF!
MAC
P 1
+25
BANG!
MAC
LAST LAP

9th February 1978

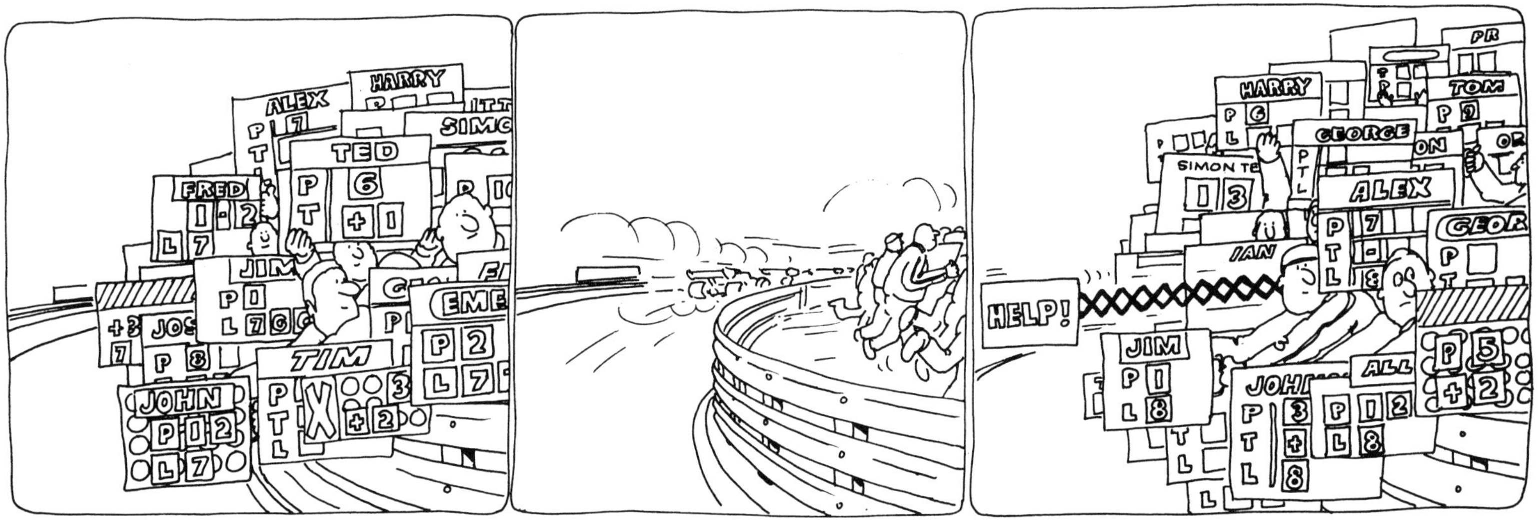
ALEX
HARRY
TED
P 6
T +1
FRED
JIM
JOHN
TIM
HELP!
HARRY
GEORGE
TOM
SIMON
ALEX
JIM

23rd February 1978

Chapter Eighteen

In The Pits

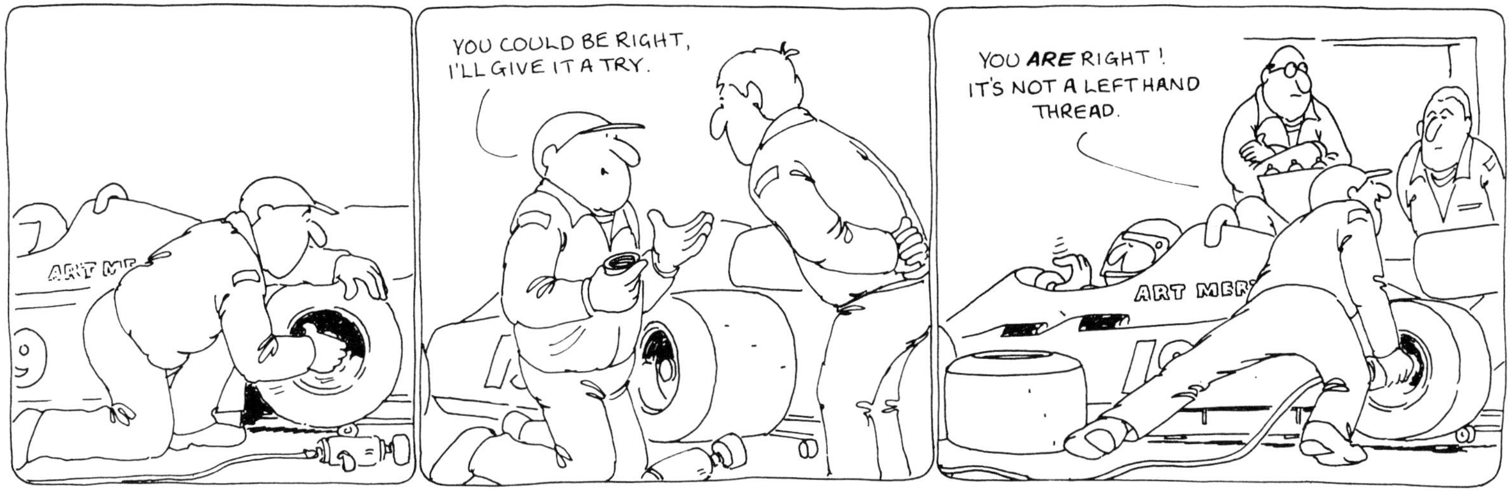

YOU COULD BE RIGHT, I'LL GIVE IT A TRY.
YOU **ARE** RIGHT ! IT'S NOT A LEFT HAND THREAD.

27th September 1979

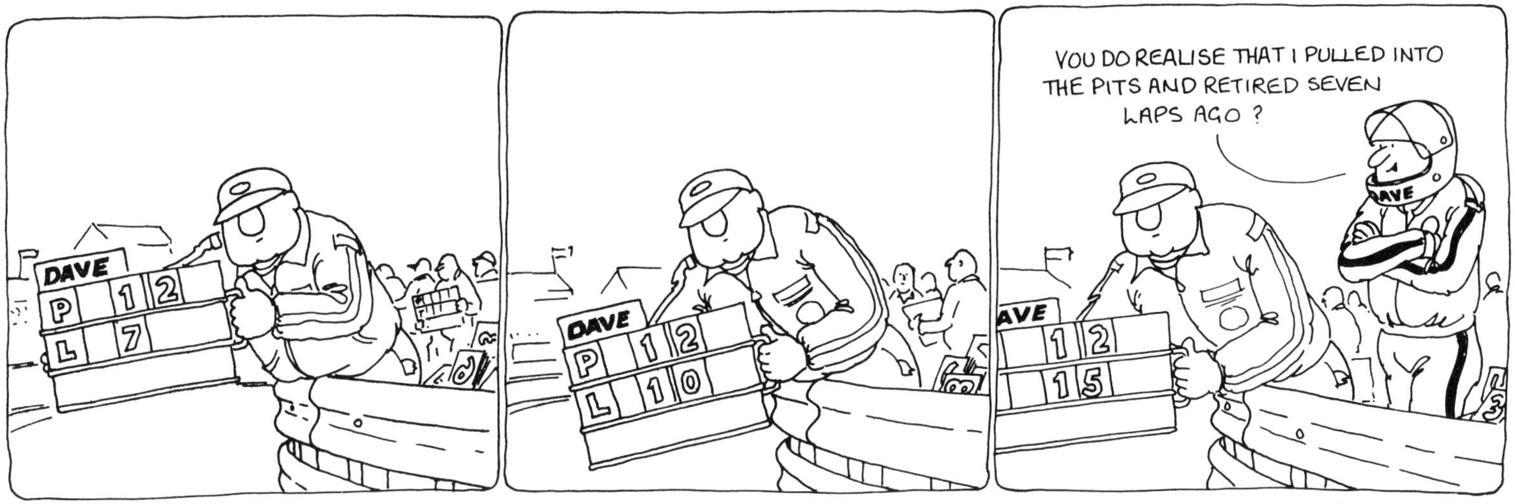

DAVE
P 12
L 7
DAVE
P 12
L 10
AVE
12
15
YOU DO REALISE THAT I PULLED INTO THE PITS AND RETIRED SEVEN LAPS AGO ?

14th August 1980

In The Pits

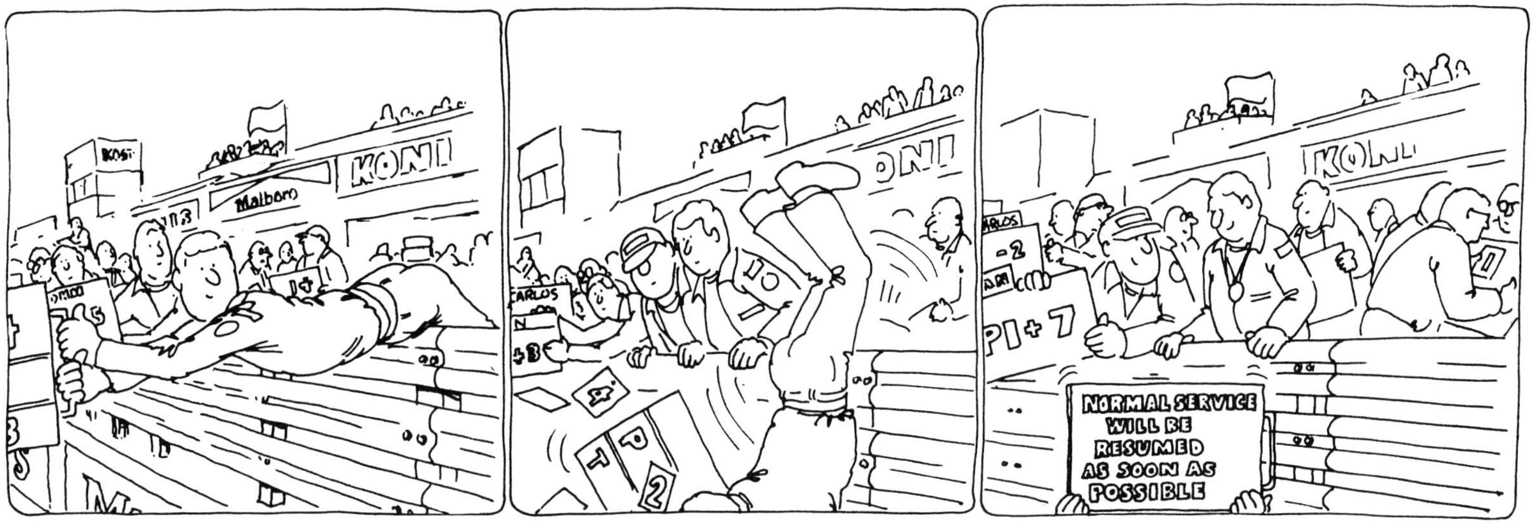
KONI
PI + 7
NORMAL SERVICE
WILL BE
RESUMED
AS SOON AS
POSSIBLE

29th May 1986

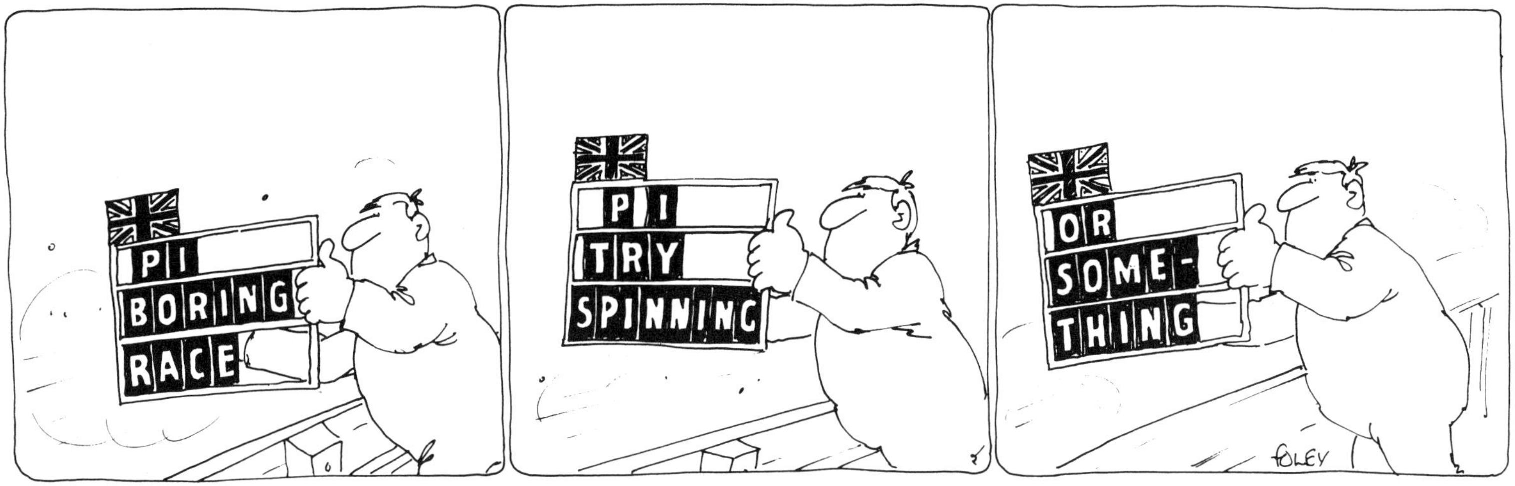
PI
BORING
RACE
PI
TRY
SPINNING
OR
SOME-
THING
FOLEY

9th July 1987

Chapter Nineteen

The Bar

IT'S YOUR ROUND

At some circuits such as Snetterton and Pembrey the bar is still a place where drivers gather. Back in the '60s and '70s the bar was where most of the racing happened.

The bar was where you could always find Tony Lanfranchi and Gerry Marshall, Graham Hill, Mike Hailwood, John Webb, James Hunt - in fact almost every driver after the race. It was here that views were formed, rumours spread and deals done. Now in 2000 and something everyone rushes off home except for Catchpole and a few die-hards who still know how to live.

NOW AS I SEE IT, TWEAK. WE'VE GOT THREE ALTERNATIVES. ONE - WE STRIP THE GEAR BOX DOWN AND FIX IT....
9
TWO - WE LEAVE IT AS IT IS AND HOPE IT FINISHES THE RACE..
9
THREE - WE SCRATCH FROM THE RACE AND RETIRE TO THE BAR
DEMON TWEAK
DECISIONS, DECISIONS, DECISIONS.
GRUNT

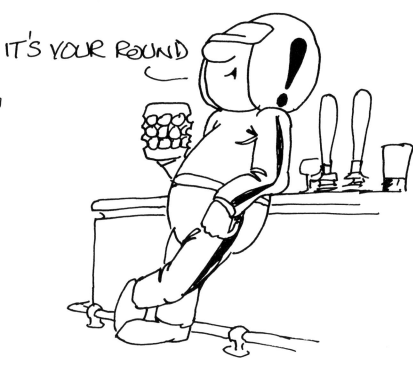

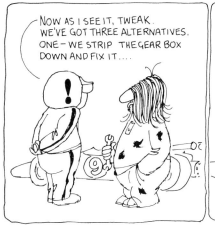

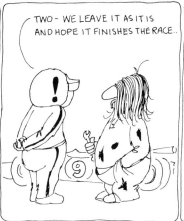

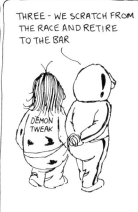

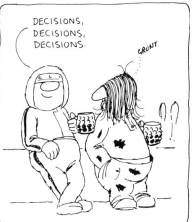

The Bar

IT'S YOUR ROUND I BELIEVE, TWEAK. I'LL HAVE A PINT
GRUNT
SHUFFLE
SCRAPE SCRAPE
GRUNT GRUNT
SHUFFLE
SHUFFLE
SHUFFLE
GRUNT
DEMON TWEAK
JINGLE JINGLE
SHUFFLE SHUFFLE
SHUFFLE
A FINE EXAMPLE OF A LOW POLAR MOMENT OF INERTIA
GRUNT GRUNT
DEMON TWEAK
SHUFFLE
SHUFFLE
SHUFFLE

27th May 1971

I HEAR HILL'S DOWN HERE, TESTING....
GRUNT
... HE'S TRYING A NEW MIX, 'WONDER WHAT IT IS?
..... MILD AND BITTER, PERHAPS?
IT'S NOT OXO THAT'S FOR SURE

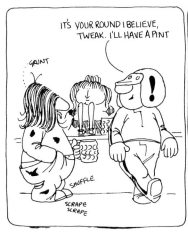

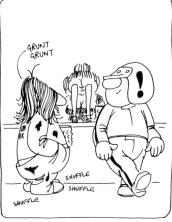

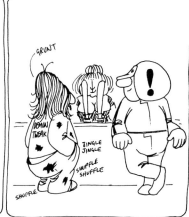

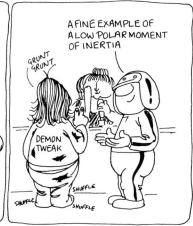

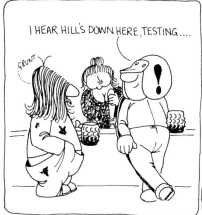

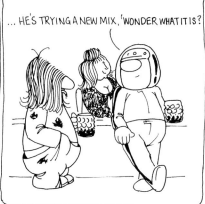

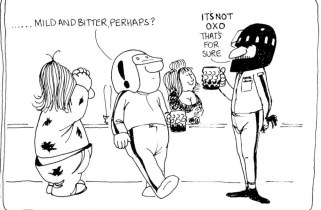

17th June 1971

Chapter Nineteen

The Bar

ABSHOLUTELY DISGUSTIN, HE SHED. SHOUD BE STOPPED, HIC! , HE SHED...
... RACING DRIVERS LIKE YOU HIC! ARE A DISGRASH, HE SHED....
BRRP! PARDON
... RASHING DRIVERS SHOUDNT DRINK (PARDON) BEFORE A RACE, HE SHED....
RASHING DRIVERS SHOUD STAY SHOBER, HE SHED....
HIC!
..... RASHING DRIVERS, SSMACING DRIVERS, I SHED, I'M THE RUDDY PILOT.

2nd September 1971

EVERYBODY KEEPS TELLING ME THAT I SPEND TO MUCH TIME TALKING ABOUT SINGLE SEATERS....
... THEY SAY I SHOULD CONCENTRATE MORE ON SALOONS ....
GRUNT
... SO I'M REFORMING.
SALOON BAR

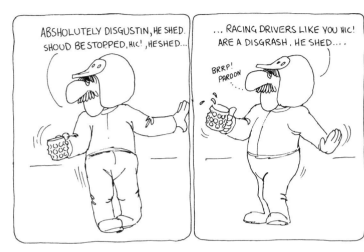

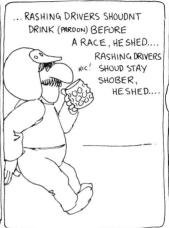

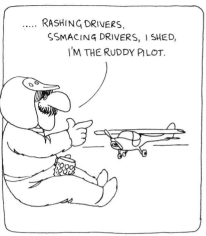

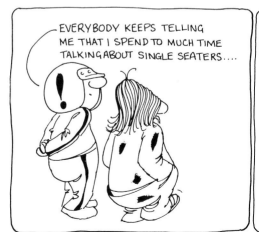

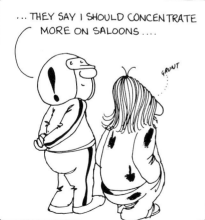

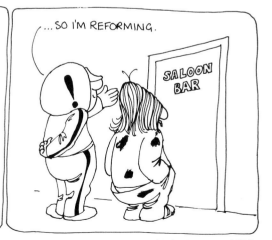

13th January 1972

I DON'T MIND DRIVERS WHO BUMP AND SHOVE OR CLOSE UP UNDER A YELLOW FLAG....
...I DON'T MIND HAVING THE DOOR CLOSED ON ME, I CAN EVEN PUT UP WITH A BIT OF BAULKING...
GRUNT
...OR RUDE GESTICULATION, BUT THE DRIVERS I CAN'T STAND ARE THE...
...BUGGERS THAT PINCH YOUR BEER.
GRUNT GRUNT

8th June 1972

THE THREE BEST THINGS IN LIFE ARE ALL DOWN TO YOU TWEAK.—'WINE, WOMEN AND RACING CARS'.....
GRUNT
....OUR RACING CAR NEEDS MENDING, YOU HAVE SCARED ALL THE BIRDS AWAY, AND....
....IT'S YOUR ROUND.
GRUNT

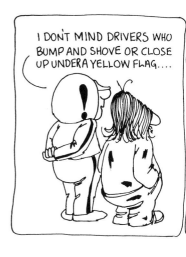

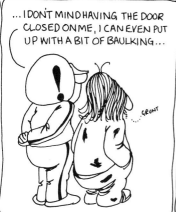

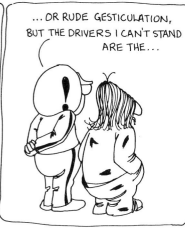

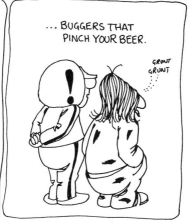

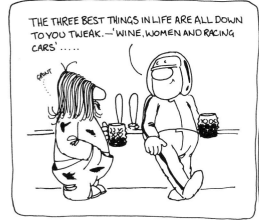

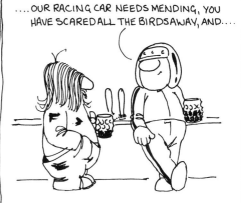

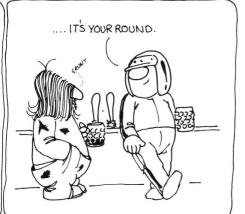

22nd June 1972

Chapter Nineteen

The Bar

YOUR BARGING TACTICS SHOULD BE BANNED THEY SAID...
MAD DOG
YOU ARE FAR TOO ROUGH, THEY SAID....
...ALL THAT PUSHING AND SHOVING TO GET TO THE FRONT IS DANGEROUS, THEY SAID...
...YOU MIGHT KNOCK SOMEBODY'S BEER OVER.

13th July 1972

THAT'S 17 MILES, ONLY 3 TO GO.
PUFF
LONDON
2,304
2,305
2,306
2,307...CHANGE LEGS...
...ONE HUNRED AND TWE-N-T-Y THR-E-E-E UGH. GASP ONE HUNRED AND TWE-EEN-TY FFFOUR.
GRUNT GROAN
MAKES YOU THIRSTY JUST THINKING ABOUT IT.

13th February 1975

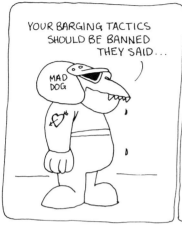

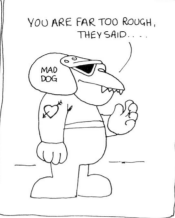

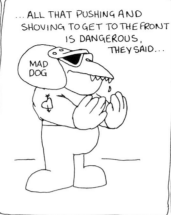

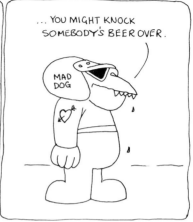

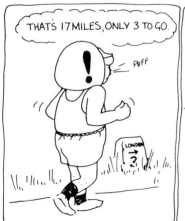

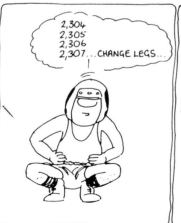

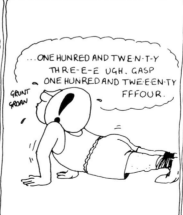

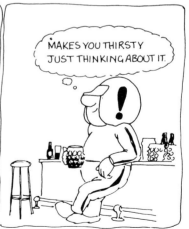

SURELY IT'S NOT JUST COINCIDENCE THAT THE LAST...
...THREE LETTERS IN THE WORD 'MAFIA' ARE F.I.A. —AFTERALL...
...THEY ARE FOREVER MAKING US OFFERS THAT WE CAN'T REFUSE.
GRUNT

5th April 1975

IT SEEMS THAT THE ARMCO BARRIER...
...WAS INSTALLED AT THE DEMAND OF GERRY MARSHALL AND TONY LANFRANCHI...
...BECAUSE THIS IS THE PLACE THEY HAVE MOST OF THEIR ACCIDENTS.

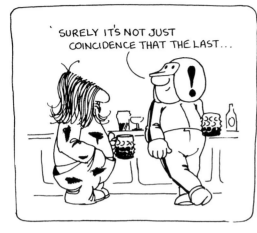

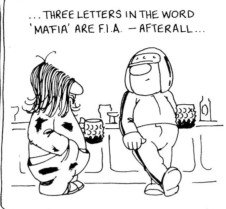

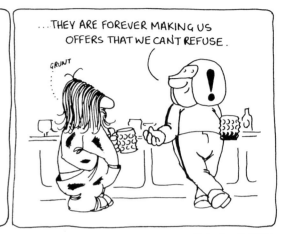

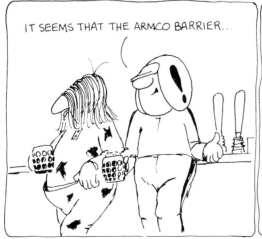

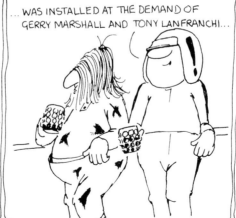

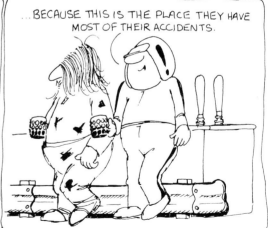

30th October 1975

Chapter Nineteen

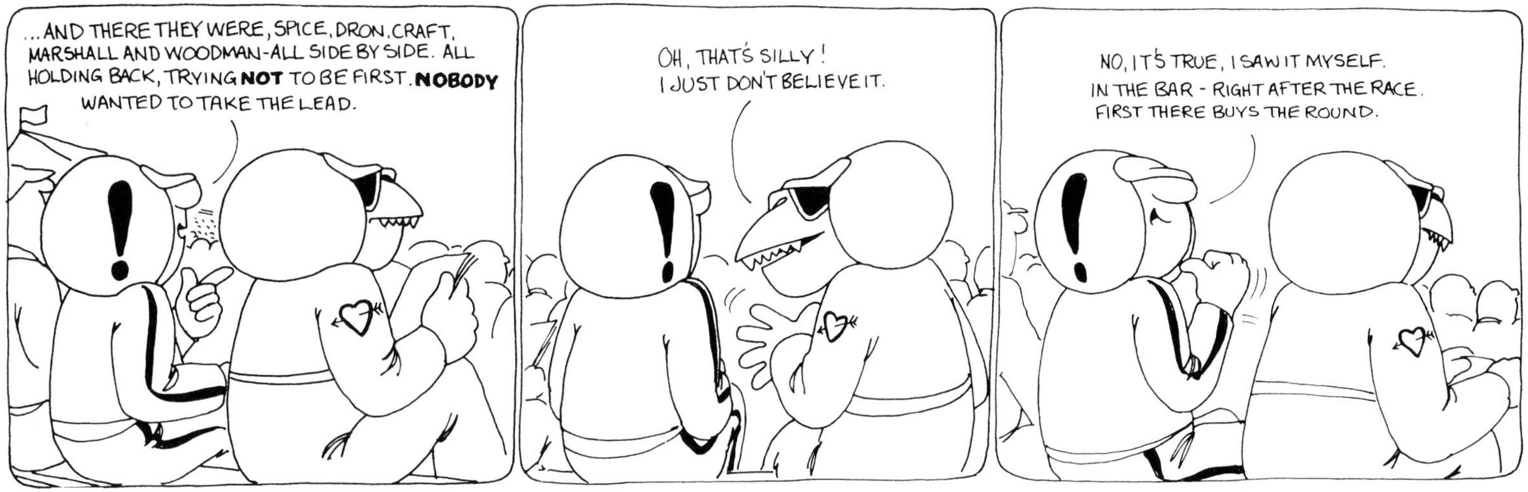
...AND THERE THEY WERE, SPICE, DRON, CRAFT, MARSHALL AND WOODMAN-ALL SIDE BY SIDE. ALL HOLDING BACK, TRYING **NOT** TO BE FIRST. **NOBODY** WANTED TO TAKE THE LEAD.
OH, THAT'S SILLY! I JUST DON'T BELIEVE IT.
NO, IT'S TRUE, I SAW IT MYSELF. IN THE BAR - RIGHT AFTER THE RACE. FIRST THERE BUYS THE ROUND.

12th May 1977

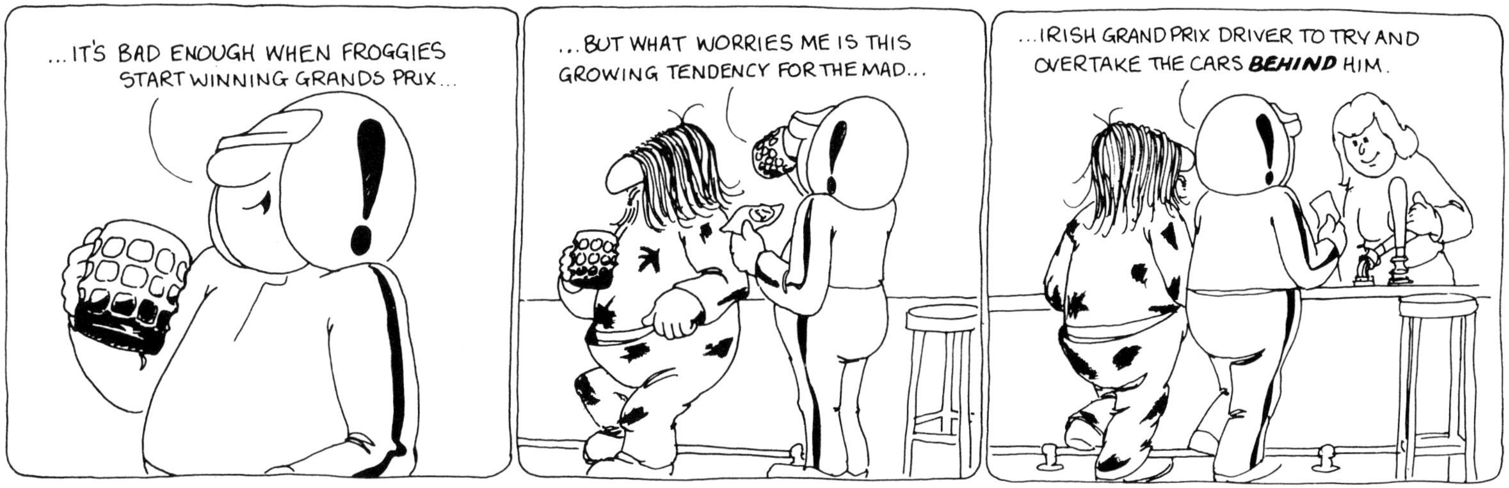
...IT'S BAD ENOUGH WHEN FROGGIES START WINNING GRANDS PRIX...
...BUT WHAT WORRIES ME IS THIS GROWING TENDENCY FOR THE MAD...
...IRISH GRAND PRIX DRIVER TO TRY AND OVERTAKE THE CARS ***BEHIND*** HIM.

23rd June 1977

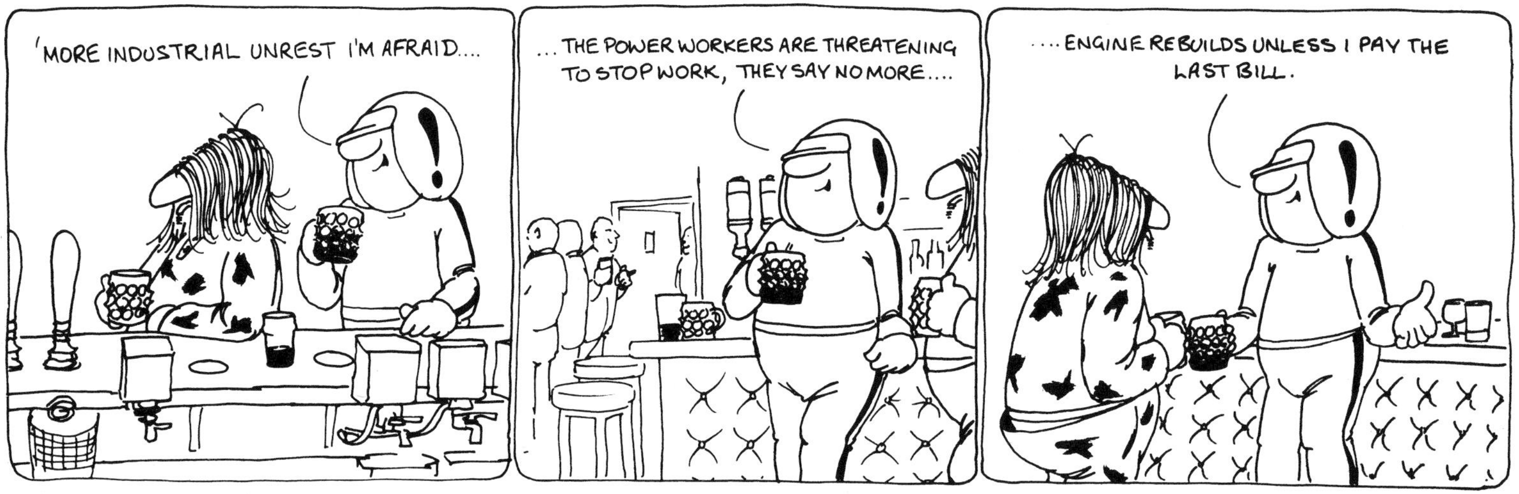
'MORE INDUSTRIAL UNREST I'M AFRAID....
...THE POWER WORKERS ARE THREATENING TO STOP WORK, THEY SAY NO MORE....
....ENGINE REBUILDS UNLESS I PAY THE LAST BILL.

10th November 1977

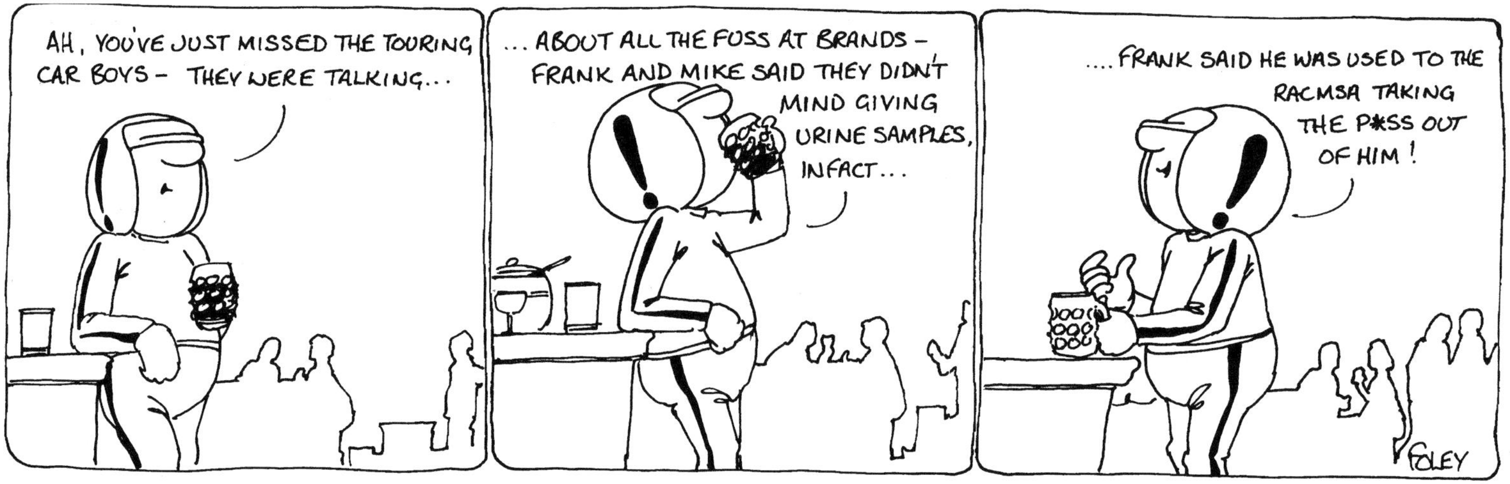
AH, YOU'VE JUST MISSED THE TOURING CAR BOYS - THEY WERE TALKING...
...ABOUT ALL THE FUSS AT BRANDS - FRANK AND MIKE SAID THEY DIDN'T MIND GIVING URINE SAMPLES, INFACT...
....FRANK SAID HE WAS USED TO THE RACMSA TAKING THE P*SS OUT OF HIM!
FOLEY

2nd August 1990

Chapter Twenty

Shunts

Ah, the best bit of all. I always get accused of rubber necking at shunts, but I think they are rather beautiful, sad for the owner of the car but a wreck is none the less an awesome thing. The real biggies like Dumbreck's back summersault at Le Mans or Villeneuve's off trying to take Eau Rouge flat are works of art. This is Mad Dog territory. He is a beautiful shunter; he has turned it into his speciality. In fact he is a racing shunters' shunter.

I WONDER IF ANYONE GOT ANY DECENT PHOTOS OF IT HAPPENING ?

HOW DID YOUR F.3. RACE GO, MAD DOG?
MAD DOG MALONE
DREADFUL. DREADFUL, AN ABSOLUTE DISASTER! I DIDN'T HIT ANYONE UNTIL LAP EIGHT.
MAD DOG MALONE

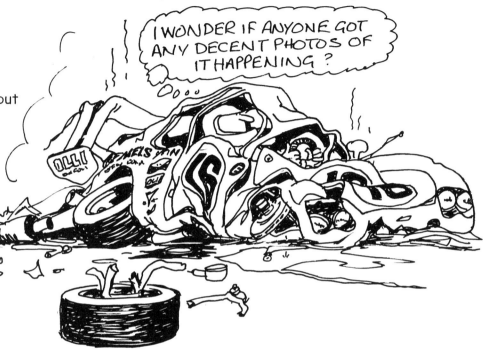

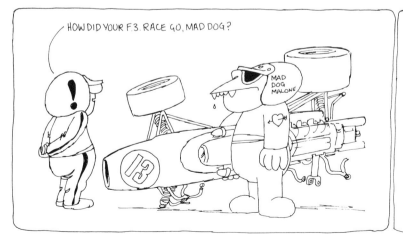

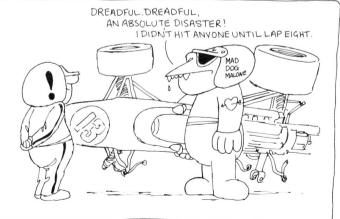

....BUT WHERE EXACTLY DID IT HAPPEN?
DRUIDS?
PADDOCK?
ST. MORITZ

8th March 1973

FREE!

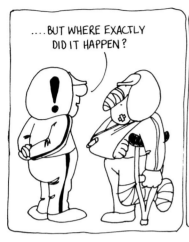

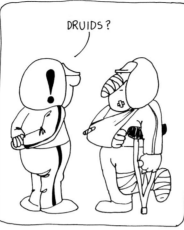

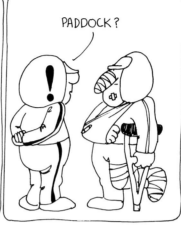

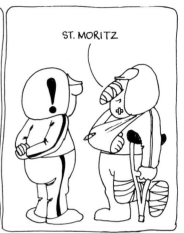

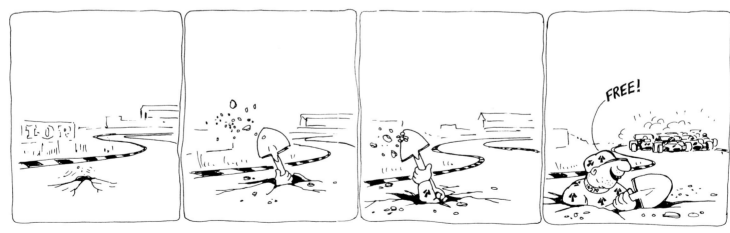

31st May 1973

Chapter Twenty

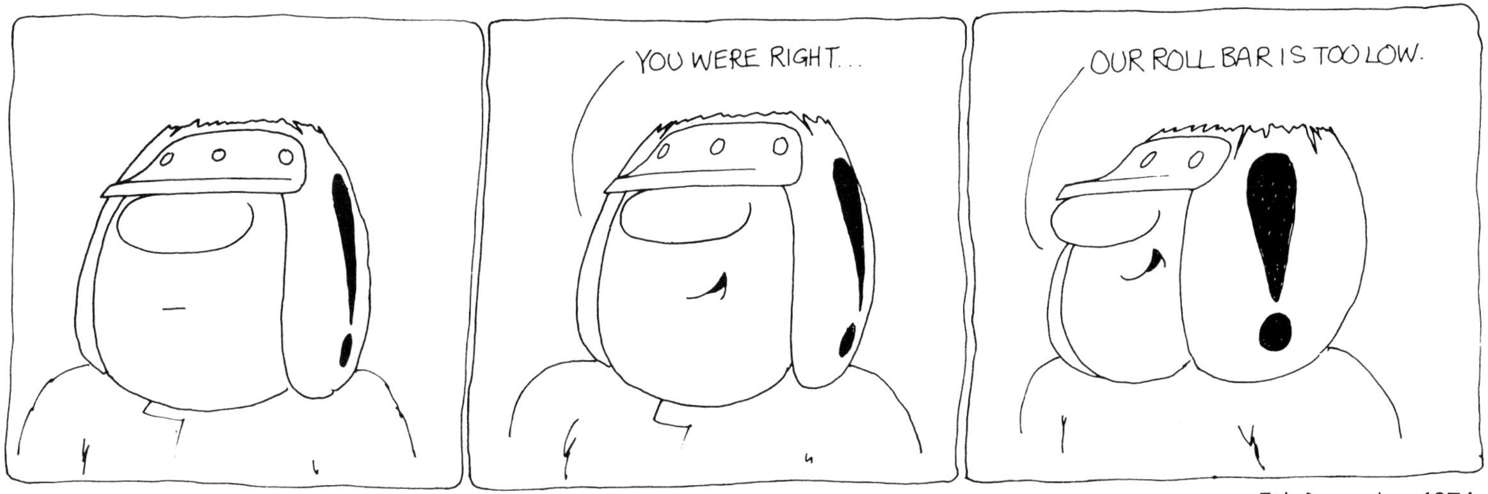
YOU WERE RIGHT...
OUR ROLL BAR IS TOO LOW.

5th December 1974

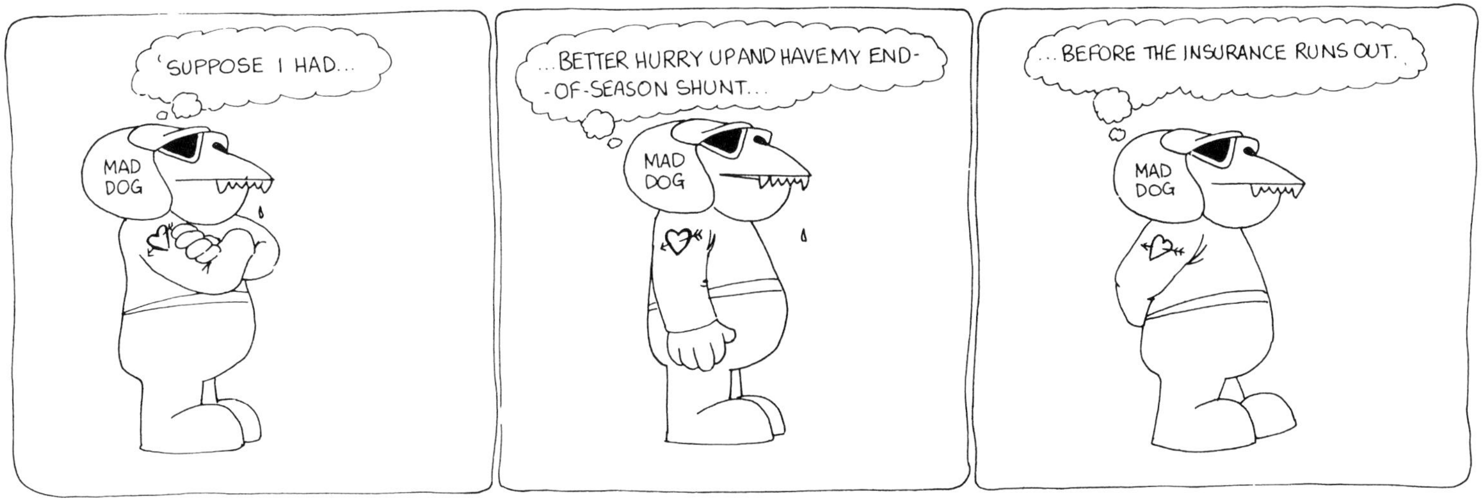
SUPPOSE I HAD...
MAD DOG
...BETTER HURRY UP AND HAVE MY END-OF-SEASON SHUNT...
MAD DOG
...BEFORE THE INSURANCE RUNS OUT.
MAD DOG

6th November 1975

Shunts

Shunts

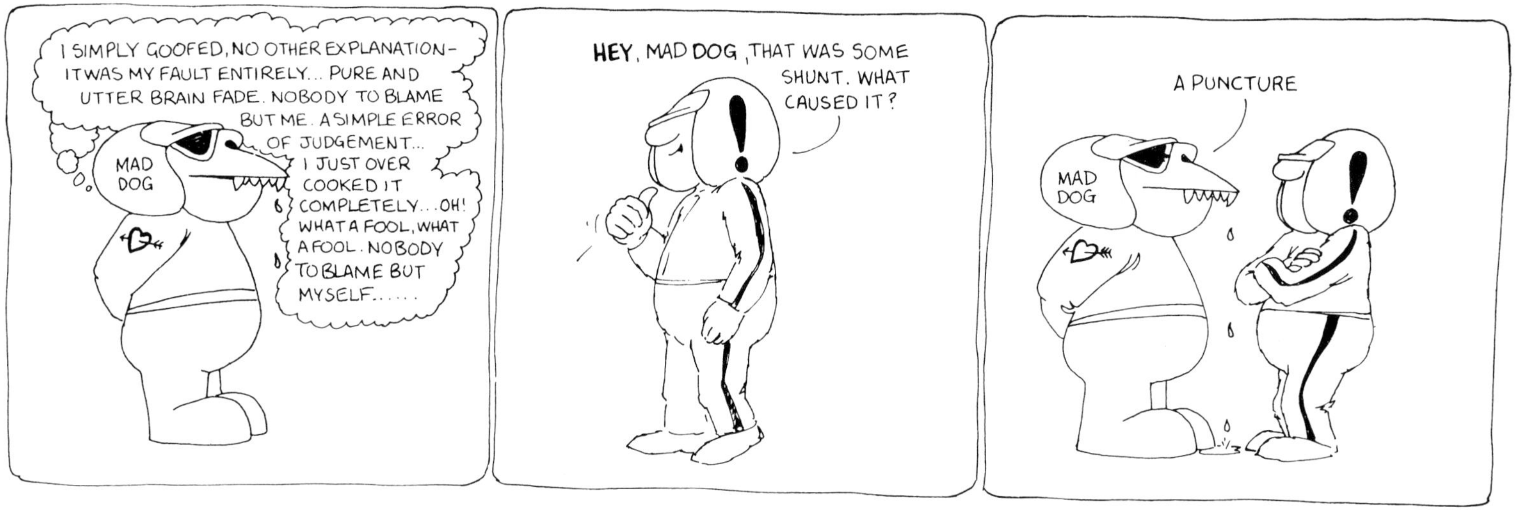
I SIMPLY GOOFED, NO OTHER EXPLANATION - IT WAS MY FAULT ENTIRELY... PURE AND UTTER BRAIN FADE. NOBODY TO BLAME BUT ME. A SIMPLE ERROR OF JUDGEMENT... I JUST OVER COOKED IT COMPLETELY...OH! WHAT A FOOL, WHAT A FOOL. NOBODY TO BLAME BUT MYSELF......
MAD DOG
HEY, MAD DOG, THAT WAS SOME SHUNT. WHAT CAUSED IT?
A PUNCTURE
MAD DOG

13th November 1975

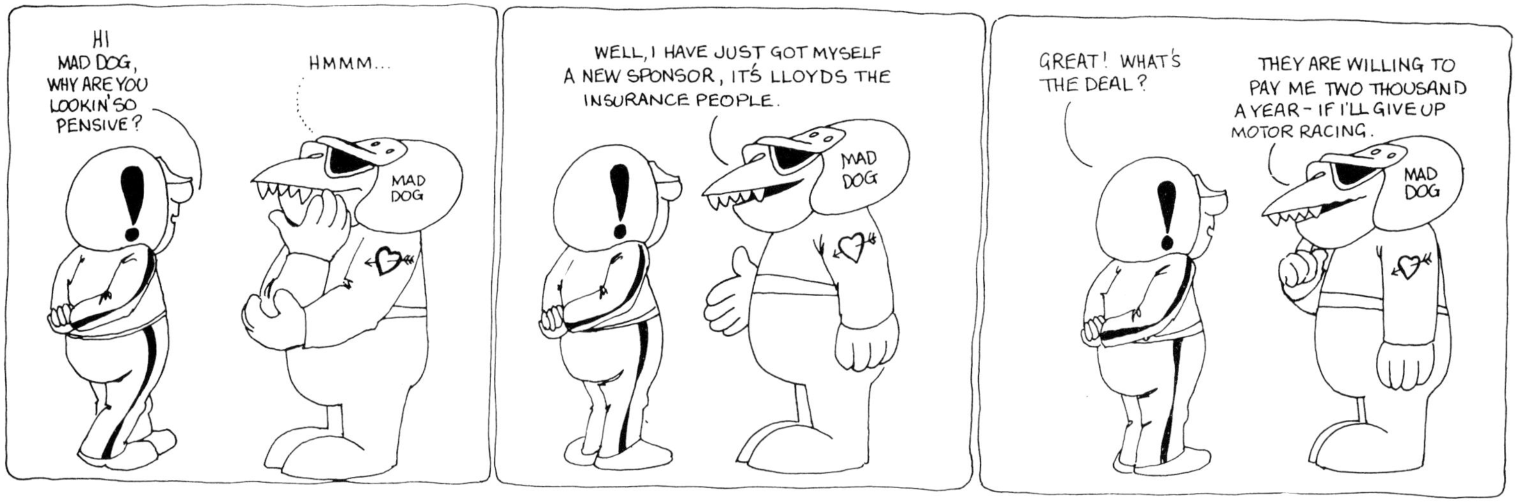
HI MAD DOG, WHY ARE YOU LOOKIN' SO PENSIVE?
HMMM...
MAD DOG
WELL, I HAVE JUST GOT MYSELF A NEW SPONSOR, IT'S LLOYDS THE INSURANCE PEOPLE.
MAD DOG
GREAT! WHAT'S THE DEAL?
THEY ARE WILLING TO PAY ME TWO THOUSAND A YEAR - IF I'LL GIVE UP MOTOR RACING.
MAD DOG

22nd April 1976

Chapter Twenty

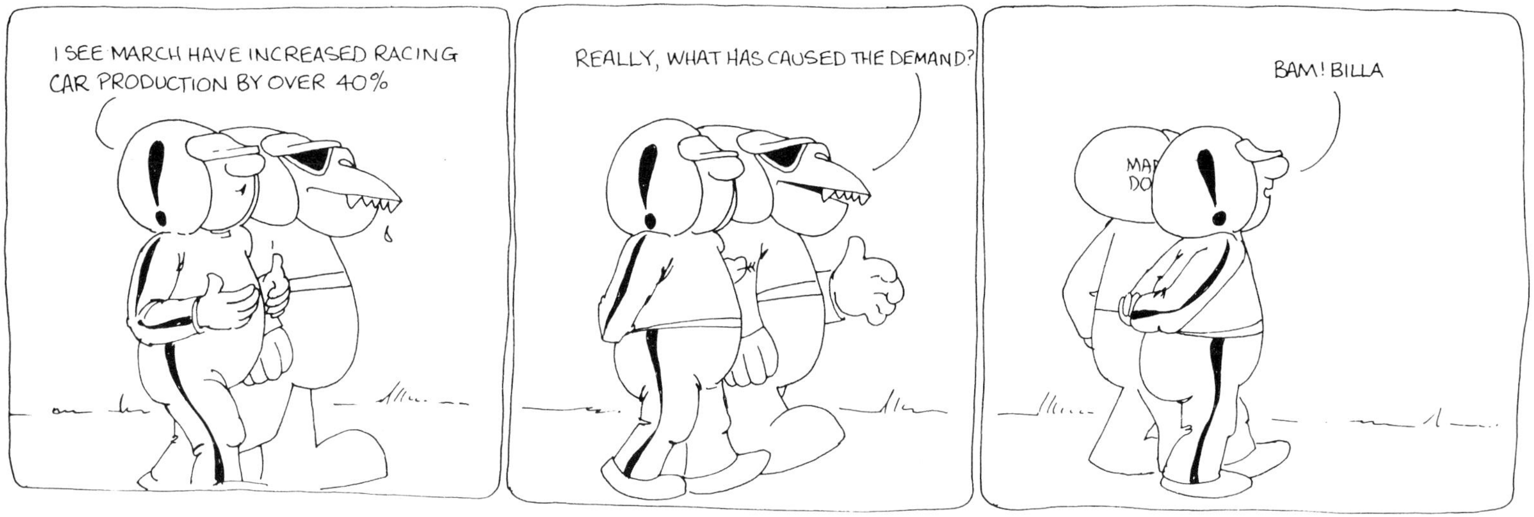
I SEE MARCH HAVE INCREASED RACING CAR PRODUCTION BY OVER 40%
REALLY, WHAT HAS CAUSED THE DEMAND?
BAM! BILLA

12th August 1976

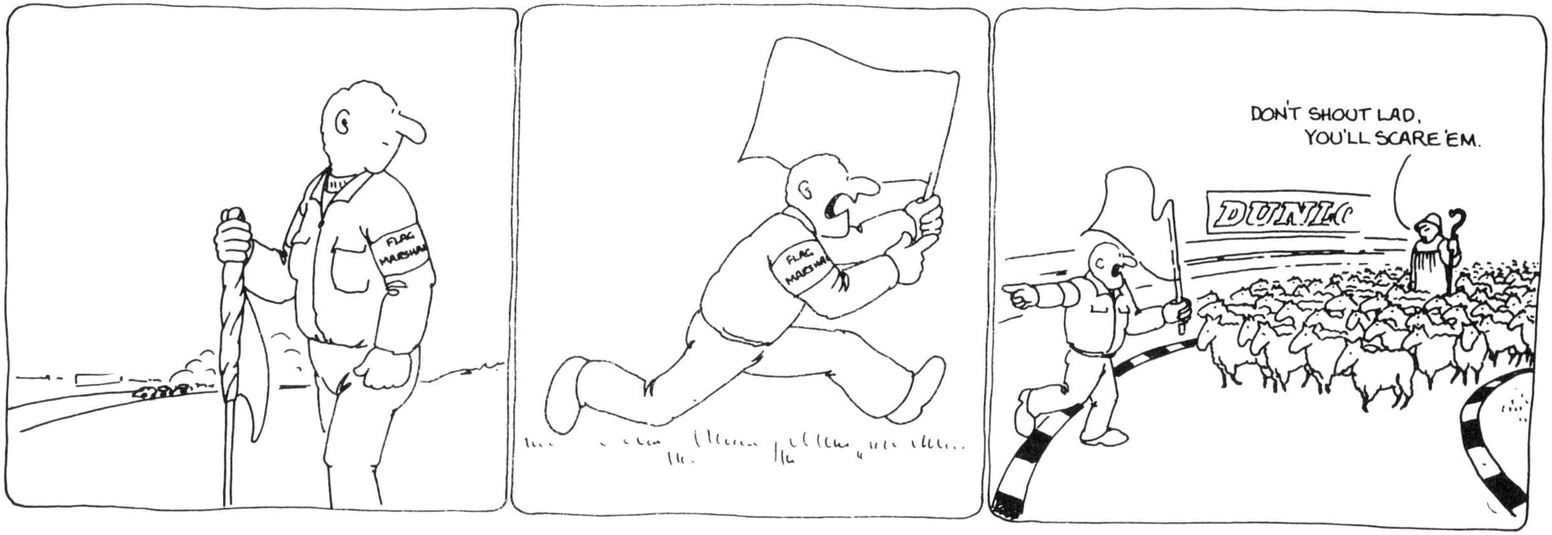
DON'T SHOUT LAD, YOU'LL SCARE 'EM.

26th January 1978

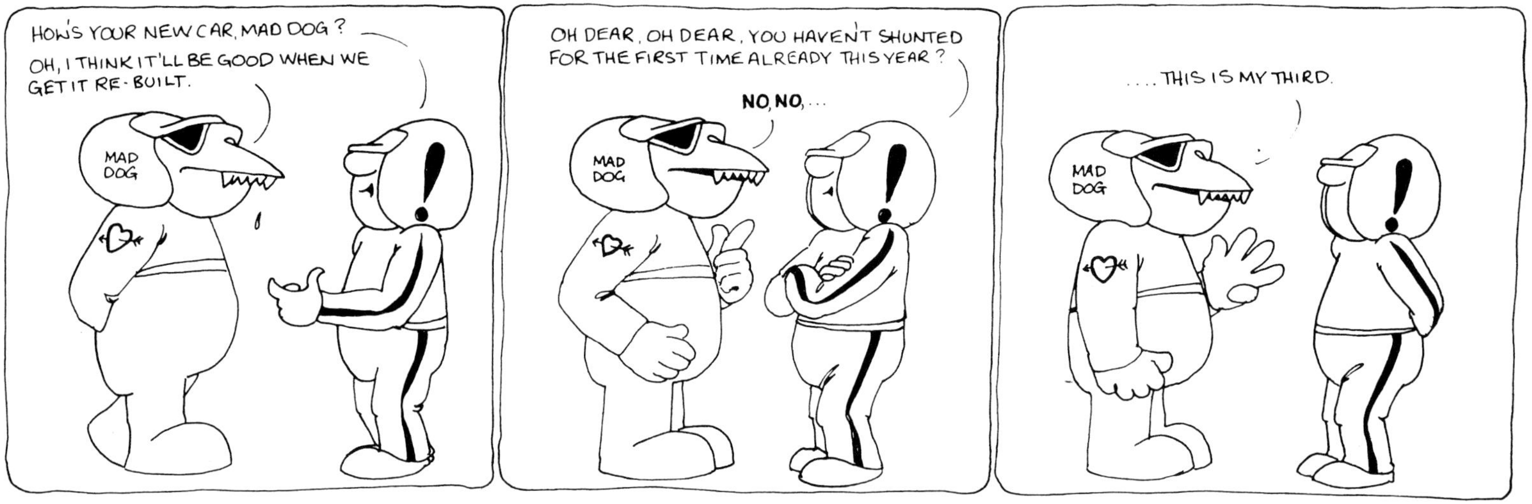
HOW'S YOUR NEW CAR, MAD DOG?
OH, I THINK IT'LL BE GOOD WHEN WE GET IT RE-BUILT.
MAD DOG
OH DEAR, OH DEAR, YOU HAVEN'T SHUNTED FOR THE FIRST TIME ALREADY THIS YEAR?
NO, NO, ...
MAD DOG
.... THIS IS MY THIRD.
MAD DOG

30th March 1978

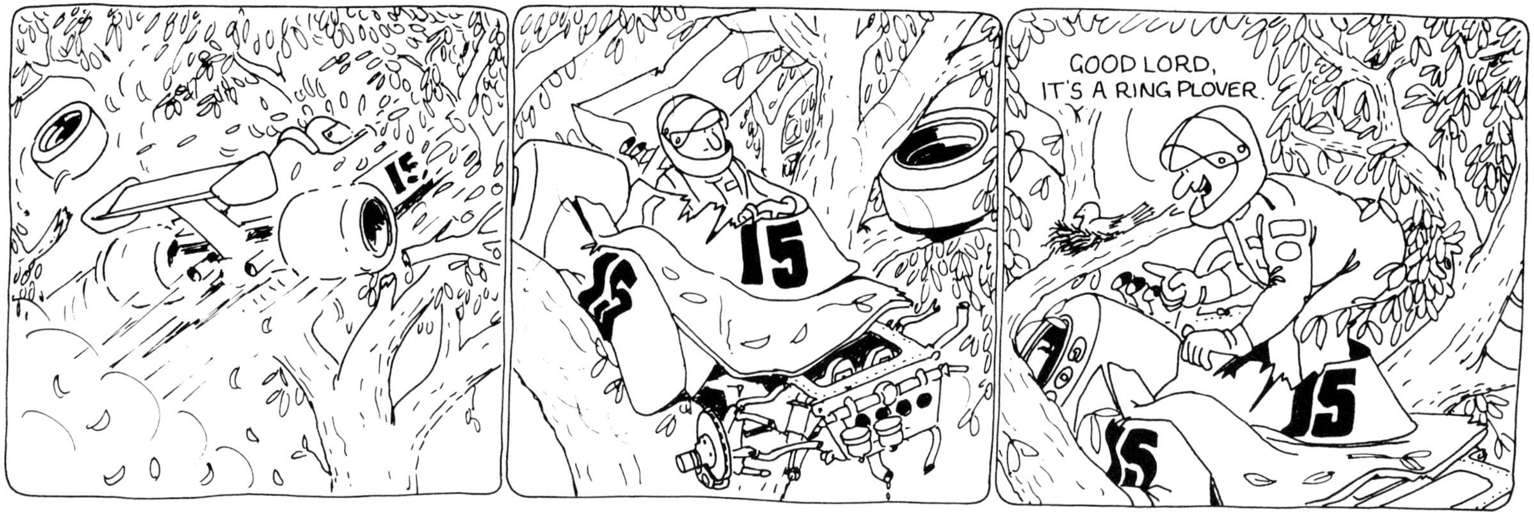
15
15
15
GOOD LORD, IT'S A RING PLOVER.
15
15

21st June 1979